This book presents a rich and ranging collection of Māori women speaking from the nineteenth-century archive. It is in various measures an inspiring, instructive and agonising read.
– CHARLOTTE MACDONALD, VICTORIA UNIVERSITY OF WELLINGTON

He Reo Wāhine brings together a wide range of nineteenth-century Māori women's voices. The extensive excerpts which fill its pages make for a rich, generative reading experience.
– ARINI LOADER, VICTORIA UNIVERSITY OF WELLINGTON

Lachy Paterson is an associate professor in Te Tumu: School of Māori, Pacific and Indigenous Studies at the University of Otago, where he teaches Māori language and Māori history. Extensively utilising Māori-language textual materials, he has published widely on Māori history of the colonial period, including a monograph on Māori-language newspapers, *Colonial Discourses: Niupepa Māori, 1855–1863* (Otago University Press, 2006).

Angela Wanhalla is an associate professor in the Department of History and Art History at the University of Otago. Her research sits at the intersection of race, gender and colonialism, with a particular interest in histories of race and intimacy within and across colonial cultures. Her most recent book, *Matters of the Heart: A History of Interracial Marriage in New Zealand* (Auckland University Press, 2013), was awarded the Ernest Scott Prize by the Australian Historical Association for the most distinguished contribution to the history of Australia or New Zealand. Her current project, which is funded by a Royal Society of New Zealand Rutherford Discovery Fellowship, is concerned with the politics of intimacy in New Zealand.

He Reo Wāhine

Māori Women's Voices from the Nineteenth Century

Lachy Paterson and Angela Wanhalla

AUCKLAND UNIVERSITY PRESS

First published 2017

Auckland University Press
University of Auckland
Private Bag 92019
Auckland 1142
New Zealand
www.press.auckland.ac.nz

© Lachy Paterson and Angela Wanhalla, 2017

ISBN 978 1 86940 866 4

Publication is assisted by

A catalogue record for this book is available from the National Library of New Zealand

This book is copyright. Apart from fair dealing for the purpose of private study, research, criticism or review, as permitted under the Copyright Act, no part may be reproduced by any process without prior permission of the publisher. The moral rights of the authors have been asserted.

COVER IMAGE Joseph Jenner Merrett, *Rangi Kawauw* (detail), 1842 or 1843, The Hobson Album, Alexander Turnbull Library, A-275-005.
BOOK DESIGN Katrina Duncan
COVER DESIGN Carolyn Lewis

Printed in Singapore by Markono Print Media Pte Ltd

CONTENTS

Acknowledgements		vii
Glossary		ix
Introduction:	Voice, Text and the Colonial Archive	1
Chapter 1:	'I am a woman who wrote this letter': Land Sales	27
Chapter 2:	'I am pierced by war's alarms': Accounts of War	72
Chapter 3:	'I am living here a Stranger on this land': Raupatu and Compensation	116
Chapter 4:	'Look at me, I am just a woman speaking': Politics and Mana	150
Chapter 5:	'I will not desist from writing to you': Māori Women's Petitions	192
Chapter 6:	'I am the prosecutrix in this case': Legal Encounters and Testamentary Acts	229
Chapter 7:	'If I die, I am dying for the Lord': Religion	265
Chapter 8:	'I am burning like fire': Private Matters	290
Epilogue:	'I am writing to you for you to hear'	318
Notes		322
Note on Sources		346
Bibliography		348
Index		358

ACKNOWLEDGEMENTS

This book has been a number of years in the making, beginning as a discussion in 2009 between two scholars of Māori history – one with expertise in Māori-language sources, the other in women's history – who wondered if these two strands could be brought together. The *He Reo Wāhine* project really got under way when the University of Otago's Humanities Division funded a summer scholarship, which allowed us to employ Alexandra King in 2010 to provide research assistance to help identify sources. That financial support and Alexandra's impressive archival research skills laid the foundations for this project, making us realise that our idea could be turned into reality. Both authors also thank the University of Otago for granting a period of research and study leave in 2014 during which time much of the book was written.

We are indebted to New Zealand's libraries, archives and museums, and the people who care for their holdings. In particular, we thank the Alexander Turnbull Library (National Library) and all offices of Archives New Zealand from whose significant and valuable holdings we have drawn much of our primary material. We also acknowledge the Hocken Collections (University of Otago), Auckland War Memorial Museum, Sir George Grey Special Collections (Auckland City Libraries), Museum of New Zealand Te Papa Tongarewa Archives, Puke Ariki Research Centre (New Plymouth City Council), Christchurch City Libraries Archives and Research Collection, and the Library of Te Rōpū Whakamana i te Tiriti o Waitangi (Waitangi Tribunal).

This volume could not have been completed without access to extensive online archives, such as the National Library's Collaborative Newspaper Digitisation Programme which supports digitised newspapers on *Papers Past*, in addition to hosting Parliamentary Papers, and the Papers of Sir Donald McLean. In particular, we acknowledge the work of transcribers and translators of the McLean material, including the Māori letters completed by E Mā: Ngā Tuhituhinga a Makarini funded by Ngā Pae o te Māramatanga. Of immense value also have been the *Niupepa Māori* website (Waikato University), He Pātaka Kupu Ture: The Legal Māori Archive (New Zealand Electronic Text Collection, Victoria University of Wellington), New Zealand's Lost Cases (Victoria University of Wellington), the Māori Land Legislation Database (University of Auckland Library) and Kete Horowhenua (Horowhenua Library Trust).

We acknowledge the many funding bodies, scholars and heritage-sector staff who helped establish and maintain these valuable online resources.

The authors thank the expert readers whose generous and considered advice and insights have strengthened this volume. Our appreciation extends to colleagues who attended seminars and conference papers presented on this project, from its initial airing at the Pacific History Association Conference in Wellington in 2012, then subsequently at the University of Otago and the University of Alberta, where feedback helped shape the manuscript. We particularly wish to acknowledge our colleagues of the University of Otago's Centre for Research on Colonial Culture, Megan Pōtiki, Paerau Warbrick, Michael Stevens, Barbara Brookes, John Stenhouse, Kate Stevens, Jane McCabe, Tom Brooking and Tony Ballantyne, as well as Merata Kāwharu, Poia Rewi, Angela Middleton and Michael Allen, who have all provided advice and guidance, or read drafts, at different points in the project.

This volume rests on considerable intellectual labour and scholarship over decades, to which our bibliography attests. *He Reo Wāhine* would not exist without the academic foundation of such works as Frances Porter and Charlotte Macdonald's *My Hand Will Write What My Heart Dictates*; *The Book of New Zealand Women* edited by Charlotte Macdonald, Merimeri Penfold and Bridget Williams; Barbara Brookes's, *A History of New Zealand Women*; and the many years of translation and scholarship of Māori texts by the likes of Jane McRae, Ngapare Hopa and Margaret Orbell.

A book such as this is a team effort. We were fortunate that Sam Elworthy of Auckland University Press was enthusiastic on first hearing of our project, and encouraged us as we brought the manuscript to fruition. We also wish to express our gratitude to all the team at the Press who helped in the production of this wonderful book, in particular Jennifer Garlick for copy-editing, Stephanie Pohe-Tibble nāna i whakatika ngā tini hē o ngā whakapākehātanga, Jane McRae for proofreading, Katrina Duncan for design, Carolyn Lewis for the cover, and Louisa Kasza for managing the process.

Heoi anō he mihi nunui ki ngā tāngata e kōrerotia nei i roto i tēnei pukapuka, ki ngā wāhine Māori anō hoki nā rātou ngā kupu i tuhi, i whakahua rānei, kia rangahaua nei e māua hei whakamārama i ngā āhuatanga o te rautau i ora ai rātou. I a koutou ngā pikinga me ngā hekenga o taua wā; i riro mā koutou ngā pīkaunga taumaha e waha kia ora ai ō koutou uri o ēnei rā.

GLOSSARY

Ariki	paramount chief
Aroha	compassion, sympathy, love
Atua	god, supernatural being
Crown grant	legally recognised transferable land title
Hapū	clan, kin group
Harakeke	New Zealand flax
Hauhau	Pai Mārire, rebel, anti-government
Iwi	tribal group
Kāhore	No!
Kāinga	village, settlement
Kaioraora	song of derision and hatred
Kaiwhakahaere	manager, agent
Karanga	woman's call as part of rituals of encounter
Kaumātua	elders
Kaupapa	purpose, subject
Kīngitanga	Māori King movement
Kit	kete, flax basket
Kōkiri	armed force
Komiti	committee
Kotahitanga	Māori unity movement, flourished in the 1890s
Kuīnitanga	government (under the Queen of England)
Kūpapa	neutral, Māori allied to the government
Mahinga kai	food gathering location
Mana	power and authority
Mana motuhake	separate authority, independence
Mana whenua	authority over land, traditional tribal area
Manuhiri	visitors
Marae	public space of a Māori village, tribal meeting place
Mate	misfortune, illness, death
Mere	hand-held club
Mōteatea	sung poetry
Niu	large flagstaff used in Pai Mārire ceremonies
Niupepa	newspaper, Māori-language newspaper
Ōhākī	death-bed statement
Pā	fortified village or position, pah
Pai Mārire	religion established by Te Ua Haumēne
Pānuitanga	notice, announcement

He Reo Wāhine

Poi	song and dance, generally performed by women, using balls attached by cords
Pounamu	greenstone, jade
Pukapuka	book, text, letter
Pūremu	adultery, sexual misconduct
Rangatira	chief
Rangatiratanga	chiefly authority, autonomy
Raupatu	confiscation
[te] Reo (Māori)	[the] (Māori) language
Ringatū	religion established by Te Kooti
Rohe	territory
Rūnanga	council, tribal meeting
Tangata whenua	people of the land, hosts, indigenous people
Take	reason, cause
Take whenua	basis of native land title
Tangi	act of crying
Taonga	treasured item
Tapu	spiritual restriction, sacred
Taua	war party
Tikanga	custom, customary
Tuku whenua	release land for sale
Tupuna	ancestor
Tūtūā	low-born
Utu	payment
Urupā	cemetery, burial ground
Wāhine	women, female
Waiata	song
Waiata aroha	song of love
Waiata tangi	song for the dead, lament
Waipiro	alcohol
Whaikōrero	formal oratory
Whakapapa	genealogy, genealogical connections
Whakamā	withdraw emotionally, embarrassment
Whānau	extended family
Whanaunga	relative
Whare	house, building
Whenua	land

INTRODUCTION

Voice, Text and the Colonial Archive

I am not a "tutuha" [sic] or person of no consequence'. Jane Maria Phillips (Ngāti Ruanui) made this statement in her 1894 petition to the House of Representatives, in which she requested redress for the loss of ancestral land confiscated by the Crown after the Taranaki wars. While Jane is one of many Māori women whose writings and testimonies can be found in New Zealand's colonial archives, especially those documents generated by encounters with the state, their experiences are not at the heart of New Zealand historical scholarship. *He Reo Wāhine* aims to produce a volume that prioritises Māori women's colonial experiences using their own 'voices'. Drawing upon publicly accessible archival and manuscript collections of documents generated by women during the nineteenth century, we ask what New Zealand history looks like if we begin with Māori women's words, speeches, evidence and testimonies.

Our focus is on the nineteenth century, for during that period Māori produced a rich set of documents in their own language, ranging from personal correspondence, manuscripts and petitions, to memoir. Historians and Māori Studies scholars have used Māori-language sources such as these to examine various aspects of nineteenth-century Māori life, claiming them as crucial sources for assessing Māori engagement with Christianity, for measuring levels of literacy, and as windows onto Māori political and intellectual culture. We have been inspired and encouraged by this scholarship to delve into the rich Māori-language holdings in public collections to illuminate Māori women's lives.

Despite the existence of a large body of scholarship on New Zealand women's history – which has worked assiduously to bring to the surface the faint traces of women's lives left in the written records – locating Māori women's perspectives through the words they wrote, or the words they spoke, is regarded as an almost impossible task, particularly because colonial archives were largely created by European men and are, as a result, dominated by male voices and viewpoints. As Canadian historian Adele Perry states, colonial archives 'reflected the societies that produced them and the ones that preserved them' in which 'men speak with greater frequency, detail, and volume than do women'.[1] The least-heard voices, however, are those of indigenous women, and New Zealand's colonial archives are no different in this respect. This does not mean Māori women were silent in the past, but reflects instead how archives were created, the collecting practices of public institutions, and the priorities of historical research in the past, which was little interested in women's or indigenous history until the late twentieth century.[2] How then do we research and write histories of Māori women, when archival and manuscript material from the nineteenth century is so patchy, uneven and unsympathetically preserved? We set out to answer this question by identifying some overlooked source materials that offer some insight into the feelings, thoughts and experiences of a selection of Māori women who lived in the decades before 1900.

Drawing from over 500 texts in both English and te reo Māori, written by Māori women themselves, or expressing their words in the first person, between 1830 and 1900, *He Reo Wāhine* explores the range and diversity of their concerns and interests, and the many ways in which they engaged with the state, as well as their understanding and use of the law, legal documents and the court system. How women's voices speak to us from texts varies. The words of some Māori women, such as witnesses in commissions of inquiry, before the land court, and in the colonial legal system, only exist because third parties, often Pākehā men, recorded them. Other women were keen participants in textual culture, writing letters to each other or to officials, with a few engaging with print culture, such as newspapers. In bringing to light women's words, we see how they sought to protect their interests, and how colonialism worked and operated more generally in their lives.

He Reo Wāhine is comprised of eight chapters arranged around particular themes, reflecting the concerns of Māori women. Although focused on whole documents and excerpts (some extended), we have provided the necessary historical context to make the selected texts, deriving from archival and manuscript collections in New Zealand's key heritage institutions, comprehensible to readers, while still allowing the original texts to 'speak'. In addition to historical context, we also detail how these sources came to enter the archive, offering a critical examination of how colonial archives were created, and whose 'voices' are better represented than others. In showcasing the rich archival and manuscript materials available for the study of nineteenth-century Māori women, our goal is to make material accessible for use as a teaching resource in history and language courses, so that it may generate further interest in researching and writing Māori women's history. In the epilogue, we return to these matters, tracing the insights provided into New Zealand's colonial history by focusing on Māori women, and we point to areas in need of further research.

—⚭—

Since the 1970s, important efforts to bring non-elite voices to the centre of history have produced fresh perspectives on New Zealand's past. Women's history benefitted from this turn to 'history from below', with scholars having explored the evolution of women's political citizenship and women's organising since the nineteenth century, in addition to prioritising new historical subjects, such as motherhood, domesticity, and women's and children's health, as well as women's work. Since the 1970s a wealth of innovative studies of women in the nineteenth century has been produced, based on extensive family archives, drawn from missionary women's writings, or focused on the institutional archives of women's groups, most of which were active from the 1880s and 1890s. Māori women, however, made only brief appearances in this scholarship.[3] Biography has probably been the most fruitful area of inquiry, but the number of books about Māori women is small in comparison to those on Māori men, particularly for the nineteenth century where chiefly leaders, anti-colonial resistance figures and politicians dominate.[4] While recent studies of the early-contact period in the decades before 1840 have demonstrated the importance of Māori women in the establishment of resource economies, especially as wives and partners of whalers and traders, the most common approach to Māori women's history has been to utilise texts created by European observers, because as historian Patricia Grimshaw rightly notes, 'few literary sources created by the women themselves survive from the [early contact] period.'[5]

We wondered, therefore, if it was possible to locate writing by Māori women, and whether they wrote or testified to how colonisation shaped their lives. We hoped that a close examination of the archives produced out of colonialism might help, in the words of historian Judith Binney, bring Māori women out from 'the shadows in which the nineteenth century European historical tradition has placed them'.[6] In seeking to bring Māori women to the forefront of New Zealand's history, we looked to the scholarship of both Māori Studies and print-culture specialists, who have revealed a rich archive of writings and compositions produced by Māori during the nineteenth-century. Very little of this work, though, has paid much attention to the gender of the writer.[7] Part of the reason for this is that much of the effort has focused on establishing and building a corpus of textual material, including the collection, transcription and translation of Māori writing, sometimes with minimal analysis of its content.[8] Much attention has focused upon particular genres of Māori writing, notably manuscripts, letters and the Māori-language newspapers, which some scholars have sought to historicise, for example, by contextualising the production of manuscript material, illuminating the orality of texts, and claiming them as key sources for accessing Māori political thought.

Knowing that a rich set of sources written by Māori in their own language existed, covering a range of genres and held by public institutions in New Zealand, we wondered whether Māori women contributed to these collections, and what they wrote about. We complemented this search by exploring whether other first-person voices existed in the archives. The answer was a resounding and very loud, yes: Māori women wrote, and they wrote about a variety of matters that affected them and their whānau. In addition to their writing, Māori women appeared before commissions of enquiry, gave evidence in court cases, and went to the Native Land Court to assert their land rights, providing historians with a rich set of sources, both self-generated and recorded by others, which could be used to explore Māori women's engagement with colonial governments, and their participation in key institutions that shaped the pattern of their lives.

In taking up writing, Māori took up a technology and practice that many indigenous peoples in colonial contexts also pursued for personal, political and creative reasons.[9] Māori women participated in this practice, producing written documents in a range of formats, writing for creative expression, to maintain connections with whanaunga (relatives), to express their feelings, and to clarify or contest their land rights. This demonstrates that while some of their writing and public speaking was political in nature, it was not limited to this, and because it was diverse it was difficult to characterise it only as coherent 'expressions of tribal identity'.[10] In short, Māori women wrote as part of a political collective, but as the chapter titles attest, they also corresponded on a range of issues as individuals, pursing matters of injustice that affected them and their families.

The emphasis on political writing and tribal identity emerges from a particular focus on post-1970s history writing in which the primary historical focus has been on Treaty of Waitangi breaches, racial conflict, land loss and the colonial acquisition of power, rather than on how mana wahine was publicly manifested, or how women lived their lives within the constraints and opportunities of colonialism.[11] In this politically inflected historiography, some regard prioritising gender issues as not only distracting, but also potentially divisive and thus counter-productive to Māori struggles for rangatiratanga.[12] Added to this, in a context of debates about decolonising the archive, the kinds of written documents that Māori produced are regarded as tainted by colonial associations, and less authentic than more 'traditional' oral modes of transmission, such as karanga (call of welcome) and mōteatea (sung poetry).[13] Māori writing produced in response to colonisation and its impacts over the nineteenth century should be read alongside, not in place of, oral sources, but both need to be interpreted critically, for neither are 'beyond or outside critique'.[14]

Collecting from the archive

We began gathering the voices of Māori women and their writings by building on the work of previous research, for example, *Women's Words*, the Alexander Turnbull Library's published list of women's manuscripts held by the library, and Auckland War Memorial Museum's *Womanscripts*, together with excellent bibliographies of Māori writing, notably Phil Parkinson and Penelope Griffith's *Books in Māori, 1815–1900*.[15] We also made use of anthologies such as Āpirana Ngata and Pei Te Hurinui Jones's *Nga Moteatea*, a four-volume collection of Māori oral compositions, and John Caselberg's 1975 collection, *Maori is My Name*.[16]

Of critical importance to our book was the around 500 examples of women's writing drawn from public collections covering the colonial period anthologised by Frances Porter and Charlotte Macdonald in *My Hand Will Write What My Heart Dictates*. Their collection includes 52 examples from Māori women, ranging from waiata to letters, reminiscences, and testimony before government enquiries, given in te reo with English translations.[17] A rich and engaging collection, one that has yet to be surpassed in New Zealand history, it was our benchmark and go-to reference book for the creation of *He Reo Wāhine*. Although our book includes some of the material that appears in *My Hand Will Write What My Heart Dictates*, it also extends it, both in terms of the range of material and the total number of Māori-produced items. As such,

He Reo Wāhine complements and expands *My Hand Will Write What My Heart Dictates*, rather than replicating it, so we suggest they be read together in order to gain a full picture of Māori women's extensive and rich writings during the colonial era.

Given that *My Hand Will Write What My Heart Dictates* (1996), *Women's Words* (1988) and *Womanscripts* (1995), were published over two decades ago, we also carefully searched the newly available online catalogues of institutions, figuring that in the intervening decades new collections may have been donated and catalogued. Moreover, new technologies, particularly digitisation, also meant existing material was now easier to discover and collate, providing the means for projects, such as this volume, to be initiated. Digitisation has allowed historians to access some of these collections and many other resources from their own desks, to search more efficiently and to create new ways of making sense of what they find.

Our online research began with the newspaper corpora, both *Papers Past* (New Zealand's newspapers) and *Niupepa Māori* (Māori-language newspapers), and other online repositories, such as the papers of Sir Donald McLean and the New Zealand Lost Cases database. In addition to texts available digitally, online catalogues enhanced our research, and enriched this book, by bringing to our attention documents collected by officials now deposited in Archives New Zealand, and also various papers held in libraries, museums and cultural institutions, for example, the Alexander Turnbull Library, the Auckland War Memorial Museum and the Hocken Collections.

Names were the key to unlocking the archive. Because many traditional Māori names (and personal pronouns in te reo Māori) are not gender specific, it was not always easy to determine whether a voice belonged to a man or a woman. Our initial research sweep involved searching for female Christian names derived from European names, such as Mere (Mary) and Ani (Annie); this was followed by further sweeps of well known Māori women with traditional names, for example, Topeora and Niniwa-i-te-rangi. Further searches identified women through gendered terms, such as wahine (woman, wife), and whaea (mother), as well as colonial terms, such as 'native woman' or 'aboriginal woman'.

As our goal was to present as wide a range of voices as possible, we did not want to limit our investigation only to texts that Māori women wrote themselves. Like *My Hand Will Write What My Heart Dictates*, we also, 'looked beyond the manuscript record to bring into the book documents which were not created "freely" by women writing of their own accord, but in which women's voices, words and experiences appear.'[18] Women signed land deeds, petitions, government forms and other documents, which purported to represent their thoughts, claims, grievances and wishes. A 'voice' can refer to sound such as speech or song, so we decided to include examples of these as recorded and stored in archives, such as waiata, statements reported in newspapers, or evidence given in the courts or to government enquiries. Nor did we want texts deriving only from women of mana. The only condition we set was that the voices had to be in the first person: I or we, or in Māori ahau, māua, tāua, mātou or tātou; or signed by the woman to indicate that the text expressed what she wanted to say. As discussed below, the way a voice is recorded or collected of course mediates its authenticity. There is considerably more archival material in which nineteenth-century male commentators, both Māori and Pākehā, detailed aspects of Māori women's lives, but this volume aspires to allow the women themselves to speak, as much as this is possible, to give their own voices the immediacy and authenticity that the words of others about them might lack. Many of the women who appear in *He Reo Wāhine* were certainly prominent in their lifetimes, and appear repeatedly in our corpus, often in dogged pursuit of land claims that took decades to resolve. But many others are little known to historians, even if they may have been well known and respected in their own communities. Our corpus tends to support Paul Meredith and Alice Te Punga Somerville's assertion that a 'rich archive of writings by less prominent [Māori] figures' exists in New Zealand's archival and manuscript collections.[19]

In addition to the temporal span, we have endeavoured to provide a broad geographical coverage from Te Tai Tokerau to Rakiura, and out to Rēkohu (Chatham Islands), across our range of themes. In all, we gathered over 500 items from publicly accessible 'bricks and mortar' and online archives. There is just a handful of items from the years up to 1850; 54 from the 1850s; then ranging from 92 to 128 over each of the following decades; 197 are in te reo Māori only, a further 110 are bilingual, and 194 are preserved in English (although most were originally produced in te reo Māori). Of the 501 items we defined 98 as reported speech or evidence. Another 308 are letters, and the remaining 95 are an assortment of memoranda, notices and advertisements, petitions, recorded waiata, land court documents, wills and other legal papers, memoirs, addresses, telegrams and other items. In organising our material, we assigned the documents a primary category relating to a set of themes: legal, social, family, economic, political, education, war or tikanga, although of course many items relate to more than one theme. We are well aware that our set is not complete. Māori women, for example, composed hundreds of waiata in the nineteenth century, although most were not published in print until the twentieth. Similarly, we are aware from parliamentary reports that many Māori, including women, appealed to the Native Affairs Committee from the 1870s, mainly concerning claims to land, but the original first-person petitions are not easy to find in the archive. Notwithstanding any lacunae, we believe that we have assembled a sufficiently wide and diverse set of data to shed light on nineteenth-century Māori women's experiences. From this collection, by no means all that the archives hold, we have attempted to provide both an interesting, but also representative range of texts illuminating Māori women's lived experiences during the colonial era.

We are aware that this material might be being read for the first time by descendants, and that some of the content could be confronting and challenging, especially items that deal with alcohol, sexual violence, adultery and suicide. Our intention is not to embarrass relatives, but to showcase the variety of writing in existence, to demonstrate the persistence of women's calls for justice, and to illustrate how they used literacy and the written word to advocate for their families and communities. In the manner of Robert Warrior, and the Hawaiian scholar Noenoe K. Silva, both of whom have worked assiduously to highlight the existence of a rich indigenous-language print culture and intellectual traditions, we also wish to bring attention to less well known sources 'in ways that respect the creative and scholarly work of the authors'.[20] This means treating difficult topics with sensitivity, which we have done by redacting names in a few instances, situating events within the context of the colonial conditions that gave rise to them, and explaining how and why these documents entered the archives.

The colonial archives

He Reo Wāhine is presented as a series of contextualised and thematic chapters that provide women's perspectives on land, war, religion, politics and the law, and touch on social and economic history, as well as on aspects of private lives. In opting to contextualise the texts and voices, rather than anthologise, we are responding to Tony Ballantyne's call for New Zealand historians to 'turn to their archives more critically, making the archives themselves the object of critical historical study', for in order to 'appreciate how our colonial archives were constructed, we must catalogue what is absent in these collections as well as what is present, and we need to reconstruct the ideological work that they have done.'[21]

Contextualising our source material allows us to acknowledge that the archives used in this volume are 'artifacts of colonialism rather than simply the repositories where the data pertaining to the colonial past is stored'.[22]

Over the past two decades historians have made the archival collections created out of colonialism the subject of study, arguing that the processes by which colonial archives were created and the information they contain are reflective of the asymmetrical power relations that constitute colonial governance, with white male voices and knowledge, for instance, prioritised over those of non-white and female subjects. As historian of southern Africa Christopher Lee notes, a document's placement within the colonial archive is not only evidence of unequal power relations, 'it is [also] a direct effect of them.'[23]

We are particularly attentive to mapping archival silences and occlusions, which requires an explanation of how archives were created, by whom, and for what purpose during the colonial era.[24] Because *He Reo Wāhine* draws mostly from government archives and the manuscript collections of colonial officials which were generated for particular reasons, Māori correspondence in these collections is often concerned with land, marking these as archives that were generated out of the settler colonial project of land acquisition. For this reason, *He Reo Wāhine* includes relatively few examples of private writing such as diaries or journals, largely because these, if still extant, remain in the hands of whānau. Letters written by Māori women to other Māori, or to Pākehā who were not attached to government, do exist but they were less likely to have been publicly collected, particularly if they related to intimate or domestic affairs. As Bradford Haami's *Pūtea Whakairo* shows, some whānau hold archives containing a range of material, including private letters and whakapapa books.[25] These taonga are often very personal to the whānau, and it is only right that they determine how these might be used. We therefore limited our searches to publicly available material. While we have very little private writing, the letters sent to public officials do reveal something of women's private worlds, their concerns and tribulations (see chapter 8).

Quite apart from lost and discarded writings, and the fact that public collections are more likely to hold particular categories of document, it is clear that those generated by certain groups of Māori women are likely to be more numerous, in particular those from women with extensive interests in land. For example, at least 55 per cent of our items have land as their primary focus. Given we are working mainly with government archives, this is no surprise, and no doubt a reflection of the collecting priorities of the institutions we accessed. It also bears the imprint of the time period, in which the colonial project revolved around dispossession, particularly of land. Related issues of injustice and economic survival are also prominent. Māori women could own land, and in fact, for a time, had more economic rights than European women,[26] so had reasons to be writing letters about land. Māori women also appeared in the Native Land Court, an institution woven into the fabric of Māori lives from the mid 1860s, as they appeared as witnesses and claimants (see chapter 1).

We also used the collections of European ethnographers who made a concerted effort to collect what they regarded as Māori history and tradition.[27] Māori women were very rarely, if ever, 'native informants', nor the collaborators or co-producers of ethnographic texts.[28] Nevertheless, sometimes women's oral compositions from the pre-contact and contact eras entered these collections, generally through the agency and authority of men. For example, Sir George Grey, New Zealand's third governor collected accounts from Māori informants for his *Nga Mahi a nga Tupuna*, first published in 1854. One chapter recounts a waiata from sixteenth-century Wairarapa, sung by Te Aohuruhuru, a young Māori woman of Ngāi Tara. Her older husband, Pāmaramara, allowed his friends to ogle her naked body as she slept. Upon waking, she was overcome with shame and committed suicide. As she was about to throw herself from a cliff she was heard to sing:

Naku ra i moe tuwherawhera,
Ka tahuna ki te ahi,
Kia tino turama
A ka kataina a au na.

[original translation]
As I was lying there exposed
The fire was lit
The house was ablaze with light
And I was laughed at.[29]

This waiata was also reproduced, with a translation, in the twentieth century: in Māui Pōmare's *Legends of the Maori* in 1934; in the Department of Māori Affairs magazine *Te Ao Hou* in 1955; and in *Rangitāne: A Tribal History* published in 1986.[30] The relaying of pre-contact voices can also be seen in Takaanui Tarakawa's account, published in the *Journal of the Polynesian Society* in 1894, of the arrival of the *Mataatua* canoe from Hawaiki in the fourteenth century. In his retelling Tarakawa gives voice to Wairaka, the chiefly woman who stepped outside of assigned gender roles to save the drifting canoe. With her immortal words 'E! kia whakatāne ake au i ahau!' (Ah! then let me act the part of a man!) she gave the locality of Whakatāne its name.[31] While female agency within these ancient accounts is interesting in its own right, this volume instead seeks to use texts that throw light on women's experiences in nineteenth-century Māori society, and how they epitomise broader developments resulting from colonisation.

Issues of voice

Quite apart from the initial filters at the point of collection or recording, a text may have gone through other processes of moderation, particularly in cases of testimony and evidence given to courts. In 1866 the *New Zealand Herald*, covering a larceny case, reported:

> Ema Puhata, sworn, Stated:—I live at Taupo. I know the two prisoners.[32]

Does Ema have more voice, more agency, than if the *Herald* had put her words into the third person: 'Ema Puhata, sworn, stated that she lives at Taupō and knows the two prisoners'? We do not know whether the *Herald* reported her words verbatim, or paraphrased them. Nor do we know how proficient she was in English, and if the words of the reported speech are hers or those of an interpreter. Ema's voice may well be modulated through interpretation, and then through the newspaper's reporting. This can be seen when there is more than one text for a single voice. Take the following testimony from two separate sets of minutes of a Compensation Court sitting at Port Waikato in March 1866 to investigate the Onewhero Block. The minutes are likely to have been taken by two of the three judges present, F. D. Fenton, John Rogan or H. A. H. Monro.

> [set 1]
> Rehara Tauroa (sworn) I reside at Waiuku and belong to the Ngatikahu tribe. I am the wife of Hori Tauroa. I claim the land from te Kakanga to Takahikahi, Ohaeroa & Onewhero. – I claim this [from] my ancestors. I was born there and lived there[.] I lived at Onewhero, te Kakenga & Takahikahi, also at te Ihutaroa.

> [set 2]
> Rehara Tauroa (sworn) I live at Waiuku. I am of N.Kahu wife of Hori Tauroa. I claim Kakanga ... Takakahi Ohaeroa & Onewhero.
>
> I claim from my tupuna. I don't know born[illegible] I lived there at Onewhero, Takahikahi, Kakanga in my childhood.[33]

It is almost certain that the court used an interpreter, although if proficient enough the judges may have also been listening directly to the original testimony in te reo. Both versions recount (mostly) the same information, but the wording is different, for example, one text uses 'ancestors' in preference to 'tūpuna'. We thus have two forms of Rehara's voice, although the actual words she spoke remain unknown.

The physical act of writing is generally an individual act, but the resultant text could also represent a collective voice. Some documents, deeds and letters have multiple names appended to them, some of which may be those of women. We cannot always be sure how much agency all the 'signatories' may have had. For example, several letters from Māori appeared in the government's *Te Waka Maori o Niu Tireni* impugning the honour of Henry Russell over land issues. The letters led Russell to sue the newspaper's editor and printer for libel. The court took evidence from Māori at a special sitting at Napier, including from one of the letter writers, Ārihi Te Nahu, a wealthy and influential chiefly woman of Ngāti Kahungunu. Her testimony points to the uncertain or ambiguous nature of individual agency with regard to nineteenth-century Māori texts.

> *I told him [Ārihi's husband] to put my name to it. I told him to put the name of Nepia te Hapuku to it. I told him to put the name of Hapuku te Nahu to it. I told him to put Tipene's name to it. These natives were not present when the letter was written.*
> *Q. – Had you their authority for putting their names to the letter.*
> *A. – Yes; we talked over the matter beforehand and they agreed that I should publish it in a newspaper. ...*
>
> *We all decided that I should word the letter. It was arranged that I should put in the names of all the people who objected to Henry Russell's conduct. I meant that when I put 'all of us' at the end of the letter. ...*
>
> *I did not say in the letter that [Russell] told me with his own mouth, but according to our Maori ideas his saying so to Hapuku is the same as saying it to myself in that he and I are one.*[34]

It was certainly not uncommon for chiefs to speak for their people. For example, when the Te Āti Awa chief Hapurona signed the terms for a truce with the Crown in 1861 to end the first Taranaki war, he claimed to represent over 60 named individuals, including 23 women.[35] Similarly Ārihi's testimony indicates writing practices in which 'her' agency was more collective than personal in that she saw her chiefly status enabling her to 'word the letter' on behalf of others (see chapter 6).

Sometimes the wording of nineteenth-century Māori writing can signify the degree of individual authorship. The missionary William Yate, for example, incorporated a number of letters from Māori in his 1835 *Account of New Zealand*, including two ostensibly co-written by married couples. However, both texts use the first-person singular to express the husband's perspective, with the wives referred to in the third person, thus indicating that the women may have had little involvement in the creation of the letters.[36]

Government documents, such as generic forms, are sometimes difficult to use to measure women's agency and voice. Consider Mere Petere's use of a Native Land Court form in 1865 (reproduced overleaf); the italicised words were added by hand, the rest of the text was printed.

The words of this form created a boundary for Mere as much as the land she claimed. Although the form, on behalf of the applicant[s], asserted 'Ko matou...' [We...] it restricted any ownership to a certificate of title, that is, the land could only be 'owned' according to English legal practice. That she signed with an X indicates that she probably dictated the boundaries, perhaps to her husband John Petley. Mere had agency in that she used the form as a means of obtaining land, but the paper form constrained her claim to an approved construction. Similarly a Māori woman writing a letter to a government official might tailor her tone and language depending on the end desired, or her position of strength or vulnerability.

Knowing the context of the texts is vital to understanding the discourse, and the underlying issues of power. In some cases texts are incomprehensible without some explanation. Rather than collect and duplicate a succession of related texts in the format of an anthology, we have attempted to discover and relay the back story of each text, or group of texts. For example, Mere Petere's Native Land Court form above is just one document in her land claim, and is discussed in more depth in the chapter on raupatu (chapter 3). Inevitably there are often gaps in the contextual information available for some texts. We cannot generally find out much more about a person if she is identified just as Meri (Mary),

He Reo Wāhine

HE PUKAPUKA TONO KI TE KOOTI WHAKAWA WHENUA MAORI KIA WHAKAWAKIA ETAHI TAKE WHENUA
===========

E KARA,-

Ko matou, ko nga tangata no ratou nga ingoa e mau i Te Pukapuka rarangi ingoa e piri iho nei, e whai take ana ki tetahi pihi whenua e tata ana ki *Opotiki* Na, he tono tenei na matou, mo to matou iwi, hapu ranei, kia whakawakia aua take ki Te Kooti Whakawa mo nga whenua Maori, he mea kia riro mai ai Te Pukapuka whakatuturu mo aua whenua.

Ki te Kooti Whakawa Whenua Maori

PUKAPUKA RARANGI INGOA

Te ingoa o te whenua	Nga ingoa o nga tangata e pa ana ki te whenua	Te ingoa o te Iwi, Hapu ranei	Te whakaaturanga o nga rohe
Waioeka	Mere Petere X	Ngatiera	– Timata te rohe ki te taha o Heta – ka haere atu ki nga maunga O Waioeka – ko te rohe ki waho kei Te Wairoa – ko te hokinga mai ki te taha ki te ra whiti ko Waioeka – Tutai Toko – kei Roto Huka – ko te taha tenei ki te ra whiti o Waioeka -------------------- ka timata ki te taha ki te roto o Waioeka ki te taha ki uta o Tamahewa – kaitimata tenei rohe puta tonu atu ki Te Wairoa – ko te putanga o tenei Pakihi

No Te *28* o nga ra
o *Hepetema* Te tau *1865*[37]

[modern translation]

AN APPLICATION FORM TO THE NATIVE LAND COURT FOR SOME LAND ISSUES TO BE ADJUDICATED

===========

SIR,-

    We, the people whose names are attached to the Names List Form below, hold interests in a piece of land close to Ōpōtiki. So, this is our request, for our iwi or hapū, that those interests be adjudicated in the Court for Māori land, with the purpose of obtaining a certificate of title for those lands.

To the Native Land Court

NAMES LIST FORM

Name of the land	Names of the people regarding that land	Name of Iwi or Hapū	Description of the boundaries
Waioeka	*Mere Petere X*	*Ngatiera*	*– The boundary starts on the side of Heta – and goes to the mountains of Waioeka – the outside boundary is at Wairoa – returning back on the east side is Waioeka – Tūtai Toko – at Rotohuka – this is the side on the east of Waioeka*

			The side at the lake of Waioeka begins on the landward side of Tamahewa – this boundary begins [and goes] all the way to Te Wairoa – Pakihi is where it comes out.

On the *28*th day of *September* in the year *1865*.

although the text itself might point to broader historical themes. Sometimes women had multiple or variant names that make finding the back story more difficult. For example, Rongo, the daughter of Ngāpuhi chief Hongi Hika, was also known as Hariata Rongo. Her mother, Turikatuku, told Samuel Marsden that Hariata also carried the name Mātenga (Marsden), for the missionary was present at Ōkuratope pā the night Rongo was born, in January 1815.[38] She may have called herself Hariata Heke when married to Hōne Heke Pōkai; the year following his death in 1850 she signed a letter as Hariata Te Pouaru (literally Hariata the Widow). In 1867 she wrote another letter as Hariata Arama Karaka Pī after her second marriage to Ngāpuhi chief Arama Karaka Pī. A newspaper report of her death in 1894 referred to her as Hariata Kahutaha.[39]

Issues of translation

Thinking critically about the creation of documents and archives also requires an analysis of the impact of translation, particularly as it relates to questions of authorship and agency.[40] Translation and interpretation are important components to consider with regard to representing Māori voices. Te reo Māori was the first language for nearly all Māori in the nineteenth century, and many spoke little or no English. Interpreters were a fact of life for Māori interacting with the colonial state, particularly over land. In 1862 the government employed three interpreters among 25 'persons employed in the administration of Native Affairs', but many of the officials listed were bilingual.[41] Native Land Courts employed interpreters who acted as clerks and secretaries to judges, and under the 1867 Native Land Act, section 7, the Chief Judge (or Governor) could issue a certificate to license suitable individuals to work within the Court, including a small number of Māori women, and 'licensed interpreters' were soon after advertising their services in newspapers.[42] By 1873 the Appropriation Act listed 22 positions of interpreter in various government departments and locations. This declined to just ten positions by the end of the century (32 years after the state took responsibility for Māori education) although the government hired in extra interpreters and translators when necessary.[43]

As we saw from Rehara Tauroa's testimony to the Compensation Court, a voice survived as a text in English, even though it was originally delivered verbally in Māori. This could also be the case for written work; in some cases an original letter exists, sometimes it survives as a hand-written transcription, and sometimes just the translation. Translation is seldom straightforward, especially if significantly dissimilar cultural understandings exist between speakers of different languages. Subconsciously or not, the translator has various things to consider, such as who the audience is, and how 'fluent' or 'natural' the rendering should be in the second language. When the level of fluency is high the reader may become unaware that the original text was first composed in a language foreign to them.[44] Of course the more natural the translation reads for the reader, the greater the possibility that cultural or linguistic nuances in the original text might be lost. For this reason we have not striven for maximum fluency in our contemporary translations; it is perhaps appropriate for the text to remind the modern reader that it was produced in a different setting. Not only was it created at a different time and in a different language, but the nineteenth-century author most likely possessed a world-view, cultural understandings and experiences quite different to our own.

Certainly in the 1860s several commentators considered official translations to be deficient. William Colenso, a former missionary turned politician, complained in Parliament that the government's translation of some legal works into Māori 'defied all attempts to understand or make any sense of it'.[45] Similarly the missionary Octavius Hadfield considered that government translators deliberately rendered Māori correspondence into poor English to suggest that the writers, 'were incapable of expressing their opinions in proper language, which is the reverse of the fact.'[46] In the latter case, the translators may have been thinking of their audience. Sir George Grey, who served two terms as governor, the long-serving Native Minister Sir Donald McLean, and other officials who were first to read the translations, were fluent in te reo Māori, and may well have found more literal and less fluent translations more useful in interpreting what the original text actually said. For example, starting a letter with 'Salutation' may seem unnatural in English, but the informed reader who knew the original language would have automatically equated this with 'Tēnā koe' in the original, a perfectly natural way to start a letter in Māori. These original official translations exist as creations of the colonial state and are therefore of interest in their own right, as part of its archival legacy; where the language is able to be understood, we have included them.

Literacy acquisition

This volume is less interested in what the introduction of new knowledge, technology and skills like writing and literacy did to people or to a culture, than what those who took up such practices did with them and for what purpose, however these cannot be adequately explored without reference to the level of Māori literacy in the colonial era.[47] Prior to the Treaty of Waitangi, Māori men's contact with literacy practices through overseas travel predated both missionary activities in New Zealand and colonial governance.[48] It is not that Māori women did not travel at all, but they were much less likely to leave records indicating an interaction with other cultures. Their engagement with texts, other than as subjects of European writings, began soon after the establishment of the Church Missionary Society's first mission at Rangihoua in 1814. Samuel Marsden's school at Parramatta, Sydney, took in men and boys from 1815,[49] but more than half the students to attend the first school in New Zealand, run by the missionary Thomas Kendall from 1816 to 1818, were girls.[50] The missionary wives also began teaching Māori girls around the same time. Missionary John King, for example, thought his wife Hannah 'will have one or two girls to instruct in writing, sewing, making any sort of clothing, to knit and spin' as well as other domestic activities.[51]

The effectiveness of this initial missionary instruction in reading and writing is uncertain. There was no standard system for writing Māori at that time, with Pākehā spelling words as they sounded to them. For example, an 1814 vocabulary lists 'Hadoodoohee', 'Ko-teedo' and 'Whyeenee' respectively for rūruhi (old woman), kōtiro (girl) and wahine (woman).[52] It was not until 1820, after Kendall and Ngāpuhi chiefs Hongi Hika and Waikato had collaborated with Professor Samuel Lee at Cambridge University, that a workable orthography was developed, which in turn facilitated not only the teaching of literacy skills but the production of printed texts in Māori.[53] Although it has undergone a few modifications, the 1820 Māori-language orthography forms the basis of how Māori is written today.

In 1826 two missionary women, the sisters-in-law Jane and Marianne Williams, established their own school at Paihia in the Bay of Islands specifically to teach girls, since, according to Marianne's husband Henry Williams 'their condition is far more degraded than the males'.[54] Literacy skills were definitely part of the curriculum: as Marianne wrote in 1828, the girls 'are tractable at school, and have yielded to us to determine when they shall sit and when stand, and whether they shall write large hand or small'.[55] Māori women also took leadership roles in these mission schools. For example, in June 1836, before leaving to visit a nearby school, Marianne 'sent for Hera, to put my infant school in her charge'. At the school up the Kawakawa River she noted, 'Katerina has the women's school, and Meri Makarini the children's', and later that Meri 'wrote a long slateful'.[56] Formal Māori education continued to be dominated by missionaries until the Natives Schools Act 1867 when the government took responsibility.

The effects of missionary education have sometimes been over-stated, including claims that Māori youth were indoctrinated by the discourses and practices of their schooling, or that the religious focus in teaching in the Māori language left them ill-equipped for the colonial experience.[57] Despite missionary desires, or the government's stated aim to assimilate through schooling,[58] many Māori acquired literacy skills with minimal or no exposure to formal Pākehā-run education, either through very short attendance at a school, or from informal lessons from fellow members of the tribe.[59] As the missionary T. S. Grace lamented in 1855, 'as for reading, writing and arithmetic' there was 'a nation of such scholars'.

> A young woman who has spent 4 or 5 years at one of our establishments returns to her kainga with a fair knowledge of reading, writing and arithmetic and knows something of drawing, geography, singing, fine needle-work, knitting, netting, and crochet; but she finds there many who are able to read, write and figure as well as she, and, as for the fine accomplishments, they go for nothing[.][60]

The level of nineteenth-century Māori literacy is a matter of scholarly uncertainty. The missionaries certainly highlighted the spread of reading, and the demand for books, as a means of promoting the success of their endeavours.[61] As Richard Taylor suggested in 1845, 'The Natives are very fond of letter-writing, and far more generally avail themselves of this way of communicating with one another than our peasantry or lower classes in England.'[62] William Wade, a former missionary in New Zealand, thought that with the straightforward orthography of te reo, Māori could be taught to read and write in a fortnight, and:

> the statement derives confirmation from the great numbers who have these acquirements, and that too amongst tribes who have had no intercourse with the missionaries. If one native in a tribe can read and write, he will not be long in teaching the others.

'The desire' he stated 'engrosses their whole thoughts'. To illustrate this, he gave an account of Māori he met on the Piako River.

> Coming to a small temporary station, I found about twenty natives engaged in fishing for eels, and curing them for future supplies. On looking into their huts I observed some of them were busy with their slates, and found that they were learning to read and write.[63]

Some scholars have accepted a widespread Māori uptake of literacy, that 'most Māori aged between 10 and 30 could read and write their own language, a higher literacy rate than in the non-Māori population',[64] and that the Māori literacy rate reached 90 per cent by the mid 1850s.[65] Others have suggested that missionary claims were exaggerated.[66] Because the printed texts supplied by missionaries were mainly religious in nature, it has been argued that a boom in reading and writing coincided with an interest in Christianity, and waned in the 1840s as Māori 'had lost interest in the Missions' teachings as a whole'.[67] Critiquing the argument that any literacy boom must have predated formal colonisation, D. F. McKenzie argues against any boom at all, basing his thesis on the small number of signatures (about 12 per cent) on the Treaty of Waitangi.[68] Lyndsay Head and Buddy Mikaere countered this view, stating that McKenzie's use of treaty signatures was misguided given that Māori most likely to have become literate were not the chiefly signatories, and that the real engagement with literacy occurred after 1840.[69] However the actual evidence is too patchy to make a definitive estimate of literacy levels. What is clear is that Māori interest in Pākehā-run education waxed and waned during the nineteenth century; enthusiasm was often linked to attitudes towards the church or government, varying in different localities at different times. Literacy, however, was a skill that could be attained without formal schooling, and could be used for a variety of purposes. Indeed, in his evidence to the Native Affairs Select Committee in 1876, Wī Parata said he was sent to the school at Ōtaki to learn English, for he already knew how to read and write in the Māori language, having been taught these skills by his mother.[70]

Writing and the written word were everywhere. Alphabetic text was integrated into many aspects of Māori life, including into tattooing, a 'literacy on the skin'.[71] Wharenui, carved meeting houses, transformed in the nineteenth century at the same time as writing was being taught in mission schools, and the written word was integrated in the form of named houses.[72] Māori used the pen to record their facial moko onto paper, which was an accepted signature on the Treaty of

Waitangi and early land-purchase agreements.[73] Māori women participated in this practice too, with at least one out of the 13 female signatories to the treaty signing with her moko.[74] In doing so, these instances 'literally mark a moment in the integration of pen and ink representation into te ao Māori, and the integration of Māori marks into the European world of paper-based authority'.[75]

Literacy practices

Deciding on how many nineteenth-century Māori could read and write is of less importance than determining how easily they could access written information and use literacy skills. Certainly we have found numerous documents that Māori women generated, but signed with an X. Most Māori lived a close communal village life and a lack of literacy did not exclude them from engaging with text if there was someone who was able to read or write for them. As Jane McRae asserts, there is 'no doubt as to Māori people's discriminating and efficient use of literacy'.[76] Books, newspapers and correspondence were sometimes read out to public gatherings, and scribes wrote letters for tribal leaders.[77] Māori women also used scribes when necessary. The lack of one skill did not preclude another. For example, Hemaima Whanako stated, 'I can read, but I cannot write.'[78] Ārihi Te Nahu could not read or write but claimed to be able to recognise an individual's handwriting.[79] She understood the power of writing too, dictating her libellous letter to *Te Waka Maori* to her husband.[80] She also placed advertisements in the local English-language newspaper,[81] and employed lawyers to deal with numerous legal issues. Her illiteracy may have placed her at a disadvantage, but did not exclude her from participating in literacy practices. The missionary T. S. Grace told of Māori women dictating letters for Bay of Plenty men taken as prisoners of war to Auckland in the mid-1860s.

> The wives and relatives of the Maoris still in prison have spent the day in writing letters for me to take. These people are not wanting in the finer feelings of our nature. As I sat by I could not help hearing them as they dictated to their scribes these letters in language most tender and touching. Two children of one poor fellow who is in prison have lately died. This sad news had now to be communicated to him. This they had done in the nicest manner, telling him not to be sad; that though the children had been taken his life had been spared, and that he had still many loving friends. Then followed a very appropriate song.[82]

The women were thus speaking and singing their words, which the scribes converted into text. Unfortunately these letters probably no longer exist, at least not in any archives we searched during the project that underpins this book.

It is likely that Māori women received assistance from missionaries, teachers, or other trusted Pākehā. For example, Ramarihi, giving evidence in 1879, stated, 'I went to Mrs. Grace, who was my teacher, to get her to write the letter for me.' Sarah Grace, the wife of Tauranga-based missionary T. S. Grace, was valuable not just for her writing skills, but also for her knowledge of Pākehā procedures. When Ramarihi needed another letter she returned to the school.

> *I wrote the letter to Mr. Clarke, Sir George Grey, and Mr. Sheehan, asking them to stop the Crown grant, and not allow it to be issued to Captain Morris.*
> 816. Did you write a letter [to] the Governor? —*Yes.*
> 817. Is that your letter to the Governor about the land of your father's at Pukepoto?—*I do not know anything about the Governors. The only Governors I know are Sir George Grey and Mr. Sheehan.*
> 818. Did you write this letter [produced.]?—*Yes, I meant it to reach Sir George Grey and Mr. Sheehan. I am an ignorant person I do not know exactly how to do these things.*
> 819. Hon. Mr. Fox.] How comes Pita's name to be at the bottom of your letter? Who is Pita? —*My brother.*
> 820. Hon. Mr. Nahe] Did Mrs. Grace write the letter? — *I went to Mrs. Grace to get advice as to what I should do about the land because I was ignorant myself. It was a daughter of the Rev. Ihaia Te Ahu, who is staying with Mrs. Grace at school, who wrote the letter. It was Mrs. Grace who advised me what to do. She was my teacher at school, and I thought she was the best person to give me advice.*[83]

While a lack of literacy was not necessarily a handicap for Māori women if they had assistance from trusted friends or relatives, when they had to rely on others they were vulnerable to fraud and manipulation. In 1897 Ruiha Kīngi and Ngāhuia Kīngi signed a lease of 38 acres at Kamo, Whāngārei, to a Pākehā man. Their lease concludes with signatures, with Ruiha signing with an X, adjacent to the typewritten words 'Signed by the said Ruiha Kingi in the presence of Edmund Thomas Dufaur a Solicitor of the Supreme Court who hereby certifies that she the said Ruiha Kingi has a knowledge of the English language sufficient for her to understand and that she does understand the effect of the foregoing'. In handwriting it is added 'and that the same was read over and explained to her[,] she being illiterate before the same was executed by her[.]'[84] Ruiha may not have had 'sufficient' knowledge of English to comprehend the legalese, and probably acted on trust. In 1901, another lawyer, Clark-Walker, and land purchaser, Kennedy, did take advantage of her. It appears that Kennedy had no money but nevertheless wrote a cheque for £300. Clark-Walker (who represented both parties) immediately lent the money back to Kennedy who promptly mortgaged the land for £200. A Native Land Court Commissioner who came across the case was particularly critical of their actions, and considered that Ruiha's illiteracy facilitated their duplicity.[85]

As literacy spread Māori wrote many letters to each other, few of which survive, or perhaps they are retained in private whānau collections. Nevertheless, *He Reo Wāhine* attests to the popularity of the letter as a mode of written communication amongst Māori, particularly in the 1850s and 1860s. The lack of paper did not impede writing during those decades, or earlier: several early visitors noted the use of 'flax letters' utilising the leaves of harakeke (Phormium tenax).[86] As G. B. Earp wrote:

> If the native has no paper, he frequently makes use of the green flax leaf as a species of papyrus, writing upon it with a pen or a nail, the writing being as distinct as it would be on paper, the scratches taking off the green polished surface, and leaving the delicate white fibre underneath perfectly distinct; the writing being thus white on a polished green ground.[87]

Early adopters of letter writing included Māori women, such as Toenga 'the only daughter of the once celebrated Waraurangi, the most powerful chief of the Nga-ti-maru tribe'. According to the artist George French Angas, she, 'like many of her sex, is an inveterate letter writer, and I remember on one occasion, to have seen her despatch a native messenger with upwards of a dozen letters, some on paper, and others on flax-leaves to her friends and relatives at the Thames.'[88]

It does not appear that any examples of flax writing still exist. The same may be said for the earliest writing efforts, such as those of the girls at Kendall's school from 1816. The earliest extant inscription by a Māori woman may be the X written by Maria Ringa in 1823 on her wedding certificate. Material objects also reveal the earliest encounters with writing, such as the writing slate recovered from under the floorboards of the Kerikeri Mission House, inscribed with the words 'Na Rongo Hongi C. 16'. The name almost certainly refers to Hariata Rongo, the daughter of the Ngāpuhi chief Hongi Hika and his senior wife Turikatuku.

Rongo attended the mission school run by the missionary Martha Clarke in the late 1820s when aged about 16, and later lived with the Kemps, another missionary family. If actually written by Rongo herself, this may be the earliest extant written text by a Māori woman.[89]

Due to the way our source material entered the archives, it, by extension, reveals much about how colonialism was practised and how it shaped the lives of Māori women. Much of the material was collected by colonial officials, lawyers, journalists and ethnographers, or was sent directly to officials, such as the governor or the Native Secretary, and so had a higher rate of survival; the other major sources are settler and Māori-language newspapers, the latter being a feature of intellectual and cultural life in Māori communities, and a source of correspondence between Māori, of which we have few examples in the manuscript collections. In light of this, the period best represented in *He Reo Wāhine* is the 1850s and 1860s, when significant numbers of texts, mainly letters, start to appear in the archives.[90] Their survival reflects the fact that these were communications sent to colonial officials, at the height of conflict over sovereignty, and the officials retained them in their collections.

For officials, language ability was a part of the tool-set of colonialism, made easier by the fact that Māori tribal dialects were mutually intelligible, which meant that the state could deal with Māori using any dialect. Although officials took an interest in the language and learnt it, and some Pākehā even grew up with it, this does not necessarily translate to a sympathy with Māori, but an acknowledgement that knowledge of te reo was required for the effective conduct of business. Additionally, having one mutually comprehensible language gave a particular shape to the textual culture. It meant the government could establish Māori-language newspapers in order to communicate to all Māori across the country, and that native department employees could give effect to native policy, in the form of land purchasing. Unsurprisingly, most of our material was originally written in te reo, suggesting it was the preferred language of communication for Māori writers when they engaged with the colonial bureaucracy.

While always mindful of the one-sided nature of the archive, we hope that the texts and their stories will be of use to a range of researchers, teachers, students and interested readers. In particular, *He Reo Wāhine*'s extensive use of items in te reo Māori also offers a resource to those seeking authentic writing produced by native speakers from a time when many had little exposure to the English language. *He Reo Wāhine* also reflects active Māori engagement with a diverse print culture, including Māori-language newspapers, letter writing and petitioning, and also memoir, or life writing. Māori read settler newspapers, requested their letters be published in them, and paid for advertisements too, often in te reo. Letters continued to be an important feature of Māori writing culture throughout the nineteenth century, but with the advent of the colonial government, land-purchase deeds and petitions, as well as government-produced Māori-language material like newspapers, ordinances and the gazette (*Kahiti*) entered the Māori world. As the colonial state asserted greater control, they also expanded their paper-based administration systems to deal with Māori land.[91] In this way, writing underpinned colonial practices of governance, and Māori, women included, wrote to officials collectively, on behalf of their families and communities, or for personal and more individual reasons. Even when individuals could not read and write, they understood the power of writing, recognising one had to engage with it in order to communicate with colonial officials. In this respect, we need to recognise that while te reo Māori has particular histories and uses within the private sphere, it was also integrated into the public world of government as a 'language of civic engagement'.[92] Just as 'print and literacy were powerful tools that indigenous and colonised groups could deploy in the face of imperial power', they were also tools exerted by the colonial administration against indigenous communities with devastating results.[93] For many Māori, then, colonialism often involved engagement with bureaucracy, legal documents and printed forms. As legal historian Richard Boast argues, looking at these documents helps to illuminate how Māori participated in a range of legal processes and institutions, while also being able to trace the impact of colonialism upon families and communities.[94]

At the same time, *He Reo Wāhine* also illuminates aspects of Māori women's intellectual and social worlds, as well as their emotional lives. It showcases the vitality and centrality of te reo Māori in written communications and the oral world, and how writing was mapped onto and integrated into existing modes of communication. It draws attention to Māori women's participation within state institutions, how they made use of the available processes for restitution, but also how they were treated under the law, and within colonial society more broadly. While we have undertaken quite extensive searches to construct our corpus of material, we are sure that much more Māori women's writing exists, especially outside of the archives held by public institutions. By tracing their words, *He Reo Wāhine* shows that colonialism was ever-present in Māori lives, but it was not completely overwhelming; there was scope for engagement and critique, as well as resistance. What *He Reo Wāhine* does is open up the variety of responses in their nuance and complexity, and also the range of ways Māori women thought about the social, economic and political transitions brought about by the pressures of colonialism.

Note on style

Unless otherwise stated, primary quotations of Māori women's voices have been italicised: where an original Māori-language text exists, accompanied by translation, the former is italicised, the latter is not. Other than the italicisation, we have tried to reproduce these texts 'as they are' in most cases and not attempted to tidy or modernise them. This has meant retaining the older forms of Māori-language orthography (such as 'kia' for 'ki a'), and not adding macrons to nineteenth-century texts. It is with hand-written material that our transcriptions may deviate slightly from the original text, such as where no print symbol exists for what was written (for example the '&' sign is used in the place of some alternate symbols) and where the punctuation or capitalisation may be ambiguous. Square brackets are used for spelling mistakes, omissions and occasionally for explanation.

CHAPTER 1

'I am a woman who wrote this letter': Land Sales

LAND WAS THE DEFINING ISSUE OF NEW ZEALAND RACE RELATIONS IN THE nineteenth century. Māori had the land that Pākehā wanted, not just for the economic aspects of settlement, but also as a means to realise Crown sovereignty and to gain effective control. Colonisation could only succeed at the expense of mana whenua, but unlike the Australian situation, the indigenous people of New Zealand were too numerous and powerful for Pākehā to simply appropriate the land. Some settlers argued, using European theorists such as Vattel, that Māori should only 'own' land they were actively cultivating. However the New Zealand government, cognisant of both Māori numbers and power, and the disapproval of missionaries and English humanitarians, always acknowledged that Māori possessed customary title to all land.[1] Such rights of ownership, based on tikanga, could be complex: tribal groups had mana over land as a form of ownership in common, although rights were often devolved to smaller groups, such as whānau, to use the land or some resources upon it.[2] It was not unusual for different hapū or iwi to claim mana whenua over the same land. The Māori forms of customary title did not translate easily into the forms of land tenure recognised by English law; if Europeans were to possess the land, native title needed first to be extinguished in order for the land to be converted into Crown land, or to become privately owned freehold property.

Pre-Treaty sales

Pākehā had already begun acquiring land from Māori prior to formal colonisation in 1840. Some Māori made 'sales' on a vast scale to hopeful Sydney speculators, or to the New Zealand Company for on-selling to its immigrants from late 1839. There were, however, a number of land transfers, both moderately large and small, from Māori to Pākehā such as traders and missionaries who were living among them. It is likely that Māori considered these deals, even when solemnised with a written deed, quite differently to the Pākehā participants. For Māori, to tuku whenua (release land) was more about building a relationship with 'their' Pākehā who, in the case of traders, were often well integrated within tribal life and had Māori wives and children. In 1841 the government established the Old Land Claims Commission to investigate the many Pākehā claims, some outrageous, some reasonable, to Māori land. Many of the claims were decided in the 1840s, but in 1856 Parliament passed the Land Claims Settlement Act so that any unresolved or disputed claims could be finally settled 'not according to strict law, but according to equity and good conscience'. The act also recognised that some cases involved mixed marriages and 'children of such marriages', and 'that inquiry should be made into such cases with a view to make a just provision for the same'.[3] The government subsequently appointed Francis Dillon Bell as the sole commissioner to investigate all claims.[4]

In 1839, the Pākehā trader Thomas Halbert acquired the Pouparae Block, about 1100 acres on the Waipaoa River near Tūranga, 493 acres of which he sold two years later to the newly arrived Anglican missionary William Williams. Because Halbert had made the original purchase, Williams left it to him to present the claim before the commission in the 1840s, something the trader failed to do. Bell therefore heard the case in December 1859 and January 1860 at Tūranga.[5] Halbert had a succession of Māori wives, and the chief counter-claimant was his fourth wife Rīria Mauaranui, an influential woman of Te Aitanga-a-Māhaki and Rongowhakaata descent with whom he began a relationship in 1837.[6] Rīria claimed on behalf of her son by Halbert, Wī Pere, who was later an influential Māori politician. Rīria stated:

> *My child had been born some time when Halbert spoke to me about buying some land for him. I said it was unnecessary to purchase the land because the natives would give it: but he answered that he would rather buy the land and then he would be sure of his son retaining possession of it – but if the land were only given, the natives could at some time or other drive him off it. We then went together to our relations, to speak about certain land (Pouparae) – and agreed to purchase a piece of land there. The talk at that meeting was that the land was to be for the child. Halbert waited some time for goods of his own*

to arrive, but as they were long time coming, he spoke to me of getting goods from Mr. Harris.[7]

It is clear that for Rīria the land was for their son, a position supported by the other Māori witnesses. For her Whānau-a-Kai hapū, the deal was about their relationship with Halbert with whom they shared a descendant, rather than the £300 in goods and money that he paid. Unfortunately, Halbert and Rīria's relationship, formalised by William Williams, did not last.

I was present at the payment being given, and it was again said at that time that the land was for the child. My child was then able to run about. After this Halbert drove me and the child away and took another woman to live with him.[8]

Halbert denied that the land sold was an inheritance for his son. Commissioner Bell chose not to make a decision. Williams wrote to Bell in 1869 asserting that Wī Pere's rights had not arisen when he purchased the land, and that all Māori claims had been dropped.[9] The Waitangi Tribunal gives several reasons why Māori might have relinquished their claims: that they believed that Halbert might be prosecuted for selling the land; that there were more important land claims needing attention; or that Wī Pere was being generous to Williams – the missionary had had to flee his mission in 1865 due to the rise of Pai Mārire, and a number of Māori and Pākehā in the area had been killed by Te Kooti in 1868 (see chapter 2).[10] Williams received his Crown Grant for the land in 1871,[11] although the Waitangi Tribunal believes that Halbert did not have the right to sell the land and effectively disinherit his son.[12]

Rīria was not the only Māori woman whose land was claimed by a Pākehā husband through the mechanism of the Old Land Claims investigations. Uncertain of their rights to land, some white men sought to establish legal title as Crown grants to land that had been gifted by marriage. Customarily such land was the woman's, to be retained for any children of the relationship, and it extended to her husband the right of occupation alone. White men with Māori wives and families – even if some were motivated to ensure the economic security of their families – exploited the land-claims system, using it to their advantage by claiming the gifted land was in fact a 'purchase'. In granting title to marriage gifts, the Land Claims Commission effectively eroded Māori women's control over their lands, and also separated the marriage gift from tribal lands.[13]

Post-Treaty sales

Under the Treaty of Waitangi, the government claimed 'the exclusive right of Preemption', which it interpreted as entitling it to be the sole purchaser of Māori land. The government argued that Māori needed protection from unscrupulous settlers, but it also feared that if settlers were permitted to buy smaller blocks directly from Māori, they would inevitably run into problems over competing claims of ownership, and possible inter-racial clashes that it would then have to settle.

In many cases the purchase agreement was largely oral in nature, with rangatira, most likely male, negotiating on behalf of the hapū with a government official. As the 1891 Commission on Native Land Laws wistfully reported, the government's 'olden style of purchase' was 'at once open and simple'.

> The proposal to purchase was made to the head chief in the presence of at least some of the lesser chiefs; the boundaries of the lands to be dealt with were described; the price to be paid was agreed to; a day was fixed upon which, in the presence of the tribe, the bargain was to be completed. The purchaser then counted the purchase-money in the presence of the chiefs and people, and placed it in a bag or bags before the principal chief, who would then distribute the money among the other chiefs, leaving them to share their portions among their own hapus and families. Frequently, great chiefs thus disposing of extensive territories would give all the purchase-money to their people, leaving nothing for themselves, and, when the gold was thus bestowed, would shake the empty bag which had held it, upside down, to show that nothing remained. 'Those were the days,' said Chief Judge Fenton, in describing such a scene, 'when the Maori chief was a gentleman.'[14]

For most of its first 25 years the government maintained its monopoly, purchasing blocks of land at low prices from tribal groupings, which it sold on to settlers at much higher prices, using the profits to finance its administration.[15] In theory, 'the government would not solicit, but merely await, an offer from a tribal group to sell some land', but in practice officials were much more proactive in their activities.[16] During this time most of the South Island was purchased, along with large areas in Hawke's Bay, Wairarapa, Wellington, Whanganui and to the north and south of Auckland.

The way in which land was purchased means that women's voices at these meetings were less likely to be heard, or at least recorded. It is in the written correspondence that their views are made known. We collected no letters by women concerning land for the 1840s, but they start to appear in the 1850s. Ani Mātenga Te Patukaikino (Ngāti Kahungunu) was direct in her request to Land Commissioner Donald McLean.

> *Aperira 16.1851*
> *E hoa e te makarini tenei ta matou kupu ki a koe[.] ko te utu mo to matou kainga 10 mano[.]*
> *Na Ani Matenga*
>
> [modern translation]
> 16 April, 1851.
> Sir, Mr. McLean, this is our word to you. The price for our property is 10,000 [pounds].
> From Ani Mātenga.[17]

Ani sent another letter. The year is not indicated, but it may have related to the same deal.

> *No Patangata no te 4 o nga ra o Hune i tuhia atu ai[.]*
> *E ta e te Makarini, tena ra koe[.] tenei ano ahau te ora atu nei[.] Na kaore aku korero atu kia koe, ara kia korua ko Kawana, kai a korua tonu nga korero ara mo to taua kainga ki te tutatanga ki te aha tanga ranei, ki te kore noa iho pea ko wai hoki ahau ka mohio, Na E ta mau e hohoro a hohoro mai, a mau e kore atu a kore atu engari pea me waka hohoro mai i nga ra wakamutunga o Hurae[.] e ta ko taku korero tena ki a koe[.]*
> *heoi ano Naku*
> *Na Ani Matenga*
> *kia te Makarini*
>
> [modern translation]
> Pātangata, written 4 June.
> Sir, Mr. McLean, greetings. I am well. I do not have anything to say to you, that is, to you and the Governor, it is up to you two to say something, that is, about our land, that is, on its current position or what is being done, or not, I have no idea. Now Sir, you can be quick if you want, or not, but you should perhaps be quick, in the last days of July. Sir, this is what I have to say.

That is all from me
From me, Ani Mātenga
to Mr. McLean.[18]

When land was sold, the money was not always all paid at one time. In the following letter, Meri Te Aokauai and another from Rangiwakaoma (Castlepoint) discuss getting money still owing to them.

Rangiwakaoma
Oketopa 20 1864

Ki Nepia kia te Makarini e ta tena koe he kupu atu tenei kia koe mo nga toenga o Maungarake ano te ..50.. pauna i korerotia ai e maua ko te kau matua ko te Wiremu Potangaroa i te Pa o te Hapuku i te Hauke[.] heoi ko aua moni me homai e koe inaianei taua 50 pauna[.] kua ki ake ano a te Wiremu kia homai e koe aua moni [.] ki te pai koe kite tukua mai e koe a te Kupa mana e mau mai[.] heoi ano
Na Meri te aokauai
    Na Tapatu Ruta.

[modern translation]

Rangiwakaoma,
20 October, 1864.

To Napier, to Mr McLean. Sir, Greetings. This is a word to you about the remaining [money] of Maungarake, the 50 pounds that the elder, Te Wiremu Pōtangaroa, and I discussed at Te Hāpuku's pā at Te Hauke. Anyway, you should give that money, the 50 pounds, now. Te Wiremu has said that you should give that money. If it is agreeable to you, hand the money to Te Kupa [Cooper] and he will bring it here.
That is all.
From Meri Te Aokauai
and Tapatu Ruta.[19]

One of the primary concerns Māori held was about asserting rights over land that was being sold, had been sold, or that someone else might sell. In some cases these concerns were expressed publicly. In 1857, the newspaper *Te Waka o te Iwi* published a letter from Miriama Hēmara, the wife of Ngāti Whātua chief Te Hēmara Tauhia. She owned land inland of the Kaipara Harbour.[20]

He Pukapuka Whenua na Miriama Hemara, o Ngatirango
   Mahurangi, Akuhata 27, 1857.
Ki a Hare Reweti, – tenei pukapuka. E kara, tenei ano te kupu ki a koe. Ki te tae mai Te Uriohau korero atu koe ki a ratou mo te pihi whenua i Aropaoa mo te pihi hou kia whakarerea, kaua e tukua, erangi kia rite te mea tawhito ka tahi ka tika. Heoi ano ka mutu.
Na Miriama Hemara

[modern translation]
Letter about Land from Miriama Hēmara of Ngāti Rango.
Mahurangi, 27 August, 1857.
To Charles Davis, this letter. Sir, here is [my] word to you. If Te Uri-o-Hau come, talk to them about the piece of land at Aropaoa, the new piece which is to be left, and not to be released [for sale] but let the old one be dealt with, and then it is right. That is all.
From Miriama Hēmara.[21]

Although the niupepa published other letters concerning land, Miriama's letter does not explain why the editor, Charles Davis, who had recently left his job at the Native Office,[22] would be talking about land to Te Uri-o-Hau, another hapū of Ngāti Whātua. What the letter does is assert her interest in an area where competing hapū and iwi were selling land. Most letters were not for publication, and sent directly to Donald McLean, then head of both the Native Office and land-purchasing operations.

Hārata Panga wrote to ensure that she received something from the sale of land at Heretaunga in 1853.

15 Hepetema 1[8]53
Ki Makawhiu kia Te Makarini e ta tena koe[.] He korero ano taku ki a koe mo taku korero ki a koe i te Turei, mo te tahi whahi o nga utu o Heretaunga kia homai mo maua ko taku hoa, kei a Hori te whakaaro kia maua, ta te mea hoki i a au tetahi whahi o tena kainga o Heretaunga ko toku matua tane no reira ko taku matua wahine no Manawatu no Horowhenua puta noa ki Porirua ko toku matua tane i pumau tonu ki Heretaunga[.] ma nga tangata o reira e korero ki a koe he pono taku korero ki a koe, ta te meahoki ko te utu whakamutunga tenei o taua kainga e oti atu ai ki a koe[.] ki te whakaae mai nga tangata ki taku pukapuka, na mau tonu e mau mai nga moni, tena ano taku pukapuka ki a Hori

kei Wareama kei a Henare, mau e mau atu ki a ia[.] E kore au e haere taua he mea ekore au i kaha ki te haere[.] ko nga moni e pai ana ahau ki te whakaae mai a Hori, £10-0-0
Ki Makawhiu
  kia te Makarini
Na Harata Panga

[modern translation]
15 September 1853
To Makawhiu, to McLean
Sir,
Greetings. I have more to say to you about my talk with you on Tuesday concerning a part of the payments for Heretaunga to be given for my husband and I. It was Hori who thought about us, but [because] I also own one part of the land of Heretaunga, from my father; my mother was from Manawatū, from Horowhenua and on to Porirua, but my father was permanently at Heretaunga. The people there will tell you that. It's true what I am telling you. And since you are about to complete the final payment for that land, then if the people agree with my letter, you yourself could bring me the money. But my letter will also go to Hori at Wareama, with Hēnare, so you could take it to him. I can't go there because I am not strong enough for the journey. The money I would like, if Hōri agrees, is £10,
To Makawhiu, to McLean
From Hārata Panga

Miriama Neinukua was concerned that land she was living on might have been sold.

Hurae 9 1857
haere ra e taku reta kia Makarini[.] e koro tena ra koe[.] he kupu tenei naku kia koe[.] tenei ka rongo au kua riro toku kainga te tuku kia koe[.] he patai tenei naku kia waka marama tia mai e koe ma nga kainga i tukua e Hupata [Heipata?] kia koe moraiiti
   kamutu
Na Miriama Neinukua
no te Aute.

[modern translation]
9 July 1857
Go my letter to McLean. Greetings, Sir. This is my word to you. I have heard that my place of residence has been given over to you. I have a question: please explain which places Hupata [Heipata?] has given over to you [unknown].
That is all.
from Miriama Neinukua
of Te Aute.[24]

When unanimity did not exist for parting with land, government agents sometimes resorted to dealing with a few chiefs in private. The concern of Hana Te Unuhi was to ensure that any sales would be done publicly.

No Takapuahia
    Akuhata 4-57
E hoa e te Makarini, tena koe, na, kia rongo mai koe, kua rongo au, e ho mai ana e koe nga utu, mo Puketapu, mo Waiongana, e mea ana au, kaua e hohorotia te ho mai o moni, kia rupeke katoa atu matou ki to aroaro ka homai ai, kia rongo hoki koe ki o matou tikanga, na, kia rongo mai koe kei whakahapa koe i au, ki nga moni atu, o nga oneone o aku tupuna, o aku matua, kei po hehe koe, ki au, he tamahine a hau ki a te Rangiahuta, hei mokopuna au ki a Tutariaria, heoti ano.
Na Hana te Unuhi
(he aha koa he namu maharatia mai ano e koe – heoti ano

[modern translation]
Takapuahia
4 August 1857
Mr McLean, Sir, greetings. Please listen. I have heard you are giving out payment for Puketapu and Waiongana. I am asking that you are not [too] quick to give out your money, until we have all assembled in your presence, then you can give it; until you have heard our propositions. So, listen lest you deprive me of the payments for the lands of my ancestors and mistake my identity. I am the daughter of Te Rangiahuta, and the descendant of Tutariaria.
That is all.
From Hana Te Unuhi.
    (Despite these gripes, please think of me. That is all.)[25]

During this period, selling land was never just a commercial transaction. Just as in early land sales where Māori sought to develop relationships with local Pākehā, Māori now sold because they wanted a good relationship with the purchaser, the government. This can be seen in the following letter, where Metīria Matara of Ngāti Toa, having sold her land, sought a site in the town for her house, and appealed for aroha (love and sympathy). She also clearly indicated her gender in her letter.

Te Kawau Hepetema 13 1852
E koro, e Te Makarini tena ra koe korua ko Kawana Kerei[.] he wahine pakeke au imua inga wakanga o tenei wenua onga motu[.] e koro, e makarini, e mohio ana koe ki tamaua rohe ko Karira i tukua atu ai kia koe i te ra taha o waiwakaiho, iaraheke[.] kua pakaru tera rohe amaua, notemea ka rongo te tokomaha o nga tangata, kawakahae katoa nga tangata ki taku tikanga[.] ka wahia ki Murumuru kei Pikipari tona rohenga mai outa ko mangorei kei pouakai tona rohe[.] ete Makarini raua ko Kawana kia rongo mai korua kua pau katoa i au te oneone te hoatu kia korua ko mangorei kua ho atu e au kia korua ko toku aroha tenei ki a korua ara ki nga pakeha[.] naku tenei tikanga na Metiria[.] me aroha mai hoki korua kiau, ki tetahi turanga motaku whare i roto i tenei taone[.] me aroha mai korua kiau, no temea he kainga tangata te wahi itu ai taku whare no Wiremu raua ko Matena[.] me aroha korua ki tetahi wahi moku hei turanga mo toku ware[.] heoi ano na takorua kotiro aroha na Metiria Matara[.]

[modern translation]
Te Kawau
13 September 1852
Sir, McLean,
Greetings to you and Governor Grey. I am a woman who is experienced in the adjudication of land in these islands.

Sir, McLean, you know our, my and Karira's, area that was given to you on the other side of Waiwakaiho, at Araheke. Well our boundary has been split, because when the majority of the people heard, they all agreed to my proposal. The boundary divides at Murumuru [and runs ?] to Pakipari [sic], inland from Mangōrei, and out to Pouākai.

McLean and Governor, listen. I have used up all the land in giving you Mangōrei; and when I gave it to you it was because of my regard for you, that is, for the Pākehā. This was my idea, Metīria's, and so show me some consideration by [giving me] a site for my house in this town. Have aroha for me because the land where my house stood was someone's home, Wiremu and Matena's. Show consideration for me by a place for me to put my house. That is all.

    From your loving girl,
from Metīria Matara[26]

Another correspondent who stressed her gender was Kataraina Kahuwahine of Pigeon Bay, who wrote to Governor Grey in 1851 offering land for sale. After listing all her land she states:

Kei mea mai koe he Tane nana tenei Pukapuka Kahore [h]e wahine au nama [sic] tenei pukapuka[.] Me aroha mai pea koe kiau no te mea kokoe te tino Kawana o Nuitireni koinei i mea atu ai tenei wahine pohara kia koe kia homaiekoe Ngautu oenei pihi whenua kiau[.]

[modern translation]
Do not think that this letter is from a man. No, I am a woman who wrote this letter. You should perhaps have sympathy for me because you are the eminent Governor of New Zealand. That is why this poor woman asks you to give me payment for these pieces of land.[27]

There was insufficient information for the government to act upon Kataraina's request. A memo is attached from H. T. Kemp, the Native Secretary, stating 'She does not say what tribe she belongs to, or whether the land is part of a reserve', and querying whether Kataraina was 'a person of any importance'.[28]

The Native Land Court

The process of sole government purchase caused some problems. Neither Māori nor the settlers were particularly pleased with the process; both felt that they might make better deals directly with each other. For the government, both the ownership of land, and its availability, were issues. When one iwi or hapū sold a block of land, the government sometimes had to pay compensation to other claimants who had not acceded to the deal. Competing claims of ownership led to friction, sometimes resulting in inter- and intra-tribal warfare. Many Māori saw

Pākehā settlement as an opportunity for trade, but became increasingly aware that as greater numbers of Pākehā settled in an area, they became less inclined to accept Māori control and demanded government protection, which impinged upon rangatiratanga. Due to both the violence between competing Māori groups emanating from land sales, and the desire to retain tribal mana, increasing numbers of chiefs became determined to resist selling land, which in turn led to the establishment of the Kīngitanga in 1858, a Māori kingship encompassing a number of central North Island tribes under Pōtatau Te Wherowhero. Matters then came to a head with the first Taranaki war, precipitated by the government in 1860 when it attempted at buy land at Waitara from a small group of Te Āti Awa, when the majority of the tribe objected to the sale.

In response to these issues, the government decided to establish a special court in which Māori could have their land claims peacefully adjudicated. The Native Lands Act 1862 created the first court, but this met only a few times. It was the Native Lands Act 1865 that gave the Native Land Court its shape for the years to come. The court's primary aim was to extinguish native title in the North Island, by converting it to a subdividable form. Once a block of land had been surveyed, the court issued certificates of title to successful claimants, who could then apply to have these converted into Crown grants. With the government waiving its right of preemption, Māori who possessed the new paper deeds could easily sell their lands to willing Pākehā on the open market.

The Pākehā judges who presided over the court, assisted by Māori assessors, determined ownership using a form of common law based on their interpretation of tikanga and tribal history, and sometimes the precedent of earlier cases. The handwritten minute books of the Native Land Court are a valuable resource in which to find women's voices, offering up considerable information about whakapapa and history, as well as details on aspects of contemporary Māori life.[29] Unlike Pākehā women, married Māori women could inherit and dispose of land in their own right.[30] Ann Parsonson suggests that 'senior women were seldom called on' to testify,[31] but women's involvement may have differed over time and place, with wāhine rangatira active participants in some proceedings, particularly later in the century.[32] However, it was the Pākehā judges who most often recorded the women's voices, and although nearly all of the Māori evidence in the nineteenth century would have been given in Māori, most of the minute books are in English. In addition to the court's minute books, Archives New Zealand also holds considerable correspondence regarding land issues.

Although there was constant legislative tinkering with subsequent Māori land laws, the major changes centred around who was able to 'own' the land once it had gone through the court's processes. The 1865 act allowed a certificate to be issued either to a tribe, or to up to ten individuals. In nearly all cases, the latter option was taken. For example,

> in Hawke's Bay 569,220 acres of the finest land in New Zealand, partly surrounding and running inland from the Town of Napier, which belonged to nearly four thousand Natives, who were living upon and cultivating small homesteads, were vested in about two hundred and fifty grantees, without any trust being declared in favour of the vast majority of the persons ascertained by the Native Land Court to be its owners according to Native custom.[33]

Although there may have been an expectation that titleholders would act as trustees for the whole tribe, there was no legal obligation for them to do so, nor any restriction on them selling the land if they so decided. The 1867 act maintained the ten-owner rule, 'but the names of all other owners were to be registered in the Court and endorsed upon the back of the certificate.'[34] While the land could not be sold until subdivided, the ten owners still received any rents and leases the land accrued. The 1873 act ushered in the final major change of the nineteenth century, when every eligible man, woman and child gained an individual share to a block of land, from which they were entitled to apply for their own subdivision that they could then sell if they wished.

The Native Land Court, governed by Pākehā judges, was the most efficient and cheapest method of transferring ownership of Māori land to Pākehā. While a few Māori did very well, gathering large estates, most came to possess little or no land, and became reliant on seasonal agricultural work for economic survival. The following excerpts show the kinds of information that women provided in pursuing their claims.

The Wairarapa was an area in which Māori leased extensive blocks of lands to Pākehā settlers. In the early 1890s the Native Land Court sat at Greytown to determine ownership of Ngā-waka-a-Kupe, a block of 60,000 acres belonging to Ngāti Hikawera, a hapū of Ngāti Kahungunu.[35] One of those giving evidence was Atareta Te Aho in 1892. We can see from her evidence that Māori women did not always have a good understanding of the Native Land Court and what was happening with their lands, often trusting relatives to ensure they received their share.

Atareta Te Iho continued

[Questioned] by JW Bathgate – After Karaurias death what arrangement was made about the rent [?]

It was divided into shares & Tully used to pay it[.] Tully is still the tenant of Parororangi.

Have you always received a share [?]

Yes.

Have you received share of rent for block let to Harris [?]

No, I have not, my name only is on[illegible] the lease.

Have you ever spoken to Harris about it [?]

Yes. I said how is it I don't get money for the rent of your kainga. Charles Harris said he gave our money to Hamuera Mahupuku the money for all of us. Hamuera did not give it to us Harris never gave me any. I spoke to Hikawera about not getting any rent. He got £20 from C Harris & gave it to me. The letter from Hikawera to Harris is now in his possession.

Who was the tenant before C Harris [?]

Long ago Kelly, then Bob Tullouck[sic] I received rent from Kelly & Tullock. Hikawera got the rent & gave it to me.

Have you received rent for Strang's lease [?]

Yes this land is at Mangahuia.

Have you received rent from other tenants [?]

No these are all [.] D.McLennan never pays me.

I received rent for Parororangi, Hautotara, & Mangahuia.

Have any of these people of N[illegible] Hikawera ever disputed your right to receive rent before this Court sat [?].

No never before.

Do you remember the last Ct. before Judge Mackay [?].

Yes. I was never asked to give evidence[.] Hikawera undertook to manage everything. I don't understand anything about N.L. Courts.

After decision was given in Ct. did any meetings of tribes take place about decision of the land [?]

When judgment was given but before names were decided, Hikawera[,] Heremaia & I spoke together, we were talking about [the] block & Hikawera proposed to put my nephew Te Raro into Mangahuia. I said no. I am still alive. Hikawera then did not persist.

Did you understand then they agreed you should get Mangahuia [?]

Heremaia did not say anything he was drunk, & I did not know whether Hikawera would agree. I first knew Hikawera had put Te Raro into Mangahuia when the acres were awarded. When the 5000 acres for the boy was arranged in Mangahuia I objected and spoke to . . .[36]

Niniwa-i-te-rangi, a Ngāti Kahungunu woman of mana, acquired considerable land through the Native Land Court through litigation. She was also an expert in whakapapa and tribal history, which undoubtedly assisted her cases. In the following excerpt, recorded at the Ngā-waka-a-Kupe hearing she explains how a piece of land was gifted to her ancestors following conflict between her iwi, Ngāti Kahungunu, and the neighbouring tribe, Rangitāne.

The land given by Turangatatu for Tupongas [sic] garment.
Te Auturuki of N Kahungunu was killed by Rangitane hapu[.] The N Kahungunu & Tuponga made a war party to avenge this death[.] They fought at Okahu and Rangitane were defeated. Turangatatu was made prisoner and was going to be killed & eaten but Tuponga who was with the war party said no and her brother also, and she threw her garment upon him. Turangatatu was brother of Te Whakamanu, there were six brothers. After that saving of his life Turangatatu gave the North part of this block to Tuponga and her brothers. He gave Tahuroa te Hauokoeko, Te Iringa, then called Te Ihu Toto but afterwards called Te Iringa, the hanging up of Nukus garment, he hung up the garment saying he confirmed the gift. Te Whiroa, Te Waiukoukou and Mangahuia, all are inside this block, and those lands are all he gave for the throwing of this garment, but he gave other blocks to other persons at the same time as follows.[37]

The history that determined initial Native Land Court decisions on ownership was supposed to end in 1840 when, in theory at least, English law had succeeded Māori tikanga. As Shelley Nikora has shown in her thesis on her tupuna, Riperata Kahutia of Te Aitanga-a-Māhaki, the court's minute books also hold accounts of more recent events, such as Riperata flying a large Union Jack over her pā in the mid 1860s, when Crown authority was being threatened by Pai Mārire (Hauhau).[38] Riperata explained in the Court,

The flag was hoisted at the grave of Te Aohuna which caused jealousy in the minds of Ngāti Maru and other tribes, about the time this flag was hoisted a Hauhau flag was hoisted on the opposite side of the river and this formed a

second reason of dispute about Te Aohuna. The British flag was hoisted by my people to signify disregard of the decision of the chiefs (Runanga) in giving the land to Ngāti Hinewhanga and Ngāti Maru. That flag was afterwards taken to Makauri, by which time Kereopa had arrived in this district and I and my people removed to Turanganui in fear of the Hauhau's[.][39]

The flying of the flag could be construed as exhibiting loyalty to the Crown, but from Riperata's testimony we can see that issues of 'loyalty' or 'rebellion' could also be conflated with more local concerns, such as land ownership.

The minute books also hold information about the land dealings of the time. Unscrupulous Pākehā, acting for either the government or private concerns, often used underhand tactics or put pressure on Māori to sell their land. This could include physical intimidation. In 1883 when the Court was hearing subdivision claims on the Tahuheru Block, Riperata's sister Kataraina Kahutia sought refuge in a Gisborne hotel from two Pākehā men pressuring her to sign over her land. They locked the door of the hotel, and out of fear she signed the document.

I did not go before Dr Nesbitt by my own accord, but was taken their [sic] by McDonald and Tucker. McDonald said to me to sign, I signed and the same with Tucker. I did sign a deed of covenant dated 2/6/1877 but was so confused by their following me I would have signed anything.[40]

Quite apart from the minutes of the court cases, considerable correspondence from women exists relating to Native Land Court business. Some iwi tried to arbitrate their own land issues through their own rūnanga, but once the court was established in an area, the floodgates were effectively open. For a case to be heard in the court, a written application had first to be made.

XXII. Upon receipt of such application notice thereof may be given by the Court and circulated in such manner as shall give due publicity thereto and in the same or in a subsequent notice shall be notified the day and the place when and where the Court will sit for the investigation of the said claim.[41]

The following is an example of a Native Land Court Notice from the *Wellington Independent* (23 January 1869, p. 6), with a modern translation.

He Panuitanga tenei mo tetahi piihi whenua kia wahia.
Tari o te Kooti Whakawa Whenua Maori.
Akarana, Nowema 10, 1868.
He Panuitanga tenei kia mohiotia ai, ko a te nohoanga o tenei kooti ki Kereitaone, i te Takiwa o Wairarapa, i te Porowini o Weretana, a te 17 o nga ra o Maehe, 1869, te whakarongona ai te tona a Matire Piripi, o taua Takiwa ano, kia wahia te whenua e mau nei i roto i te Karauna Karaati o te o nga ra o 186 [blank], i tuhia i whakaputaina ki taua wahine ki etahi atu hoki, ko taua whenua kei Moiki, i taua Takiwa ano, ko Moiki ano hoki te ingoa.
  He mea whakahau,
     Na Tiki,
    Kai tuhituhi o te Kooti

[modern translation]
This is a Notice about a piece of land to be divided.
Office of Native Land Court
Auckland, 10 November 1868.
This is a Notice to inform that this court will sit at Greytown, District of Wairarapa, Wellington Province on 17 March 1869 to hear the claim of Matire Piripi of that District for the land held under the Crown Grant of the day of 186 [blank], in which it was recorded, and awarded to that woman and others. That land is at Moiki, in that District, and is also known as Moiki.
By order,
   [A.J.] Dickey
     Clerk of the Court.

Receiving notice was important; under the rules of the court, failing to make a claim disqualified owners. Attendance was therefore mandatory or land might be lost. In 1868 Ihapera Hinurere and two others of Whangaruru wrote to Judge Francis Dart Fenton complaining that the notice of the court sitting at Whāngārei had arrived late. Ihapera therefore requested another hearing at Paihia.

Whangaruru Akuhata 31
E hoa e te penetana e tureiti ana nga panuitanga kia matou mo matapouri no te 4 o nga ra o akuhata katae mai te tahi no te 30 tetahi a kahore matou e tae atu kinga hanarete ki Whangarei i mea mai hoki te panuitanga hei te 30 o akuhata te hanarete koia matou i kore ai E tae i tu rei ti aua pani [sic] engari

me tuhi mai mate manene e whaka wa ki paihia kia tu tata ai nga pani [sic]
te tae mai kia matou engari kia hohoro ia nga panui tanga kia matou
Na ihapera hinurere
Na te reneti te Kihi
Na hemi tea

[modern translation]
Whangaruru 31 August [1868]
Mr Fenton, Sir.
The notice about Matapōuri came to us late. One came on 4 August, another on 30 August, and we couldn't make the hearing at Whāngārei. The notice said that the hearing was on 30 August. That's why we weren't there, as those notices were late. But you should write via a messenger that it will be judged at Paihia so that it is close by. The notices didn't come to us, be quick in sending notices to us.
From Ihapera Hinurere,
Te Reneti Te Kihi,
Hēmi Tea.[42]

Although there were forms that applicants could use, some, such as Amīria Kihi, wrote directly to the Native Minister. A clerk was instructed to write to Amīria 'that applications of this kind should be forwarded to the Chief Judge, to whom they should apply'.

Waitara
Maehe 4 1892
Ki te Minita Maori
Ehoa
He tono atu tenei na matou na (Amiria Kihi) me aku tamariki kia tukua mai he Kooti ki Waitara nei kia whakawa tia tenei poraka a Titirangi ki Waipapa (Nama Tahi 1) Ngatirahiri Poraka i runga i to matou mate ko aku tamariki i te wehenga i Turangi kaore i kooti tia kia korerotia ai nga take a matou. Koi matou e tono atu nei kia aroha mai koe ki to matou mate[.] Ko aku tamariki kore rawa he whenua hei tunga whare a mahinga kai ranei. Mo aku tamariki he inoi nui atu tenei na matou kia aroha mai koe ki to matou mate. Ka tuku mai taua kooti hei whiriwhiri i to matou mate. Heoi na matou.
na Amiria Kihi
na Raiha Raumoa
na Wiremu Ropiha

>   na Te Riu Teira
>
> me etahi atu maha noatu matou e noho mate atu nei kia tere te utu mai i ta matou tono
>
>   na o hoa aroha

[official translation]
>   Waitara
>   March 4th, 1892.

The Hon
   The Native Minister
Friend
      This is an application from me, Amiria Kihi, and my 'tamariki' (children) for a court to sit here at Waitara to hear Titirangi Block at Waipapa (No. 1) Ngatirahiri Block because my children and myself are experiencing hardship through the cutting off of Turangi without first of all ascertaining the owners before the court. This is my reason for asking you now to be kind to me and my children for there is no land whereon my children may build houses or cultivate food. We pray that you will favourably consider our 'mate' and send the court to inquire into the nature of the same.
Sufficient
Amiria Kihi
& ors

Written applications could also be sent for investigations into land to be reopened, as in Hārete Tāmihana's request in 1883.

>   *Tauranga*
>   *Hurae 22 83*
> *Ki a Maketanara*
>   *Tumuaki Kaiwhakawa*
>   *E h[o]a Tena koe*
>   *He tono tenei naku ki a koe e hiahia ana ahau kia kahititia Te Ngakau o Te Otea wahi o Opureora Tauranga mo te aranga o te Kooti a Enoka Tokoahu me ta Ngatitamehariua me ta Te Puru ki reira whaka wakia ai taua piihi whenua*
> *Heoi ano*
>   *Na Harete Tamihana*
>   *Na Muru Para*

[official translation]
    Tauranga July 22nd, 1883
J.E. Macdonald, Esq.
  Chief Judge
Sir
   Salutations to you. This is an application to you from me. I desire Te Ngakau o te Otea, part of Opureora, Tauranga, to be advertized against the rising [sitting] of the Court of Enoka Tokoahu, and that of Ngatitamehariua, that of Te Puru, that that piece of land may be heard there,
  Enough.
  From Harete Tamihana
   and another.[44]

When Rīpeka Tīria Hihina wrote, it was to receive the Crown Grant awarded to her sister.

[original not included, official translation]
    Waipa
      Waitotara, May 29th, 1877
  To Mr Fenton
      Greetings. This is an application of ours to you that you may send the Crown Grant of land belonging to my younger sister Mata Hihina as soon as possible. The letter which you received some time ago was not mine. Reply soon. This is all. From
    Ripeka Tiria Hihina
     and another[45]

Several officials scrawled notes across this document trying to determine what block of land the writer was referring to, and saying that another writer, 'Maata Tiria applied to succeed Mata Hihina' in several sections of land at Waitōtara.

In 1872, Miriama Tamaterā of Rangiriri wrote to Fenton about obtaining the actual piece of land she had originally been awarded. This may have been land awarded by the Native Land Court, or perhaps by the Compensation Court.

Rangiriri
25 o nga ra o Maehe 1872
Kia te Penetana – Kai Whakawa Ehoa Tenakoe – he kupu atu tenei naku ki

akoe mo taku piihi whenua e tata ana ki Wahi ki te awa, e mea ana ahau me homai kiau te takotoranga o aku tupuna o aku matua te rima te kau eka, ki te taha o ta Nini Kukutai, i whakaritea e te Kawanatanga maku, i te homaitanga tuatahi, i muri ka hoatu kia te tangata ke, kia Reihana te Rawhiti, e mea ana ahau, me homai ano kiau taua piihi, ko nga tupapaku te take, kaore au e pai ana ki te whenua iuta ki te taha o te roto, na te mea i whakaae a te Kawanatanga maku ake taua piihi tuatahi.

 Heoiano
  Na to hoa
  Na Miriama Tamatera

[official translation]
   Rangiriri
   March 25th., 1872.
To Mr. Fenton
 Judge
  Friend, Salutations to you. This is a word of mine to you about my piece of land near the Wahi River. I wish that you would give me the place where my ancestors and parents are laid – the fifty acres at the side of Nini Kukutai's (land) which the Government arranged should be for me at the first giving (of land), afterwards it was given to another person, to Reihana Te Rawhiti, I ask to have it given again to me, on account of the dead (there). I do not like the land more inland at the side of the lake, because the Government consented to my having that first piece.
 This is all
  From your friend
   Miriama Tamatera[46]

The possibility of individuals attempting to defraud fellow claimants led some women to write to the court. Miriama Irai wrote to the Chief Judge, Fenton, in 1877, to warn him about a man attempting to claim her lands.

  Ohui
  Oketopa 29-1877
E Kara E
Te Penetana
Tu mu aki o Akarana e Pa tena koe he kupu atu tenei naku kia koe mo te tangata haere atu ki kona tini ha nga ai mo aku pihi whe nua i

konei[.] Ko Piahana Tiwai te tangata hai tini Hanga koe ku are koe ki tena tangata mo taku pihi e tata ana ki Opotiki[.] hoi ano ka mutu[.]
Na Miriama Irai
Na Miriama Rewe

[official translation]
Ohui
October 29th 1877.
Friend Mr Fenton.
Greetings. This is a word to you about a person who is going to deceive you about my lands – Pihama Tiwai. Take care that you are not made a fool of by him about my piece of land at Opotiki. This is all. It ends.
    From Miriama Irai
      Miriama Rewe[47]

Māori women also contested surveys of their land. There were two key objections to surveying related to the Native Land Court. One was the cost that claimants had to bear. This was such a discouragement to Māori that the Secretary for Crown Lands, W. S. Moorhouse, even suggested (to no avail) that the Crown should cover the cost of surveying for claims to the court.[48] Māori also objected to surveyors turning up on their land, as it could mean that the government, or perhaps another individual, coveted their land. Maraea Hēpara wrote to Judge Fenton in 1876 about her land in the Dargaville district. She was unhappy with the destruction caused by the surveyor, and that Parore, the man who requested the survey, was in cahoots with a local Pākehā and after her land.

[original missing; official translation]
        Te Houanga
        March 28th 1876

To Mr. Fenton
Chief Judge of
Native Land Court

Friend,
    Greetings. I have a word to say to you about Mr. Graham – to inform you that my cultivations have been cut through by him. The Kumaras, maize and peachtrees have been cut through by him, and the fences completely broken down.

Now, sir, I am not a mere squatter (pahihi) upon this land – it has descended to me from my ancestors – I am not a mere squatter that it should be right for him to cut (his lines) through my cultivations. Now, Mr. Henry Kemp is the cause of this work about which Parore and I have disagreed; because it was he who told Parore to have the land surveyed; and on that account my cultivations have been cut through by Parore and Mr. Graham's line. Sir, if this procedure is right according to the law it is well, but I do not consent to this action of Mr. Graham's. However, do you, the Government communicate with Mr. Graham as I shall soon suffer from this action of Mr. Kemp's because Parore and I will not cease contending about it. For this reason I write to you about Mr. Graham, so that he may be sent back by you. Another reason that I wish him to go back, is, that he purposes to cut lines through the leased land. However, I do not consent to have that land, Mangatara, again surveyed, as it is all included within the boundaries of the flax lease. If the law upholds this work, I shall say it is a native custom. If it is right, do you write to me, so that I may understand about it.

This is all I have to say.

    From Maraea Hepara
    Te Houhanga, Kaihu, Kaipara[49]

Officials wrote a number of notes on this translation, asking whether the lands had been through the court yet, and whether Mr Graham was authorised to undertake the survey. It was noted that he was working for Parore and 'if there are any opponents, they will no doubt be heard in Court'. A letter must have been sent to Maraea, as she replied soon after.

Te Houhanga Mei 17 1876
Kia Te Penetana
Tena koe Kua tae mai tau reta patai kia au mo Mango tara[.] e hoa ko tenei whenua no te tau 1869 ka ruri tia e Te Panati te putanga kei te tikitiki tai tua ka whakatu kite kotiu Te moko noho mai pu toetoe moe atoa Wai Rapa kura Tau mata kaha wai Wai Kawe ka whakatu kite Mara Ngai Marere Atu ki korari whero te awa o Kaihu[.] Kote raina tenei atoku tupuna[.] E hoa ko tenei whenua na Te Rokena i whakawa i te Aroa ko Mita hikairoi te Ate ha i te tau 1870 e hoa he mea tika ranei Tenei ki te Ture ma te tahi tangata ke e raina tahae taku whenua kia mea ai koutou nana te whenua e Hoa e kore au e mangere mo taku whenua ake ano –
Na to hoa

Na Maraea Hepara
Kia Te Penetana
Tumuaki
Kaiwhakawa

[official translation]
> Te Houanga
> May 17th. 1876

To Mr. Fenton,

   Greetings. Your letter asking about Mangotara has arrived. Friend, this land was surveyed by Mr. Barnard in 1869: the boundary runs as far as Tiritiritaitua, then goes on towards the North to Te Mokonohomai, Putoetoe, Moeatoa, Wairapakura, Taumatakaha, and Waiwaikawe; then turns and goes on towards the East to Korariwhero, the Kaihu River. This is my ancestor's boundary. Friend, this land was adjudicated upon by Mr. Rogan and Hikairo, Assessor in 1870. Friend, is this right according to the law, to let another person survey my land clandestinely that you all may say 'yes the land is his'. Friend, I will not be lazy about my land never, never, from your friend
   (Sig) Maraea Hepara.[50]

Once a group of claimants had been given a Crown Grant to a piece of land, they might choose to revisit the court to subdivide it, or live on it in common. In the following letter Raiha Pūaha wrote to A. J. Dickey, a clerk in the Native Land Court, about one of the owners surveying the land with a view to unfairly disadvantaging the other owners, and asked him for guidance on what she should do, and for the records of the original hearing. Appended to the letter is a man's name, Atanatiu Kairangi, indicating a scribe composed the letter.

Porirua, Wellington
Akuhata 3 1882
Kia Tiki Etita o te Kooti
   E Pa tena koe.
Ko ahau ko Raiha Puaha ka tuhi atu nei ki a koe, he whenua to matou ko aku hoa ko te Urukahika te ingoa kei Porirua, tokorima nga tangata nona taua Whenua, ko ahau ano tetehi, he Whenua kua oti te Karauna kia matou, he Whare toku kei taua Whenua ka rua tekau nga tau e tu ana, kei taua Whare

ano ahau e noho ana i naianei, Ko tau Whare kua whakahoutia e ahau ki nga moni e toru rau pauna (£300)[.]

Heoi i te otinga nei o taku Whare ka Ruri tia e tetehi o nga tangata o taua Karauna taua wahi i tu ai taku Whare – E toru nga take o tana Ruritanga, Tuatahi kia riro i a ia taku Whare, Tuarua, kia riro i a ia te wahi pai katoa ara te Pakihi, Tuatoru kia riro i a ia te taha ki te Rori katoa, ko nga eka hoki ma te tangata kotahi, erua tekau ma wha eka, 24. 3/4 – 8[.] Ko matou hoki ki tana, me noho ki te taha ki te Maunga, I mea atu matou ki taua tangata kia whaiputanga ano matou ki te Rori[.]

Te ingoa o taua tangata e whakararuraru nei i a matou Ko Rene Oeunuku[.] Ko ia hoki te tangata i whakataua e te Kooti ki nga eka e rua i te Kooti tuatahi o taua papa whenua[.]

Me hemea kei kona nga korero o taua Whakawakanga me whakaatu mai e koe. Kihai pea i whaitohungia ana eka ki roto ki te Karauna, E Pa, kia aroha mai koe ki au – No konei ahau e tuhi atu ai ki a koe kia whakaatu ria mai e koe he ritenga moku no te mea he wahine ahau e tuhi atu nei ki a koe – Ko aku hoa hoki he koroheke he kuare – Kua rongo hoki matou kua mutu a Penetana – Ko te tangata e mahi kino nei E rua nga eka i whakatau e te Kooti mana, mau pea e titiro iho i nga korero o te Kooti tuatahi. E pa kia puta mai to aroha ki au[.]

Hei kona ra
    Na Raiha Puaha
Atanatiu Kairangi

[official translation]
    Porirua, Wellington, August 3rd.
        1882
Mr. Dickey
    Editor of the Court.
Sir
    Salutations to you. I, Raiha Puaha, now write to you. There is land here at Porirua belonging to me and my friends, called Te Urukahika. It belongs to five persons of whom I am one. It has been Crown Granted to us. I have a house upon that land. It has stood there for 22 years, and I am living in it at the present time, That house has been renewed by me at the cost of (£300) three hundred pounds. But on the completion of my house, the spot on which it stands was surveyed by one of the persons in that Grant.

There are three objects of his survey:–
1. That he may obtain my house.
2. That he may obtain all the good land, that is, Te Pakihi.
3. That he may obtain all the road frontage.

The acreage for each person should be 24 acres 3 quarters and 8 perches.

According to him we must live on the mountain side. We told that man to leave us access to the road.

The name of the man who is disturbing us is Rene Ouenuku: and he is the person to whom the Court awarded two acres at the original adjudication upon that block.

If you have the records of that investigation tell us if those acres are not specified in the Crown Grant. Sir, take compassion upon me.

Therefore I have written to you, that you may tell me what I ought to do: for I am a woman, now writing to you, and my friends are old and simple. We have heard that Mr. Fenton has ceased (resigned).

The man who is doing this evil had two acres awarded to him by the Court. Look into the evidence of the first Court.

Sir, Show your compassion toward me. Farewell.

    From Raiha Puaha

Atanatiu Kairangi[51]

Contestation over surveying sometimes led to physical confrontations between owners. In 1874, Miriama Turahere was charged with assault after attempting to prevent the survey of land she had an interest in at Poverty Bay, illustrating how the Native Land Court was particularly destructive of relationships within Māori society.[52]

Horowhenua land dispute

In the case of Horowhenua, hapū and iwi competed before the court over large blocks of land, with women as the active participants in the conflict. Issues around land ownership between iwi that surfaced during colonial times sometimes derived from deep-seated antagonisms predating 1840. For example, Muaūpoko were one of the principal tribes residing in the southern North Island until about 1818, when a number of northern tribes began migrating south. Ngāti Toa and Ngāti Raukawa killed many Muaūpoko, driving them from their lands. However Te Whatanui, the Ngāti Raukawa chief who settled in Horowhenua, made peace with Muaūpoko, many of whom returned to their lands in that district. Take raupatu, land rights based on conquest and holding land, was a valid claim to land according to Māori tikanga; the claims of a defeated tribe permitted to live under the protection of the new occupiers were significantly impaired. The Native Land Court recognised this tikanga as it stood in 1840, after which English law supposedly held sway. In the Horowhenua-Kapiti district Ngāti Toa and some Ngāti Raukawa considered Muaūpoko as a subject tribe. It appears that Te Whatanui (who died in 1846) was more magnanimous, with Muaūpoko living alongside him in peace,[53] while he contested ownership of the land with his Ngāti Raukawa kin.[54] In neighbouring districts Ngāti Apa and Rangitāne also lived, whose occupancy pre-dated 1818, and Te Āti Awa and Ngāti Toa, two of the migrant tribes, as well as other Ngāti Raukawa hapū.

The court began sitting at Ōtaki from 1866.[55] It appears that Ngāti Raukawa attended the Native Land Court on 5 February 1869 to assert their claim to the Porokaiaia Block, between the modern towns of Levin and Foxton. Among the claimants were three women, including Kararaina Whāwhā, a descendant of Te Whatanui, and her sister Tauteka, who had been married to one of Te Whatanui's sons, but was now married to the chief Mātene Te Whiwhi. Also in court was a Pākehā, 'Mr. Albert Henry Nicholson [who] appeared as agent for the claimants', Kararaina Whāwhā's brother-in-law.[56] Nicholson was then living with Kararaina and her children.[57] On 6 February, the judge awarded the land to the three women.[58]

Soon after Tauteka and Kararaina planned to take more land to the Native Land Court. Tauteka wrote a brief letter to C. W. Richmond, the Minister of Native Affairs stating:

> Now this is one word to you. We are willing that the surveys be commenced at once; if you disapprove, write to us by Monday's mail.[59]

She also enclosed a letter from Wiremu Pōmare, a Ngāpuhi chief but also a descendant of Te Whatanui, saying he would be coming down to Horowhenua later in the year to settle land issues, and calling on Kararaina and Tauteka to, 'Be strong in the matter of our lands, lest through ignorance you allow others to take it'.[60] He also added, 'The pakeha, whom our parent located at Horowhenua, let him not be ejected; leave him still to occupy in the "mana" of Te Whatanui.' This Pākehā was Hector McDonald.

The sisters commissioned a surveyor, but Muaūpoko and one of Te Whatanui's descendants, who also claimed the land, responded by writing a letter to Richmond.

The lead signature belonged to Rīria Te Whatanui, but appended to the names was 'and also Muaupoko', indicating that those writing claimed to represent the whole of that tribe. Like many Māori women, Rīria leaves few traces in the colonial record. Another letter suggests she is Te Whatanui's daughter, but his daughter was Rangingangana who married the Ngāpuhi chief, Pōmare II,[61] in which case Wī Pōmare would be her son. More likely Rīria is a granddaughter of Te Whatanui, as his son Tūtaki was also known as Te Whatanui. Wī Pōmare had also written to Rīria, telling her to hold fast, and 'do not be afraid at people trying to eject you'. We can only assume that Pōmare, having asked Rīria, as well as Tauteka and Kararaina, to 'hold fast', was attempting to act as a mediator, and to safeguard the rights of all of Te Whatanui's descendants. Rīria's letter is as follows:

> [original missing, official translation]
> To Mr. Richmond, –   Horowhenua, 17th March, 1869.
> Our parent, – Salutations to you and your runanga. This is a word to you. If you should hear of any persons going thither to get a pakeha to survey Mahoenui, do not let him (the pakeha) come hither. It is exceedingly wrong of certain persons to ask for such a thing. Give heed, we claim on one side of the boundary, and Nerehana te [Te] Paea on the other side. If it were our wish to have it surveyed it would be right. This is a fixed word – if it were our wish to have it surveyed it would be right.
> But if you see how far this is right or wrong, write.
>
> > Riria Te Whatanui,
> > Te Wiiti,
> > Tamati Maunu, and
> > Muaupoko also.[62]

Henry Halse, an Assistant Under-Secretary of the Native Office, replied suggesting that they allow any surveys to continue, and encouraged them to come to the Native Land Court to assert ownership over the land. Hetariki Mātao wrote again to Richmond stating that the land belonged to Muaūpoko and Rīria Te Whatanui, and that: 'the action taken by the wife of Matene Te Whiwhi was this: She came here and has been chaining the land to ascertain its area. This is wrong – very wrong indeed.'[63] For good measure Rīria wrote to the surveyor, George Frederick Swainson, and Hōne – most likely one of the surveyor's co-workers.

[original missing, official translation]
To Mr. Swainson and Hone, –   14th April, 1869.
Friends, – Cease your survey work. O Swainson, go away, and you also, Hone, leave off, lest you come to trouble, owing to your wrong work. Wiremu Pomare did not say that Horowhenua was to be surveyed. Tuainuku is also absent. Your work is a robbery. O, Hone, neither your grandchild nor your son said a word to us about surveying the land.
From Riria Te Whatanui.[64]

Rīria again wrote to Richmond, explaining how she was restraining the Muaūpoko from rash action. She also refers to 'the European', that is, G. F. Swainson.

[original missing, official translation]
To Mr. Richmond, –   Horowhenua, April, 1969.
Friend, – I have sent a copy of my letter to the people who are making roads at Horowhenua, and also to the European, without effect. Do you send that European away. Friend, Mr. Richmond, trouble will be brought upon us, the Natives, through the work of these women. The Muaupokos are urging to cut up the chain, and will not hearken to my advice to remain at their own village. They are urging to break the chain, to break the theodolite. Friend, if you do not put a stop to the work of these women and the European also, great trouble will come upon us, the Natives, – greater than ordinary troubles. Friend, Mr. Richmond, put an end to this work at once, put an end to this work at once, put an end to it entirely at once.
From Riria Te Whatanui.[65]

Hetariki Mātao also wrote 'to Ministers residing at Wellington', echoing Rīria's request.

In October Tauteka and Kararaina, together with Whatene Te Kaharanga and all Ngāti Pareraukawa, wrote to the new Native Minister, Donald McLean, complaining about Hector McDonald. Despite Wī Pōmare's directive that the settler remained under the mana of Te Whatanui and should not be ejected, the sisters were keen to see him gone.

[original missing, official translation]
To Mr. McLean, –   Horowhenua, 4th October, 1869.
O friend, – Salutations. – This is my word to you. It is about a certain European who is living here at Horowhenua. He is a European who is causing us trouble

at this time. His name is Hector McDonald. Formerly he had a lease, now he is simply squatting. His time expired on the 24th of May last, in the year 1869. He is now only squatting. Our desire is to have the land surveyed, and that European tells Muaupoko that the chain for Horowhenua is not to be allowed to be brought here. Therefore I say that you must send some person hither to tell him to go away; for in the event of his not going away, if my hand strikes him I will have done no wrong. Therefore I say to you, send some person hither to tell him to go away lest that European remain here and the trouble increase with us the Maoris; so that the trouble may be left for us, the Maoris, alone, and then it will be right. O friend, Mr. McLean, we have applied to you to send away that European, because through this trouble we are on the point of taking up arms. That European tells the Muaupoko not to allow the chain for Horowhenua to be brought hither, and we wish our land to be surveyed, that it may be brought properly before the Native Land Court. But that European, together with Muaupoko and also Ngatiapa, is making a disturbance about it. If this letter reaches you, reply quickly. Do you hearken. The disturbance about our land is growing into or will result in a great crime. Sufficient. This is a list of names.

    From Whatene Te Kaharanga.

    Kararaina Whawha.

    Tauteka.

    Indeed from all of us,

    Ngatipareraukawa.[66]

In reply to a letter from G. S. Cooper, a Native Office Under Secretary to 'cease to interfere' in a disputed land claim,[67] McDonald wrote to William Fox, who was both Premier and a local settler, explaining that:

> I rent a run of the Whatanui, and lived on it for the last twelve years; the [sic] Whatanui [the son] died last January; as soon as he was dead, two women – Caroline [Kararaina], living with a man named Albert Nicholson, and Tautika Matene, Te Whiwhi's wife – claimed the land and tried to turn me off. Caroline and Tautika were three days at my place, pulled down my fence, and threatened to burn my house down over my head.[68]

Te Whatanui, he suggested, had promised the land to Muaūpoko, who 'will not admit any one but Whatanui's daughter and her husband to be owners of Horowhenua'. He claimed that, 'Those women and old Matene are angry with me for not acknowledging them as my landlords' but blamed the dispute on Nicholson who wanted the run for himself. Like Rīria, McDonald had tried to restrain the Muaūpoko from breaking Swainson's equipment, and was waiting for Wī Pōmare to come from the North. McDonald wrote again saying that Ngāti Raukawa had stopped the sisters from conducting the survey, and that a large meeting had been held at Horowhenua pā which Te Keepa Te Rangihiwinui and Kāwana Hūnia also attended.[69]

The involvement of these two chiefs on the side of Muaūpoko signalled an escalation in the tension, and marks the disappearance of the women's voices from the colonial record. Te Keepa (also known as Major Kemp) was a powerful government loyalist and affiliated to Muaūpoko on his father's side; his ally Kāwana Hūnia Te Hākeke was of Ngāti Apa. Despite attempted mediation by Wī Pōmare, other Māori chiefs and government officials, the two sides built forts and indulged in accusations and harassment. In August 1871, the tribes left it to Donald McLean to mediate.[70] The block went before the Native Land Court in 1872, with Muaūpoko gaining most of the land, although much of it in Te Keepa's name.[71]

Joshua Jones and Mōkau

Māori women were better able to maintain rights to property than Pākehā women, but this also meant they could be exposed to the same temptations and pitfalls as Māori men when dealing with their lands. The following case study illustrates some of the experiences of Māori women in dealing with their lands, and the pressures and unethical methods they faced from unscrupulous Pākehā trying to induce Māori to sign land deeds. One practice was to supply alcohol to Māori, although this was likely to remain undisclosed in most circumstances. One occurrence of plying Māori with alcohol was discussed at a Royal Commission in 1888 investigating claims by Joshua Jones (also known as 'Mokau Jones') that he had been disadvantaged by officials' interpretation of Māori land law when obtaining a lease for the block of land between the Mōkau and Mohakatino Rivers on the southern border of the King Country.[72] Jones had befriended Ngāti Maniapoto chief Wētere Te Rerenga, and was interested in leasing the land, especially for its coal, limestone and timber. Wētere Te Rerenga was a Kīngitanga supporter and had been implicated in an 1869 attack on the redoubt at Pukearuhe and the murder of the missionary John Whiteley, but he gained the approval of Rewi Maniapoto to put the 56,500-acres

Mokau-Mohakatino Block No 1 through the Native Land Court in 1882, in order to forestall possible claims from the neighbouring tribe, Ngāti Tama.[73] The court provisionally awarded ownership of the block to Wētere and 99 other people. Jones negotiated a 56-year lease with some of the owners but, under the Native Lands Act 1873, could not successfully complete the negotiations until either all the named owners signed, or the court had subdivided the land to identify the willing lessors.[74] A number of Māori women gave evidence of Jones' meeting with Māori at Mōkau in 1882 in order to gain signatures. Their testimony focused primarily on the two 36-gallon kegs of beer (327 litres in all) that Jones had provided to those who attended the meeting.

> PARE HUAKIRAU, and Mr. BUTLER, the Interpreter, having been duly sworn, PARE gave evidence as follows:–
>
> I am the wife of Puketea Pupurutu. I do not remember putting the mark on the deed which is said to be my mark. I was at Mokau when the Maoris were signing the deed. Dalton [an interpreter] asked me to go and sign my name. While the talk was going on inside the whare we were outside drinking the beer. My thoughts were all confused. I knew what Dalton said to me. He said, 'You had better go and sign the deed, as it will not be good unless you hold the pen.' I said, 'What will I gain if I sign the deed?' He went back to the house. I did not go with him. I was lying helpless. My legs could not carry me through drinking the beer. Someone else must have made the mark. I am sure I did not. Did not go near to touch the pen.
>
> HINEHOEA, and Mr. BUTLER, the Interpreter, having been duly sworn, HINEHOEA gave evidence as follows:–
>
> I am the wife of Te Oro. I did not make the mark on the deed now shown to me which is said to be my mark. I was at Mokau the day the Maoris were signing the deed. I was drinking the drink provided by the pakeha. I mean Jones. I did not know whether any one asked me to sign the deed. I drank so much beer that I do not know what was done. Jones gave me beer himself. As soon as I began to get drunk I went and helped myself. I dipped it out of the buckets with a panniken.
>
> KAU, and Mr. BUTLER, the Interpreter, having been duly sworn, KAU gave evidence as follows:–
>
> I am the wife of Hare Piripi. I live at Mokau, and claim to be one of the owners of land there. I have never signed the deed produced. I remember the day when

the deed was signed by the Maoris. I was drinking beer that day. I drank a good deal. I drank until my head went around. I do not know that any one asked me to sign the deed.

NGAWHAKAHEKE, and Mr. BUTLER, having been duly sworn, NGAWHAKAHEKE gave evidence as follows:–

I am the wife of Heta Tokiriri. I did not make the mark on the deed now shown me, which is said to be my mark. I was at Mokau on the day the Maoris signed the deed. I was one of those preparing food that day. Grace [an interpreter] came to me and asked me to sign my name. I said I am very busy baking bread. He then went away. I suppose they signed my name in the house, as both Grace and Jones knew me. Owing to me being busy and the beer I had drunk, I did not go to the house where the signing was going on, or touch the pen. I drank a good deal of beer that day. I could get as much beer as I liked as long as it lasted. You know what Maoris are; they never stop until it is all gone. They drank at day and at night until the whole of the beer in the casks was gone.[75]

The testimony from all the women was consistent that they had been drinking, but had not signed the lease. Other evidence was conflicting. Captain William Messenger, who was present to witness the signing, did not recollect any women signing. Wētere, who had been friendly with Jones at the time of the signing, stated:

... anyone could have a drink, whether he signed or not, that day. The beer was run into buckets, and the buckets carried round, with a pannikin to drink from. The only Native whom I saw drunk was a woman called Parehuakarua [Pari Huakirua]. I saw her lying down outside the storehouse. I am sure she was drunk, as she was fighting with her husband. We considered that the beer was given us in celebration of the signing of the lease; it was a present ... I did not see Parehuakarua sign. I cannot say whether it was before or after she signed that she was drunk.[76]

Notwithstanding the appointment of Hāmuera Mahupuku, a Ngāti Kahungunu chief and court assessor, as one of the three commissioners, the commission considered that '[t]he statements made by some of the Natives as to the drinking ... are, in our opinion, for the most part untrue, or, at all events, greatly exaggerated'.[77] It did question the ethics of 'the introduction of intoxicating drink into a Native settlement in connection with a land-transaction' but did 'not believe, however, that the beer was intended to be used for any improper purpose in the way of obtaining signatures to the deed.'[78]

The commission was sympathetic to Jones, resulting in Parliament passing the Mokau-Mohakatino Act 1888 which instructed the Surveyor-General to provide an approved plan of the block so that the Native Land Court could subdivide the block based on those who had signed the lease. In the meantime Jones was free to continue obtaining signatures.[79] Notwithstanding this legislative intervention, Jones continued to struggle to obtain his lease as Māori attitudes to him hardened, with further governmental enquiries in 1907 and 1911. The land was eventually sold, but not to Mokau Jones.[80]

Perspectives on the Native Land Court

Native Land Court processes often forced families to give evidence to prove a better claim than their neighbours and relatives. Fraudulent claims were sometimes made, and Pākehā land sharks preyed on Māori, attempting to induce them into debt to get their 'piece'. Once one individual took a claim for land before the court, all other interested parties were required to attend in order to protect their rights. The process was expensive, with claimants responsible for fees to lawyers, surveyors and the court itself, in addition to paying living expenses while the cases were heard. Successful claimants often had to sell land to cover their costs. Māori were clear in their criticisms of the court. Niniwa-i-te-rangi, despite her successful litigation in the court, wrote about the financial burdens to the niupepa, *Huia Tangata Kotahi* in 1894.

> *Kaati tena, ka ki ake au i etahi peka o te Kooti Whenua Maori, ahau ka ono aku tau e noho ana i te taone, taku mahi he kooti whenua, ka tae mai au ki te taone ka utua e au taku whare e mea nga moni i te wiki he miiti maku e mea nga moni i te wiki ka haere enei mea.*
>
> *He moni te Huka   He moni te Rohi*
> *He moni te Ti   He moni te Pata*
> *He moni te Tiamu   He moni te Miraka*
>   *He moni i nga Pakeha mahi Ika.*

Na ka puta mai te pire ki ahau i te wiki mo enei mea katoa neke atu pea i te tekau pauna taku moni e Pau ana mo enei mea i au e noho ana i te taone.

Ko nga eka o te whenua i tukua atu ai ki te kooti kaore i rahi, hei te whakataunga mai a te kooti iti rawa atu te whenua i riro mai i au heoi kaore i ea nga kai e tangohia mai ana e ahau ki tenei whenua, ka whakaaro nui te ngakau me pehea e rite ai nga moni a nga pakeha na ka rapu atu te nga kau ki etahi pitopito whenua ata i tua atu o tera...

[modern translation]
Enough of that, I will talk of the costs of the Native Land Court. I was six years living in town, involved in the Land Court. When I came to town, I paid for board each week, and for meat, as well as these things.

Money for sugar, money for bread,
money for tea, money for butter,
money for jam, money for milk,
money for the Pākehā fishmonger.

So when the bill for all these things in the week came, it was maybe more than 10 pounds that I was spending each week while living in town.

The acres of land submitted to the court were not large, and when the court made its judgement I only obtained a small portion, and at the end the food that I had taken was not covered by this land, and I thought hard on how I could square the debts of the Pākehā, and I considered some other pieces of land beyond that [piece under claim]...[81]

Niniwa was wealthy and may well have had an entourage to feed, but this was still a considerable sum in the late nineteenth century.

In 1891, Mary Tautari, a 'native schoolteacher' of mixed descent, gave evidence at Kawakawa, Northland, before the 'Commission appointed to inquire into the subject of the Native land laws'. Although several other women raised grievances about their own lands, she commented in her evidence about the operation of the court and its effects. The following is an extract from her discussion with Commissioner William Rees.

1044. Is the working of the Native Land Court satisfactory in determining these sub-tribal and hapu boundaries —*No, and for this reason: The man who has acquired a knowledge of how to act in the Land Court carries his claim to the land* to a successful issue, while those who are deficient in that kind of knowledge fail to establish their claims, and thus lose the land of which in many instances they are the rightful owners.

1045. Do you mean to say that clever and unscrupulous people know how to so manage their claims before the Court as absolutely to obtain judgment in their favour by making a fair appearance?—*Yes. I have myself gone to the Native Land Court, and sat there during the progress of a case, just to see how it went on, and I have actually seen people who ought to have had the land absolutely lose it. It is the cross-questioning that kills them. It is impossible for them to answer it. If, however, a proper inquiry were made, I am certain every one would get his rights.*

1046. What do you mean by a proper inquiry? Do you mean an inquiry conducted by the heads of the tribes?—*Yes, I mean an inquiry at a general runanga, which should have the necessary authority for the purpose.*[82]

Mary also discussed lands that had previously been sold directly to the government, and how northern Māori now had little to show for it. She also refers to the Ngāpuhi chief and government assessor, Marsh Brown (Maihi Parāone Kawiti), who gave land to the government to make peace, although she does not elaborate on the circumstances.

1050. There is a great part of the land in this northern district sold to the Government?—*Yes. Formerly a lot of it went to the Government as a sort of gift or makepeace with the Government. My husband had a deal of land given by his tribe to Marsh Brown to give to the Government.*

1051. And the Government have also purchased land?—*Yes. They purchased a great deal. In fact, they said they would not take it for nothing, but preferred to pay something.*

1052. Have they now anything left to represent the money which they derived from their sales of land – anything on which they spent it —*No, they spent it all on drink. They drank fearfully in those times.*

1053. They have not purchased anything else with the proceeds of these land-sales – other land or stock, for instance?—*No, except a flour-mill up at Taumerere [sic], which they bought for £1,500. They have always asked such an enormous sum for leasing it that it has remained on their hands idle.*

1054. Do you think the wiser plan of dealing with the Native lands would be not to sell them, but to lease them in order to get a revenue from them —*That would be a very good thing – to only lease, so that their land would not be taken from them. They* have the idea that the Government wish to take their land from them. They say that by the Treaty of Waitangi they were to have the power of dealing with their lands, and that they have been done out of it.[83]

The government was not above its own underhand activity.

1068. People whom you knew to be entitled to the land according to Maori custom and usage —*Yes. There is the case of this Puhipuhi Block, for instance. It was only because the Government had advanced money on that land to certain people that the land actually passed to the people who received that money and yet they had no right to it. It looked very like as if the Government favoured the people who had received the money.*[84]

Mary believed that subdivision of individualised blocks of land would suit her, but she was quite aware that it was not a practice many of her contemporaries were used to. However, she proposed if Māori themselves were managing the process then it would be more likely to succeed.

1057. Do you think, in relation to the leasing of their lands, that it would be wise to have Committees, formed of the leading people of the different tribes, to act with the Government Commissioners, so as not to have these multitudinous signatures to everything?—*That would be a very good plan.*
1058. It would save all these expenses of subdivisional surveys would it not?—*Yes.*
1059. Has the individualisation of title been attempted up here?—*Yes and it seems to fail.*
1060. First of all, is individualisation of title according to Native custom?—*No the land was formerly held by the hapu. They would say, 'Your hapu will have that portion to cultivate, and ours will have this other portion;' but these divisions would only be for the purposes of cultivations.*
1061. Then, the individualisation of title is an entirely new thing among the Maoris?—*Yes, altogether.*
1062. It seems to be feared?—*Yes. My own people tried it very hard under Graham Tawhai, at Hokianga, and there is a large block at Waima which they took and subdivided.*
1063. Do you not think that the plan should be to lease alone?—*Yes; but as regards individualisation, is it not better for me to have my own shanty, so to say, to myself I have an interest in two blocks – one of 7,000 acres and one of 11,000 acres. I should like my portion cut out.*

1064. Mr. Mackay.] Of course the subdivision of land like that would not be so expensive? —*No.*

1065. Mr. Rees.] In regard, then, to the sub-tribal and hapu boundaries, you think that the Natives themselves would be both competent and more successful in defining boundaries than the Native Land Court?—*Yes.*

1066. That they would not be deceived —*Yes all the parties would speak out freely, and would obtain a better hearing. They would not either, be confused by cross-questioning.*

1067. Do you think that, before the runanga, the people who make up clever stories would fear to do so there?—*They would be more afraid of doing so there than before the Native Land Court. These are people who constantly attend the Courts and who know how to manage cases there, whereas those who have not acquired that knowledge are quite ignorant of the procedure of the Court, and will ask what they have to do in going before it. Perhaps, then, they will be led in the wrong way by these clever, designing people, and put on a wrong track altogether. I have thought of this matter for a long time, for, as I have said, I have sat in the Court and witnessed these things. I have seen Natives lose their land straight out in that way.*[85]

Niniwa-i-te-rangi also gave her views on the Native Land Court in 1898, to Parliament's Natives Affairs Committee as a submission on the Native Lands Settlement and Administration Bill.[86] *Te Puke ki Hikurangi* printed a report of the questioning in Māori, which differs from the 'official' parliamentary version, although the gist is largely the same. Niniwa would have given her evidence in Māori, with her responses translated for the parliamentary report. The committee released a Māori-language version of the report but this only contained its recommendations, and not the text of submissions given.[87] *Te Puke* published its text two months after the hearing, but does not state whether this Māori-language text is a verbatim report, notes taken at the time, or a summary of the English-language text. It is therefore difficult to determine which best reflects her 'voice', the slightly more extensive English text or the more natural-sounding Māori. Like Mary Tautari, Niniwa believed that Māori-run committees should deal with Māori land, as well as have the authority to review previous judgments by the court.

Tiwini:–
Q. Ko tehea te mea pai, ko te Komiti Maori ranei ko te Kooti ranei hei whakatau mo nga paanga Whenua?

A. *Taku whakaaro ko te Komiti Maori te mea pai.*
Q. *I rongo koe ki te kai korero o raua ia koe kia wha nga Komiti mo enei Motu?*
A. *Kaore.*
Q. *Ki to mohio he iti rawa, pea te wha Komiti?*
A. *Ae, he iti rawa.*
Q. *I rongo koe mo nga kupu e whakahe nei mo nga Ateha ote Kooti?*
A. *Ae.*
Q. *Kia tere ai te oti o nga whakatau paanga wehewehe Whenua me maha ake pea i nga Tiati, aua Komiti?*
A. *Ko nga Komiti o nga takiwa taku e korero nei.*
Q. *Me utu ano pea nga Komiti?*
A. *Taku mohio kaore he utu.*
Q. *Ka penei pea ratou me te Moa kaore he kai, he hau anake te kai?*
A. *Ae, he nui nga Komiti e mahi ana kaore he utu, engari mehemea ano ka eke ki nga-Tima, ki nga Tereina, katahi ka tika kia utua.*
Q. *Ma wai e utu?*
A. *Penei taku whakaaro me waiho ano ma te Maori e utu.*
Q. *Me pehea nga kai tuhituhi, me nga kai Whaka-maori?*
A. *E korero ana au mo nga Maori anake taku kupu.*
Q. *Otira he maha nga Pakeha e uru ana ki nga Keehi?*
A. *Ae pea.*
Q. *Mawai e utu?*
A. *Taku whakaaro ra me mahi he tikanga e te Maori.*
Q. *Me pehea te mahi ma te Komiti?*
A. *Kite kitea e ratou e ahua raruraru ana etahi waahi me mahi ratou kia pai aua raru- raru.*
Q. *E penei ana to kupu, ko nga whenua i he nga whakatau o mua me hoatu he rarangi hou ki tenei Ture hei hura i etahi tu whenua pera kia mahia ano.*
A. *Ae.*[88]

665. [Cross-examined by] Mr. Stevens.] Are you in favour of Native committees instead of the Native Land Court dealing with the question of land titles?—*I prefer the Native committees.*
666. You heard what was said by a witness that there should be four Native committees for the whole of New Zealand?—*I should not like to say at present whether I think there ought to be four or more committees.*
667. Do you not think that four would be too few; that with only four Native

committees it would take a great many years to settle all the questions of subdivision, for example —*I think that four would perhaps be too few, and that there ought to be more.*

668. You also heard the objections made to the actions of the Assessors?—*Yes.*

669. Would it not be necessary to have more Native committees than there are Native Land Court Judges at present in order to settle the question, of Native-land difficulties and disputes?— *The Court travels about the country from place to place, but the committees we speak of would, be located in particular parts of the Island, and would not move about.*

670. Would you not require to pay these Native committees —*I think they would not require payment; they, being Maoris, would not want to be paid.*

671. Are they like the moa bird, and live on wind?—*They would be like other Maoris, and would not require to be paid for everything they did. Of course, if they used European conveyances, such as railways and cabs, they would have to pay for them, and also if they had to put up at hotels they would have to pay their expenses there, but not otherwise.*

... 672. Then, you think that the colony should be relieved of the cost of the Native Land Court as at present constituted, and that the Maoris would do the work themselves for nothing?—*Yes; I would say let the Maoris do the work themselves.*

673. Would they require recording clerks and interpreters, as they have in the Native Land Court now?—*What would interpreters be required for if it is Maoris dealing with other Maoris with regard to land? It would be for the European side to find an interpreter if a European took a land case before the Maori committee.*

... 678. What would you propose that the Maori committee should do with those lands that the Court has already dealt with —*If they found that in some cases the Court dealt unsatisfactorily with them, I suppose the committee should be given the power to amend the titles.*

679. Then, the object of the committees would be to review all the work that the Court has done?—*Yes that would be one thing for the committee to do – to rectify the errors and mistakes of the work of the Native Land Court.*

680. Then, in any proposed new legislation you wish to give power to the committees to open up any cases where there was dissatisfaction expressed by any of the parties —*Yes. I think the committee ought to have power to do so.*[89]

Unlike Mary Tautari, Niniwa favoured a more corporate approach rather than subdivision. As a chief of high status, her rangatiratanga would be better maintained through holding the land in common.

Q. Ki to whakaaro me takoto huihui tonu nga paanga i roto ite whenua, me wehewehe ranei?

A. *Ki taku whakaaro me noho huihui tonu, engari ko nga paanga eka o te tangata e whakatau.*

Q. Me pehea te mahi paamu, ka hiahia etahi tangata ki te whakanoho Hipi, Kau, whakatu whare ranei e taea ai te mahi e kore ai he raruraru?

A. *He Iwi pai te Maori ki te rite te whakaaro ki te whakanoho Hipi, Kau aha ranei ka pai noaatu.*

681. With regard to the holding of land by the Natives, do you think they should hold them in common, or do you think that each individual should have his own land for his individual needs —*I think that they should hold the land in common, and that the area for each man should be specified, but that the land should remain in one block.*

682. Do you propose that those people who hold a block of land in common shall use and occupy the land, and cultivate it, and run their stock on it while they are holding it in common —*The Maoris are people who easily agree with each other, and they could arrange to place stock and sheep on the land without any dispute.*

Niniwa was then quizzed about the status of her own land. The Māori text is shorter and does not discuss fencing of individualised sections. While the English text suggests that she can determine the future of her share of the land through a will, the Māori text avoids this.

Moka:— He nui ou whenua.

A. *Ae.*

Q. Kei te noho wehewehe?

A. *Kaore engari ko nga eka e wehe ana ko au me etahi atu kei roto.*

Q. Ki to mahara kaore e tipu mai he raruraru a muri atu ki te kore e wawahia atu kia motuhake ou whenua i naianei?

A. *Kaore au e mohio atu ki tera wa.*

Q. He Tamariki au?

A. *Kaore, engari he whanaunga.*

Q. He pai rawa pea te wehe i ou hea kia pai ai te Wira ki tau i pai ai?

A. *Ko aku Whenua kua takoto wehe, engari kei te takoto topu tonu tooku Whenua.*

Q. Kaore koia e pai ana kia koe kia takoto wehewehe nga Whenua Maori katoa ka pai?

A. *Ae, ma ratou ra e wehewehe ka pai.*

Q. *Mehemea e mau ana i runga ite ritenga Maori, ko tehea te mea pai ko te ritenga Maori ko te ritenga Pakeha ranei?*

A. *Ko te ritenga Maori.*[92]

687. [Cross-examined by] Mr. Monk.] Have you got much land?— *Yes.*
688. Is it individualised?—*The areas are separated, but the block is still in one title.*
689. Are there any co-owners with yourself in the one title?—*Yes.*
690. Do you not think that some day, after you have gone, there will be some difficulty in dividing it up? —*I could not answer for that. I am now only speaking for the present time. I could not speak for the future.*
691. Have you any children?— *No.*
692. I suppose you have relatives?—*Yes I have a great many relatives.*
693. Do you not think it would be better for yourself if you had your own portion individualised, so that you could will it or do what you liked with it?—*My lands are in this position that they are separated and yet they are lying tapu – that is, in one block; but if I were dying I would be in a position to will the land to any one I liked.*
694. Then, it must be individualised. You must mean that the boundary-lines have not been run through but that is not occupying the land in common?— *The lands are subdivided, but they are lying in one block.*
695. You mean that there are no dividing-fences, and you are all occupying it in common —*Yes.*
696. Do you not think that it would be better if all the Natives held their lands in that way, so as not to be afraid of any future litigation affecting their titles to their lands?—*Well, perhaps so, if they would do that, and fence their lands in.*
697. It is not a question of fencing, but of ownership – I mean define the ownership. Would you feel that your position would be as good if you were holding your land under Native rights as in the manner you now hold it, by direct deed from the Native Land Court —*I would prefer the Maori tenure.*[93]

The questioning became more aggressive, although this is more apparent in the English text. Niniwa was unable to answer all the questions, but the Māori text does suggest that 'the bill be sent to the meeting at "Waitangi"'. By this she means that the Kotahitanga movement should have the opportunity to discuss the bill, a point not specifically stated in the English text.

Q. I ki koe mate Komiti e mahi nga whakatautau Whenua me ata rehita marire pea e tika ai kia mau tonu ai mo nga tau inaha e haere ake nei?
A. *Ae.*
Q. Kei whea he Tari, he kai-tuhituhi hei mahi i aua mahi?
A. *Engari tena ma te Komiti e whakarite he tikanga.*
Q. Kei te mohio koe kote Kawanatanga te mea tino kaha hei tiaki mo enei mea katoa ka pena ranei te Komiti Maori.
A. *Ae, ma te mate ra ano ote Maori e ngaro ai.*
Q. Kite pahemo atu te Komiti ka rapu nga Uri ki aua pukapuka mo 150 tau ki muri ake nei me pehea e kitea ai?
A. *Kaore e taea e aua tena te mohio atu.*
Q. Koia nei ra te uaua kaua e titiro kite taha kotahi engari me titiro nga taha katoa kaua te Maori e korero noa?
A. *Ma te Komiti ra e whiriwhiri tena mea.*
Q. Ko ia nei ra te uaua, kaua e korero noa ake, engari me tino marama rawa ki nga mea katoa mo a muri atu?
A. *Kaore au e mohio ki nga mea a muri ake nei.*
Q. I roto i nga korero katoa a nga kai korero, kaore rawa au i marama ki enei mea e korero nei koutou, me nga mea mo a mua atu?
A. *E tika ana engari rawa ko te Pire nei me tuku atu ki te hui ki 'Waitangi.'*
– Ka mutu nga patai. –[94]

701. You speak of a Native committee. If we are to decide the Native-land interest now, do you not realise how necessary it would be to register the decisions and the titles which are arrived at for the sake of future generations —*Yes, that is so and the Maori committee would have to do that.*
702. But would the committee be in possession of offices and documents which would be, so to speak, perpetual —*I will answer that briefly. The committee would have to appoint officers and attend to all the matters you mention.*
703. But would the committee have the character and power which the Government has? A Government never dies?— *The committee would exist as long as the Maori people exist, and when the Maori people die out the committee would die out too.*
704. But it is the character of a Government that it should be perpetual in its power in order to be efficient. For instance, some of your descendants a hundred and fifty years hence might want to know what the committee had done in these days where would they go to find the document? Where would the records be

kept?—*I could not answer that question.*

705. But you should have a clear conception of the power and operation of the committee to know whether it would be the best thing to have?—*Yes, that is so but I say let the committee be appointed, and let them go into that question and decide upon it, and upon what committees in future should do.*

706. You imagine that the committee should do certain things and not do others, and you should have a clear idea of how the machinery would be established to carry that out properly —*That is a question which I have answered to the best of my ability. The tribes of the Island have not yet assembled together to discuss that view of the matter.*

707. The trouble we have had in all the evidence we have heard so far is that the witnesses do not seem to have any clear conception of the machinery which would be efficient for carrying out the system they propose? —*Yes, that is so but we have asked that the body of the Bill be adjourned to some future time, and in the meantime we will consider these questions.*[95]

Conclusion

The acquisition of Māori land was a primary goal of Pākehā settler capitalism in New Zealand. The process began with sales to traders, missionaries and speculators, but after British annexation in 1840, the government held a monopoly on purchasing until the mid 1860s, when it created the Native Land Court to convert Māori land into an asset that could be traded directly with Pākehā. The relentless pressure from government agents, then private Pākehā concerns, to procure this land informs the history of Māori dispossession, and efforts to retain their land. This history has tended to privilege the role of men, and ignore that of women with regard to land, for two reasons. That Māori men often spoke for their communities on land issues to colonial agents meant that women's voices are less prevalent within the official archives. More importantly, perhaps, because Māori held their land in common as whānau, hapū and iwi, rather than through individualised titles, land loss is seen as affecting people as a collective rather than one particular gender. There is truth in this, but the danger is that by focusing on tribal groupings, the history becomes completely blind to the experiences of Māori women. As this chapter has shown, women, as part of Māori society, were also personally involved in land issues.

As extracts in this chapter illustrate, some Māori women, just like the men, wrote to government officials about their land in the mid-nineteenth century, but it was the bureaucratic processes associated with the Native Land Court that began to collect Māori women's voices in greater numbers. This parliamentary creation, imposed in order to free up Māori land for Pākehā colonisation, required Māori, men and women, to attend the court in order to prove their ownership of land that had formerly been tribal domains. With an emphasis on individual property rights, each Māori claimant was forced to defend their own personal rights, and a few people, such as Niniwa-i-te-rangi, were able to garner considerable wealth. For most Māori, however, the court, with its tolerance of sharp practice, was destructive to both personal and communal wellbeing, as the testimonies of Mary Tautari and Niniwa make plain. However, as later chapters on the Compensation Court and parliamentary petitioning show, the Native Land Court was just one setting where women argued for the possession of land they felt rightly belonged to them.

CHAPTER 2

'I am pierced by war's alarms': Accounts of War

Warfare was a recurring feature of New Zealand's nineteenth-century history that often involved Māori women, sometimes as participants, sometimes as victims. These wars comprise six phases. The first, the 'musket wars', involved only Māori groupings. Although sometimes Pākehā precipitated or facilitated conflict, and occasionally Pākehā joined in, the wars were fought by Māori over Māori take (causes). The musket wars occurred primarily in the 1820s, and declined in the 1830s as firearms became ubiquitous. Inter-tribal conflict continued after formal colonisation in 1840, although infrequently. The second phase involved a series of wars in the 1840s. In Northland, conflict developed as colonial authority clashed with the mana of Ngāpuhi chief, Hōne Heke Pōkai. In the Cook Strait area, the warfare was mainly over land, as settlers moved into disputed areas. In many cases the government forces claimed victory, but they were generally unable to subdue their foes. Taranaki was the crucible for the third phase of war, when Governor Browne precipitated a war against Te Āti Awa in 1860 over a disputed land purchase. One year of inconclusive fighting was followed by two years of armed truce before conflict resumed. Because the Kīngitanga had assisted Te Āti Awa in the 1860–61 war, Governor Grey decided to invade the Waikato in order to crush the movement, resulting in the Waikato war (1863–64).

In 1862, a new religious movement, Pai Mārire, arose in Taranaki. Although the aims of its originator, Te Ua Haumēne, were peaceful, within two years it had developed into a militant resistance movement. This fourth phase began in Taranaki, thereafter spreading to the Bay of Plenty, Hawke's Bay and the Wairarapa. The New Zealand government had relied on the British Army regiments to bear the brunt of most of the fighting, but agreed on a 'self-reliant policy' in 1865, with its own colonial forces alongside Māori allies taking over full responsibility for the fighting in early 1866. The action between the government side and Pai Mārire (also known as Hauhau) was marked by more brutality than earlier campaigns.

The fifth phase from 1868 saw the government dealing with two separate Māori war leaders, Tītokowaru, who bamboozled the colonial forces in South Taranaki for several years, and Te Kooti, who waged a guerilla campaign in the East Coast, Bay of Plenty and Central North Island until 1872. The final phase is often not counted as part of the New Zealand wars, although the relevant events involved troops or armed constabulary. In 1881, colonial troops invaded Parihaka, a pacifist settlement that had been resisting land confiscation. There were also other incidents that could have come close to fighting during the nineteenth century: Tūhoe objections to surveying in 1895, and resistance to dog taxes in the Hokianga in 1898.

Unfortunately, despite extensive searching, we did not find women's texts relating to all the different phases of warfare. Although Māori women occasionally led taua (for example, 'Epee' of Ngāmotu in the 1840s)[1] the role of leading warriors or soldiers in battle, or negotiating terms with the enemy, was generally left to men. As a consequence women's views about these conflicts were less likely to be preserved within the colonial archive, leaving a somewhat fragmentary record of their experiences. Several waiata and a narrative composed many years after the event give some sense of the nature of inter-tribal warfare complicated by muskets. We have little written material from women from the first two decades of colonisation, despite a number of armed clashes between the Crown and Māori. Testimonies are perhaps the most significant source for accessing women's views on war, as well as their experiences of it. At times the government treated captured Māori combatants as prisoners of war, dealing with their tribes collectively. At other times it interpreted Māori actions as individual criminal acts, resulting in court cases. In the Papakura and Tūranga cases discussed below women were among those who bore witness in the courtroom. The government did not investigate only Māori combatants. This chapter also contains Māori women's testimony about the Pōkaikai incident, in which aspersions had been cast over the conduct of military personnel. The archive is more likely to include such texts, and of course we should always be aware of the context in which they were produced. But in the absence of other written sources, they provide a partial window on Māori women's experiences of war.

Topeora's kaioraora

The acquisition of muskets by Māori in the early nineteenth century changed the nature of society. Although the motivations behind inter-tribal warfare remained the same as the time before firearms,[2] tribes possessing guns had a distinct advantage, psychologically as well as with weaponry. Iwi or hapū might be driven from their lands, or migrate, and captives might be killed or enslaved as before, but the new technology, particularly when one side lacked it, caused this to happen more quickly and dramatically. At this time slaves became more valuable economically, for growing potatoes, a newly introduced crop, to feed the warriors, and for dressing muka, flax fibre, to be sold to traders so warriors could obtain more firearms. As an example of these changes, Ngāti Toa, under pressure from neighbouring (and related) Tainui iwi, left their ancestral lands at Kāwhia, migrating to the Kapiti area. Together with Ngāti Raukawa, and Te Āti Awa and other Taranaki iwi, they pushed the existing tribes off much of the land from Rangitīkei in the north to the southern coast of the North Island using muskets. Ngāti Toa, under the leadership of Te Rauparaha, then turned their attention to the South Island, gaining a large wedge of land incorporating its northern coast.

A traditional form for women to give voice to their feelings is through song, such as a waiata tangi, a lament for a slain kinsman, or kaioraora, to vent hatred of tribal enemies. A defeat, or murder of kin, diminished the mana of a hapū or iwi, until the matter was revenged. Te Rauparaha's niece, Topeora, was a gifted composer, singing pertinent waiata at tribal meetings. She was also known to participate in battle.[3] In the period before Ngāti Toa's migration south, a group of Ngāti Toa women were killed by Ngāti Pou. Topeora composed the following kaioraora in response to the deaths, which Te Rauparaha subsequently avenged.

HE KAI-ORAORA NA TOPE-ORA.

Kaore hoki koia te mamae,
Te au noa taku moe ki te whare,
Tuia ana te hau taua
I a Te Kahawai, whakaoho rawa.
Kia kaha, e te iwi kaha-kore
Te hapai o te patu,
Kia riro mai taku kai ko Titoko.
Ka nene aku niho

'I am pierced by war's alarms': Accounts of War

Puhi kaha ko Ue-hoka
Ka kohekohe taku korokoro,
Roro hunanga no Pou-tu-keka,
A horo matatia e au
Te roro piro o Tara-tikitiki.
Whakakiki ake taku poho,
Ko Taiawa, me ko Tu-tonga.
Waiho mai ra aku huruhuru,
Te puahau o Te Tihi-rahi.
'A kai atu ko Kuku, ko Ngahu,
Ko te tupuna i tupu ai
O mahara tohe riri.
E tapu ra te upoko o Te Rua-keri-po,
Te homai hei kotutu wai kaeo.
Ki Te Kawau,
Ka tukutuku i te ia
Ki Tarahanga,
Ki te kai-angaanga i Ngati-Pou
Ka hirere taku toto
Ki runga ki te tumuaki koroheke,
Te Rangi-moe-waka tohe riri.

[original translation]
Topeora's Cursing Song

Alas! how great this constant pain,
That prevents all sleep in my house,
For I am pierced by war's alarms,
Due to Te Kaha-wai; 'tis this arouses me.
Then be ye strong, ye listless people
In skilfully plying your weapons.
And hither bring Titoko, as a meal for me,
My teeth will gnash and tear
My throat, with eager desire, is tickling
For the hidden brains of Pou-tu-keka,
The stinking brains of Tara-tikitiki
Will I swallow still uncooked.

Kai-awa and Tu-tonga, both,
Shall fill me up inside.
My hair shall form a top-knot
To degrade the head of Te Tihi-rahi,
Kuku and Ngahu, will I gladly eat,
The ancestor from whom did spring
Thy thoughts of angry strife.
Sacred is the head of Rua-keri-po,
But as a dish for mussels shall it be
At Te Kawau, at our home.
Then turn my thoughts to the current
At Tarahanga, on Waikato's bank,
Where dwelt those cursed heads, Ngati-Pou,
There shall my blood spout forth
On to that old man's head, on to
Rangi-moe-waka, originator of strife.[4]

The battle of Ōmihi

After Ngāti Toa had established themselves in the Cook Strait region, Te Rauparaha led a force in 1829 to attack the Ngāi Tahu people living at Kaikōura. Ngāti Toa's take was ostensibly that the Kaikōura chief, Rerewaka, was harbouring a fugitive, Kekerengū, and had boasted that he would rip open Te Rauparaha's belly with a shark-tooth knife. However Patricia Burns suggests that the war party was also interested in acquiring much-prized pounamu (greenstone jade).[5] On Te Rauparaha's approach, the Kaikōura people fled south. According to W. T. L. Travers, '[t]hey were overtaken by the war party at a pa called Omihi, where they were attacked and routed with great slaughter, numbers of prisoners being also taken'.[6] One of the survivors, Ema Turumeke, recounted the story of her escape to her daughter, and the story was subsequently published in the *Journal of the Polynesian Society* in 1894. If still alive when her account was printed, Ema would have been about 80 years old. It was not unusual for the writings of Māori men to appear in the *Journal*, but these were generally in Māori, with an accompanying translation by a Pākehā man. Ema's account is unusual because it was translated by her daughter, Metapere (also known as Mabel), who rendered it into the third person, thus mediating Ema's voice through her own writing.

NARRATIVE OF THE BATTLE OF OMIHI,

As Related By Ema Turumeke to her Daughter, Mrs. C. J. Harden, and Translated by the Latter.

THE narrator of the following episode of the tribal wars of the Maoris, is an old woman still living, named Ema Turumeke, who at the time of the incidents referred to in this history, was about 14 or 15 years of age. Born at Kaitangata near Kaiapoi, between the latter place and Rakahuri, on the Ashley River, she, when quite a child, migrated with her parents to Omihi, near Amuri Bluff, south of Kaikoura, and lived with a tribe of people called the Kurukau-puke-puke.

During her stay there, a North Island Native named Te Keke-rengu, belonging to the Ngati-ira tribe, arrived there, having fled from his own people for some transgression. There he found refuge, but with disastrous results to his protectors, as the sequel shows.

Some time after his arrival, towards the close of a certain day, a body of men were espied rapidly approaching the Kainga. The demeanour of these men was such as to admit of no doubt as to their hostile intentions. They had landed from their canoes at Waihara-keke, close by, and proved to be the Ngati-toa and their allies, headed by the redoubtable Te Rauparaha. Rapidly arming themselves, the Kurukau-puke-puke advanced to meet them, and a short and sanguinary encounter took place, in which the Ngati-toa were the victors, losing on their own side, however, one of their chiefs named Huka (of the Ngati-ira tribe, father of Te Kekerengu). Some of Te Rauparaha's men carried firearms, obtained from intercourse with the white men, who were in the habit of visiting Kapiti for trade, and for whaling. Many prisoners were taken by the victors, among them being the chief Rerewaka, whose boastful speech, 'I will tear out his entrails with barracouta teeth,' on a former occasion, led to Te Rauparaha's raids on the South Island. Te Rauparaha made slaves of those captured, our friend, Ema Turumeke, and her mother (who was carrying an infant at the time) being among the number. The prisoners were taken to Makura, near Omihi, where they were regaled with potatoes, fish and kumura [sic]. Others of the slaves were not so fortunate, as they were killed and eaten instead. The victors sat a considerable distance from their slaves when eating, deeming it beneath their dignity to dine with them.

Early one morning, a day or two after the fight, Ema's mother was set free—the wife of her captor climbing on the roof of a whare, and commanding none to detain her, as she had released her. Ema's mother was thus allowed to depart, taking the infant with her. At mid-day on the same day Ema made her escape, fortunately eluding those who pursued her by escaping into the bush. During Ema's short detention, Te Rauparaha dispatched six of the Ngati-toa warriors belonging to Kapiti Island to Kaiapoi, for the purpose of reconnoitring, evidently intending to attack that stronghold when a favourable opportunity presented itself. This expedition was under the command of Te Pehi. The Kaiapoi people, however, were on the alert, and, surprising the scouts, killed Te Pehi and some others, the rest escaping back to Makura, where Te Rauparaha was awaiting the report of their observations. Enraged at the loss of his men, and the failure of their mission, Te Rauparaha caused some of the slaves to be slain.

But to return to Ema. After making her escape, she ran through the bush for a long time till she came to a potato garden. Thinking she was now safe from further pursuit, she climbed the fence, but, being alarmed by hearing the cracking of some twigs, she quickly hid herself in the hollow of a friendly Tarata tree which grew near. Trembling with terror, she saw from her retreat the figures of three men passing. One was some distance ahead, and was armed with a Taiaha *(or club); following him was one with a* Patiti *(or tomahawk), the last man carrying a musket.*

They looked about, and so close were they, that Ema could hear them talking and speculating as to the whereabouts of some of the escaped slaves. Presently, one of the men caught sight of Ema's footmarks, and called to the others, 'Here are the tracks of one of the slaves' Ema trembled from head to foot, and scarce dared to breathe; but, to her great relief, they moved away, failing to find where she was secreted. It was a long time, however, before she could summon sufficient courage to leave the tree that had proved such a haven of refuge for her. When she emerged from her hiding-place, she ran yet further into the bush, but eventually turned back to the sea-shore. Being afraid of discovery, she retreated again to the bush. Four times did she retrace her steps, each time to be again, by some mysterious influence, attracted to the cliffs. Boldly scrambling her way down, she gained a crevice, out of which grew three Totara trees. Here, to her great joy, she found her mother and infant, alive and unharmed. The two, taking the infant with them, went into the bush, where they rested that night.

During the night, her mother told her that her atua *had warned her not to stir from the spot where they were camped, as the cannibals would pass that way on the following afternoon. This, strange to say, proved to be the case, as about the time expected, she drew her daughter's attention to four men who were passing about 200 yards off. They watched and saw them sit down and cry, calling to any slaves that were within hearing to come to them, as they also had escaped. It was a ruse on their part, but the women, being warned by the* atua, *did not respond to their call. Thus they escaped the trap set for them. The men soon rose and departed, and the women set out for Kaihika. On their way thither, they fell in with a woman named Pukoro, who was crying for the loss of her son who had been shot in the fight. They sat down for a tangi and remained with her that night.*

Next morning they all set out for Kaihika, where they found the young fellow lying. He had been shot through both thighs, and was unable to move. He presented a dreadful sight, as the maggots were crawling through his wounds. Death, however, soon put an end to his sufferings, after which Pukoro returned to Makura. Ema and her mother continued their wanderings, till they were startled at hearing someone commanding them to keep on the crest of the hill they were crossing. Seeing it was the enemy, they ran off down the hill, and came across some of their people lying almost dead with hunger and fatigue. They gave them some roots, and bade them fly quickly as the enemy were on their track. They all ran into the bush, but Ema, who was carrying the baby on her back, could not keep pace with the others.

Darkness coming on, she lost sight of the others, and sitting down she cried bitterly. Presently she saw a woman approaching carrying a torch. This proved to be her mother returning to look for her children. Resting till morning, they started before sunrise, arriving at Waiau-uwha River, and turning off there they came down to the beach at Tauhinukorokio, and journeyed till they reached Waimata. There they stopped that night, and next morning started for Oamaru near Omihi, where we must leave them for the present.

In the meantime, the Kaiapoi natives had assembled to chase the scouts, and attack Te Rauparaha at Makura. On their approach, the Ngati-toa and their allies drew off in their canoes, taking the slaves with them. They landed at Waikuku, north of Kaikoura, and from thence went to Takahaka. Landing here they captured some slaves that had escaped from Makura, and also slew some of the Kaikoura natives, among them being the chief Waha-Aruhe (fern-root mouth). After this Te Rauparaha returned to the North Island.

At Oamaru, Ema and her mother found others of their people, but during the first night of their stay there, they were alarmed by loud reports like the sound of guns, which the people ascribed to the atua of the slain. Next morning, their fears being allayed, they all decided to settle there. Here Ema found her father, who had also escaped the massacre.[7]

A captive's song

Formal colonisation, initiated by the signing of the Treaty of Waitangi, did not mean that English law was immediately accepted across the country. Warfare between tribal groups, although diminished, occasionally flared up. Land was often the cause of disputes, but older tribal antagonisms still remained. While colonial officials or missionaries made disapproving noises, the government lacked the necessary resources to police Māori districts. In 1842, Ngāi Te Rangi murdered Ngaki, the young son of the Ngāti Whakaue chief Tohi Te Ururangi, at Katikati. Tohi Te Ururangi, who had not signed the treaty and did not consider that English law applied to him, led a war party against Te Whānau-a-Tauwhao on Tūhua (Mayor Island) in the Bay of Plenty in order to seek utu for the murder.[8] In the mid-1840s Edward Shortland served in the Western Bay of Plenty as the sub-protector of Aborigines. He was a government official tasked with encouraging Māori to accept English law, and to 'amalgamate' into the new colonial systems. While there, he collected ethnographic information which he published in *Traditions and Superstitions of the New Zealanders* in 1854, which included this waiata attributed to an unnamed female captive. In the song she is sitting on Mount Parahaki, between Maketū and Rotorua, remembering what she has lost, and thinking of her current position. The version of the waiata below was published in the government's newspaper, *Te Manuhiri Tuarangi* in 1861.

Waiata,
No Tetahi Wahine Herehere o Tohi Te Ururangi, Maketu

Kaore te aroha
E whaki nei.
Puna te roimata
Ka hua i aku kamo.

Aha te Kaiuku,
Nana rawai ho mai. [Nana ra waiho mai]
Tahi eke nei au
Te hiwi ki Parahaki;
Marama te titiro
Te motu ki Tuhua.
Tahi au ka aroha
Te hiwi ki Taumo
Kia Tangi-te-ruru;
Kia whakakai
Au makao Taniwha [Au maka o Taniwha]
Ka pai au, ka purotu,
'Wai te kaipuke,
E waihape atu ra?
Nou na, e te Hu,
He hau na Pohiwa;
E rere ana ia
Te tai ki Iuropi.
Homai, e Toru, tetahi kia au.
A humehume tahi
Te kahu a te Tipua.
Kati au ka hoki
Ki aku pipi pora,
Ki aku kore noa iho.

[newspaper translation]
Song.
By a Female Prisoner of Tohi Te Ururangi, Maketu.

My regret is not to be expressed
Tears like a spring, gush from my eyes.
I wonder whatever is Te Kaiuku (her lover) doing,
He who deserted me.
Now I climb upon the ridge of Parahaki,
Whence I clearly see the isle of Tuhua
I see with regret the lofty Taumo
Where dwells Tangiteruru.

> If I were there, the shark's tooth
> Would hang from my ear.
> How fine and pretty I would look.
> But see, whose ship is tacking?
> Is it yours, O Hu? you husband of Pohiwa,
> Sailing away on the tide to Europe.
> O Toru! give me some of your fine things,
> For beautiful are the clothes of the sea-god.
> Enough of this:
> I must return to my rags,
> And entire destitution.[9]

Shortland provides the following explanations. Taumo is the name of a hill, and pā, on Mayor Island of which Tangiteuru was chief. The 'maka o Taniwha' refers to the teeth of a local species of shark that were highly valued as jewellery. Pohiwa, also known as Toru, was the daughter of Rangihaeata's sister, who was married to a white man, and was renowned for her fine clothes. Tipua is thus a metaphor for Pākehā.[10]

The Waitara dispute

It could easily be argued that of all the regions, Taranaki suffered the most through warfare during the nineteenth century. Northern Taranaki suffered from Waikato raids in the 1820s resulting in much of the population either being taken north as slaves, or migrating south to lands provided for them by Te Rauparaha in the Kapiti-Cook Strait region. When the New Zealand Company established its colony at New Plymouth in 1840, it considered it had bought vast swathes of empty land, but the Māori population returned, as slaves were freed, and exiles returned. The government's inquiry into 'old' land purchases resulted in a relatively small area set aside for New Plymouth settlers. Pressure was placed on Māori to sell land, to enable the colony to expand. The musket wars, with slavery and exile, had disrupted the cohesiveness of Te Āti Awa, the iwi in whose rohe New Plymouth was established, and disagreements between opposing groups wishing to sell or hold their land had led to fighting and murders. In 1859 a minor chief, Te Teira Mānuka, offered 600 acres of land at the mouth of the Waitara River for sale. Making the sale was perhaps more important for the settlers than acquiring this relatively small piece of land. As the District Commissioner Robert Parris wrote, 'Teira is getting very anxious about his offer which is regarded as a turning point of the land question in this Province, if bought, the Natives say all will go and vice-versa – if not, none will'.[11] The government investigated the land's 'title', but rather than following the existing practice of acknowledging tribal ownership in common, they ignored the opposition of the tribal leader, Wiremu Kīngi Te Rangitāke, and determined that Te Teira and his people were the sole owners.

Both contemporary commentators and subsequent histories tend to posit Te Teira as the prime mover of the sale, but he would have been unable to sell without the support of his immediate kin group. To justify the claim, the government published in its niupepa a list of eleven 'owners' together with their whakapapa, and although only males were listed, appended were the words '[o]tira na matou katoa o Ngatihinga o Ngatituaho enei korero' ('[t]his communication, however, is from all of us of the Ngatihinga and Ngatituaho').[12] On the subsequent land deed, completed 24 February 1860, the Māori signatories were referred to as, 'We, Chiefs and Men of New Zealand, whose names are hereunto subscribed'. The Māori version 'ko matou ko nga Rangatira Maori me nga tangata maori hoki o Niu Tireni e mau nei nga ingoa i raro nei' uses 'tāngata' for 'men'. Although 'tāngata' sometimes refers to males, its meaning more generally alludes to 'people': of the twenty signatures and marks of people agreeing to the sale, at least six belong to women.

> A hei tohu ano tenei Tukunga kua tuhia nei o matou ingoa.
>
> (Signed)   Tamati x (his mark) Raru
> Rawiri x (his mark) Raupongo
> Te Teira Manuka
> Hemi Watikingi Pataka
> Paranihi
> Epiha te Hoko
> Weterere
> Hori te Kokako
> Rewiri x (his mark) Kaiuri
> Erueru Raurongo
> More x (his mark) Whatu
> Hita Tupoki
> Hera x (her mark)

Ripeka
Hira
Rakira x (her mark) Te Ringa
Makareta x (her mark) Te Motu
Rameri x (her mark)
Wikitoria x (her mark)
Te Watene x (his mark)

I tuhia i te aroaro o
   (Signed) Robert Parris, District Commissioner.
John L. Newman, Settler.
E. W. Stockman.[13]

We do not know how much input the women had in making the decision to sell, but their rights were significant enough for their names to be included on the deed.

A year of war came out of this sale of the land at Waitara. Other Taranaki iwi and warriors from the Kīngitanga came to assist Te Āti Awa in the fight to keep their land. The British Army could not bring Te Āti Awa to submission, but the tribe and its Māori allies could not exist on a war footing indefinitely. The Te Āti Awa leader, Te Rangitāke, did not make peace, but withdrew to live with Ngāti Maniapoto within the Kīngitanga realm. It was left to the tribe's fighting chief, Hapurona, to bring hostilities to a close. The government's terms, at least in English, appear severe. However in the Māori text 'submission' was rendered as 'whakaae' (agreement). Certainly not all Pākehā were happy: the *Colonist*, for example, considered the government's policy 'had been dictated by motives of expediency'.[14] Hapurona signed, but his declaration stated, 'I, Hapurona, speak for myself, for all these men whose names are here unto subscribed, for the women and children', followed by 64 names, 23 of which were women's.

Women

Karoraina,	Apikaira,
Maraia,	Hariata,
Mere Poka,	Ka,
Heni,	Ani,
Ka,	Here,
Hara,	Metepera,
Hana Nepo,	Mere,

Ramari,	Mata,
Rakapa,	Roihi,
Reti,	Oriwia,
Hariata,	Peti.
Peti,	

From me,

Witnesses { More, Donald McLean, Native Secretary.

From Hapurona [15]

John Gorst, a contemporary commentator, was dismissive.

> The Treaty, or Convention, or whatever it was, bore the title – 'Terms offered to the Waitara insurgents,' and was signed by Hapurona and twenty-four men, by 'Maria, Jane, Betty,' and sundry other women, and several children, all of whom, according to the text of the document, had been for twelve months carrying arms against Her Majesty the Queen.[16]

However, as with the Waitara purchase deed, women's names were included because they were considered to be members of the iwi. Whether they had personally borne arms was irrelevant, when they were part of a collective that had.

Ambush at Papakura

The truce in Taranaki was broken in 1863, but Governor Grey had been preparing for war, and decided that a pre-emptive strike against the Kīngitanga in the Waikato would avoid the sort of war that the British Army had previously been bogged down in. On 12 July 1863, the British Army under General Cameron crossed the Mangatāwhiri Stream, precipitating the Waikato war. Two days later, the army defeated a Māori force at Koheroa near Pōkeno, but it was not until the end of October that the army moved again, towards Meremere. James Belich disputes the commonly held assumption that Māori did little to impede Cameron's communications behind his lines, and that any attacks were 'unco-ordinated and strategically pointless revenge raiding by young Maoris living north of the Waikato, who had been expelled from their homes after 9 July'.[17] Rather he suggests that small groups of roaming Māori tied down the British forces, thus stopping the army from moving for three months, during which time the Kīngitanga force at Meremere were able to complete their defensive fortifications.[18]

On 14 October 1863, the *Daily Southern Cross* reported 'another murder by the rebels', occurring on the Papakura to Wairoa (Clevedon) road, in which a war party had killed '[a]n old and respectable settler, named Job Hamlin, brother to Mr. Hamlin, the missionary', and badly tomahawked a fourteen-year-old boy.[19] By the end of July 1864, although fighting was still occurring in Taranaki, hostilities against the Kīngitanga had effectively ceased in Waikato and fighting had stopped in Tauranga. In October the government issued a proclamation granting a pardon to those Māori who were prepared to swear allegiance, give up their arms and give up some land. However, the pardon did not extend to those people involved in a number of named murders, including that of Job Hamlin.[20] In May 1865, Wiremu Te Oka was charged with Hamlin's murder and that of several others.[21] Te Oka appears to have been released on providing information that led to the arrest of two men, Hōri Taka and Mātiu, who were put on trial.[22]

The key witnesses for the Crown were two Māori women, Kuia and Ahimanawa, who gave evidence at the depositions, reproduced below, and provided similar accounts at the actual trial. A court reporter stated that 'the examination of the native witnesses being necessarily a slow process, and some time being spent in discussing the precise meaning of Maori words'.[23] Kuia, who had carried food for the war party, gave evidence first.

Kiua [sic], sworn, said: I am the widow of Te Patui, and know both the prisoners. At the end of the year 1863, I was with them at Rawhitiroa. Ngapoaka, Tamati, Te Rewhehe, Pene, Awamu Karaka (men), Penenia, Tamari, Maria (women), were also with them there. The men all went on the road between Papakura and Wairoa to lay in ambush. They started after breakfast, and each took a loaded gun and cartridge box with them. The cartridge boxes contained powder, ball, and caps. Each of them had tomahawks also. The women went to Wairoa to eat tawara [kiekie flower bracts]. On their way we saw the men on the Wairoa road, at the place where the white men were assaulted. I saw both the prisoners there myself. We were about twice the length of this Court-house from them. We were amongst the manuka trees on the right hand side of the Papakura and Wairoa road. The men were in the road on the opposite side to where we were, and both prisoners were then armed with guns and tomahawks. This was about the middle of the day, what the pakeha calls dinner time. When we had done eating we came out into the road and I saw some white people. There were two – one boy and one man – not very far apart. The man was on foot driving a bullock dray and the boy was on horseback. They were driving the cattle, which were drawing a cart. The man was on the right hand side of the road going from Wairoa to Papakura. When I first saw them they were in the hands of the natives. Wiremu Tuwehiwehi was the one who had hold of the boy. Immediately after that Tamati assaulted the boy and after that Matiu, one of the prisoners. Wiremu Tuwehiwehi fired his gun and then pulled the boy off the horse. Then Tamati ran up and struck him on the head with the muzzle of the gun. Matiu then ran up and helped Tamati in beating him with the gun. Wiremu Tuwehiwehi then struck the boy on the face with a tomahawk. The prisoner Hori Taka was also there assisting. The boy groaned. They left him lying on the road. The other party of Maoris were chasing the man. Arama Heni went after the man. I saw them chasing him along the road, but on hearing the guns I and the other women ran away. We did not run in the direction of the body, but in an opposite direction towards Rawhitiroa. I afterwards saw the prisoners with other natives. They returned to Rawhitiroa immediately after the murder. The women arrived at the place first. They had conversation respecting the death of the old man. The prisoners were there and spoke on the subject. They commenced it. They all said that they had killed the old man and the boy. They said nothing more on the subject. I recognise the boy as the one who was with the old man. The other women who were with me on that day are now with the king. I do not know where exactly.

Cross-examined by Hori Taka: I did see you there during the assault on the boy. You went with this party from Rawhitiroa. You resided at that place. We had all one place of residence. I did see you there before that fight. The prisoner Hori said he was not present at that murder, but he could name those who were.

Cross-examination continued: These are the persons who went to that murder—yourself and the other prisoner, because you were living at the same place. I saw you with my own eyes[.]

Cross-examined by Matiu: I saw you there. I distinctly saw you going. We had only one place of residence, and we all went together.[24]

Ahimanawa, an older woman, had not accompanied the party but corroborated Kuia's testimony.

Ahimanawa sworn, deposed: I am a married woman. My first husband is dead at the Galloway Redoubt [Wairoa]. My present husband's name is Kaingait[i]. I do not remember coming from Aroaro to Rawitiroa in the latter end of 1863. I saw the prisoners at Aroaro that time. The prisoners belonged to the Kohereki tribe. The two prisoners went from Aroaro on an expedition of plunder. Arama Karaki, Peni, Hori te Rangi, Paratene, Wi Koka, and others went with the prisoners. I saw them going as an armed party, and they said they were going to kill pakehas. They went from Wairoa towards Papakura. They had guns and cartridge-boxes. I saw nothing else. Each man had a gun and a cartridge-box. I remained in the place (Te Aroaro.) I was unwell. They all returned after the white men were killed. They were away three days. On their return they related what had occurred during their absence. The prisoners were present during the conversation. They stated that they had killed two Europeans. I heard Arama Karaka and Heni and several other Maoris speak on the subject. I heard the prisoners state the same. They said it was Mr. Hamlin and a boy, whom they had struck on the face. After this they all dispersed. They said Mr. Hamlin was shot.

Cross-examined by Matiu: I saw you go with the party; I also saw you go with them to murder and plunder, for you were one of the party. What I and the previous witness have said is perfectly true. There were many other Maoris present when the story was told. They were king natives, and are all with him now.[25]

Ahimanawa's words, 'they were king natives', suggest that the war party was part of the wider Kīngitanga strategy to cause disruption behind the 'front'.

When the case went to trial the judge instructed the grand jury, who were to determine if the trial should proceed, not to consider issues of war: 'but it is, gentlemen, my duty to charge you and I do so simply, that you will inquire into that murder upon the same ground and the same rule of evidence as if it were a charge brought against one European for the murder of another.'[26] The trial was held and the two men found guilty and sentenced to hang.[27] Luckily for the two men, political events were moving in their favour. Two weeks before they were sentenced, the government issued another proclamation offering pardons to Māori who had been involved in fighting the Crown. Again it listed a number of murders whose perpetrators would be excluded from the pardon, except Job Hamlin's name was no longer included.[28] Just a month after they were sentenced, their pardon came; their irons were struck off and they were released, much to the chagrin of their fellow prisoners, and Auckland's press.[29]

It is not clear why the two women spoke out against Hōri Taka and Mātiu in court. The other Māori involved had moved to the King Country, and were effectively shielded from the government's intervention. The women may have decided to remain in their own home area – which would have meant subjecting themselves to a degree of Pākehā control – and perhaps gain some land back through the Compensation Court. Giving evidence was one way of demonstrating that they were not 'king natives'.

The attack on Pōkaikai

After General Chute's Taranaki campaign during the first half of 1866, the British Army was effectively garrisoned while New Zealand colonial troops and their Māori allies took over the fighting. Major Thomas McDonnell led the military forces, both Māori and Pākehā, in the Pātea area (southern Taranaki) inhabited by Ngāti Ruanui, who had consistently resisted the Crown through the earlier conflicts of the 1860s. However by mid 1866 some hapū were seeking peace, and Te Ua, who had initiated the Pai Mārire movement, was also encouraging peace. Ngāhina Nātanahira and Tito Hanataua, rangatira of Tangāhoe who lived at Pōkaikai, had begun negotiations with McDonnell who expected immediate submission. Rather than accompany McDonnell to Wellington, Nātanahira travelled to Taranaki to see the Civil Commissioner, Robert Parris. McDonnell was angry at what he perceived to be a snub to his authority. Rangiamohia, a Māori woman also known as Rangiwhakaangi, who was the wife of one of the Māori soldiers but related to the people of Pōkaikai, visited the village in order to deliver a letter from McDonnell. McDonnell, asserting that she had been mistreated while undertaking her mission, ordered a surprise attack on the sleeping village of Pōkaikai on the night of 1 August 1866 with a force of about 214 men.[30] Three Māori were slain, and one trooper was accidently killed by his comrades. When Māori reported this to the government Parris was sent to investigate, resulting in a Commission of Enquiry in 1868. Thomas Gudgeon, who had taken part in the raid, considered it an 'insignificant skirmish' and, but for unfounded accusations that 'unnecessary violence and cruelty' had occurred, it would soon have been forgotten.[31] The commission interviewed a range of people, including Parris and McDonnell, as well as some of the soldiers and the village's defenders.

Three Māori women gave evidence: Maata Moerewarewa, a young woman who was the wife of Nātanahira, Mereana Matau, from the village, and Rangiamohia.

Rangiamohia's involvement is significant, because it demonstrates the complex relationships between Māori groups, and that Māori women could be mediators in military situations. McDonnell and other witnesses had stated that her mistreatment was the catalyst for attacking the village, but it is possible she did not explain her experiences to McDonnell, or that he misconstrued them. The danger of misinterpretation was amply shown when Aperaniko, a captain in the Native Contingent, gave evidence.

> She complained of having been ill-treated at Pokaikai, that she had been beaten and her clothes torn by her own relatives. [Deponent then, according to the Interpreter, added the word 'if' at the end of the sentence, and the Interpreter explained that the addition of that word 'if' would now make the sentence run – If she had not relatives in the village she would have had her clothes pulled off, and she would have been killed.].[32]

Rangiamohia's husband, Arapata Te Rata, was even less concerned. Her encounter with her relatives followed Māori protocol: 'she and the Pokaikai people had a cry (a *tangi*), and afterwards she sat down and ate food. After she had finished eating, Tukino came up to her and said "It is well that you came here; if the Keteonetea people had seen you on the road they would have stripped you of your clothes and taken away your horse."' Rangiamohia was alarmed at having to pay a toll for having entered Hauhau territory, but Arapata stated, 'We the privates were not angry, but perhaps our chiefs were.'[33] Rangiamohia's evidence was thus vital to the commission.

> Rangiwhakaanga, having been duly sworn, was examined.
> 223. *The Chairman.*] What is your name, where do you reside, and to what tribe do you belong —*My name is Sophia; I reside at Aramoho, near Wanganui and I belong to the Patutokotoko hapu of the Wanganui tribe. I am the wife of Arapata.*
> 224. Are you called by any other name —*They sometimes call me Mohi, and sometimes they call me Rangiamohia but my proper name is Rangiwhakaanga.*
> 225. Did you ever proceed to Pokaikai, about two years ago?—*Yes, I did go to Pokaikai.*
> 226. State what you know about your visit to Pokaikai. —*One day, before the attack upon Pokaikai, I was with my husband, who was at the time serving with the Native*

Contingent at the camp of Manawapou. We both started on horseback, and when we reached Hawera my husband returned to Manawapou, and I continued my journey alone. When I approached Pokaikai I met some of the Pokaikai people they were on their way to shoot cattle at Taiporohenui. When they saw me they returned with me to Pokaikai. It was about noon. When I reached Pokaikai I went to the house of Martha, the wife of Natanahira. All the people of the village came to Martha's house, and I gave them a letter which Lieut.-Colonel McDonnell had entrusted to me to deliver to them. After they had read the contents of the letter, the man who read the letter then said, It will not do for us to go there yet; we had better wait till Natanahira comes back from Taranaki, then all the people will go there to carry food. Tukino was the person who said this. He said to me, It is well that you came to Pokaikai, and did not go to Keteonetea, otherwise they would have stripped you of your clothes and taken away your horse; you had better give us payment for your having broken through our Kati; by Kati I mean the line which the Hauhaus draw on the ground praying to their God, and this line constitutes the boundary which no one not a Hauhau may cross. I became alarmed, and I gave Tukino two shillings, which I believe to be the usual toll. Martha had cooked some food for me, of which I had partaken. The people of Pokaikai, after I had paid the two shillings, caused my horse to be saddled, and I rode away back to the camp at Manawapou; Hamiora accompanied me back to camp. On my return to camp, I told Lieut.-Colonel McDonnell what had passed. It was about sunset when I reached camp. I told Lieut.-Colonel McDonnell what I have detailed above.

227. Did you make any complaint to Lieut.-Colonel McDonnell, or to your husband, or to the men of the Native Contingent, on your arrival in camp, of the treatment which you had received? —*I made no complaint; I merely said what I have detailed above.*

228. Have you any relatives at Pokaikai?—*Yes my mother belonged to their hapu.*

229. How came Tukino to make you pay toll if you were related to the villagers?—*I cannot tell; but I suppose they made me pay toll because I was on the side of the Government, and they were Hauhaus, and they had held no intercourse with Europeans,—had not even seen a European since the beginning of hostilities.*

230. Were you threatened at Pokaikai with any ill-treatment, such as stripping you of your clothes, or of taking your life?—*No the only ill-treatment which I received was the asking me to pay toll.*

231. Did the men in camp appear to be angry after they heard your tale —*I told my tale to Lieut.-Colonel McDonnell, and he told it to the Native Contingent, and the first thing I saw was, that the force started for Pokaikai.*

232. Did you bring back any written answer to the letter which you delivered to Tukino —*I brought back a written letter from Tukino.*

233. Did you know the contents of the letter, and of the reply? —*I did not hear the letter read. Tukino opened the letter, and then took it away into a house, and he returned with the reply closed.*

234. Did you ever say to any one in the camp that the villagers of Pokaikai threatened if your husband, Arapata, went to Pokaikai, they would tomahawk him? —*No all I said then I have detailed now.*[34]

Māta Moerewarewa's evidence corroborated that of Rangiamohia, in that she said her encounter with her relatives had been peaceful, and that there had been no suspicion that they would soon be attacked.

Martha, wife of Natanahira, having been duly sworn, was examined.

80. The Chairman.] What is your name; to what hapu do you belong; and where do you reside?— *My name is Martha. I am the wife of Natanahira. I belong to the Tangahoe hapu of the Ngatiruanui tribe, and at present I reside in Matangarara.*

81. Do you know anything about the attack on the village of Pokaikai, in August, 1866?—*I was present in the village when the attack was made.*

82. Were you taken prisoner on that occasion?—*Two days before the attack on Pokaikai a woman named Rangiamohia (Mohi) came to the village – she is a relation of mine by the mother's side. After the usual courtesies, crying and eating, were gone through, Tu Kino asked her to pay certain fees as toll for passing a boundary which the Hauhaus had established at Matangarara (a boundary line had been established by the Hauhaus, commencing the other side of the Tawhiti Stream and ending at Matangarara, across which no one not a Hauhau was allowed to pass without paying toll). Rangiamohia offered Tu Kino two shillings in silver, and Tu Kino replied 'this sum is more than is required for the toll.' She rejoined, 'I know this custom of demanding toll, keep the money.' She then asked Te Ratoia, her cousin, to put the saddle upon her horse. Tu Kino repeated the order to saddle her horse. When the horse had been saddled, my father, Aperahama, told me to give her some potatoes to take to the British camp at Mawanapou [sic]. Rangiamohia had come from the camp, and my father of his own accord wanted me to present her with some potatoes for the use of the camp. She had come to us as a Pakeha, and we wanted to make her a present of the potatoes for the use of the Pakehas. The people of the village said to my father 'Do not give the potatoes to-day, but wait till to-morrow when we shall know whether Tito consents to the*

potatoes being given.' Tito was sent for the same day, and he gave his consent and said *'Let the potatoes be dug up to-morrow.'* In the meantime Rangiamohia had left Pokaikai on her way back to Mawanapou [sic], and she was not present when Tito arrived in the village. On the following morning we made kits of flax, and were engaged all day in that work. Three kits were filled with potatoes that evening and we purposed to fill the other kits the next morning, but the attack on the village was made that night, at midnight, when the people were asleep. The sleep was the sleep of fools, for the words of the Governor, sent through Te Ua, had lulled us. My children were lying around me in fancied security. One of the children, a little girl, ran out of my house, and the rifles were pointed at her and fired at her, but she was not hit. My father and mother went out of their house, and were both shot dead. No shot was fired by the Maoris. My little girl after going out of my house ran towards the house of my father and mother, and they were both shot as they ran out of their house. I was in my house when I heard the two volleys fired. I went out of my house, and saw my father and mother lying dead just outside the door of their house. Their house was six or seven yards from my house. I then saw Captain McDonnell, and he said to me *'Come to me and you will be safe:'* At first I refused, but he called me a second time and I then went to him. It was moonlight at the time. Captain McDonnell then left me for the purpose of going to his own men, and I remained standing at my own door with a second child in my arms. At this time an European took hold of the ornament which was in my left ear, and in pulling it the cartilage of the ear gave way. (Deponent here showed her left ear, and the cartilage had been broken through.) I said to that European *'Do not rob me whilst I am alive, you had better shoot me with your rifle.'* The ornament not coming away, he took a sharp instrument and cut the cartilage of the ear to enable him to take possession of it. My hand was also cut at the same time, but it has healed up and left no scar. I had lost sight of the little girl who had run out of my house at the commencement of the attack, and I and Lieut.-Colonel McDonnell went to look for her, but we could not find her. I complained at the time to Lieut.-Colonel McDonnell that it was very wrong to attack the village whilst my husband, Natanahira, was absent, having gone to Taranaki to Mr. Parris to make peace, and Lieut.-Colonel McDonnell replied, *'Who is Mr. Parris, I am the person with whom peace should be made.'* Lieut.-Colonel McDonnell and I went to the spot where my father and mother were lying dead, and I said to him, I wish to have them buried, and the Lieut.-Colonel's men buried them at once. The Lieut.-Colonel then told me to go with him to Manawapou, and I begged of him to order the houses to be spared. Before the bodies of my parents were buried I expressed a wish to be *allowed to wrap them in some clothes. The Lieut.-Colonel said to me, 'My men will see to that.' I am not aware whether any clothes were supplied or not. The houses in the village were burnt, and all the property, guns, &c., were either taken away or burnt, and we went to Manawapou, as prisoners, with no clothing on. [Deponent afterwards stated that those who escaped went away without clothing, but that the prisoners who were taken to Manawapou had clothes on.] Ten prisoners, women and children, were taken to Manawapou. At Manawapou the Native Contingent cooked for us, and when it was daylight I went to Lieut.-Colonel McDonnell and asked his permission to go and look for the little girl whom I had not been able to find. The Lieut.-Colonel consented, and leaving one child in the camp, and taking the youngest with me, I went to Pokaikai. Not finding my little girl in the village I went into the bush and found her unhurt. Another of my daughters who had escaped with the fugitives had been hurt by a splinter running into her hand. That daughter is approaching womanhood, and she said that the splinter was caused by a bullet striking a piece of wood near her. When I left Manawapou to look for this daughter Lieut.-Colonel McDonnell asked me to take a letter from him to Tito, with a message from him to the effect that if he and his people did not come in and surrender he would send the prisoners to the Chatham Islands, making an exception in my favour. I was to be sent to Wanganui, to remain there until my husband's return. I was in fact no longer a prisoner. I delivered the letter to Tito, and the message also, and I also told him that if they did not surrender they would all be followed into the bush as if they were wild pigs. Tito agreed to the proposal of the Lieut.-Colonel and sent a lad into the camp.*

83. Lieut.-Colonel McDonnell.] Do you swear on your oath that the ornament in your ear was torn or cut out by any European of the force on the night of the attack of Pokaikai?—*Yes, I do swear and I saw the European in the Camp at Manawapou, when I went there as a prisoner.*

84. Did you on the spot and during the night of the attack on Pokaikai hold any conversation with Captain Newland, Captain McDonnell, or myself, on the subject of your ear ornament—*I had never seen either of the officers above named before, and I had no conversation with them on the subject during that night; but on the following morning after daylight, I showed the blood to Lieut.- Colonel McDonnell and the men of the Native Contingent.*

85. You have stated that you went that night with Lieut.-Colonel McDonnell to look for your little daughter; how do you now state that you did not know Lieut.-Colonel McDonnell, because you had not seen him before?—*On the night of the attack I did not know who it was that said to me, 'Let us look for your little daughter,'*

but I now know that the officer who made that speech to me is Lieut.-Colonel McDonnell.

86. Do you know now Captain Newland and Captain McDonnell?—*Yes; I do know them both now.*

87. Did you show on the following morning at Manawapou the blood to either Captain Newland or Captain McDonnell, or to any one else?—*I did show it to Lieut.-Colonel McDonnell; the two others I did not at that time know personally. Lieut.-Colonel McDonnell was the only officer whom I knew at the time, he having been pointed out to me as their chief by the men of the force.*

88. Did you not propose to me, the morning after the attack on Pokaikai, that you yourself should return to your tribe and endeavour to induce them to surrender—*Yes, I did.*

89. Did I not say to you that I was afraid that you would not return, but that I would run the risk of your absconding?—*Yes, you did say so; and I was in fact released as soon as I reached Manawapou. The Colonel had reached his tent before the prisoners arrived. On my arrival, being in great grief about the death of my parents and my missing little daughter, I went at once to the Lieut.-Colonel's tent, and I was then and there released.*

90. The Chairman.] Did Rangiamohia, of whom you say that she came to Pokaikai as a Pakeha, and paid Tu Kino the two shillings toll, say nothing to you and your people about the affairs of the Pakeha, such as coming in and surrendering at the Camp at Manawapou?—*We were then living in peace. Rangiamohia said nothing about coming in and surrendering.*

91. With what intent did she then come to Pokaikai?—*Rangiamohia told us that it was her great love for us which induced her to visit us.*

92. If you were living in peace, what is the meaning of Tu Kino demanding money, and receiving two shillings toll from Rangiamohia your relation, who came to visit you out of her great love for you, on the plea that she had crossed a boundary line established by the Hauhaus—*That boundary had been established, and it was the intention of our people to do away with it when Natanahira returned from Wellington.*

93. Do you remember what occurred to Merieana [sic], a girl of Pokaikai, on the night of the attack —*She was fired at by an European whilst in a house the bullet grazed her side. She had a bayonet wound near the collar-bone, another bayonet wound on the left cheek, and a tooth was also knocked out. She then turned upon her side, and the Europeans discovered that she was a woman.*

94. Was she taken as a prisoner to Manawapou or left behind in the village

> —*She was left behind in Pokaikai in my house, the only house left standing in the whole village. She was attended by Dr. Suther, who dressed her wounds, and she is now alive and well in this village.*
>
> 95. Mr. Commissioner Graham.] Was Rangiamohia at Pokaikai on the evening or on the night of the attack?—*She was not.*
>
> 96. Mr. Commissioner Cargill.] Was Rangiamohia abused or ill treated by any of the Pokaikai Natives on the occasion of her visit?—*Not an ill word was uttered; tears fell upon both sides.*[35]

Māta's main concern is for her children, and her dead parents. She also remonstrated about the attempt to forcibly steal the taonga from her ear. It appears that a Pākehā volunteer, Bezer, attempted to steal the earring but was arrested by Captain Newland. She was subsequently recalled to identify the earring. Her testimony also points to the dynamic nature of the relationships between Māori groups, in this case her dealings with Lieutenant Wirihana of the Native Contingent.

> *It is the very same ornament. Captain McDonnell, the brother of the Lieut.-Colonel gave this ornament to Wirihana, of the Native Contingent, with instructions to restore it to me. Wirihana gave it to me at Hawera, on the occasion of the return of my husband from New Plymouth, and of his visiting the Lieut.-Colonel's camp at that place. Wirihana also, at the same time, gave me back a greenstone ornament and seven pounds sterling which I had intrusted to his care when I was starting from Manawapou with the letter addressed by Lieut.-Colonel McDonnell to Tito, and with a view to finding my missing little girl. I presented Wirihana with that greenstone ornament to show my sense of the obligation which he had conferred upon me by taking care of my property during my temporary absence.*[36]

Although her testimony is rather vague about Mereana, according to James Belich, Māta 'notes that her fate was nothing to that of another woman, Mereana Matau, whom she suspects was raped while wounded by several colonists'.[37] In his *Dictionary of New Zealand Biography* entry on McDonnell, Belich also points to 'the excesses of his drunken troops, which probably included the multiple rape of a wounded woman'.[38] Indeed, when Mereana herself gave evidence, she is very circumspect about what might have happened after her initial wounding.

Mereana having been duly sworn was examined.

138. The Chairman.] What is your name, where do you reside, and to what tribe do you belong—*My name is Mereana Matau. I reside at Taiporohenui, and I belong to the Tangahoe hapu of the Ngatiruanui tribe.*

139. Do you know anything about the attack upon Pokaikai in August, 1866—*I formerly resided in the village of Pokaikai, and I was present when the above mentioned attack was made by the Europeans. It was about midnight. I was asleep, and on waking up a bullet grazed my left side, causing a slight flesh wound. I was standing on my feet inside the whare preparatory to rushing out and making my escape. After receiving this wound I fell and was lying on the floor of the whare when I received four bayonet wounds, one of which knocked out a tooth, the other a slight wound under the left eye, and two slight prods of a bayonet above the right breast. [Deponent here showed a vacant space in her left jaw on the upper side, and slight scars in the other spots indicated.] When my tooth was knocked out I cried, and I was, from my voice, recognized to be a woman. When the affair was over I was taken from my whare to Martha's whare, where the women and children who had been taken prisoners were assembled. While I was lying in my own house I fainted, [deponent used words which literally mean 'I could not hear the voices of men, but I was breathing,'] and the surgeon of the British Forces came to me and administered some stimulants, [the word waipiro was used] and I revived, and my wounds were bleeding. The surgeon put a bandage round my side, and caused me to be conveyed to Martha's house, and there spreading a bed for me he laid me down upon it. I was perfectly naked when I was wounded, just as I was when sleeping, and when the surgeon arrived to attend me an European brought a blanket and threw it over me. I was left in the house of Martha, and not taken with the rest of the prisoners to Manawapou, the reason being that I was considered not strong enough to walk that distance. No other clothes were given me excepting the blanket.*

140. Lieut.-Colonel McDonnell.] Did you express a wish to Martha or any one else to be permitted to accompany the prisoners to Manawapou? —*I expressed a wish to Martha to be taken along with the other prisoners, but Martha said Lieut.-Colonel McDonnell wishes you to stay behind because you are not strong enough to go.*

141. Were you kindly treated after you were wounded?—*I do not know by what motives the Europeans were actuated, but the surgeon came and attended me, and I was healed as I have stated above.*

142. Was any food, such as bread, or was any tobacco left with you —*No bread nor meat, but three pieces of tobacco were left in my hand by the Europeans as I was lying in Martha's house.*

143. You have been reported as having died of your wounds. Are you not alive and in good health, and now living under the protection of a person of the name of Whitelock, an European, formerly of the Patea Rangers —*I am alive and well, and am living with Whitelock, and have been living with him for months*.[39]

Mereana's evidence refers to 'when the affair was over' – which may relate to the shooting – and that she 'fainted', but the text does not mention any sexual assault. The Pākehā evidence was such that the commission's official report stated that 'the women and children who were taken prisoners were kindly treated' and 'that no wanton outrage was committed by any enrolled member of the force'.[40] This latter judgement may be technically correct; some participants, such as Bezer who attempted to steal the earring, were not considered 'enrolled members' but volunteers.

However other evidence points to possible foul play, and that some information may not have been revealed at the commission. The commissioners asked all the military men about the consumption of alcohol, and they readily admitted a gill (quarter-pint) of rum had been given to each man at the outset but, as McDonnell asserted, 'the night was bitterly cold and a gill would be next to nothing in a long march.'[41] Most did not observe any drunkenness: as former private, Frederick W. Rolfe recalled, '[t]here might have been a few men under the influence of liquor, but the main body was sober and fit for duty.'[42] The commissioners also asked about a Pākehā volunteer attached to the Native Contingent, named Grey Spencer, about whom a consensus prevailed that he was a drunkard, liar and a rogue. When asked if Spencer had been drunk, McDonnell attested that 'I cannot swear that he was the worse for liquor, but he certainly behaved to me in an extraordinary manner on the occasion' and Captain Newland considered that 'he was rushing about in an excited state'. Both Gudgeon and Dr Walker, the surgeon who was present, thought he was drunk.[43] The reported questioning was rather random, with no suggestion about what Spencer was meant to have done. McDonnell recounted:

> I went into the whare and stirred up the fire with my foot, and saw a naked woman in one corner of the whare, there was some blood on the upper part of her body and she was apparently dead. I went close to her and saw that she was merely in a swoon, and Mr. Spencer, who was attached to the Native Contingent, entered the whare and I left it. Some time afterwards I returned to the same whare and found the same woman, along with several other women, smoking their pipes.[44]

No questions were asked about why Spencer entered the whare, or what he might have done. However, Aperaniko stated that, 'Capt. McDonnell [Thomas's brother] stood in a doorway of a whare, preventing Europeans going in, because there were some women inside.'[45] This suggests that he was attempting to stop the soldiers from molesting the women.

The commission cleared McDonnell and his troops. The authorities believed his tactics were successful in pacifying Māori, and by 1868 had rewarded him with the appointment to Lieutenant-Colonel. As the *Wanganui Herald* considered, '[b]rave men are not cruel; it is not their nature', and McDonnell 'has proved himself better able to bring Maoris to their senses, than any officer, either Imperial or Colonial, they have ever had to contend against.'[46] However, despite the lack of hard evidence recorded in the commission's report, the *Wellington Independent* considered: 'the gallant colonel . . . has been traduced by a lot of scoundrels, one of whom in particular named Spencer Grey, alias Grey Spencer, has come out very badly.'[47] One of the three commissioners, George Graham, protested the official report, stating that be believed 'that the Tangahoe people were sincere in their intentions to make peace', but wanted to negotiate with Parris rather than McDonnell, who did not sufficiently explain why he attacked the village.[48] Certainly Tangāhoe were unequivocal; when Nātanahira subsequently argued for his hapū's lands to be excluded from confiscation, he 'considered that my offence [rebellion] had been satisfied by the murder of our people at Pokaikai by Colonel McDonnell. It was while I was absent on a message of peace to Governor Grey that my people were massacred by Colonel McDonnell.'[49] In their *Taranaki Report*, the Waitangi Tribunal supported this assessment. It considered Pōkaikai an example of the 'slaughter of unarmed persons . . . after it had sought neutrality or peace', which is reflected in the Ngāti Ruanui *Deed of Settlement* negotiated between the tribe and the Crown that agreed 'the surprise night attack by Government forces on Pokaikai, where Maori were killed . . . occurred at a time when Maori thought hostilities were ended'.[50]

The letters of the Pakakohi women

Pakakohi formed a small tribe from the Pātea area, who like others were caught up in the Taranaki conflict. Certainly in June 1867 the *Taranaki Herald* considered the tribe to hold hostile intentions, but in September reported that they 'now had come in and are decided for peace'.[51] The following year when Tītokowaru's war was in full swing the tribe formed a part of his force in the latter stages of his campaign. It was unclear how committed the tribe were, and whether Tītokowaru compelled their chief, Ngāwaka Taurua, to join the fight.[52] The fighting in Taranaki ceased with Tītokowaru's still-contentious abandonment of the Taurangaika pā in early 1869.[53] At this point, '233 Pakakohi men, women, and children came down from the hills and surrendered on the basis of promises they would not be harmed. Of these, 96 were tried for treason and 74 were sentenced to death, the sentences being later commuted to imprisonment in Dunedin.'[54] These prisoners of war, labouring on Dunedin's public works projects, were not released until 1872; as Dunedin historian Bill Dacker notes, 'their stay was the longest and their suffering the greatest, as 18 died'.[55]

On 8 September 1870, the government sent a message to Isaac Newton Watt. A former Speaker of the Taranaki Provincial Council, Provincial Secretary, Member of the House of Representatives for New Plymouth, and Captain of the Taranaki Volunteer Rifles, Watt was married to Rai, a Te Āti Awa woman. In 1863 he took on the post of Resident Magistrate (RM) in Bluff, then in 1869 shifted to Dunedin also as RM, as well as Sherriff of the Supreme Court.[56] The message stated that the government intended to ship the Pakakohi women to Otago, with the 'Intention to send women and children first and place them on land, & few old men not sentenced might possibly accompany them, but no others'. Once the prisoners had served their sentences, they would join the women. The message concluded: 'Subject confidential at present, Taiaroa said land would be given up when I was at Dunedin. No particular hurry to reply. "Settle" means permanently.'[57] The plan was thus to shift the tribe from Taranaki onto Ngāi Tahu land near Dunedin.

Despite the secrecy behind the project, the Pakakohi women soon found out and wrote to the Native Minister.

> *Putiki Wharanui Hepetema 12 1870*
> *Kia te Kawanatanga kia Temakarini me tona runanga e tika ana tau kupu kua rongo nei matou kia kawea matou ki Otakou kia rongo mai koe me to runanga katoa ekore matou e pai ko konei ano matou he ngari kohe matou hoa ara te iwi e noho mai ra i Otakou kia tukua mai e koe e Temakarini me to runanga katoa e kore e tika tenei kupu kia kawea matou ekore rawa e tika tenei tikanga au e Temakarini*
> *Heoi ano ka mutu*
> *Na te iwi Whahine katoa.*

[official translation]
Putiki-wharanui
September 12, 1870
To the government—to Mr. McLean and his Council. Is it true – that you have stated that we are to be taken to Otago? Give heed you and your council we don't want to go. We would rather stay where we are. It would be preferable to send our husbands who are now in Otago back here again. Mr. McLean and Council it is not right to propose to carry us off to that place. That purpose of yours is not all correct Mr McLean.

    That is all.

From all the Women.[58]

Watt investigated the proposal. He found H. K. Taiaroa, the local Ngāi Tahu chief somewhat 'awkward' at the prospect of giving up land for a permanent settlement and supervising the Taranaki prisoners, but the magistrate nevertheless recommended acquiring the lease of Māori reserve land at the Otago Heads and releasing the prisoners there immediately on good behaviour.

On 30 October the Pakakohi women wrote again to McLean about their first letter.

Mehemea kua tae atu ranei, kaore ranei, mehemea kua tae atu, heaha te take i kore ai e whaka utua mai e koe taua reta, no te mea e mamae no te ngakau koia matou i tuhi atu ai i taua reta kia koe me to Runanga mo runga i to kupu i rango na e matou kia kawea matou ki Otakou kia matou tane koia matou i mea ai kaore matou e pai kia haere ki Ota kou, engari ko a matou tane me whaka hoki mai kia matou no te mea kua rite to whiunga ia matou kua rupeke ratou ki te mate ki Otakou, koia matou i mea ai kia waka hokia mai e koe nga oranga ake kia matou.

[official translation]
Have you received it or not? If you have why don't you reply to it because it was the uncertainty that caused us to write to you respecting the statement by you which we heard viz. that we were to be taken to Otago to our husbands. So we said that we did not want to go to Otago but that our husbands should be brought back to us because sufficient punishment has been inflicted by you upon us in sending them to Otago to die. We therefore ask for you to send back to us those who are yet alive.[59]

With local Ngāi Tahu reluctant to acquiesce and the women unwilling to go, the plan was abandoned. The government released the surviving Pakakohi prisoners in 1872, allotting them a reserve within the confiscated Taranaki lands.[60]

War in Poverty Bay, 1865–1869

The new religion Pai Mārire reached the Poverty Bay district in 1865. Some important chiefs considered that the movement threatened to destabilise to their own authority and the region's prosperity, with the potential to lead to government land confiscations. However, Pai Mārire attracted supporters within the Māori population, offering some a meaningful way of resisting Pākehā settlement, and others an alternative to the missionary religion, which to many Māori was now too implicated in colonisation and war. Later in her life Maraea Moreti[61] (Maria Morris) of Te Aitanga-a-Māhaki gave an account of her life, referred to as the first autobiography by a Māori woman.[62] In it she tells of the coming of Kereopa Te Rau, a Pai Mārire emissary, and her flirtation with the new faith. Maraea states that Kereopa wanted to kill Bishop William Williams, whose mission station was at Waerenga-a-Hika, just north east of Gisborne.

> *Kereopa came with the intention of killing the good Bishop & brought a large party of Hau pai mariri [sic] natives (who were afterwards called Hauhaus) with him, & had the head of a European, for the natives had revived a barbarous custom, long laid aside by them – that of preserving and drying in smoke the heads of their enemies. Kereopa said that the head was the house of their God, who spoke to them from it, & they pretended to consult it about all their actions. It was brought here for Hirini Te Kani who was one of our chiefs. When Kereopa arrived & camped at Taureka he erected a pole & hoisted the Pai mariri flag on it.*[63]

The niu pole was a feature of Pai Mārire ceremony. According to Bronwyn Elsmore, the pole was a conduit for the divine acquisition of all the world's languages.[64]

> *A large number of the natives at Poverty Bay soon joined the Hauhaus, & there was a great disturbance throughout the whole district. I joined the Hauhaus for I had a great desire to get an insight into the new religion. My husband had*

> been brought up by the Bishop, & I had been educated at the Three Kings in the Wesleyan Institution there & ought to have known better.
>
> Pera [her husband] was very angry with me & said 'Maria you are mad' [illegible] [']leave me alone['] I replied [']I know what I am doing' so I ran round the pole & danced & sang with the others & thought it was fine fun especially where two or three hundred joined hands & walked round & round the pole singing & when the song ended we held up our right hands while we repeated a prayer which ended thus 'Pai mariri riri riri hau['] but I could not understand the meaning of the words. That was the only service they ever had.[65]

Bishop Williams escaped, and the Pai Mārire fortified the position. Maraea's account suggests that her involvement was principally amusement. Similarly Hēni Te Kiri Karamu (Jane Foley) who had fought against the British Army at Pukehinahina (Gate Pā) in 1864 also later dabbled. As she later wrote:

> I also at one time studied the Paimarire religion, I was acquainted with it so far that my nearest & dearest friends joined it, and I lived among them which surprised them the more that they were not successful in making me a medium as it were or a subject, but I did study the prayers and songs if they may be called, or incantations.[66]

Certainly Maraea had no qualms leaving when the situation escalated. Sir Donald McLean was then the most powerful man on the East Coast of the North Island, both Superintendent of the Hawke's Bay Province and appointed as the 'General Government Agent with wide powers to control the *Pai Marire* movement on the east coast'.[67] McLean gave an ultimatum for the Hauhau to submit. Maraea stated:

> I left them there, for I did not really believe in it and went with my husband to Owhata a Pah belonging to Paratene Potote the friendly chief.

Māori kūpapa (referred to by Maraea as 'friendly natives') and Pākehā Volunteers attacked and besieged the Hauhau position at Waerenga-a-Hika. This, the principal government action against the Pai Mārire in Poverty Bay, lasted six days before the defenders submitted.

> When we heard that the Pah was taken, & that many of the Hauhaus were prisoners, we went to see them. I found a large Maori house full of wounded men & prisoners chiefly men & women.
>
> Te Kooti was a prisoner too at head quarters. He had not joined the Hauhaus, & fought with the natives on the friendly side against them at the same time he was found secretly supplying the natives at Kohanga Karearea with ammunition & was therefore kept a prisoner.
>
> The prisoners to the number of 200 were sent to the Chatham Islands & Te Kooti was sent with them[.] The Hauhaus on the East Coast remained quiet for some months after this defeat, & there was peace at Poverty Bay.[68]

Under McLean's powers he was able to transport the prisoners without trial to Rēkohu (Chatham Islands), about 780 kilometres east of mainland New Zealand. Included was Te Kooti Arikirangi who had been fighting on the government side. Judith Binney suggests that Maraea's husband, Pera Taihuka, had 'maliciously fingered Te Kooti' resulting in his banishment.[69] Her evidence is a letter from Te Kooti to McLean, but this document only suggests that Pera (and not Te Kooti) was among those supplying munitions to the Hauhau.[70] Notwithstanding this, Te Kooti built up much resentment over his exile.

What follows is a narrative of Te Kooti's return to New Zealand in July 1868, and the violence this provoked in the following six months mainly in the Poverty Bay district, using the voices of a number of women. One of the voices comes from Maraea Moreti's reminiscences; this text ends abruptly, so may be just a part of a (now lost) longer manuscript. It was also most likely written in the late 1880s, after Maraea had become a Salvationist (see chapter 7). She was educated and bilingual so may have written in English, or it may have been translated. Te Kooti's struggle lasted almost four years to May 1872, when he settled in the King Country safe from the government's forces. Some of his alleged followers, however, were arrested and stood trial, and it is from the evidence given by Māori women, including Maraea Moreti, that the remaining voices are sourced. The women would have spoken in Māori, but it is the newspaper court reports, based on interpretations, that remain. While their accounts do not impart a clear sense of temporal progression – what appears to be a short period of time could in fact be weeks – their accounts do provide a sense of what they experienced.

Also sent with the Hauhau prisoners to Rēkohu in early March 1866 were some of their wives and children. In an official file compiled in August only the 116 men are named, but it notes that there were also 49 women, 34 children and

4 boys. One man, one woman and one child had died before the survey was taken, but four children had been born.[71] More men, women and children were subsequently sent. It is not totally clear exactly what status the women had. They were sometimes referred to as 'prisoners', although their own words imply that they saw the men as prisoners, rather than themselves.

> [Rīria Kaimare] My husband was also at the Chatham Islands. He was a prisoner himself and a Hauhau. I stopped at the Chatham Islands about three years. I do not know how many prisoners there were in all. I was in the habit of mixing continually amongst them.
> ...
> [Wikitōria Topa] My husband was a prisoner at the Chatham Islands... We were not separated but were all together at the Chatham Islands.[72]

Notwithstanding this, the women appear to have been under the same level of discipline and surveillance as the men. For example, when a case of venereal disease was discovered, all the men and women were subjected to compulsory inspection, an indignity normally only reserved for known prostitutes.[73]

According to Rīria, Te Kooti's influence grew after their arrival at Rēkohu, as he began to develop the Ringatū religion from the Pai Mārire faith that the prisoners had practised. A notable feature was the ringa tū, or the upraising of hands during prayer.

> Te Kooti only obtained his authority and influence over the rest of the prisoners while they were at the Chatham Islands. He was not an influential man before. Merely an ordinary man.
> ...
> His word was always obeyed at the Chatham Islands. I heard him say that all the prisoners should turn to his form of worship (that is the Hauhau form of worship) which is to be found in the Psalms, in Isaiah, and part of it in the New Testament. It was partly practised by us before we were taken to the Chatham Islands. We had not any books, but merely prayed and held up our hands.[74]

On 4 July 1868, the prisoners at Rēkohu disarmed their guards, seized the supply ship, the *Rifleman*, and the guard's redoubt and magazine, from which they collected what food, weapons and money they could find. On the following day they set sail for Poverty Bay. In all 162 men, 64 women and 71 children escaped; just three men and one woman remained.[75] The weather was not favourable and after throwing greenstone overboard as a sacrifice in an attempt to change the winds, Te Kooti then ordered that his uncle, Te Wārihi, be bound and thrown from the boat. Te Wārihi's wife, Wikitōria Topa recounted:

> *My husband was thrown overboard and drowned ... I followed my husband on deck and saw him being bound and afterwards thrown overboard. I clung to him and tried to protect him.*[76]

The weather improved, and the *Rifleman* made land at Whareongaonga, a small Māori settlement about 23 kilometres south of Tūranga, on 10 July. It was a place to regroup, and acquire a few more weapons for Te Kooti's relatively under-armed force.[77]

> *[Rīria Kaimare] There was not a pa there, but only whares. They were Maori houses, and did not belong to Europeans. The men afterwards got more guns. They took them from the Government or friendly natives. The arms were taken unwillingly from the friendly natives. The Hauhaus frightened them and then took the guns away. When the Hauhaus landed they went into the houses and lived there, and stayed about a week. They did not erect any fence or palisading, or build any earthworks about the houses.*[78]

Not all the women were keen to continue the struggle, including Te Kooti's wife, Maata Te Ōwai.

> *[Maata Te Ōwai] When we left Whareongaonga I wanted to remain behind, but Te Kooti made me go, and I cried very much.*
> ...
> *[Rīria Kaimare] I did not hear my husband, or Te Kooti, or any of the others express any fear about being retaken. I wished to leave them at Whareongaonga, but Te Kooti said that if I or any others left, we would be cut to pieces. All heard Te Kooti saying this. This was my cause of my remaining with them.*[79]

While the escapees were at Whareongaonga, Captain Biggs sent in one of his Māori troopers, Pāora Kati, 'to call upon the Hauhaus to give up their guns and come in to the Government', a demand Te Kooti refused.[80] The group then moved inland. The government forces pursued Te Kooti's party, engaging them three times at Pāparatū (20 July), Te Kōneke (24 July) and the Ruakituri River (8 August), each time ending in defeat. This allowed Te Kooti to establish a secure position at Puketapu pā, north of Lake Waikaremoana, where he stayed for almost three months. From Rīria's and Wikitōria's testimonies it appears that the women were not involved in the fighting, and their evidence suggests they were not always fully aware of all that was happening around them.

> [Rīria Kaimare] When we went the women and the children were placed in the middle, and the soldiers went before and behind. I call them soldiers because they went like soldiers, and were called soldiers by the rest of the Hauhaus. They had guns with bayonets to them. They went as if they meant fighting if they were opposed.
>
> . . .
>
> When we got to the top of the hill, we heard people fighting and guns firing in the stream below. The women were then left behind at the top of the hill, and all the men went down to fight.
>
> . . .
>
> After the fight was over, a pah was built up on the top of the hill. The pah was built by Te Kooti's people. They dug up the ground and threw up earthworks. All the people were engaged in this. The prisoners were employed among the others, I did not see any earth bags. The place was called Puketapu, and we stopped there some weeks. The bush was cut down all round the pah for some distance.[81]

The Government, facing a more perilous situation in South Taranaki with the Ngāti Ruanui war chief, Tītokowaru, attempted to come to terms with Te Kooti. However the negotiations failed due to mutual suspicion and the ineffectiveness of the Government's go-between, a French Catholic priest. In early November, Te Kooti decided to attack Poverty Bay. Belich suggests that he was motivated by the failure of the peace negotiation; Binney maintains that Te Kooti had wanted to gain sanctuary in the King Country but had been rebuffed by Tāwhiao, the Māori King.[82]

On 9 November, Te Kooti's whole party set out towards the coast, and captured the Māori settlement of Patutahi. The following evening a war party attacked Te Kooti's former home at Matawhero, a mixed community of Māori and Pākehā about seven kilometres west of Tūranga (Gisborne), where they killed 32 Pākehā and 22 Māori, including men, women and children, and then left taking a number of Māori as prisoners. Two days later Te Kooti moved on to nearby Ōweta where he executed four chiefs, and added most of the settlement to his now large number of prisoners. Two women who were taken prisoner at Matawhero, Ema Katipa and Maraea Moreti, gave evidence at the 1869 trial, and Miriama Whakahua made a statement for another trial in 1871. As noted above, Maraea composed reminiscences of her life, which also discussed the Matawhero incident.

As Binney suggests, the court testimonies were hardly disinterested statements. Being implicated in a rebellion could result in being excluded from land shares through the Native Land Court, so the evidence was 'of those who sought not to identify themselves with Te Kooti, the testimonies of people trying to protect themselves'.[83] Some witnesses, however, were happy to testify – in order to identify those accused of killing their loved ones. As Maraea Moreti stated,

> *[I] wanted to gain sufficient evidence to hang them all if they should ever be taken prisoners again, & here may I say that I have been twice to Wellington to give evidence in the Supreme Court against Hauhaus.*[84]

Maraea wrote her reminiscences after joining the Salvation Army, which may also have coloured her views. In 1871 Miriama Whakahua provided a sworn statement to the authorities at Tūranga, prepared for the trial of Rēnata Amuamu, detailing the murder of her husband, Tūtere Konohi.

> [Official translation]
> Statement of Miriama Whakahua Aboriginal Native of Turanga Poverty Bay
>
> On the day of the Massacre at Turanga by Te Kooti's people in the year 1868 I and my husband Tutere were living at our place at Waitaria[.] My husband was sick at the time and unable to move about. In the middle of the night we heard firing in the direction of Matawhero and we also saw Houses burning. We knew it was the Hau Haus from the firing in the night. We were very much afraid. In the morning William Wyllie arrived on horseback at our Whare and told us that the Hau Haus were at Matawhero[.] I advised him [W]ill – his mother and others to make their escape through the Bush. We could not go as I was lame and my Husband was too sick to move. Soon afterwards Te Kooti with Renata Amuamu and others arrived at our Whare. On their arrival they chased a child belonging

to Pehimana Taihuka – who ran towards us. They shot him, they fired a volley at him and Renata Amuamu was one of the firing party. I saw him fire. They afterwards Bayoneted my husband Tutere. Renata Amuamu and Te Wairama (I have forgotten his Christian name) called to me to come away before killing my husband[.] they dragged me away from him. When I had been dragged about ten yards distant from my husband I saw Renata Amuamu and Te Wairama kill my husband and Ema Poho's child. I distinctly saw Renata Amuamu bayonet my husband through the chest[,] he then bayoneted the child of Ema Poho who was clinging to Tutere. Wairama was also one who pierced them with a Bayonet[.] After killing my husband and the two children they left me and went in pursuit of Mr Wyllie and family[.] Soon after they left. Hone Toke came and told me that they were going to catch Mr Wyllie alive and cut him up. He told me also that Tamai and Rangi were the executioners of all the Europeans and Natives who were to be killed at Turanga. The same day a Kokiri headed by my brother Henare Kapapango came and took me away.[85]

her
Miriama X Whakahua
Mark

Maraea Moreti lived at Matawhero. When they heard firing they thought it may be a 'drunken spree', and several men went to investigate.

On reaching home about 5 am they told us that the Hauhaus were coming upon us. We were a large party, and our leading chiefs We [Wi] Pere, Himiona Katipa & others were with us. We rushed out of our houses in our night clothes, & fled in all directions across a field. I heard a voice call out E Maa ma e tu (an order to stand) & thinking it was a friendly native who knew my native name E Mara, I stood & the man came & took me by the shoulder, when to my surprise I found he was a stranger named Te Whiu – this I found out afterwards while I was a prisoner.[86]

Maraea and other prisoners were gathered together at the settlement. Her court evidence, recorded in newspapers, is rather brief and rather stoical.

My husband was also taken prisoner. The prisoners were separated, the men from the women. The men were afterwards shot by Te Kooti's order.[87]

These contrast with her reminiscences which are more comprehensive and more emotional, and with slight differences in detail.

> *When Harata (Piripi's wife) saw [Te Kooti] riding down she stood up & welcomed him in the Maori style; he had a bottle of brandy in one hand & a long stock in the other, & his knee was supported in the stirrup leather as his foot had been wounded in a recent engagement[.] He did not return our greeting but called the prisoners['] names out one by one, said 'Harata stand to the left['], & she went. Te Kooti then told her husband & children, & my husband to go & stand by her. I thought they were going to be tried for having joined the friendly natives & went & stood by Pera but Te Kooti told me to return to my place by the other prisoners. Then Te Kooti said 'God has told me to kill women & children, now fire on them' & about 60 guns were instantly aimed at them & fired[.] I heard a fearful scream, & on looking back I saw my husband fall close to me; I saw Harata too with her arms pressed closely to her side, & Piripi lying by her with a child on her back. One little girl was only wounded & I saw her crawl out from amongst the dead, & one of the men ran up & thrust a bayonet through her back[.]*[88]

The prisoners were taken back to Patutahi, where the violence continued. Ema Katipa states:

> *I remained at Patutahi four days. I saw my husband at Patutahi. When he came up here, he was immediately taken prisoner by the Hauhaus. He came there to see me and my children. I was taken from Patutahi to Pukepuke. I did not see anyone when I got there. When my husband was taken prisoner, an armed Hauhau went before him and behind him. He was also taken as a prisoner to Pukepuke, where he was taken away from the rest of us, and shot and sworded. I did not actually see him killed.*[89]

The situation for the women taken must have been frightening. Many, like Maraea, had children there. No evidence was given concerning sexual assaults, but Maraea states that Te Kooti did suggest that she become another of his wives.

> *While I was listening Te Kooti looked up & saw me & said 'Maria don't you have another husband except me'. [N]o no I replied. [I]s that the reason you killed my husband because you wanted to marry me? I will never*

marry you[.] [H]e replied 'Maria if you talk like that I will cut your head off'[.] My uncle was standing near & said 'Maria go away do not be impudent to him he is a Devil'[.]

Ema and Maraea spent some time as prisoners. Ema considered the religion practised by her captors, which Te Kooti was developing into the Ringatū faith, as 'a bad creed' primarily concerned with war.

[Ema Katipa] The Hauhaus said that they prayed to the great God of Heaven, to Jehovah. They named the name of Christ and Jehovah in their prayers. They prayed about killing the Europeans, and asked God to deliver their enemies (all the Government people) into their hands; That appeared to be the matter of their thoughts and the object of their prayers.[90]

[Maraea Moreti] When the prayers were not going on we remained in the tent, but when prayers were said we came out of the tent and joined in them. Te Kooti ordered us to go.[91]

All the women's testimony also points to the nature of Te Kooti's leadership. This was partly based on fear and charisma, but also on the promise of regaining land lost to the Pākehā. Te Kooti's military success also led to others joining his party.

[Maraea Moreti] . . . we all joined Te Kooti with our lips to save our lives but not with our hearts[.][92]

[Maata Te Ōwai] Being the wife of Te Kooti I should of course know him well. His was the authority over the people. I have heard him threaten any who wanted to leave him, and on that account they were frightened at him, and turned to him. His authority and intimidation was continually exercised over them . . . All the men were in very great dread of Te Kooti, because he said that he was under the protection of God, who would give all the Government people and the friendly natives into his hands.[93]

[Ema Katipa] I heard Te Kooti say that God would give the Turanganui country, and all the best places of the Europeans, back to him and his people.[94]

[Rīria Kaimare] A great many people came and joined us while we were at Puketapu, who had not come with us from the Chatham Islands.[95]

> *[Wikitōria Topa] The Ureweras came to us there [Pāpuni]. They came with their guns. Their pa is at Te Whaiti, Ruatahuna. They are not Hauhaus, but are opposed to the government.*[96]

On 17 November, Te Kooti withdrew his party inland from Poverty Bay, 'burdened with at least 400 non-combatants, and a great deal of plunder, including sheep and cattle', establishing himself at Mākāretu.[97] As Maraea recounted:

> *Early the next morning a scout was sent out, & just before sunrise the bell was rung for prayers. After two or three Psalms had been sung, & several prayers said[,] Te Kooti stood up to preach a sermon to his people, said 'The Secret' that is God had told him in the night that a man & woman & a child must be killed, & offered as a sacrifice to God. Sometime afterwards I heard from some Hauhau prisoners who were taken by the Volunteers that Te Kooti intended to have killed Wi Pere & myself & my child that morning but before his sermon was ended we heard the report of a gun & saw our scout on the hill just above the camp shot dead by a party of friendly natives who had come and attacked the Hauhaus, headed by the native chiefs of Napier Henare Tomoana, & Renata Kawhapo [Kawepō], & Poverty Bay chiefs.*
>
> *. . .*
>
> *The bullets fell like hail around us & we took refuge under a low hill, & close to the bank of the river which flowed past the camp[.] Te Kooti did not go out to fight that day, but concealed himself with the women & children under the cover of the low hill. A great many were killed & I saw many wounded brought to Te Kooti during the day who spat on his fingers then touched each wound, repeating a prayer as he did so in an unknown tongue[.] I could not understand it, for it was neither English nor Maori & sent them to the river to wash[.]*[98]

Neither the kūpapa force of Ngāti Kahungunu and Rongowhakaata, nor Te Kooti's force, were able to gain ascendancy, and a standoff prevailed for nearly two weeks.[99] The confusion however provided an opportunity for some of the prisoners to escape.

> *[Ema Katipa] I ran away frightened from Makaretu, while the fighting was going on, and I went to the Government people at Oweta. Others made their escape besides myself from Makaretu.*[100]

> [Maraea Moreti] Just after dark that evening all the prisoners scattered & stole silently & stealthily one by one from the camp. Himeona Katipa's widow Ema, & Ririha[,] We [Wī] Pere's mother & two or three others followed me. We walked for some distance in the shallow part of the river. After awhile I looked back & missed my friends Ema & Ririha & found that they had crossed the river & fled to the hills. We heard afterwards that they wandered for many days in the bush living on fern root, & berries, at last they made their way to the Bay of Plenty.
>
> . . .
>
> When the moon set we left the water & camped for a short time for we were weary. At day light we fled to the hills[.] I carried my child on my back all the time[.] One man carried a bag of flour on his back but we were afraid to cook any of it during the day lest the Hauhaus should see the smoke of our fire[.] At night we made dampers & baked them in the ashes for the children[.] The grown up people had no appetites & scarcely took anything except water[.][101]

The group split again: some headed north towards the Bay of Plenty, but Maraea and a small group travelled east down to Poverty Bay.

The kūpapa force, reinforced by Ngāti Porou, took Mākāretu on 6 December, but Te Kooti was able to extract most of his party, including some prisoners, and travel further inland to Ngātapa, an old pā that the group set about refortifying. Rīria Kaimare gave an account of the fight in her court testimony.

> Te Kooti and his party all collected there. Some fighting took place there immediately. I made my escape and ran away down the side of the hill, as soon as the fight commenced. After the fight was over, we all remained at Ngatapa.
>
> . . .
>
> The pa was then removed higher up the hill at Ngatapa, and all three of the [defendants] were employed in building it and in throwing up embankments and earthworks and making defences round the pa. Sacks were also filled with earth, and piled up on the top of each other and laid close alongside one another. There was an attack made upon the pa; it was made by the Government people, who surrounded the pa. I was inside tha[t] pa.
>
> . . .
>
> I was very much frightened at Ngatapa. I went where the women were, on an embankment. . . . The embankments formed the pa. The women were on the

> highest embankment, and the men were in the embankment nearest to the Government troops. . . . Some of the women were cheering the natives on. These that were frightened hid themselves. I was one of the very frightened ones. I was lying down in the tent, and did not see the rockets that were fired into the pa. The bursting of a rocket near the tent that I was in alarmed and wounded me in the back. I was in the tent during the greater part of the fight. The fighting continued for several days.[102]

The court testimonies were primarily concerned with the supposed crimes of the defendants, rather than the women's life stories, and do not give detail about how and when they left Te Kooti's party. Rīria is the only woman to mention it, saying:

> I afterwards went away with my father and mother. We went into the bush and two days after we were in the bush I saw [the defendant] Rewi there; and after that I also saw [the defendant] Matene there in the bush.[103]

The attack in early December on Ngātapa failed, with the kūpapa troops being compelled to withdraw. A mixed Māori-Pākehā force set out again, and successfully besieged the pā, which fell on 5 January. The government troops captured 135 women and children, and 140 men were also taken prisoner: 120 of these – some of whom had been Te Kooti's prisoners – were summarily executed as utu for Matawhero and other killings. Te Kooti escaped with a small group of sixty men and some women, subsequently revitalising his campaign, which ranged across the central North Island while under constant pressure from kūpapa pursuers.[104] He was granted sanctuary in the King Country in mid 1872, and finally pardoned by the Crown in 1883 as part of their rapprochement with the Kīngitanga.

The court testimonies and Maraea's reminiscences accentuate the bloodshed associated with Te Kooti's activities in November 1868, especially the raid on Matawhero and the killings of prisoners, events that historians have attempted to grapple with. James Cowan, for example, noted that '[m]ost of the prominent settlers, including the military officers, lived at or near Matawhero; among these were several men against whom Te Kooti nursed an undying grudge for his deportation to Wharekauri [Chatham Islands]'.[105] Belich posits that the Matawhero raid 'objectives were primarily military: to dislocate the enemy defence', giving Te Kooti 'unchallenged control of the district for a week'.

However the 'unnecessary killing of harmless non-combatants' arose from the desire to gain utu over his imprisonment and the subsequent lack of support from his own tribe, to intimidate the local kūpapa, and 'the mysterious dictates of his God'.[106] Binney also describes the events in terms of utu, but relating to land: Te Kooti owned land at Matawhero from which he was dispossessed by both Māori and Pākehā after his transportation.[107] Most of those killed were implicated in these land dealings. She claims that some of the Māori murdered had 'fingered him as disloyal', or had been too aligned to the government, and the killing of women and children was 'usual in warfare'.[108] There is no doubt that Te Kooti had been unjustly treated, but his revenge alienated many of the Māori of Poverty Bay, who in turn vigorously pursued and fought him. His actions also resulted in considerable trauma for his followers and his victims, including those women whose voices appear above.

Conclusion

Warfare in New Zealand changed through the nineteenth century, from the inter-tribal musket wars, to conflicts borne out of the pressure of colonisation, with Māori at times fighting the British Army, armed settlers and colonial militia, or other Māori government allies. Despite the fact that fighting never enveloped the whole country at any one time, or that the numbers involved were small from a global perspective, the impact on communities and individuals touched by war, including women, could be immense. Although nineteenth-century warfare in New Zealand was often sporadic, small-scale and localised, these extracts written by women show that for Māori women exposed to war, the impact was deeply felt. Although the archive is patchy, nonetheless the women's voices featured here tell powerful narratives of war: of losing loved ones, suffering injury or capture, and being subject to forces beyond their immediate control. Women may not have necessarily been on the front line, but they certainly felt the effects of war, and lived with its consequences.

CHAPTER 3

'I am living here a Stranger on this land': Raupatu and Compensation

In late 1863, as the British Army was fighting its way up the Waikato River in order to crush the Kīngitanga, Parliament passed the New Zealand Settlements Act. This law enabled the governor to proclaim a district to be in rebellion against the Crown, and to 'take or reserve any Land within such District and such Land shall be deemed to be Crown Land freed and discharged from all Title Interest or Claim of any person whatsoever'. In effect, the law allowed the wholesale confiscation of large areas of land in Waikato, Taranaki, Tauranga, and subsequently in the Whakatāne-Ōpōtiki, East Coast and Hawke's Bay districts, from tribes fighting the government. The government was to dispense some of the land to the troops who had been recruited on the promise of land grants. These 'military settlers' were supposed to farm their land, while their presence ensured the existing Māori populations kept the peace. The conversion of the confiscated territories into Crown land effectively extinguished the existing native title with its complex layers of proprietary rights and the arguments about ownership that dominated the Native Land Court. The act also contained provisions to establish Compensation Courts to compensate on its own terms those Māori who had not taken up arms or assisted the 'rebels'. Its provisions initially provided only money as compensation to successful claimants; land was later awarded, although 'broken into discrete parts and allocated to individuals in prescribed shares'.[1]

The actual proclamations occurred between December 1864 and January 1867.[2] Auckland authorities were quick to capitalise on their windfall, with the first auction of land, that of Ngāruawāhia 'or Newcastle, as it has now been called' taking place at Cochrane's Land Mart in Auckland on 9 September 1864. This was less than five months after the battle of Ōrākau, and several months before the official declaration of confiscation.³ At the sale a Māori woman, 'well dressed after the English fashion, with a scarlet cloak and bonnet' interrupted the proceedings by reading out the following:

> Ko au, ko Timata, ka whaka he au ki te hokonga o etahi whenua ko Ngaruawahia te ingoa. Te rohe o tetahi taha kei Waipa, ki te awa ko tetahi rohe kei te awa o Horotiu. Ko au te take o tenei whenua, ko taka [sic] tama, ko aku tamahine me etahi atu whanaunga. E mohio ana te mano he tangata rangimarie no te Kuini. No kona au ka karanga me tiaki oku whenua, ta te mea he tangata au no Kuini, akua whakaaetia aku whenua e te tiriti o Waitangi. Ka whaka he nei, a kia kaua aku whenua e hokona e ahatia, ite mea kahore i whakaaetia e hau[.] Ki te mea ekore taku whakahe e whakarangona. Ki te kore au e whakatikaia, ka rere tapu kupu ki a te Kuini, toku rangatira nui. Timata.
> Akarana, Hepetema 9, 1864.⁴

The text of the speech was signed by Timata, and witnessed by her Pākehā husband, William Prior, who then read out an English-language translation of the document.

> I hereby protest against the sale of certain lands known as Ngaruawahia, bounded on the one side by the Waipa River, and on the other by the Horatiu [sic] River. I claim the land for myself, my son, my daughters, and other relatives. It is well-known to thousands that I have ever been a peaceable subject to the Queen. I therefore claim protection as a British subject, my rights being guaranteed to me by the treaty of Waitangi. I protest against any of my lands being sold or disposed of in any way without my consent. And if my protest is not attended to, and my rights respected, I shall appeal to the Queen, who is my great Chief. (Signed) Timata.
> Auckland,
> 9th September, 1864.⁵

The sale then proceeded uninterrupted, with high prices gained for the blocks on sale. Several months later Timata submitted a formal petition praying for the restitution of her land, and compensation for its loss.⁶ Although the original petition cannot be located, it is likely that it was closely based on the text of the speech she read out in protest at the auction.

In 1866 Frederick Whitaker, Auckland Superintendent, informed his Provincial Council that 'it is gratifying to learn that Auckland [Province] has got possession, not only of the whole of the Waikato and Tauranga lands *for nothing;* but in addition, of the lands confiscated at Opotiki'. It was estimated that they had 1,217,473 acres in the Waikato, 'of which 603,173 will be required for military settlers, immigrants, and natives'. The Tauranga and Ōpōtiki lands were reckoned at 50,000 and 480,000 acres respectively, of which '[t]he military settlers and natives will probably require about 70,000 acres to satisfy their claims'.[7] This was of course conjecture. In the Taranaki Province, another 1,300,000 acres were confiscated, of which 70,000 were required for military settlers, and 150,000 were estimated as sufficient for 'friendly natives'.[8] In the Hawke's Bay province 270,000 acres of the Mōhaka-Waikare block were confiscated, although most of this was returned,[9] and over 56,000 acres was 'ceded' by Ngāti Kahungunu and Ngāti Porou chiefs, some of which was returned.[10]

The confiscation and compensation process worked differently in each locality. In the Waikato and Bay of Plenty out-of-court settlements were not unusual; courts were used in Waikato and Taranaki, whereas 'special commissioners were given powers to carry out investigations and inquiries' at Tauranga. In Hawke's Bay, the Provincial Superintendent, Donald McLean, brokered a deal with local chiefs meaning no investigations were undertaken.[11] Despite ongoing military activity, the government effectively abandoned this punitive policy after the Hawke's Bay confiscation and East Coast cessions. Most investigations into compensation occurred in the years immediately following the proclamations, but officials were still dealing with the repercussions of this policy well into the 1880s.

Compensation: Waikato

The nature of the compensation process is difficult for historians to document, because, according to Richard Boast, 'Much of the detail is irrecoverable, and [because of this] there is very little evidence about how Maori engaged with the process and what they thought about it' and 'the fragmentary records of the process make the process hard to understand'.[12] Notwithstanding these issues, a number of voices of Māori women who claimed compensation can be heard in the settler newspapers, judges' minute books and archived documents of the period for the Waikato and Bay of Plenty districts.

Rīria (Lydia) of Te Ākitai (Ngāti Tamaoho) was involved in a number of cases related to the Waikato confiscation. She is identified as 'the mother of Ihaka': Īhaka Takaanini Te Tihi, who was 'a government assessor and Keeper of the Native Hostelry in Auckland'.[13] In the Māori reserved lands of Pukekohe the case boiled down to the degree Īhaka may have been guilty of treason in 1863 when government forces invaded the Waikato. Despite their government connections, both he and fellow assessor Mohi Te Ngū were moderates within the Kīngitanga, and had raised the alarm about a fortification that the Crown was building within Waikato territory prior to hostilities. Such was the Government's concern at that time about Īhaka's loyalty that it cut his assessor's salary. Just as the army was about to invade, Francis Dillon Bell and other government officers visited Māori communities in the district immediately south of Auckland to deliver an aggressively worded proclamation. It demanded that Māori give up their arms and sign a declaration of allegiance to the Queen, or vacate their lands and withdraw to Waikato. It is small wonder that Rīria saw the situation as fearful, and the people as having been driven off their lands.

> *The first witness examined was Ryria, the mother of Ihaka, one of the claimants, who deposed: I possessed land at Pukekohe. Mohi and Ihaka had cultivations there. I do not know the boundaries[.] Te Keene does. The whole of the land belonged to the ancestors of those named. We were driven away by the Europeans in consequence of the war. We were not told to go. We left through fear. We do not intend to return. Ihaka left three children.*
> *[Cross-examined] By Mr. Crawford: The five claimants are all of our tribe, Te Akitai. The name of the hapu is Ngatipare. We had cultivations at the time of the war. Te Hapimana had cultivations there. I recollect when Pukekohe was sold. It was sold by Ihaka, Te Keene, Te Hapimana, and Mohi. The land now claimed was reserved for us all. I was with Ihaka when Mr. Bell went out to administer the oath of allegiance at Kirikiri, and the same night we were apprehended. Mr. Bell had promised to return the following morning. Ihaka did not take the oath. He was waiting for Mr. Bell. Ihaka was not in company with Mohi and the armed party. Mohi was stationed elsewhere.*
> *[Cross-examined] By Mr. Brookfield: Te Hapimana had a large clearing at Pukekohe at the time he was turned away. I saw it. The produce was for the tribe. We were afterwards released by the Government. We were not required to take the oath.*[14]

Her evidence alludes too to their flight towards Waikato. However, they were encumbered with a number of kaumātua and sick people, including Īhaka. While Mohi and the able-bodied men were able to escape to Waikato, the others, including Īhaka, were 'apprehended'. This misfortune ultimately proved fortuitous, as it enabled Rīria to claim a non-rebel status. Rīria and her family received £3,944 for their claim, while £1,500 was paid to other parties.[15]

Rīria also made representations when claims were made on the Tūākau Block. Although Thomas Beckham declared that the claims of Te Ākitai were 'total fiction',[16] her evidence gives a few clues to her earlier personal life.

Riria: I claim the Tuimata block on behalf of myself and children. I have no claim on Tuakau. I have three children. I belong to the Ngatipari tribe. I do not know how long it is since I was married. It was the time that Te Rauparaha was in Auckland. I was married according to Maori custom before that. We were married by the Bishop.[17]

Governor Grey kidnapped the Ngāti Toa chief, Te Rauparaha in 1846 and held him in Auckland in 1847–48, which roughly dates her Christian marriage. As the Catholic Bishop, Jean Baptiste Pompallier, was overseas at this time, 'the Bishop' refers to the Anglican, George Augustus Selwyn, indicating that she was very likely of that faith.

The Patamahoe [Patumāhoe] Block was another for which Rīria appeared before the Compensation Court in 1865.

Riria, sworn, said I lay claim to compensation for Patamahoe, for myself, and children. Paora Te Iwi, Paora, Tuaire, Ahipene, have also claims. I claim through Ihaka. Heta is my younger brother. We were cultivating there two years before the war, after the death of Poharama. I don't know that Hakopa has any claim. It is quite true he resided on the land and cultivated there. I don't know when he went first on the land. When we went there he had been in occupation some time. He belongs to the Ngatihauna [sic] tribe, a different tribe to Ihaka's, but his wife is connected with the same tribe as Ihaka. I don't know whether he claims through himself or his wife. Let him speak for himself.

Cross-examined by Mr. Crawford: Heta is not a brother of Ihaka's. He is a son of Tipine's younger brother. Tipine was Ihaka's father. I do not know whether Tipine had a claim on the land. I have put in a claim for Heta, because he is a son of the younger brother, while Ihaka is the son of the elder brother.

Puakitehau was the brother of Poharama and Te Tipine. Poharama was the oldest. Tipene is dead. He had children, but they are dead. Poharama had a son, Te Ropia, but he is dead. He had other children, sons and daughters, but they are dead. Te Ropia left children. Hone Ropia, Te Tipene, Inoka, and Hera, who is with the King. Hone Ropia is alive, and with the King. Te Tipene is also with the King. Turira never was married, and is dead. Waata is dead, without issue, he went over to the rebels, but he died a natural death. Te Matai had other sons beside Paora, Te Iwi, and Waata. Maka is a cousin of Poharama.[18]

In her statement Rīria gives details of familial relationships, and in several cases, identifies individuals who are 'with the King', that is, in exile in the King Country. She was thus subtly alluding to her own non-rebel status. The court awarded Rīria and her children £350 for her claims to this block, while £370 went to other parties, of which £250 went to Pāora Te Iwi and Aihepene Kaihau mentioned below.[19] She received nothing for her claims in the Tuimata Block,[20] but £30 for the Wairoa Block.[21]

Court processes and documents

The court's processes followed closely those of the Native Land Court, with Judge Fenton in charge of both, and '[p]recedent developed in one jurisdiction was routinely applied in the other'.[22] In another Waikato case, Ngāti Tīpā claimants assembled at the Civil Commissioner's Office in Auckland, with Judge Rogan presiding. Ani Pūtutu gave her evidence, describing the names of localities in a manner reminiscent of the Native Land Court, while an official converted her speech into an English-language text.

> *Ani Pututu   claim read (witness deaf)*
> *   Hori wrote out the claim & was called to make a statement.*
> *Hori Kukutai   deposed that Ani asked him to write the claim for her.*
> *Noa Kukutai   (called) The lands described in Ani's claim are at Waipa,*
> *I cannot describe the boundaries, only a portion of them. Ani can describe them.*
> *Ani Pututu   (recalled) I do not belong to Piringia [sic] I belong to*
> *Ngatitipa[.] I can describe the boundaries of the land[.] The boundaries of*
> *Te Rohe[Roho?] It commences at Otorokiokio [illegible] thence to Manguawhia*
> *then to Karamu thence to Te Ranguatawhiti, then to Otupawhero, thence*

to Te Awaiti, thence to Te Kohukohu, then to Te Uku[illegible], thence to Ruatuna, thence to Kahuitara, thence to Te Tomo, thence to Waipapa, thence to Ohinerora, thence to Raiina ---- (Waihakari, Whakapuapua and Whakangiringiri are in these boundaries) thence to Tuhimata, thence to Pukimapai, thence to Tiotera[illegible] thence to Te Hapua, thence to Pakaroa, thence to Pokairoiroi thence to Te Whaotomo, thence to Te Titoki, thence to Oruatohungia thence to Paiateram[illegible] thence to Otutai, thence to Kahunui, thence to Timoukataina[illegible], thence to Waipuna, thence to Otutone, thence to Whitianga, thence to Otawhiwhi, thence it descends to Te Mania, thence to Aaraara, thence to Te Punia, thence to Te Ruki a ngawhao, thence to Te Puta, thence to Karangapaihau inland thence to Te Kopi, thence to Owhakope, thence to Nga Ruahine, thence to Waiorua[.] Thence to Ngamokopuna, thence to Rotorangi, thence to Putoitoi, thence to Waerangi, thence to Pukekura, thence it turns to Te Taura, thence to Rotorini, thence to Ngawharekaitawara, thence to Karangapaihai, -- Te Ruaruru[illegible] -- Pekapekarau -- Pukamatai -- Waimaru -- Ruakotari -- Ruakaka -- Tuakura -- Te Kohu -- Mangawhero -- Taurangamiromiro -- Te Ahana -- Ngaroto -- Pareahi -- Maungawhakatari -- Pukatea -- Pikopiko -- Waipaki -- Ngawhakawawha -- Maungakawhau -- Teiringa -- Makomako this is the end of the boundary of my piece of land. Miriama claims with me.[23]

The 'paperwork' for successful claimants differed in each confiscation area. In the following example relating to the Waikato confiscation, the judge has written out a receipt in English for the claimant to sign. Ani Mihipō Pātene signed the receipt, written in English, with an 'X'. Also written on this receipt (marked 'Duplicate') are the words 'Scrip with Weteni Mahikai for £15-' so it is not clear whether she shared this money, or was to receive some land instead.

Ngaruawahia
7 January 1869
I the undersigned do hereby acknowledge to have received from Judge Mackay Jr Esq the sum of twenty five pounds being amount awarded to me by the Court for my claims to confiscated lands at Ngaroto and at Waipa West, Pironga [sic], & Waikato
Ani Mihipo Patene
her X mark

Ngaroto –   £15. 0. 0
Waipa &c   10. 0. 0
            £25. 0. 0

No of cheque 5

Compensating with money soon proved expensive for the government, and regulations were changed so that land (or scrip, a promise of land) could be awarded instead. However, as Boast notes, the government granted land to military settlers before any Māori had a chance to claim, so that in some places, such as Ōākura in Taranaki, there was insufficient land available for Māori claimants.[24]

An urupā at Patumāhoe

The loss of ancestral lands weighed heavily on hapū. On 21 June 1865 Ana Pāora Te Iwi, the wife of Aihepene Kaihau, wrote to Frederick Weld, the New Zealand Premier, about the Compensation Court. She had two concerns; the first related to an old urupā (burial ground) within the Patumāhoe block.

> *he kupu taku kia koe monga Tupapaku i roto o Patumahoe kia whakaputaina e koe ki waho tatemea e koreeahei ia Matou te Hahu no Na mata noa atu ratou I mate ai i takoto ai i to ratou kainga e kore e kitea e matou. He kupu atu tenei na Matou kia koe kia Whakaputaina mai te Karauna Karati mote wahi i takoto ai o Matou Tupuna[.]*
> *Ko nga eka i takoto ai ratou kia 40[.] kua ki atu hoki Aihe Pene Kia te Penetana Kia kapea nga Tupapaku ki waho[.] Kihai nga Kaiwhakawa i Whakae ko te take tenei i Pouri ai Matou ki o matou Tupapaku no te mea kihai i puta mai ta ratou koha kia Kapea ki waho[.] ka pa ia nei he Tupapaku hou e ahei ia matou te kimi[.] No konei matou e mea ai mau e Whakahoki mai te wahi i takoto ai o Matou Tipuna[.] Heoi tena[.]*
> *E hoa kei pouri koe ki ta matou kupu tate mea kua riro atu ia koe te whenua me o matou Tupuna[.] Heoi tena[.]*

> [official translation]
> I have a word to you about the dead at Patumahoe that you may exclude their graves – we cannot remove them as they have been so very long dead and are still

lying in their own place – we shall not be able to find their remains – this word of ours is to ask you to give us a Crown Grant for forty acres of the piece in which our Ancestors are laid – Aihepene asked Mr Fenton to exclude the graves of the dead (from confiscation) but the judge did not consent to do that – this is the cause of some grief that they did not show us that favour – had they died lately we might be able to find their remains – we therefore ask you to return to us the place in which they are laid –

O friend do not be grieved at our word, because you have the land also (the remains of our ancestors[ )].²⁵

Charles Heaphy, a government surveyor, was asked to investigate and the following month wrote in the file that, 'No burial places are apparent on the ground', but he also stated that the block (701 acres in size) had already been allocated for new immigrants. Judge Mackay, perhaps a little more sympathetically, also noted on the file, 'Referred to Major Speedy to inform the writers that if they wish to have a burial ground reserve they must point out the spot – and a reserve will be made, but not 40 acres. If there are more places than one – <u>reserves</u> will be made. They must not delay making the selection.'

Ana wrote again in August to Judges Fenton and Mackay, saying,

> *i rongo au kia Meiha Pire kihai i marama ia korua te takiwa ki o matou tupuna ara i Patumahoe[.] ko te korero a Meiha Pire kia hau e kiana korua mehemea he wahi iti ka tahi ka marama ia korua ko tenei e hoa ma e taea hoki e matou te aha i te nui ano ote wahi i ta koto nga Tupapaku[.]*

[official translation]
I have heard from Major Speedy that you are not clear regarding our Ancestors (burying place) at Patumahoe – this is Major Speedys [sic] word to me – that you should say if it was a small piece you would then see the matter clear – Now friends what can we do as the place is large where the dead are laid we cannot make it less now.²⁶

Despite Ana suggesting that she would keep pestering the Native Office until she got justice, a note appended to the file stated, 'It has been explained to her. Her application is unreasonable and unlikely to be complied with.'

Dubious claimants

Ana's other grievance was with the eligibility of certain low-born people to make claims to the court. In her first letter she states,

> *Rere whakarongo mai kia korerotia atu e ai O Matou tikanga Maori kia mohio koutou[.]*
> *E hoa kei te titiro pouri matou ki nga tikanga o te whakawa tango whenua ate Kawanatanga[.] te he i kitea e matou ko te whakataunga ate whakawa ki nga Ware ki nga tangata hehe nei ratou ki nga whenua ara ki Patumahoe ki Pokeno ki Maketu[.] he hunga nei hoki ratou he ngarengarenga ite oranga o matou Tupuna a tae iho ana kia matou matua[.] Kaore hoki ratou e karangatia ki nga whare korero ao matou Tupuna ao matou matua[.] Taratou nei karangatanga he mahi kai i nga kai i te Moana i nga kuri ano hoki o uta[.] kaore ano hokihe wehe-wehenga Whenua i te oranga o matou Tupuna kia whiwhi nga Ware[.] kei nga Rangatira anake hoki nga Whenua ara kei o matou nei Tupuna heoiano to nga Ware tikanga he noho noa iho i runga i te Whenua[.] me nga tangata ke ano hoki e haere atu na ki te korero kia koutou no ratou te Whenua kaore matou e mohio ki enana tu tangata tatemea he tino Taurekareka rawa ratou[.] koia matou ko oku hoa Wahine Rangatira ara ko nga uri o Hinewai O Rangi Heihei ka titiro pouri atu ai ki enei tu tangata[.] Heoiano te mea i marama ia matou ko te Tamaiti a Ihaka[.] whakaaroa e koe i te Oranga o Nuitireni[.] heoi ano nga tangata e haere atu ana kia koutou ko Mohi raua ko Ihaka ta te mea no roto raua i nga Tupuna Rangatira e korerotia atu e au nei[.] Heoi Tena[.]*

[official translation]
Now listen while I tell you of our 'Maori' customs that you may understand one – O friend we are looking with sorrow to the way in which the Compensation Court disposes of the land (claims)[.] the error we complain of is the awarding by the Court to the plebeians the right to the lands they have no (just) claim to – viz to Patumahoe to Pokeno and Maketu to those parties who were subservient to our parents and Ancestors and who were not admitted into their councils – their duty was to cultivate food for them[.]

There was no division of land made in the time of our parents or Ancestors that these plebeians should have a right (to hold lands) – The chiefs alone have the right to the lands. That right was our Ancestors – all that the plebeians had to do with it was living on it – Other men also come to you and tell you the land is theirs – we do not acknowledge that class of persons because they are really slaves – therefore we and our female friends of rank the descendants of Hinewai of Rangiheihei look with vexation towards that class of men (slaves) – The only person we acknowledge is Ihakas [sic] son – do you take into consideration when New Zealand was in health (ie before the war) the only (class) of men who had intercourse with the Government were such as Moihi [Mohi] and Ihaka Te Kanini [Takanini] because they descended from Ancestors of rank of whom I have been speaking[.]²⁷

Her second letter also queries the money given to one of the claimants, and compares it to what her own husband and father received. This may have been due to tribal differences, however, rather than differences of class.²⁸

he patai tenei naku ki a korua no te whea Whenua ia na nga moni ia Hawira Maki[.] ki te mea mo Maketu katoa kahe engari kia tika ano ki tona wahi te utu mo ana moni[.] kotenei ehoama wahia nga moni i karangatia ki te ingoa o Hawira hoatu ki nga tangata iuru ki tera whi [sic] ki tera wahi a tae noa ki Pokeno[.] kei mea korua he hura naku ia korua tikanga kua oti na te whaka takoto e korua kahore he whaka atu kia mohio tia ai a korua ti kanga ki nga tangata inoho irunga itepai ki nga tangata ano hoki nona tera wahi tera wahi[.] he aha te take i wha ka nuiai nga moni ma tena tangata ma Hawira[illegible] he iti nei tona wahi ko nga moni i nui[.] he aha te take i iti ai ma Paora raua ko Aihe notemea ia raua nga wahi rahi o Maketu a tae atu ano ki Pokeno[illegible] he aha te take ikore ai te tahi ma te Tamaiti a Ihaka note mea noroto ia io matou Tupuna[illegible] engari hoatu kia Aihe kia Paora kia Rapata kia Hori kia ki taratou Tamaiti kia Ngotu Ihaka nga moni erite ana ki oratou hiahia[.] kia mahara ano hoki korua kia matou koku Tuakana[.]

[official translation]
This is the question of mine to you for which land did Hawira Maki have the money? If for the whole of Maketu it is an error – rather let his own piece be payment for the money – Now o friends divide the money awarded in Hawira's name and give it to those who have claims to that and other pieces to Pokeno – do not think I wish to overturn your decisions that you have already laid down without your making known what your intentions are towards those who have remained peacefully that they may be understood by those who are the people to whom that and other pieces belong[.]

What is the reason that so large a sum of money was given to that man Hawira whose piece was small and the money great[?]
What is the reason that it was small for Paora Te Iwi and Aihipene for to them belong the larger portions of Maketu extending to Pokeno – what is the reason there was not anything given to the son of Ihaka for he is from our Ancestors – better give to Aihipene to Paora to Rapata (Kaihau) to Hori (Tauroa) and to their child Ngotu Ihaka the money equal to their desire and that you also remember me and my elders[.][29]

In her first letter, Ana was also keen to establish her people's loyal status in contrast with the more dubious Īhaka Takaanini Te Tihi.

E hoa kei pouri koe kei whakaparahako ano hoki kia matou nei korero[.] he korero tuturu tenei na matou[.] e hara ite mea e korero pena ana matou me nga tangata o Mohi raua ko Ihaka i Mahue iho nei ki te Kupapa[.] ta ratou mahi he korero whakahihi.
Rere whakarongo mai kia mohio koe ki nga uri o enei Tupuna i Mahue ki te Kupapa ioati pono ano hoki ki te Kuini[.] ki hai matou i hopukia, i hoki mai ranei ite ara e maro atu ana kite Kingi engari i noho tuturu Matou i runga i nga kainga o te Wahine Matua a Pohutu ara o Hine Wai[.]

[official translation]
O friend do not be vexed neither disregard our statement which is the truth – We are not speaking as do the people of Moihi and Ihaka who were left with the Neutrals[.] their words are words of strife – Now listen that you may understand who were the descendants of those ancestors who were left with the Neutrals who also took a faithful oath to the Queen – we were not taken prisoners[,] neither did we return from the road which led straight to the King – but who resided truthfully on those residences which (formerly) belonged to the head wife of Pohutu that is Hinewai[.][30]

Ana uses the word 'kūpapa' to define Īhaka, who had been detained while on the road to Waikato, in distinction to her people who had remained and took the oath of allegiance to the Queen. One meaning of the term 'kūpapa', 'to lie flat', aligns with the concept of keeping out of a quarrel, but the term later became associated with 'friendly' Māori in general, including those who allied with the Crown. From the twentieth century, the term has been used more pejoratively as 'collaborator' with the colonial regime.

Compensation: Bay of Plenty

Confiscation in Tauranga came in response to Ngāi Te Rangi's stand against the government during the Waikato war, while in the Whakatāne-Ōpōtiki district confiscation resulted from Pai Mārire (or Hauhau) activity. In 1865 Pai Mārire emissaries visiting Ōpōtiki incited the murder of the missionary Carl Volkner, who was suspected of spying for the government. This incident provoked an invasion by the militia troops, the trial and execution of a number of chiefs, and confiscation of about 480,000 acres of land.

One of the first claimants was Mere Petley (or Petere), the wife of John Petley, a former imperial soldier turned coastal trader. In the same month the troops arrived Mere wrote to the governor, perhaps attempting to ensure her rights would be protected.

Hepetema 18 1865
E hoa E Te Kawana
He pukapuka whakamahara tenei ki nga whenua oku i Opotiki. Kei te taha a Heta, ka timata te Rohe, ka haere atu ki nga maunga o Waioeka, ko tona rohe kei te taha ki waho nei ko te Wai-Roa; ko te hokinga mai o te taha ki te Rawhiti ko Waioeka, kei Tutai-Toko. Kei te taha ki te Ra-to o Tutai-Toko ko te Rohe tenei puta tonu ki Maro-Wai-Wai, kei Roto Haka ka mutu. Ko te taha tenei ki te Rawhiti o Waioeka, ka timata ko te taha ki te Ra-to o Waioeka kei te taha ki uta o Tawa-Hewa ka timata tenei Rohe puta tonu atu ki te Wairoa ko tona putanga o tenei awa ko Pakihi[.] Ko te take o tenei Whenua ko te Rangi-wawata toku tupuna.
Hoiano
Na Mere Petley

[modern translation]
18 September 1865
Friend, the Governor.
This is a letter to inform you about my lands at Ōpōtiki. The boundary starts on Heta's side, and goes to the mountains of Waioeka, its outside boundary is Te Wairoa. Coming back to the eastern side it is Waioeka at Tūtaitoko. On the side of the west of Tūtaitoko the boundary goes to Marowaiwai, and finishes at Rotohaka. This is the side on the East of Waioeka. The side on the West of Waioeka starts at the side inland of Tawahewa, and this boundary goes along to Te Wairoa,

and this river comes out at Pakihi. My rights for this land come from my ancestor,
Te Rangiwawata.
Enough
From Mere Petley.[31]

At the top of the letter the official wrote, 'This land is not yet confiscated, therefore it is useless sending this letter to the Governor. If Natives wish to procure a title to unconfiscated lands they should apply to the Native Land Court. If the land is confiscated they should apply to the Colonial Secretary for Compensation.' Mere immediately made an application using a standard Native Land Court form (see Introduction).[32] As the district was confiscated in January 1866, applicants had to wait until 1867 to have their claims heard.

Pēti Parāone (Elizabeth Brown) Tāhere also used a government form in order to claim land in the Ōpōtiki area, one that had been created for confiscated land, although in the Waikato district rather than the Bay of Plenty.

> [underline indicates handwritten text.]
>   <u>Akarana 14 July 186 6</u>
> Ki te Hekeretari o te Koroni,
>   Kei Akarana.
>   He kupu whakaatu tenei naku kia koe mo toku pihi whenua i roto i nga rohe o te whenua kua tangohia e te Kawana mo te hara o nga iwi o Waikato. E hiahia ana hoki ahau kia whakawakia e te Kooti Whakarite toku tikanga ki taua pihi. He oti ano.
>   Na to hoa,
>   Na <u>Tahere</u>
> <u>(Elizabeth Brown)</u>
>
>   Ko te ingoa o te whenua ko <u>Mararuhi</u>
>   i te takiwa ki <u>Opotiki</u>
>   ko nga rohe i timata ki <u>Marainui</u>

> [modern translation, underline indicates handwritten text]
>   <u>Auckland 14 July 1866</u>
> To the Colonial Secretary
>   In Auckland
>   This is an application from me to you about my piece of land in the areas

of land taken by the Governor for the crimes of the tribes of Waikato. I desire
my rights to that piece to be judged by the Compensation Court. Enough.
From your friend
From Tāhere
(Elizabeth Brown)

The name of the land is Mararuhi
in the district of Ōpōtiki
the boundaries starting at Marainui.[33]

Tāhere probably did not fill in the information herself, because when she received land in compensation she signed the handwritten agreement with an 'X'. Unlike the Waikato receipts written in English, some of the Bay of Plenty agreements are in Māori. The Commissioner J. A. Wilson most likely wrote this document which, as attested by several witnesses, was read out to her.

Opotiki 4 Aperira 1867
Kua oti te whakanoa e au aku pukapuka katoa tango utu mo aku whenua i tukua e au ki te Kooti whakawa mo nga whenua kua tangohia e te Kawana i te takiwa o Bay of Plenty mo te hara o etahi tangata, ara kua whakanoatia taku take ki roto o te rohe o te Kawana – Na te take i noa ai kua oti te homai e te Wirihana Komihana ki ahau erua tekau ma rima eka whenuaki Ohui.
Peti Paraone Tahere x

[modern translation]
Ōpōtiki 4 April 1867
I have abrogated all documents to gain compensation for my lands that I submitted to the Court for lands taken by the Governor in the Bay of Plenty district, for the transgressions of others, that is, I have abrogated my claim within the [confiscated] district of the Governor. With the claim removed, Commissioner Wilson has given me twenty-five acres of land at Ōhui.
Pēti Parāone Tāhere.[34]

Māori or Pākehā?

Meriama (sometimes Mereana, or Mary Ann) White also claimed confiscated Ōpōtiki land. She was the wife of Bennett White, a storekeeper and shipper, who escaped death at the hands of Pai Mārire adherents in 1865 when James Fulloon was murdered, but two years later suffered the same fate himself.[35] Just two months before his death, Meriama gave evidence for her claim in court.

> <u>Meriama Waiti</u>. *claims at Mataka &c. [claims 41, 42, 43]*
> *I have been married to Bennet [sic] White about three years. I was the wife of another white man for seven years. It is a considerable time since I was among my own people. I consider myself a European. It was at considerable outlay in surveying my claims. I make the claim through my ancestors. The land (pink col. on the plan produced[)] is mine. Te Hapa was her father. My claim begins at Mataka, Panepoaka, then along the tops of hills to K[??]panga, descends Otuaia and joins the middle of Ohui, then to Te Hua a te rangikapakapa. Te Hapa belonged to Ngatirua. He is dead[.] The lands were settled on me by Panuiamarama[.] Te Hapa was not a chief.*
> *[Cross examined by Mr. Wilson] I lay claim to the land solely through my ancestors. No other person has a claim to these lands. I never bought land: I claim not by tribe but through forefathers. I belong to Ngatirua hapu and not to any other tribes. Both my grandfather and father cultivated in several places on the land[.] Am not aware any land has been sold to Europeans. If any has been sold it was wrong to do so. My father never sold any of it. Father was living in this place when Europeans came here in Titoko's time.*
> *[Cross examined by Mr. Marston] Am ignorant of the value of the land. It is good quality. £200 was given for land and houses at North Shore. There is a good road to my land[.] I am aware that land has been sold there.*[36]

Although she states her hapū affiliation and bases her claim through whakapapa, Meriama stated that, 'I consider myself a European'. This may have been a genuinely felt conviction, although we cannot be sure exactly what she meant. Bennett White had had a store in Whakatāne, a small town where it would have been difficult to avoid contact with other Māori, even if they were not 'my own people'. Her assertion may have been to indicate that she had adopted Pākehā customs, or may have been a ploy to ensure a better chance of success. The use of the English language was a practice that might demonstrate the adoption of tikanga Pākehā, but it is not clear what language she used in Court. One imagines that a judge quickly taking minutes wrote a text similar to what he heard, and that a testimony in English might well be different to the sort of language reproduced by an interpreter. However there seems to be little difference between the minutes of her speech and those of others. Despite having not lived with her people for some time, she does not appear estranged. Taipua who gave evidence after her stated that 'she claims through her forefathers. The tribes did not dispute her claim'.

In some cases, it is through correspondence that we have some evidence of women's involvement in the compensation process. In 1866, Elizabeth Fulloon, the daughter of early settler John Fulloon and Koka Te Mautaranui of Ngāti Awa and Tūhoe, claimed land in the Whakatāne district. It is clear that Elizabeth (or Riripeti) as an āwhekāihe (half-caste) occupied a space in the intersection between Māori and Pākehā societies. Her knowledge of Pākehā practices and the English language no doubt stood her in good stead when dealing with bureaucracy. She was also sister to James Fulloon, 'one of the first people of mixed descent to achieve standing in the public service', who was murdered by Pai Mārire adherents in Whakatāne in 1865.[37] Elizabeth received, from her brother's death, an annual pension of £50.[38] According to Judith Binney, Elizabeth disapproved of her brother's relationship with a Māori woman, and her refusal to acknowledge her brother's daughter, Emeri Maraea, prevented the latter from making her own claims for confiscated lands for many years. The two women clashed years later when Elizabeth had her brother's body reburied in the Whakatāne town cemetery. Elizabeth's actions were, according to Binney, 'a rejection of her Māori affiliations'.[39] In 1878 Elizabeth, who had lived mainly in Auckland from the early 1860s, married the government official Thomas H. Smith who had extensive experience in the Native Department, and would become a Native Land Court judge.[40]

In 1866, in her mid twenties, Elizabeth made her claim for land to the Colonial Secretary as required by law.

Tauranga 4th July 1866.
Sir
I have honor to make application under the provisions of the New Zealand Settlements Act, for compensation for my claims to lands confiscated in the District of the Bay of Plenty – these lands were owned by my late mother

Koka and brother Mr. James Fulloon, and are situated in the neighbourhood of Whakatane. I am not at present in a position to define the boundaries to which I am entitled; but will take an early opportunity of furnishing further particulars.

    I am Sir
    Yours very respectfully
    Elizabeth K. Fulloon.[41]

This was accompanied by another request, of a slightly more personal nature.

Tauranga 4th July 1866

Sir
    I have the honor to inform you that my brother the late Mr. James Fulloon owned a piece of land at te Wairere Whakatane containing about four acres (the plan whereof is here unto annexed)[.] As my mother and brother are both burried [sic] within this piece. I beg most respectfully to request that it may be granted to me.
    I am sir
    Yours very respectfully
    Elizabeth Koka Fulloon[42]

When the time came for the claim to be investigated, Elizabeth wrote a short declaration stating that she chose a James Baker as her agent to represent her.

I authorise Mr James Baker to act for me, in all matters connected with my claim to land at Wakatane, [sic] and to receive compensation for the same.
    Elizabeth Fulloon
December 29th 1866.[43]

It was James Baker who signed a memorandum with the Crown Commissioner, J. A. Wilson, on 6 May 1867, in which Elizabeth 'agreed to withdraw and renounce all her claims for compensation for lands confiscated in the Bay of Plenty district'. In return she received £150 and 50 acres on the Whakatāne flat, as well as a plot where her relatives were buried, 'not [to] be less than ¼ of an acre, or more than ½ an acre'.[44] Official Compensation Court forms signed by Judge James Mackay the following month duly authorised the agreement.[45] In 1892, Emeri Maraea Mautaranui (Emily Maria Fulloon or Mrs Buckworth) petitioned Parliament 'for compensation to the extent of £500 for losses sustained through the confiscation of her father's land and his murder whilst he was in the Government service'.[46] Emeri petitioned a number of times before gaining redress (see chapter 5).

Ruta Te Manuahura's struggle for compensation

The Compensation Court cases sometimes dragged on for years, as can be seen in this series of documents from Ruta Te Manuahura. Her persistence, however, paid off. In her third letter to McLean, the Native Minister, she stated that her claimed lands lay in Waikato, but asserted that she had committed no crime against the state. After the Waikato campaigns she married a Te Arawa chief, Philip Tapsell, who had fought alongside the government against the Kīngitanga forces.[47]

> Maketu
> 31 Hurae 1876
> Ki a Temakarini
> E koro tena koe e koro ko te tuatoru tenei o aku reta kia koe ki te Kawanatanga mo aku piihi whenua i Waikato i riro i te rau o te patu a te Kawanatanga, ara ko Tiritiri ko Miropiko ko Waipahihi ko Hukanui ko nga ingoa enei o nga piihi whenua[.] E toa [tonoa?] nei e au ki a koe ki te Kawanatanga, kia whakahokia mai ki au na te mea noku ake ena whenua no toku whae na te mea e hara ahau i te wahine i whai hara ki ti Kawana tanga hei take e puritia ai au piihi whenua[.] Ko te toru tenei o nga tau e tono ana ahau kia koe ara ki te Kawanatanga he aha ra te take i kore ai e whakahokia mai[?]
> Na ki te kite koe ki tena reta kia ??? te whakahokimai na te roa hoki o to whakahokimai i waiho ai hai taimaha ki toku ngakau mea whenua[.]
> Na Ruta Manuahura.

> [official translation]
> Maketu 31 July 1876
> To Sir Donald McLean
> Oh Sir
> Greetings Oh Sir this is my third letter to you to the Government about my pieces of land at Waikato they were confiscated by the Government. The lands are Tiritiri,

Miropiko, Waipahihi and Hukanui[.] These are the names of the pieces of Land I want returned by the Government[.] These lands are mine individually inherited from my mother – I am a woman that has not committed any offense against the Government that they should hold the land[.] This is the third Year year [sic] I have been trying to get this land returned by the Government. What is the reason the land is not returned[?] when you receive this letter do you reply[.] It is because my letters are not answered that matter is a weighty-affair with me[.]

Ruta Te Manu Ahura.[48]

Several months later she wrote again.

> Maketu
> 22 Oketopa 1[8]76
>
> Kia Ta Tanara Makarini
> E koro hei noi atu te nei kia koe mo aku puka puka kare ano ihoki mai ia koe mo aku whenua iriro i te rau ote patu a te Kawana tanga iwaikato[.] Ka maha hoki aku reta ka tae atu ki te Kawana tanga ara kia koe[.] Kua mutu ngara ruraru iho mai e te Kawanatanga kia te arawa[.] Kia marama ta korua ti tiro mai[.] Na reira ahau ka tohe kia ku pihi kia whaka hokia mai e koe[.] Na te raru raru hoki imua te tae atu ki reira[.] Kua rongo au kua hoki etahi wahi ona whenua kinga ta ngata nona[.] he aha koe iwhaka rongo ai ki ta te Kingi imau patu nei ki te Ka wanatanga[?] Ko ahau e noho manene ana ite nei whenua[.] Koa ku whenua koi te na Kua riro na ia koe[.] E koro e noho pani ana[.] Ko toku matua kua mate me toku matua wahine kua mate[.] He wahine ahau he nui aku ta mariki[.] Kaore oku whenua ikonei imaketu nei[.]
> Kote ingoa oa na pihi kua tae atu kai a koe te puka puka[.] E koro ma kia mana mai i a korua ta ku reta[.]
>
> Na Ruta te Manuahu[ra]

[official translation]
    Maketu 22 October 1876
To Sir Donald McLean
Oh Friend
    This is to ask you about my letters to which I received no answer. The[y] are about my land that has been Confiscated by the Government at Waikato[.] I have written several letters to the Government that is to you, The Arawa troubles with the Government are now over[.] Do you impartially

look at this matter[.] I ask to have this land returned to me[.] It was on account of confusion that I did not go there[.] I have heard that some of the Land has been returned to the parties laying claim to the land. Why did you listen to the King party who took up arms against the Government[?] I am living here a Stranger on this land[.] My lands are gone to you[.] I am an orphan[.] Both my parents are dead[.] I am a woman with several Children but have no Land here at Maketu[.] The names of those pieces of land are with you[,] they were sent by letter[.] Do you reply to my letter[.]
from Ruta Te Manuahuru[sic][49]

In her letter she suggested that land was being returned, but to those, unlike her, who had fought against the government. The 'Arawa troubles' alluded to no doubt refer to Te Arawa hostility to extensive government land purchasing in its territory. Such was Te Arawa's response that the *Auckland Star* suggested that the tribe was close to rebellion so that, in June 1876, 'The Government . . . directed the suspension of all land purchase operations in the Arawa districts.'[50] This was not of direct concern to Ruta's claim, but she may have felt that the Government's non-response may have been tied to her marriage to Tapsell, and her residence in Te Arawa territory.

In about 1882, the Government had agreed to compensate Ruta, part of which was an award of '75 acres of "good average land" in Waikato'.[51] However she did not think this was sufficient, and petitioned parliament for more. The Native Affairs Committee who investigated her petition considered her award 'liberal' and 'that it is the fault of the petitioner herself that she is not in possession'.[52] Ruta persevered, looking for land closer to where she lived at Maketū to satisfy the remainder of her claim.

Maketu oketopa 4 1883
Kia paraihe minita mote taha maori e koro tena koe[.] awhea ano te Kawanatanga whakarite ai ite whenua maaku[.] kanui taku tatari roa kaore ahau e mohia [sic] kite take e whakaroa nei te Ka wanatanga ite whenua maaku[.] awhea koe hoko ai ite nei whenua ite rauotehuia[?] me tono e koe te kai ruuri kia wahia taua whenua kia marama ai nga eka maaku[.] heoi ano te whenua e hiahia tia ana e au nate mea kei konei ahau enoho ana[.] e tata ana ki te kotahi te kau nga tau ina ia nei kaore ano te kawanatanga kia whakaoti[.] heoi ano[.]
Na Ruta te Manuahura.

[official translation]
Maketu
October 4th, 1883.
To Mr Bryce
Native Minister
Friend Greeting
When will the Government arrange about giving me the land I am to have? I have now waited a long time and do not know what the cause of the delay is. When are you going to buy Te Rau-o-te-Hua [sic] [?] Do you send a surveyor to divide that land so that I may know where mine is situated: this is the land I would prefer to any other because I am living here. It is now ten years since it was arranged that I was to have the land and the Government have not yet carried it out – Ended[.]
from
sgn. Ruta Te Manuahura[53]

By 1885 she had negotiated a piece of land at Te Puke, close to Maketū, although she was not totally satisfied with it.

Maketu hepetema 29 1885

Kia te paranihi minita mote taha maori e Koro tena koe[.] kua tae mai ate paramena kia au kia tiro hia nga whenua ate Kawana tanga ite puke[.] kua tae ahau kite titiro itaua whenua kua kite ahau ite ahua ote whenua, e pai ana te ahua otiia heoi ano te mea naana i whakakino taua whenua kitaku titiro kote tahi awaawa hohonu mete tahi repo kei waenga nui tonu otaua piihi otira e mea ana ahau me tapu mai ano e te Kawana tanga etahi eka hei tapiri mote wahi kino kia rima eka[.] ki te whakaae tekawana tanga kite nei ka whakahoki ahau mate kawa natanga ano e tono mai te kai ruuri hei tapahi i nga eka maku iputa hoki te kupu ate kawa natanga kia kimihia tetahi wahi pai maku na reira ahau itono ai kia tapiri tia mai taua wahi kino[.]
heoi ano
Na Ruta Manuahura

[official translation]
Maketu
Sept. 29th 1885.
To Mr Ballance

> The Native Minister
>
> Friend,
>
> Greeting to you. Mr Brabant has asked me to look at some land belonging to the Government at Te Puke. I have been to look over the said land, and have seen what kind of land it is. It is good land, that is, I consider it to be so. I think the only objection is that there is a deep gulley, and a swamp, right in the centre of the land. I consider that the Government should give me five more acres in lieu of the bad portion that cannot be made use of. If the Government agree to this, I shall also agree that the Government should send out their own surveyor to cut off the land for me, because the government said to me that a piece should be selected for me. Therefore it is that I ask that five more acres be given me in lieu of that that cannot be made use of.
>
> That is all,
>
> Ruta Manuahuru [sic].[54]

Ruta's persistence clearly grated with the Native Office. H. W. Brabant wrote that Philip Tapsell and his wife 'are very hard to please', and W. J. Morpeth, another official, noted on the file that '[t]his land claim of Ruta's has given the Department a great deal of trouble for a long time owing to the difficulty there is to please her'. The land, 68 acres in all, was valued at £3 an acre, and Morpeth considered that 'she ought to be satisfied, and I quite concur with Mr Brabant's suggestion that Ruta be offered the 68 acres in final settlement of her claim'.[55]

Sale of a compensation award in Taranaki

Confiscation effectively extinguished the native title of land, so when the Compensation Court awarded this land back to Māori it now possessed a more saleable status, with the owners often coming under pressure to sell. In Taranaki the government resolved to purchase as much of the returned land as it could, giving its agents few restrictions on how they might achieve this.[56] In 1871 the Government employed G. B. Worgan, a Napier surveyor, to purchase or lease the compensation lands in Taranaki.[57] Although Worgan worked for the government, he also moonlighted as an independent agent and irregularities in his practice soon became apparent. The following year Colonel Andrew Hamilton Russell headed a Royal Commission into Worgan's activities, which led to the latter's suspension.[58] Prior to the enquiry, the Wanganui Resident Magistrate, James

Booth, had talked with two elderly Māori, Mere Awatea and her brother, Erueti Te Pewa, who told him that they had received £400 for their land, but were still waiting for the remaining £600. When he questioned Mere again at the commission hearing, her story had changed.

> Mere Awatea deposed on oath
> Examined by Mr Booth –
> Did you have an award of 400 acres of land by Compensation Court between Whenuakura & Patea Rivers?
> Yes
> Did you sell that land?
> *I did not sell that land[.]*
> Who sold the land? or is it sold?
> *It is sold.*
> By whom?
> *It was sold by Wirihana[.]*
> Do you know to whom the land was sold?
> *It was sold to a European, I do not know to whom.*
> Do you know what sum of money the 400 aces of land was sold for?
> *I refer to the land of my Brother as well as myself was sold for £1,000–.*
> Did you sign the deed when the land was sold?
> *I did.*
> Was the £1000– paid to yourself and your Brother when the Deed was signed?
> *It was paid into my hands.*
> In what form was the money paid, notes, or gold?
> *As far as I can remember it was paid in notes[.]*
> How much did you receive as your portion?
> *Wirihana took from the Town[illegible] £200– I received a further instalment [sic] of £200– in a Public House from Wirihana, Major Kemp being present[.]*
> Was this money all for yourself?
> *This money was for both of us.*
> Have you received any more than the £400–?
> *I do not remember when I received any more money, But I received £400 more since.*
> Does that altogether make £800– that you have accounted for?
> *I think that is correct, but I do not count. I received £200 from Wirihana at Aramoho, & £200– in a Public House in Town & £400– also in the same Public House. All the money was paid to me by Wirihana.*

> When did you receive the last installment of £400–?
> *About three months ago.*
> What is the relationship between Wirihana and yourself?
> *Wirihana is my nephew.*
> Was it your wish that Wirihana should have the disposal of your money?
> *Yes.*
> Are you aware the land sold for £200– more than you received?
> *I do not know.*
> What do you suppose the land was sold for?
> *I thought it was sold for £1500–*
> Where do you think the remainder of the money is?
> *In Wirihana's hands for me.*[59]

Booth later wrote a memorandum to William Fox, the chairman of the West Coast Commission investigating Taranaki land issues, which revisited the case of Mere Awatea and Erueti Te Pewa and 'the notorious George Buckland Worgan'.[60] Booth stated that, 'Shortly after the inquiry was over there was a great noise & disturbance outside the Court house'. Worgan had told Mere and her brother that he and Wirihana would go to jail if they testified that they had not received the outstanding £600.

> Worgan moreover promised that if they swore they had received the whole of the purchase money, he would hand over the unpaid balance as soon as they came out of Court.
> When however they asked for their money he said 'why you have received the whole of the money and sworn to it before the Commissioner.' My opinion is that the facts are pretty much as stated and Mere Awatea & Erueti Te Pewa received £400- for their 800 acres and no more[.][61]

By 1881, Worgan was in jail for an unrelated forgery. Both Mere and Erueti were dead, but their descendants were unable to gain any redress. Fox considered that 'by their own wicked and foolish conduct [Mere and Erueti had] relieved the Government from all responsibility in the matter'.[62]

Compensation in Taranaki: a continuing struggle

Individuals who had applied for land grants through the Compensation Court were often not content with the awards. Taranaki was no exception. In some cases people were not awarded land, or were never allocated the acreage they had been awarded, or land received was insufficient for the needs of whānau. The grievances over compensation awards often dragged on for years. One woman, Mere Naera Pōmare, wrote to Sir George Grey. The letter is not clearly dated, but Grey was Premier from October 1877 to October 1879, so Mere may have written during that period. Like many Māori she addressed him as Kāwana Kerei (Governor Grey) although Grey's second governorship had ended in 1868, and he had now become a colonial politician.

> *Onaero   Hurae 26*
> *wahi o Taranaki*
> *Kia Kawana Kerei*
>   *E koro tena ra koe[.] Ka nui toku aroha atu ki a koe, ara, ki te matua o aku tuakana i te mate.*
> *E koro. He kupu atu tenei naku ki a koe. e kore ranei koe e pai ki te whaka marama mai i taku patai atu ki a koe kinga whenua o taku whaea o te Rauoterangi ratou ko ona matua me ona tupuna. Kua riro katoa i te rau o te patu a te Pakeha[.] I ngaki ano au i runga i aua whenua i mua atu i te rironga i te Pakeha. Heoi kaore nei aku take i riro Mau atu ai i te Pakeha enei whenua i Urenui i Onaero, wahi o Taranaki nei. Heoi e koro whakaaturia mai e koe te ritenga ki a marama au. Me pewhea ra e hoki mai ai enei whenua ki a matou ko aku tamariki. Ahakoa kotahi to meneti aroha tia mai e koe. me etehi atu ritenga onga whenua maori e hoatu ana ki te Paremata.*
> *Heoti tera. E koro whakautua mai taku reta. Ka mutu[.]*
> *Te Rauote Rangi*
> *Na Mere Naera Pomare*
>
> *Kia ora ra i raro i te maru o to tatou Ariki.*
>
> [modern translation]
> Ōnaero   July 26
> located in Taranaki
> To Governor Grey

Sir, Greetings. I hold much affection for you, that is, the father of my elder siblings who have passed on.

Sir, I have another issue for you, whether you would be so kind to give an explanation to my question to you about the lands of my mother, Te Rau-o-te-rangi, and her parents and ancestors. This has all been forcibly taken by the Pākehā. I cultivated on those lands before they were taken by the Pākehā. I gave no cause that these lands at Urenui and Ōnaero, here in Taranaki, should have been taken by the Pākehā. And so, sir, can you show me what the processes were, so I can be clear. What should be done so that these lands are returned to me and my children. Although you may only have one minute [to spare], please have compassion for me, and some of the other issues about Māori land being sent to the parliament.

That is all. Sir, please answer my letter. Ended.

Te Rau-o-te-rangi.

From Mere Naera Pōmare

Greetings under the protection of our Lord.[63]

In 1880 the new Government, under John Hall, was under pressure from Māori based at Parihaka under the leadership of Te Whiti-o-Rongomai and Tohu Kākahi, who were employing passive resistance techniques in an attempt to maintain mana whenua. In response the Government appointed the West Coast Commission to look into promises that government officials had made to Māori in Taranaki. Mere Naera Pōmare used the commission as an opportunity to argue for her lands.

305. Mere Naera Pomare, wife of Ngaere, said: *I have something to say with regard to the block of land called Onaero. At the close of the first war, I came to reside at Onaero on land owned by my grandfather on my mother's side. From Onaero I went to a place called Kaweka, at Urenui, which belonged to my grandmother. At the commencement of the second insurrection I went to Kapiti, near Wellington. After that a notice was issued of a sitting of the Compensation Court, and calling upon all Natives who had claims to make to attend the Court and prefer their claims. I did not attend, but my husband at that time (Inia Pihia) and my father and mother attended. Mr. Rogan was Judge of the Compensation Court. The claim preferred by my mother (Rau-o-te-rangi) was not admitted. She lived with my uncle. The Court awarded me 100 acres at Onaero, but none at Kaweka. I now ask that the Commission should give me some land at Kaweka, as the 100 acres at Onaero are insufficient for the support*

of myself and family of eleven children. I further request that the lands awarded by the Compensation Court to the Ngatimutunga tribe should now be allocated, as a very long time has elapsed without anything having been done. The land is situated between Titoki and Urenui, and is probably about 3,000 acres in extent; but I am not quite positive as to the quantity. The reason I am so anxious that this matter should be settled is, that so many of us are now living without any land.[64]

Ākanihi Kurakitoro (Agnes Simeon) also complained of not receiving her award of 100 acres.

All our land has been taken by the Government. Nothing has been given by the Government to the Natives who have remained loyal throughout. That is why I now come to lay our troubles before you. We have been waiting for many years, and we now come to try and get something done. In the year 1866 the Compensation Court sat at New Plymouth, and I attended it there. The Court then recognized our titles, and gave out a number of acres for us. We received the awards, but have never received the land. We thought that these lands were awarded to us on account of our loyalty. We did not sign the claims we sent in, with any idea that we were to give up altogether our rights and titles to the land.[65]

Maraca Pēkamu was about 18 years old and living in the South Island when the Compensation Court sat, and did not attend its hearings. She saw the commission as an opportunity to obtain a land grant.

358. Did you not go before the Compensation Court ?—*No; because I was not here. I was living at Port Underwood, in the other Island, and knew nothing about the matter.*

...

362. If you got a piece of land, would you go and live upon it ? —*I wish to go and remain upon it. If I did not, I would stock it. My age is thirty-two. I was quite young when the last sitting of the Compensation Court took place, and was living in the other Island. I knew nothing about the sitting of the Court, because there were no people in my neighbourhood.*[66]

Many of these women would continue to pursue their claims for compensation or the return of confiscated lands through other official channels, notably by petitioning Parliament (see chapter 5).

The 'European Compensation Court'

In the 1860s, two different Compensation Courts were operating in New Zealand. The court described above, relating to land, was sometimes termed the 'Native Compensation Court', although a few Pākehā also made claims to it. Individuals could also make claims for property destroyed, abandoned or commandeered during the period of military activities to what was sometimes described as the 'European Compensation Court', headed by Commissioner Thomas Beckham.[67] As Richard Boast points out, it was primarily Pākehā settlers who benefited from this form of compensation.[68] However, Māori also applied although, unlike the Pākehā, their loyalties might be called into question. In June 1865 Beckham reported that he had investigated 372 European claims totalling £136, 370/2/6, which he calculated down to £71,002/16/2. The Māori claims, which 'have been somewhat more difficult to determine', came to £7,454/10/6, which Beckham reduced to £2,432/19/6.[69] By the time he had finished Beckham had awarded £78,415/15/8 to claimants, although the claims were later reinvestigated and reduced further to £58,688/3/7.[70]

Māori women were among those who made claims for war damages, although in the case of Maraea Tukuiho, her husband was instructed to make the claim in his own name.[71] Claimants were expected to make a claim in writing; those from Māori were generally short and to the point. In 1865 Hera Pounara made a claim relating to fighting the previous year in Tauranga. It is not clear from the letter if she wrote it herself or dictated her words to another person.

> Tauranga Mei te 24 1865
> Koaku taonga e nei i nga ro i te whawhai ki Tauranga[.]
> e 1 hoiho tautahi £10 pauna[.] e 2 poaka e £6 pauna . . . 16 kete Riwai e £4. e45 Puhe witi £13.10 . . . e 20 Kete Kumara 5. 0. 0
> Na Hera Pounara
> Ngaituwhiwhio

> [official translation, somewhat at variance to the original]
> Tauranga May 24 1865
> These are my goods lost during the war at Tauranga[.]
> 1 one year old horse £10- 0
> 2 pigs   4 [£6]
> [16 kits potatoes   £4]

45 Bushels wheat   13– 10
20 kits Kumaras   10– 0
Hera Pounara
of the Ngaituwhiwhio[72]

The Pākehā newspapers sometimes discussed the worthiness of Māori claims to the 'European' Compensation Court. For example, the *Daily Southern Cross* suggested 'some rather strange claims' had been heard, 'but the native claimants certainly eclipse the Europeans in the nature and imperativeness of their demands'. One that 'illustrates the cool assurance of the writers' was a letter from Mere Awitu and three others.

Waipapa April 27, 1865.
Sir George Grey, Governor,
  Sir,--Salutations. Listen you. We wish the half of the value of our property to be paid to us now, on receipt of this letter, because we have heard that we shall not be paid now when peace is made: that is why we are uneasy about our property, because there will not be peace yet. Pay us now in the time that we and our children are in need. Let the half be paid now – 3 horses, 60 pigs, 3 patches potatoes, and 1 cow from Maramarua. From Hauraki there were 4 boxes of clothes, 1 box of books, and 4 pigs. The total value of the property is £160. Let us have £30 now, and let the balance, £130, be adjudicated upon. Another grievance is the time we have remained in Auckland. We have been here from the 8th March to the 27th April. These are the months we have waited in Auckland. From

        WIREMU KEPA,
        WIREMU KORONEHO
        MERE AWITU
        MAORA RANGITUMA[73]

The 'demanding' tone of what was undoubtedly a translation merely reflects the difference between the two languages, and the Māori habit of brevity. Mere and her friends no doubt considered they had a valid claim, and that receiving a small portion immediately would not have seemed unreasonable when they were in need. Besides, if they were required to stay in Auckland in order to make their claim, they would have been incurring further costs.

One of the first actions of the Waikato campaign was the capture or destruction of Māori canoes on the Manukau Harbour.[74] Ākinihi Taro of Māngere claimed £150 for canoes destroyed by Pākehā at Waiuku, as well as another £100 for the food consumed by the men who had built them.

> [Cross-examined] By Mr. Boardman: *I used to live at Mangere with Te Wherowhero, and afterwards with Tamati Ngapora. Tamati and others of my friends went to the war in Waikato. I saw last month one of the men who went in the canoes, and who assisted in the making. Some have been killed in battle the rest are with the King. The people did not tell me that they would go. They did not arrange to go. But the Governor told them to go to Waikato, and they went.*[75]

As with Rīria's evidence mentioned earlier, Ākinihi refers to the Governor's ultimatum to the Māori living south of Auckland, which she interpreted as an order to leave their lands. Some of the men died in the fighting; others were 'with the King'.

Turuhia Nahunia claimed £15 for a gun stolen by a Māori man for the defence of Rangiriri. She claimed that she used the gun to shoot pigeons, which prompted Beckham to enquire if she also had been involved.

> The Commissioner: Was it to shoot pakeha pigeons?— Witness: *No, the women did not shoot; I was always loyal.* — Commissioner: Did the women not load the guns while the men shot? — Witness: *Yes, but I did not load any.*[76]

In a number of cases, Māori women made claims for farm animals and other goods that they had lost due to the men going off to join the Kīngitanga forces.

> **CLAIM OF MATIRE TOHA.**
> *Matire Toha deposed: I reside at Mangarei and sometimes at Awitu. I was residing at the former place in 1867, when the losses occurred. I resided at Mangarei during the war, and up to the present time. The goods for which I ask compensation were at Awitu in the charge of Hone Kingi, Te Kapene, and Mokina. They left when the Governor expelled the people from the Manukau district. I left 200 kits of kumeras, £100; 50 bags of maize, £50; 4 kits of taros, £20. I had four houses, one my daughter's, two my servant's and one my own whare. Their value was about £20. About a month after Mr. Puckey and I went there and the food was all gone.*[77]

The men responsible for her property had been killed fighting on the Kīngitanga side, but their departure had resulted in her losses. Her husband, who had died in the 1840s, had owned the land on which she had resided, but which had now been confiscated.

At the same hearing, Tīmata Tītoko also made a claim. She was married to a European, but her brothers had joined the Kīngitanga, which had resulted in her losses. She is most likely the same Tīmata who unsuccessfully objected to her (confiscated) land being sold at auction in 1864.

> *Timata Titoko, sworn, said: I live at Mangarei, and was at Auckland during the war. My horses and cattle were at Rangiriri, in charge of two people, one of whom is dead, the other, Kihi, is now in town. There were two mares and an entire horse, worth altogether £130. A carpenter's chest of tools was worth £100, and was at Kaitotehe, near Taupiri, at the house of my relative's. There was also three cows and a bull sent to Rangiriri in Governor Browne's days.*[78]

But as Tīmata 'could not give the slightest evidence as to the value of the horses or cattle', we can presume her case did not meet with success.[79] Te Wama Amohanga, married to William Astle, claimed over £200 for the loss of various farm animals and items. One of her cows was 30 years old.

> The Commissioner: Was that the grandmother of all the cows in New Zealand. Did it give any milk?
> *Witness: Yes a good deal. It is now lost. The soldiers ate it.*
> The Commissioner: They would find it tough.
> *Witness: I had 50 pigs, very large; some were 20 years old. The pots I had ten years ago, when I was married. The sheep were very old. I got 60 bags or 6 large bales of wool from 20 sheep.*[80]

She had left the area before the war started, but as the *Herald* noted, 'the property was lost because [her] relatives and others joined the rebels because they were kingites'.

The newspaper also discussed a possible impropriety concerning a resident magistrate and claimants. In 1865, when Beckham was hearing the Waikato claims, there were rumours that R. O. Stewart, the Resident Magistrate at Port Waikato, who was married to a Māori woman, Marian McKay, had perhaps been assisting her Māori relatives in making their claims. Beckham had questioned claimants about their relationships, which led the *Herald* to report, 'from the examination on Saturday it is evident that questionable friendly natives will not pass so easily through Mr Beckham's hands as they apparently do through those of the Chief Justice in the Confiscation Compensation Court, sitting in an adjoining building.'[81] The accusations concerning Stewart lead Marian to write to the *Daily Southern Cross* to deny any involvement.

> *I see by the papers that in Mr. Beckham's Compensation Court, natives have been making use of my name. Some say in their evidence that they are related to me and the* New Zealand Herald *remarks on the 15th, that 'Mr. Stewart (my husband), in marrying a native woman, seems to have married a whole host of her relations.' Now, as I am not a public personage, I do not like my name to be brought up in a court or in the public papers unless I had to do with the case in hand. One of the claimants who has been at the court returned here yesterday, and tells me that Mr. Beckham asked these ridiculous questions about me. None of the natives of Waikato are related to me except Walter Kukutai, as he is partially descended from a tribe at Whakatane, to which my mother belongs. Only two of the claimants are connected with me by their marriage; – William Marshall, who is married to my sister; and Wilson Te Rotoroto, whose wife is a distant cousin of mine. I have asked William about what went on in the Court, and he says that Tamihana Tunui never said anything about me whatever. Whatever those natives have said, I don't blame them so much as the magistrate for putting such questions.*[82]

We can imagine that her husband might have helped her in 1878 when Marian, described as 'a half-caste woman of the Ngatipukeko tribe', petitioned Parliament in her own right for confiscated land in Whakatāne.[83]

Conclusion

Just as women were affected by the period of fighting during the New Zealand wars, they were also impacted by the aftermath of confiscation and compensation. On the one hand Māori could claim for war damages along with Pākehā, but it appears that they got little from the process. The confiscation of land, by far, was of much greater significance. Although the New Zealand Settlements Act 1863 and associated legislation that enabled confiscations were technically legal, the way that the government proceeded with the confiscation and compensation was not.[84] In its apology to Waikato-Tainui in 1995 the government admitted that its actions had been 'wrongful', causing ongoing pain and distress.[85] Quite apart from the fact that many Māori became rebels because government forces attacked them, hapū that did not take up arms against the Crown also had land taken. The compensation was often unjust and inconsistent: some people missed out; awards were unfair or insufficient; and the whole process was handled quite differently from one region to another. Women, along with men, were required to submit themselves to a judicial process over which they had little control in order to salvage what they could of their legal land rights. Having eliminated native title and its complications, the government immediately commenced buying up land recently returned to claimants. It is small wonder that raupatu continue to rankle with iwi who lost their lands as a result of war.

CHAPTER 4

'Look at me, I am just a woman speaking': Politics and Mana

According to Te Rangihīroa '[a] *rangatira* was such by reason of birth', and the senior position in a tribe, that of ariki, 'was reserved for the first-born son of the senior family of the tribe'. Whakapapa is thus an essential foundation for mana, the basis of leadership, although achievements could also enhance one's position. A woman, he suggests, 'could not succeed to the active leadership of the tribe' but 'was treated with the greatest respect as a female ariki'.[1] But as Api Mahuika has pointed out, women of his tribe, Ngāti Porou, did take leadership roles both on account of their whakapapa and their accomplishments.[2] The numerous entries on Māori women in the *Dictionary of New Zealand Biography* and *The Book of New Zealand Women*, as well as the work of Patricia Grimshaw, Sandra Coney, Charlotte Macdonald, Tania Rei, Angela Ballara, Miranda Johnson and Barbara Brookes all provide overwhelming evidence of women's political leadership during the nineteenth century.[3] Gender roles in Māori society were often complementary, and tapu precluded some occupations for women. For example, even today when tangata whenua welcome manuhiri onto a marae, the role of leading women is to karanga and for men to whaikōrero. In most iwi (Ngāti Porou and Ngāti Kahungunu are exceptions) women do not whaikōrero; most tribes would argue against putting those who give birth to future generations at risk by exposing them to the metaphysical verbal warfare of the marae.[4] To a certain extent the culture of orality transferred into written political discourse: the overwhelming majority of Māori writing on official tribal business, either to newspapers or to government officials, was by men.[5]

Pākehā culture recognises and values public speaking, so it can recognise whaikōrero, whereas karanga has no real equivalent in Western culture. It was therefore not difficult for Pākehā male powerbrokers, such as missionaries and colonial government officials, to comprehend Māori public political leadership and discourse as men's work; it was what they were able to see in the Māori world. It was also natural in their own world-view, in which 'married middle-class women [were] confined to the domestic sphere while men became associated with the public sphere'.[6] Māori interaction with the colonial world thus privileged the status of men. Leadership and spiritual roles in the missionary churches were also reserved for men. When the government invited rangatira to Kohimārama in 1860 for a month-long conference to discuss political issues, although women may have been present, none are recorded as having stood and spoken for their iwi. When the New Zealand Parliament created four seats for Māori in 1867, no woman in New Zealand had the vote.[7] The patriarchal power systems inherent within colonialism were thus overlaid on Māori society, and would have accentuated or distorted gender differences already present. Notwithstanding these forces, some Māori women, particularly those with illustrious whakapapa, wielded considerable power during the nineteenth century. As the following discussion demonstrates, some Māori women operated as individuals on an equal footing with men, while in other cases they operated through women's rūnanga or komiti to pursue political goals.

Te Paea Tīaho and the Kīngitanga

Te Paea, also known as Tīaho, was the daughter of the Tainui ariki, Pōtatau Te Wherowhero. As a teenager during the musket wars, she was part of a female peace mission to Ngāti Kahungunu.[8] She later married the Ngāti Tamaoho chief, Ēpiha Pūtini Te Rangiātaahua and lived near the new settlement of Auckland. In 1858 central North Island tribes selected Pōtatau to be the Māori King. When he died two years later, Te Paea moved to Ngāruawāhia, the Kīngitanga capital.[9] According to John Gorst, who was planted as a government magistrate within the Māori kingdom in 1862, some Kīngitanga supporters sought to have Te Paea installed as monarch, but it fell to her brother Matutaera (later known as Tāwhiao) to take the role of second Māori king.[10]

There was considerable Māori sympathy for the Kīngitanga, but formal support was more varied, both between and within tribes. For example, most of Waikato supported the King, who was also their tribal leader, but chiefs near the river mouth remained loyal to Queen Victoria and the government. In the Tauranga area, Ngāi Te Rangi supported the King, but neighbouring Te Arawa were mostly for the Queen. In the Kapiti region, opinion was more divided, and chiefs actively campaigned for both the Kuīnitanga and the Kīngitanga.[11] In 1861, Topeora, a leading female Ngāti Toa chief, wrote to Donald McLean to declare her antipathy to the new movement, which she saw as disruptive of the status quo.

> ... *tenei au te noho atu nei i konei kei te pokea au e nei iwi taurekareka poka noa ki te hanga kingi mona kaore au e pai kia haere mai enei iwi taurekareka ki konei whakararuraru ai i toku kainga he kainga kuini oranga noku tenei kainga ...*
>
> [modern translation]
> Here am I living here, beset by these slave tribes, with no authority to set up a king for themselves. I do not like these slave tribes coming here and upsetting me in my area. This place is loyal to the Queen and belongs to me.[12]

Even within the Kīngitanga there were divisions. Gorst, although his government position at Te Awamutu formed part of Grey's wider strategy of undermining the movement, had some sympathy for the Kīngitanga. However, in his 1864 book, *The Maori King*, he suggested that two principal factions existed: a group of moderates led by Wiremu Tāmihana (which included Tāwhiao and Te Paea), and a militant section under Rewi Maniapoto of Ngāti Maniapoto. The former sought to maintain peace with the government, the latter he considered 'the most violent of the king's partizans'.[13]

It is clear that Te Paea had considerable mana on account of her whakapapa, which she used in order to keep the peace. For example, when Ngāti Maniapoto seized timber that Gorst's men had cut to expand the government school at Te Awamutu, Te Paea requested that the timber be given to her. Rewi could not 'refuse her so trifling a request'. By putting the timber under her mana, Rewi was now powerless to touch it.

> 'Now,' she said, 'I shall give the timber to Mr. Gorst.' She wrote and sent a messenger to beg that I would fetch my timber which she was holding for me. 'One thing,' said this lady in her postscript, 'I have forgotten; please give me a little tobacco.'[14]

1863 was a turning point in New Zealand's history. The first Taranaki war had ended, but remained unresolved, with government forces occupying the disputed land at Waitara. As a counter, Māori held a block of land at Tātaraimaka previously acquired by the government and sold to Pākehā. A number of events kept tensions high. Gorst's presence at Te Awamutu, effectively a government challenge to the King's mana, made the Kīngitanga unhappy, but they became particularly angry when he established a niupepa, *Te Pihoihoi Mokemoke*, which mocked the King and the movement.[15] In addition, Governor Grey pursued a dual policy to defeat the Kīngitanga. He first employed a peace strategy of establishing self-governing rūnanga for iwi in an effort to draw them away from the Kīngitanga. At the same time he prepared for war, placing a fortified redoubt at Te Ia on the Waikato border, constructing a military road towards the kingdom, building up his armed forces, and acquiring armoured gunboats that could penetrate the Waikato River. Tensions escalated when a Kīngitanga taua not only removed a party of builders who were constructing a government blockhouse within the Kingdom's boundary, but also expelled Gorst and his printing press. The spark for the renewal of war, however, occurred in Taranaki. Grey sent in troops to re-occupy Tātaraimaka, but, despite hinting that he would return Waitara to Te Āti Awa, he continued to hold that disputed land. When Taranaki Māori retaliated by attacking a small group of soldiers, Grey had his take to pursue war, but did not direct the army to Taranaki to deal with the situation there. In the first Taranaki war (1860–61), Kīngitanga warriors had gone south to fight the army while their own lands remained peaceful, something Grey wanted to avoid, so in July 1863 the army launched its attack on Waikato in an attempt to crush the Kīngitanga once and for all.

Considerable communication occurred in the months leading up to the war, some of which involved Te Paea. Many texts are just fragments of the conversations. In early February 1863, Te Paea (more generally known to Pākehā as 'Princess Sophia') led a delegation to Auckland to talk with Governor Grey. The *Daily Southern Cross* report of this meeting implies that the three-and-a-half hour meeting was social, and the paper was more concerned with Te Paea's apparel than her conversation.[16] It is the Kīngitanga's own newspaper that reports the real reason, the possibility of Wiremu Nēra Te Awaitaia, a pro-government Waikato chief, selling land. The Kīngitanga would have felt compelled to react, and Te Paea counselled against Grey accepting any offer.

Ka ki mai kawana, e Pae kua tae mai a wiremu Te awaitaia, ki a Akarana nei ki te kore ro i te taha o waipa, e hokona ana e wiremu ki au, ano ra ko te Paea, kei whakaae koe ki tena korero, kaua e ho atu he moni; e kore te whenua e ho atu e te iwi, he papatupu tena pihi, kei waitetuna te rohe, kia koe ki au, ano ra ko kawana, e tika ana ka ore au e pai, e ngari ma nga runanga katoa te ritenga, ka whakaae au ki te hoko whenua, ka huri[.]

[modern translation]
The Governor said, 'Pae, Wiremu Te Awaitaia has come to Auckland to speak about selling one side of Waipā to me.' Te Paea said, 'Do not agree to that suggestion, do not give any money: the tribe will not give [you] the land. That is tribal land, the boundary is at Waitetuna, between you and me.' The Governor replied, 'You are right. I will not agree, but will leave it for all the Rūnanga to determine, and then I will buy the land.' That is all.[17]

When Ngāti Maniapoto seized Gorst's press, the two wings of the Kīngitanga were at odds over the implications of this action. Gorst's reports to Grey, and his subsequent book, show that Te Paea was prominent in the intra-movement debates, although unfortunately her voice is largely in the third person.

> A great discussion has been going on at Kihikihi between Rewi and his followers, together with Reihana on the one side, and Te Paea, Potatau [Tāwhiao], and Patara, of Ngaruawahia, on the other. Rewi's side are urgent for an immediate descent on the Ia (with the view, as I am told, not of attacking the troops, but of making a raid on the settlers), while Te Paea and Patara strenuously oppose the plan.[18]

Gorst also states that Te Paea put all the blame on Rewi and Ngāti Maniapoto, and at a meeting at Ngāruawāhia, 'she rushed, tears running down her cheeks, into the adjoining house, and addressed the meeting in a very loud voice, abusing their acts and designs for about an hour.'[19] The moderate voice prevailed; it was the British Army that attacked first, not the Kīngitanga.

Te Paea and the moderate faction may have desired peace, but this did not mean submitting to the government. In May 1863 James Fulloon, a Native Office official, mentioned to her that Nini Kūkūtai, another pro-government chief, was planning to move to Te Ia, which would effectively place the settlement under his mana and protection.

> She said quite indignantly 'What is he going there for? Does he think that, he will keep Waikato back, if they had an intention of attacking Te Ia? No, he wants to provoke them, for they have been wrangling some time past, and would be only

too glad to bring on a collision – especially after what they had lately done that of stealing (*keia*) Wetere's canoe.'[20]

Te Paea was undoubtedly disappointed when General Cameron crossed the Mangatāwhiri Stream to begin the Waikato war. She wrote a letter to Wiremu Nēra Te Awaitaia, her kinsman on the government side, which was read out to a meeting of settlers at Raglan.

No Ngaruawahia,
Hurae 14, 1863.
KIA WIREMU NERO,— E koro tenakoe tena koatou [sic] ko tamariki ko te iwi hoki tenakoe ekoro kia rongo nui koe kua tutu kiki tau aki ai koe mana ki mua rere ko Te Ia kua whiti kia e te pakeha 3,000 hoia nana i whaka whiti kua tu ngapariki kei te Koheroa tae noa mai ki te ko ngutu awao whanga marino e rua nga paraki kei te ko ngutu awao whanga Marino no te rua o nga wiki ka whiti ngia a Manga Fawhni [-tawhiri] no te po ao noaki i te mane kua tu hepa ahiahi noake kua kapi katoa i te pa e whaka tae ana kia whiti i tetehi o aua awa heoi kahiri [ka huri] tena ko Tamati Ngapora, ko Ihaka, ko Mohi ku[a] oti era te rauna he punui kei te tia ki a ratou heoi kahuri e koro te [na] koe e hoa ma tena korua aku tupuna tena koutou ko tenei e koro kua marama, kua marama, te whaka aroa o iwi mokai kua rite ki tau e koro tena koe heri [sic] na.
TEPAEA TIAHO.
Ki te Kumatua [sic], Kia a Wiremu Nero.

[newspaper translation]
Ngaruawahia, July 14. To William Nero O father! greetings to yourself, your people, and your children Listen to me. Your advice has been adhered to (when you told us not to be the first, but to let the Governor commence to cross our lines). Three thousand soldiers have crossed the Mangatawhiri, and have put up barracks at Koheroa, reaching to the mouth of the Whanga-Marino. There are two barracks at the latter place. At the conclusion of two weeks, they crossed the Mangatawhiri, and at night they built a fort which they had finished by Monday morning. Monday evening they had the ground all covered with tents. They are trying to cross one of those creeks (Maramarua). Tamati Ngapora, Ihaka, and Mohi have given in their allegiance. That hundred (Maoris) have a large gun with them, at Mangatawhiri, to take care of them. O father! salutations to my ancestors, and to you all. Now, O father, this is clear, quite clear to the understandings of all your tribes which are

under you (*mokai*), and it has come to what you have said. Farewell.
(Signed)
Sophia Tiaho.
To my Father
To William Nero.[21]

The war unified the Kīngitanga, at least initially. The newspaper declared that Te Paea was 'stating the faith of Ngaruawhahia [sic], so plainly, i.e., that the Governor invaded their territories when the troops crossed the Mangatawhiri', at odds with the government position that it 'asserted the right of the Governor to govern the colony'.

Within a year the government occupied and confiscated most of the Waikato lands, and the Māori king and his people lived in exile with Ngāti Maniapoto in what became known as the King Country. Rather than continue the war, the government left the Kīngitanga in isolation but with independence, making occasional attempts to negotiate a peace.

Te Paea retained her influence. In 1867 Grey wrote to Tāwhiao, Te Paea and others in order to arrange a meeting. According to a Māori letter to the *Daily Southern Cross*, 'Te Paea [the Princess Sophia] said to the Maori King, "Do you reply to Governor Grey's letter in writing" and Matutaera, the Maori King, said, "I will not write a letter to that man. Was it not he who drove me into the wild woods to roam about?"' However he agreed that Te Paea should meet Grey at Taupō, where she argued for the return of the confiscated land.[22] By 1869 it was Rewi Maniapoto who was more inclined to make peace with the government. Te Paea's importance can be seen when Rewi and others attempted to organise a meeting with the Governor; it was first delayed until Te Paea arrived, and then abandoned when she declined to participate.[23]

Te Paea Tīaho and the Ōhinemuri goldfields

Te Paea was also influential outside of the lands still held by the Kīngitanga. Tensions were rising in the Ōhinemuri (Thames-Waihī) district due to Pākehā pressure on Māori to 'open' the area to gold mining. Before the war, this district had been part of the greater Kīngitanga domain. It was now nominally under government authority, although many Māori there remained resistant to Pākehā encroachment.

One of the most defiant about the gold mining was Mere Kuru, a chiefly woman of Ngāti Tamaterā. The government officials had been ineffective in their negotiations over the goldfields, so in 1868, a delegation of miners, unhappy with the government's progress, travelled to an (unnamed) village under the chief, Rāpata, to try their hand themselves. After some talk, they provided some ale, brandy and rum.

> When the stuff had all been consumed, which, as both parties participated, was very soon, an old woman, named Mere Kuru, who was said to be a sister of Te Hira's, came over the river, and said to Rapata: You are doing wrong by allowing these white men to come here. Why is the flood tide come up to this place? Are we to be swamped by these pakehas?
>
> Rapata, addressing Mere Kuru, said: You are right.
>
> Old Woman, addressing the Deputation: What is the reason that you have come up here?
>
> Deputation: The reason we have come is, because this is a council of pakehas which has been appointed to seek to obtain the gold of Ohinemuri.
>
> Old Woman: Off you must go, back to Hauraki, and there, let me advise you, set to work. Leave this place for us, where we can dwell in peace. Go back to where you came from, to Hauraki, and see that you stay there. Be you willing to go, and we will be willing to stay in our own place. You have from Hikutaia right out to the ocean, and that is surely big enough for you.[24]

At another meeting to discuss the issue that year she simply declared:

> The gold will not be given up; there is death in giving it up.[25]

When John Williamson, Superintendent of the Auckland Province, visited the following year, the male chiefs gave speeches, but Mere's protest was more dramatic, as the *Herald* reported:

> At this stage of the proceedings, the Hauhau party, headed by Mere Kuru and Maata – two of the principal chieftainesses of the district – stood up and gave us a truly

savage style of Maori war dance. The above named ladies dancing in front of the rest of the party, and making the most horrible grimaces imaginable. The whole performance concluding with the chant,

> When the land is gone, whither shall the people go?
> Hold it! Hold it!

They then lifted their Hauhau flag and left abruptly.[26]

Mere Kuru also led a group of 'Amazons' who chased off a party of surveyors in the district in 1870.[27]

In 1869, Mere's brother, Te Hira Wharewhenua, 'handed over' the Ōhinemuri lands to Te Paea, in effect placing them under her protection, although she appeared rather noncommittal about taking on the responsibility.[28] The following year, Wiremu Te Wheoro, a Waikato chief who acted as an intermediary between the Kīngitanga and the government, met Te Paea while travelling to the King Country.

> In the evening I addressed Tiaho thus, 'I learn that the matter of Ohinemuri is in your hands.' She answered 'Yes.' I then said, 'If that be the case, then withdraw your objection; let Ohinemuri be opened, lest it become a source of trouble and annoyance to us all; and for this reason, that the majority of the people are for opening up Ohinemuri, while Te Hira stands alone in holding it back, and his strength lies in your supporting him.'
> She replied– 'What you say is right. I agree to it. I myself will send a message to Te Hira and Mere Kuru. Manuwhiri and myself have already written to Te Hira to say that if he were willing to open up Ohinemuri, he should do so without reference to us. But Te Hira is not willing to let it go – even on those terms.'[29]

Although Ōhinemuri was nominally under Te Paea's mana, she was still leaving the final decision to the local chief. The goldfield was finally opened in 1875, the same year that Te Paea died.

A foreshore dispute

Pākehā settlement in the Thames area was not just about gold. In 1869, a rūnanga of Ngāti Maru women wrote to Governor Bowen.

Waiotahe, Akuhata 5, 1869.

E hoa e te Kawana, --Tangata pai, tangata kino ranei tenakoe. Ka hua mau e atawhai nga tangata, o Hauraki, ara ko ou atawhai tenei. Ko a matou pihi whenua ma matou ano te tikanga mo a matou pihi. Kaua e apohia noatia ekoe a uta te moana. Kaua he ritenga motu a matou moana. Koe e tahae, kaua to matou whenua e tahae tia e koutou e nga pakeha. Engari whaka honeretia au tamariki, no te mea i ki koe kia kotahi tonu a taaua ritenga, ae ana au to tamaiti, i runga i ou whakaaro maha, neke kotore ana koe to matua, Tena te ngohi kiete [sic] moana he koura, te putanga mai ite rua neke kotore ana. He patai tenei, na tou Kuini ranei te ritenga, nau ano ranei, Ka ahua ko te tangata anake tau e patu ai patu rua ana koe ko te tangata ko te whenua. Aue! taku whenua e! koti koti ora te kainga, kaore e ngaro te moke tangata. Aue te rorohi e! Heoiano.-- Na te runanga wahine o Hauraki. – Na MARAEA PUREWA, na MIRIAMA KONEHU, na MATA PARAONE, na TURUHIRA RAPANA, na HERA APERAHAMA, na MATA TE KURA, na HERA PAREMATAITI, na Matou katoa

[newspaper translation.]
Waiotahe, August 5, 1869.
Friend the Governor, good man or bad man, greeting. It was supposed that you would be kindly towards the people of Hauraki (Thames), that is to say, your kindness to consist in this to leave with ourselves the arrangements about our own pieces of land that you should not grasp without cause both the land and the sea. Let there be no interference on your part with our lands on the sea (beach). 'Thou shalt not steal.' Do not you Europeans steal our land, but honour your children, because you said that our interests should be one. I, the child, consented to this but you, with your many thoughts, you the father, are moving backward [i.e., breaking your pledges]. There is a fish in the sea, the lobster: when it comes out of its cave it crawls backwards. This is a question. Is it your Queen, or does this purpose emanate from you [i.e., taking possession of the beaches on the sea shore at the Thames]? It was imagined that you would kill men only, but you are killing both the men and the land. Alas, my lands are divided, whilst I still live, and the solitary ones of the land have not been destroyed! Alas, the affliction! Sufficient. From the council of women at Hauraki (Thames).--(Signed) MARAEA PUREWA, MIRIAMA KONEHU, MATA PARAONE, HERA APERAHAMA, MATA TE KURA, HERA PAREMATAITI, and the whole of us.[30]

The *Daily Southern Cross*, which printed the letter, states that it had 'been forwarded to Wellington', which suggests that Ngāti Maru sent a copy of the letter to the newspaper. It appears also that the women were acting in concert with the men. On the same day the women sent their letter, the 'runanga of Ngati Maru', eight male signatories, also wrote to government to assert that they had never given up the beach, which remained a food-gathering place for them, and asking on what basis it was being taken.[31] We cannot be sure if the women met regularly as a separate rūnanga, but on this occasion Ngāti Maru considered a dual approach worth trying.

While the women's letter relates to land, it also questions the Governor's role in New Zealand politics. Since the sitting of the first New Zealand Parliament in 1854, there had been tension over where executive power lay – with the elected settler politicians, or with the Governor. Although Māori men had just gained the vote when this issue arose, most Māori still looked upon Queen Victoria (and the Governor as her appointed representative) as the site of Pākehā mana, rather than the settler Parliament. The government's discourses played upon this belief, accentuating the Queen's love for Māori, and portraying the governor as a father figure.[32] It is for this reason that the women posit themselves, somewhat ironically, as 'the child' and critique 'the father', who is walking backwards like a lobster. The women want to know whether he is responsible for the taking of the foreshore at Hauraki, and whether the Queen has sanctioned this action.

Takiora's letters

As stated, unresolved issues from the first Taranaki war (1860–61) precipitated the invasion of Waikato in 1863. Once the British Army had driven the Kīngitanga south into the King Country, and occupied the Waikato lands, it turned its attention back to Taranaki. In the meantime a new form of resistance, Pai Mārire (Hauhau), had emerged in the region, in which opposition to colonialism was integrated with a new form of religious belief. The second Taranaki war continued until late 1866, during which time the struggle became more bitter and brutal, with New Zealand-raised forces – Volunteers, Militia, and Māori kūpapa – taking over the fighting from the British Army. The Crown confiscated most of the land in Taranaki, but was not initially in a position to occupy it all. Its practice was to push Māori out from one location, consolidate their hold, then do the same again in another place, in what has been termed a 'creeping confiscation' policy.[33]

War again broke out in June 1868, when the Ngāti Ruanui chief, Riwha Tītokowaru, initiated a successful campaign in South Taranaki. When Tītokowaru's forces abandoned fighting in 1869, the third Taranaki war effectively came to an end.[34] The response in Taranaki to land confiscation transformed in the 1870s into more pacifist forms of confrontation, in particular the ploughing and fencing of lands occupied by settlers. Two Parihaka prophets, Te Whiti-o-Rongomai and Tohu Kākahi, led the non-violent resistance, and Tītokowaru also eventually allied himself to the Parihaka cause, becoming a key organiser of the protests.

Takiora, also known as Lucy Lord or Lucy Grey,[35] with her husband Te Mahuki, assisted the government forces as a guide and interpreter during the second Taranaki war. Te Mahuki was killed in 1866, but Takiora continued to guide colonial forces and provide information during the third Taranaki war, against the interests of her own tribe of Ngāti Ruanui.[36] She may also have been the mistress of Major Gustavus von Tempsky, who was killed during an ill-fated attack on Tītokowaru's pā, Te Ngutu-o-te-manu, on 7 September 1868,[37] and she was involved in the last action of the war, when kūpapa forces shot two old men at Ngāpahi on 27 October, 1869.[38]

Takiora inhabited both the Māori and the Pākehā worlds, but may not have felt fully accepted in either. Her mother, a Ngāti Ruanui woman, was taken as a slave by Ngāpuhi to Northland during the musket wars. Takiora was born there to a European father in the early 1840s, and although she had returned south by the early 1860s, may have felt like an outsider. This may explain why she aligned herself to the Pākehā side during the wars. In 1870, the situation was very tense. The colonial forces were still pursuing Te Kooti in other parts of the country, and although fighting had stopped in Taranaki, it was an uneasy peace, with Tītokowaru's intentions unknown. The Native Minister was desperate for information on what Taranaki Māori were up to, which Takiora was happy to provide.[39]

In 1870, Te Whiti convened two large hui at Parihaka attended by Robert Parris, Taranaki's Civil Commissioner. For the second meeting, Parris thought that 'a good muster of natives who acknowledge allegiance to the Government, would be likely to have a wholesome effect, and I accordingly induced a large number of friendlies to attend the meeting'.[40] In all, 700 Māori accompanied the commissioner, including Takiora. Parris also knew that Tītokowaru was going to attend, which he thought put him in 'an unpleasant position ... as I cannot avoid meeting him'.[41] Tītokowaru had still not come to terms with the Government after his military campaign, but the Government was not prepared to risk more conflict. As the Governor wrote to London, Tītokowaru's 'fastness [is] in the almost impenetrable forests about forty miles west of New Plymouth, where he will be left unmolested so long as he remains quiet'.[42] Neither, at this stage, had Tītokowaru fully accepted Te Whiti's message of peace. Takiora wrote a full account of the meeting for the Native Minister, Donald McLean.

Waihi
26th September 1870
Kia Te Makirini

Korero tenei naku mo taku taenga ki te Runanga ki Parihaka ko te tikanga ou [sic] taua runanga, kahore a Parete i mohio. Ki te mohio a Parete, ko te Kuini raua ko te Kingi kia hinga. Ko te Whiti raua ko Titoko hei Kingi mo nga Pakeha mo nga Maori e tika ana tona mohio. Ko te tino tikanga o taua runanga Ko te Kuini mo nga Pakeha, o Hawera, o Manawapou, mo etahi Pakeha atu e noho ana i runga i nga whenua o nga Maori, me hoki nga Pakeha ki tona whenua.

Ko te tikanga mo te Kingi, mo nga Kingi Maori o te motu nei, me hoki ki tona whenua, ki tona whenua, ki te noho tonu te Pakeha, ka noho tonu te kino.

No te 18. [sic] i timata te Runanga, no te 22, i tae mai a Titoko, me tona ope, e ono tekau ki Parihaka. Ko te ra i tae mai ai ia, ka timata te korero mo te Rori. Ka whawhai ki Ngatiruanui raua ko te Ngatiawa ka ki nga ratou, i tukua kia puta otira na Tito te auataua i whakaae kia hanga.

Kihai i pai a Titoko i taua ra ki te whakarongo i nga korero a Parete, he rangi raruraru na te Kawanatanga raua ko te Hauhau[.]

No te mutunga o nga korero ka haire [sic] matou ki te tangi, no te mutunga ka kite a Titoko i au, ka karanga ki au, 'Haere mai te Tienera o nga Pakeha.' Ka kite au i reira, taku tungane, ko Wairau, Ka ki mai kia au (i korero puku ki au) 'Kia tupato koe ko ta matou haere mai, ehara i haere mai mo te Runanga, i haere mai matou ki te titiro i te ahuatanga o te whenua i te peheatanga ranei.['] Kaore a Titoko e whakaatu i tona whakaaro i naianei. Ko tona ritenga ma te Pakeha, ki mua. Tirohia mai, e koe, kei te haire atu a Titoko me tona ope ki Whanganui, ko tona titiro kia kite ia i te panga o te ringaringa Pakeha ki aiia, ki te kahore, ka mohio ia kua pai.

Kaua e whakarongo ki tenei korero, e korero whakawai[.]

Ki tenei marama, ki tera ranei ka tae atu ki Whanganui, E rua nga ara ko te haere ai ia na roto i te motu, ko te hokinga mai, ko na waho mai. Ki te raru raru maku e tuhituhi atu e pukapuka ki akoe ki te kore koe, kia tuhituhi au kia Pereki, Kati, me haire koe, kei raruraru koe. Kei Omoturangi [Omuturangi] a Titoko e noho ana i naianei kahore e hoki wawe ki Waitara. Kei te kohikohi ai ia i nga tangata i naianei i roto i te kupapa, kia huihui katoa ona tangata ki raro i aua parirau.

I kite au i nga tangata katoa o te ope a Titoko, engari ko Titoko me Wairau enako[anake] i hariru ki au i haere mai ki te whakaputa i ta raua pouri ki au, ki te korero te kino o te iwi ki ahau. Kahore i haere mai taku iwi ki te hariru ki au. Mehemea kahore ratou i kite Pakeha ko te mate au, i a ratou, hei utu mo te Ngutu o te Manu, mo te Ngaene[.] ko Tito te Auataua raua ko te Ngohi aku matua tiaki i ahau. nga raua i ora ahau, E kore au e kite ia Titoko, na te Ngohi ahau i pupuri atu kia kite ahau i aku matua, ia Titoko ma.

No te taenga mai o Titoko, ka marama ahau, ka mutu taku pouri, ka korero mai ratou, i, ia ratou pouri mo taku kino kia ratou.

Ka korero a Titoko ki ahau, ka ako mai ki au. Kati taku korerorero ki te Kawanatanga. Tona kupu kua rongo ia kia Whanganui, ko au te kai mahi o nga Pakeha otira te taha Kawanatanga. Ko au te kai whakaatu o nga ritenga Hauhau. Ko tona kupu me tango ahau ki Waitara, kei noho ahau i konei, kei korero i ia ratou mahi, i ia ratou whakaaro, ki te Kawanatanga. Na te whanau mai koe i roto i taku tuahine i ora ai koe penei, kua mate koe i au i naianei. mehemea he tangata ke ahau, kahore ia e titiro ki au, engari ma te mata o tona pu ahau e titiro.

Tona ki mai ki ahau. 'Kia tupato! Tupato! Tupato!'

Na te Rahoroi (24) i mutu ai te runanga, ka hoki mai matou te taha Kawanatanga, me Titoko hoki waiho atu e matou ki Maungakirikiri moe ai, haire tonu mai matou ki Oeo. No te Ratapu ka tae mai ratou ki Opunake, e noho atu ana ahau[.] kia kite atu ahau ia ratou ka hoki mai ahau. Ka ki mai a Hone Pihama ki au, me hoki mai au ki Waihi, kei tangohia ahau ki Waitara. No te Mane ahau ka tae mai ki Waihi, no te Turei a Titoko ki Oeo. Ma te Wenerei ki Omoturangi ma te Taite ki te Ngutu o te Manu ki te kohikohi i ana taonga.

Kua riro mai i ai ia ona tangata i Parihaka, nuku te apiapi ki Oeo, me Kaupokonui.

Ko hui ia te kupu a Titoko ki roto ki ta Te Whiti, kua kotahi te korero, Kaore i te mohiotia ta Titoko kupu, i tika ranei, kahore ranei ko te tono tikanga o taua runanga he whakatu ia te Whiti hei Kingi mo te Maungarongo. Ko tenei korero ko te mau tonu. Tana kupu, kua mutu tana hoari, ko tana hoari, kei tona maunga ko te mau tonu tana korero engari ma Parete e hoatu ki akoe te nuinga o ana korero.

I ki te Whiti kia Titoko kia, whakatakoto tona pu ki raro, Ka ki a Titoko, Kahore! Me haire au, me taku rakau, kaore e takoto taku rakau ki te whenua, ka mau tonu ki taku ringa.

He kupu ano tenei. i taku taenga mai ki Oeo ka rongo ahau kia te Horo nga Huinga, no Titoko tenei tangata[.]

Mehemea i kitea te tangata a Parete i tuku mai ai ki Patea ki te kawe pukapuka mai, kua hopukia, kua tangohia te mera, kua tukua mai ko te tangata enake. Oti tenei mo nga hoiho, taku rongo ki ta ratou kupu, ko nga hoiho o nga Pakeha i mawhitiwhiti e haere ana, ko te tangohia e ratou he utu mo o ratou hoiho i riro i roto i te whawai. kua timata te mahi tahae hoiho a nga Hauhau o konei. Hoieano[.]

E te Makarini kia matau koe ki tenei pukapuka, he mea korero huna ki ahau, Kia mohio koe, kei rongona, kei mate au.

Kotahi te Runanga kei muri na te Whiti aua[?], kei Parihaka mo te kawana kia haere mai ki Parihaka, Ka mutu tera runanga ka haere Te Whiti ki Ingarangi.

Hoieano

Ka mutu

Lucy Grey

Ma te rongo korero hou ka tuhi tuhi ano ahau

[modern translation]

Waihi,

26th September 1870.

To McLean:

This is what I have to say about my going to the council at Parihaka. If Parris did not know what it was about. Parris thought that it was that the King and Queen were to fall, Te Whiti and Tītoko [Tītokowaru] would be king for the Māori and the Pākehā and he would be right. The real purpose of that council is that the Queen would rule over the Pākehā of Hāwera and Manawapou, and those Pākehā living on Māori land should go back to their own land. The proposition for the King, the Māori kings, is that each should return to their own land, and if the Pākehā stay, then evil will also remain.

The council started on the 18th, and on the 22nd Tītoko arrived at Parihaka with his party, sixty strong. On the day he had arrived, they had started talking about the road. Ngāti Ruanui and Ngāti Awa were opposed to allowing it to go ahead but Tito Te Auataua [Hanataua] agreed that it could be built.

On that day Tītoko did not want to listen to what Parris had to say, and it was a day of discord on account of the Government and Hauhau.

When the speeches were over, we went to weep together, and when that was over Tītoko saw me, and called out to me 'Come here, the General of the Pākehā'. I saw there my brother, Wairau, who said to me (privately), 'be careful, we have not come here because of the council, but to see how the land lies.['] Tītoko will not reveal his thoughts now. His plan is to let the Pākehā do that first. See here, Tītoko and his party are going to Whanganui to see if the Pākehā lay a finger on him. If they don't, he knows it's alright.

Don't listen to what they have to say, it is just to lead people on.

This month or the next, they will go to Whanganui. There are two routes: he will go there on the inland road, and come back along the coast. If there is trouble, I will write a letter to you. If not to you, then to Blake. Well, you should go in case you get into bother. Tītoko lives at Ōmuturangi now, and won't return soon to Waitara. He is collecting men now from among the kūpapa, to have all his people together under his wing.

I saw all the people in Tītoko's group, but only Tītoko and Wairau shook hands with me. They came to show their sadness to me, and tell me of the people's dislike for me. My people did not come and greet me. If they hadn't seen Pākehā there, they would have killed me, as revenge for Ngutu-o-te-manu and Ngaene. It was Tito Te Auataua and Ngohi who protected me, and who saved me, so that I wouldn't see [the wrath of] Tītoko. It was Ngohi who held me back so I would see my parents, Tītoko and the others.

When Tītoko arrived, I cheered up and stopped being sad. They talked to me about how sad they were at the wrongdoing I had done them.

Tītoko talked to me and instructed me to stop talking to the government. He said that he had heard from the people of Whanganui that I was working for the Pākehā, that is, the government, and was telling them what the Hauhau were up to. He said that I should go to Waitara, and not stay here in case I talked to the government about what they were up to and what they were thinking. [He said] [']You are alive now because you are related to me through my sister. You would be dead now if I was a different man.['] He wouldn't look at me, but the end of his gun would[.] His word to me was 'Be careful! Be careful! Be careful!'

The rūnanga concluded on Saturday the 24th and we, the government people, returned, leaving Tītoko to sleep at Maungakirikiri, while we went on to Ōeo. We got to Ōpunake on the Sunday. I stayed until I saw them, then returned. Hōne Pīhama said to me that I should return to Waihī, in case I was taken off to Waitara.

On Monday I got to Waihi, and on Tuesday Tītoko was at Ōeo. On the Wednesday he was at Ōmuturangi, and on the Thursday he went to Te Ngutu-o-te-manu to collect some of his belongings.

He took his people from Parihaka, and the group shifted on to Ōeo and Kaupokonui.

What Tītoko says comes from what Te Whiti says, they speak as one. It is not known if what Tītoko says is correct or not, but the real objective of that rūnanga is to establish Te Whiti as the King of Peace, a stand that they maintained throughout. He [Te Whiti] says that he has finished fighting, and was now just sticking with talk, but Parris will give you a full account of what he said.

Te Whiti told Tītoko to lay down his gun. Tītoko said 'No! I should go on, with my weapon, and I won't be laying it on the ground, but will continue to hold it in my hand.'

There is something else. When I was at Ōeo that there were meetings with Te Horo; he is one of Tītoko's men.

If the man Parris sent to carry letters to Pātea was discovered, he would have been seized, the mail taken, and just the man released. This is the case about the horses; I heard them say, that the Pākehā horses that escaped would be taken in return for their horses taken during the fighting. The horse stealing started with the Hauhau here. That is enough.

Mr. McLean, you should know that there are things in this letter that were spoken secretly to me. You should know, in case others hear, and I am killed. Te Whiti is having another council at Parihaka, and for the Governor to come to Parihaka. When that council is finished, Te Whiti will go to England.

   That is all

     I conclude

       Lucy Grey

When I have any fresh news I will write again.[43]

From Takiora's letter, McLean learnt that Te Whiti, although not willing to acquiesce to governmental control, was espousing peace and no longer supported the Kīngitanga, and that Tītokowaru was not yet publically prepared to follow Te Whiti's pacifist teachings. This may have been an elaborate performance for the benefit of Parris and his party, as she stated that Te Whiti and Tītokowaru spoke as one. Takiora also mentioned road building. Roads were essential to the colonial project: they opened up districts for Pākehā settlement, and allowed better military control. In some locations Parris sought

Māori acquiescence by offering the building contracts to local hapū.⁴⁴ She also mentions horse rustling, which she blames on the 'Hauhau', although Parris's report mentions that a group of Pākehā also took the opportunity of the Parihaka meeting to steal horses.⁴⁵ Takiora is also keen for McLean to know her personal situation. Her own people resented that she had assisted the government's forces, and were aware that she was continuing to provide information. She felt unsafe, protected at this hui only by the presence of the kūpapa. Tītokowaru admonished her, but also recounted their shared whakapapa links. Takiora wrote again soon after.

    8th Tīhema 1870
Kia Temakarini
    E koro tena koe, kua tae mai tau reta ki au whakapai hoki mo taku tuhituhi atu ki te kawanatanga[.]
    E koro kei a koe te whakaaro mo taku mahi[.]
    Kei te haere au ki Taranaki ki te whakarongo korero mo te whenua, te whakaaro o Titoko ko te hoki te whenua ki aia[.]
    Te tahi kei te taware a Titoko i te kawanatanga kia wareware tona ngakau kia matau koe kia tukua mai e koutou a taurua ratou ko taua iwi[.]
    Ka timata te kino (he ki) huna tenei (ka oho katoa te motu kia matau te kawanatanga[.] Kei te haere ahau ki Taranaki a popo – a haere tonu atu ki Waitara[.] maku hoki e tuhituhi atu kia koe[.] ko te hoki mai ano au ki Patea a tera wiki[.] Kei patea taku kainga[.]
    Lucy Grey

[modern translation]
8 December, 1870.
To Mr McLean

    Sir, Salutations. Your letter has come to me thanking me for writing to the government.

    Sir, it is for you to consider what I do.

    I am going to Taranaki to listen to talk about the land. Tītokowaru considers that the land will return to him.

    One thing, Tītoko is trying to fool the government into forgetting about his past attitudes, and for you to release Taurua and that tribe.

    The evil has started (this is secret)[.] The government should know, the whole land is aroused. I am going to Taranaki tomorrow, then on to Waitara. I will write to you. I am returning to Pātea next week. I am living at Pātea.

Lucy Grey.[46]

In this letter Takiora discusses Ngāwaka Taurua, the chief of the Pakakohi people of the Pātea district, who surrendered during the third Taranaki war. As discussed in chapter 2, Taurua and 200 Pakakohi men and boys were sentenced to two years' hard labour, and transported to Dunedin to serve their sentences, before being released in 1872. They returned the following year to reserves set aside from their confiscated lands.[47]

It would be difficult to describe Takiora as a 'spy', as her activity appears to be relatively commonly known. McLean would also have got the sort of information Takiora was providing from other informants such as Parris, but her letter would have given him another angle, with more nuance and perhaps a better understanding of what Māori thought. She may also have heard things earlier than other informants. Several more similar letters from her sit in McLean's papers. In July 1872 she wrote about Māori unhappiness with surveying, and the likelihood of trouble. She was continuing to listen for information, and ended her letter with, 'Ki te tino tuturu taua korero ko te patu atu au i te waea' (if that report is really true, I will send you a telegram).[48] The following month, she reported bits of information she had gleaned, for example, that Te Kooti, still a fugitive, had sent several letters to Taranaki about visiting various locations, including Parihaka, and that it was 'kūpapa' Māori, rather than the 'Hauhau', who had burnt a whare that surveyors had been planning to use.[49] Takiora also passed on information to government officers, such as Blake, who then relayed it to McLean.[50] It is possible too that Takiora passed back information the other way. The following year several Taranaki Māori sent a letter to Tītokowaru warning him that Parris had sent out a posse of Pākehā men to look for him. The final words of the letter are 'The information is from Takiora'.[51]

It is difficult to know exactly what Takiora got in return for providing information to McLean. She certainly tried to call in favours when she could. In January 1871 she wrote to complain about being evicted from her house at Waihī (near Hāwera) by Captain Noake, and was now required to live with a Pākehā woman at Pātea. She added:

ko te toru hoki tenei o aku tau e mahi ana ki te kawanatanga waihoki kahore ahau e mohio ki taku hara[.]

[modern translation]
This is my third year working for the government, and furthermore I don't know what I have done wrong.[52]

Interestingly, several letters sent in 1872 are addressed from Waihī, so she may well have had her house returned. That year she also met McLean to discuss land. She wanted land for herself, but also took the opportunity to speak for her hapū.

> He then asked me where I wanted the land, and I said I wished for some land at Ketemarae. That was the place of my grandmother and my mother.... We then went into conversation about the Waimate Plains. I asked him for some reserves for my tribe, Kanihi, who were then living at Kaupukunui, and who were without land...[53]

However, soon after she wrote to McLean protesting against the surveying of her 50 acres for the purpose of laying two roads across it, and asked to have a personal meeting to discuss it.[54]

Sir Donald McLean was able to operate effectively within the political space between the Pākehā and Māori worlds because he cultivated a range of informants, Māori and Pākehā-Māori, as well as officials, surveyors, missionaries and others who lived and worked within Māori communities. From 1869 to a month before his death in 1877 he served a succession of ministries, who valued his abilities to deal with Māori while they got on with the job of developing the colony. Takiora was just one of his informants, but well positioned in a highly volatile region.

McLean was no doubt an important political patron, but Takiora continued working for the government after his death in January 1877. In 1879 she is listed as employed within the Native Land Purchase Department on a salary of £120 per annum, although this position was discontinued in 1881.[55] While some chiefs were prepared to sell land, there was considerable and active passive resistance from those aligned to Parihaka. In 1880, the Taranaki Civil Commissioner Charles Brown, giving evidence to the Royal Commission on Confiscated Land, was questioned about payments to Takiora.

> 1077. As part of the same system, and connected with the list of payments on account of the Waimate Plains, we find a few items about which we wish to ask you. Takiora Dalton, who, apparently, also appears in the list as Lucy Grey,

has received £325 12s. 6d. during the last two years. In what capacity did she receive that money? —*Part in respect of her claims, and part as salary, when Mr. Sheehan ordered her to be put on pay at £10 per month.*
1078. To be put on pay for what? —*For reporting any information that came in her way from the Waimate Plains.*
1079. Had she been employed in a similar capacity before? —*Yes.*
1080. While holding a Government appointment? —*No; but she stated before the Commission that the land at Hikutere was given to her for her services by Sir Donald McLean. That land was sold, I think, for £400.*
1081. What kind of services do you yourself consider that Mrs. Dalton is capable of performing: can she influence the sale of the Waimate Plains? —*No; but, for instance, she came to me and said, 'I had a letter from Blake, and he is coming up with Brissenden next month, and they are going in to buy the Ngaere Swamp;' so I immediately made a payment on account and had it gazetted, and that shut them out. I was afraid that, if Brissenden got his finger in the pie outside the confiscation line, I should not know where to stop him.*
1082. The payments to Harerota of £140, and to Mere Hawaiki, are of the same nature, are they not? —*Yes; for the purpose of getting information for the service of the Government.*
1083. Have you seen a letter, which is in the possession of the Government, addressed to Mrs. Dalton by E. T. Blake?—*Yes.*
1084. Do you know his handwriting? —*Yes; the letter produced is in the handwriting of Captain Blake. It is as follows: 'Whanganui, 9th September, 1877. – (Extract.) – Never mind about your share. Watch for the other side; nothing must go across there. Brown is very whakahihi [up himself]; but you and I can't be much good if we can't stop his game. You watch and stop things till I get up . . . Why should the Natives care for Brown? Let him rip, and you stick to the land. . . . Watch Te Ngaere: keep that out of Government hands. We can make a fortune out of that, and you are one of the principal owners there. – E. T. Blake.'*
1085. Was the person to whom that letter was addressed Mrs. Takiora Dalton? —*Yes. She handed me the letter in presence of Captain Wilson, whom I asked to attach his signature to the letter at the time in order to verify it.*[56]

It is clear that the government still found Takiora useful in its aim of gaining possession of the contested Waimate Plains. Brown also accused Captain Richard Blake of trying to induce the Taranaki Māori into resisting the government's attempts at surveying, although the implication from the letter of his brother Edward was that they could all make more money selling it privately. Takiora decided to remain loyal to her government paymasters.

Given the continuing resistance from Parihaka to confiscation, resulting in mass arrests, imprisonment and transportation without trial, it is not surprising that Takiora's relationship with her own people was at times fraught. In September 1881, the *Star* reported that Takiora was at Māwhitiwhiti pā 'residing with her hapu on land reserved by the Royal Commission'. The newspaper reported that 'a dispute has recently arisen between her and other members of the hapu, resulting in the inpounding of her sheep and the driving off of all cattle belonging to Europeans running on the land with Takiora's consent.'[57] This had arisen from Takiora laying poison to kill dogs that were worrying her sheep,[58] but also at a time of rising tensions and fears of another armed conflict. Less than three months later, John Bryce, the Native Minister, led armed troops into Parihaka in an attempt to extinguish the Māori passive resistance movement, arresting Te Whiti, Tohu and Tītokowaru, and driving all the people out. In her later years, Takiora may have emotionally distanced herself more from her Māori side, even objecting to the use of the name 'Takiora'.[59] When she died in 1893 she was interred in New Plymouth's public cemetery rather than in an urupā.

Māori women's Komiti

Māori women's Komiti (committees) mushroomed in the last decade of the nineteenth century. Komiti had existed prior to this. As Vincent O'Malley states, '[t]he old mechanisms of tribal governance – runanga, or tribal assemblies – were reinvented in ways that made them more appropriate to the altered geopolitical landscape, and entirely new institutions, committees deriving from European society, absorbed, adopted, adapted, and realigned to suit Maori priorities.'[60] It is perhaps not surprising that men also dominated these new formations. However, examples of influential women leaders are not wanting, and as already noted, Ngāti Maru women formed their own rūnanga in 1869. Māori women participated in temperance movements in the 1870s and 1880s,[61] but it was the decision of the Kotahitanga movement to allow women to organise their own groups that saw '[a] great flowering of committees' in areas where the Kotahitanga was supported.[62] The Kotahitanga emerged out of several decades of Māori organising – including iwi that supported the Crown during the war – to push for autonomy and better land rights, as guaranteed by the Treaty of Waitangi. In the 1890s, the tribes formalised a parliamentary structure, with meetings around the country, before the Māori Parliament settled at Pāpāwai, in the Wairarapa.[63]

Māori women had to push for recognition within this new structure. It is likely that the suffrage campaign influenced Māori women to assert themselves with regard to their own Parliament. As Tania Rei has shown, some Māori women signed the suffrage petitions in 1892 and 1893, and also enrolled as voters when suffrage was achieved in 1893.[64]

Angela Ballara details in her article on Māori women within the Kotahitanga, how in May 1893 Meri Mangakāhia addressed the Māori Parliament, four months before New Zealand women achieved suffrage, proposing that Māori women should gain the right to vote for their own members and sit in the House. Ākenehi Tomoana supported her motion.

> *Meri Mangakahia:* E whakamoemiti atu ana ahau kinga honore mema e noho ana, kia ora koutou katoa, ko te take i motini atu ai ahau, ki te Tumuaki Honore, me nga mema honore, kia mahia he ture e tenei whare kia whakamana nga wahine ki te pooti mema mo ratou ki te Paremata Maori.
>
> Ka whakamarama ahau i te take i tino tino [sic] ai ahau kia whakamana nga wahine maori ki te pooti, a kia tu hoki he mema wahine ki roto i te Paremata Maori.
>
> 1. He nui nga wahine o Nui Tireni kua mate a ratou taane, a he whenua karati, papatipu o ratou.
>
> 2. He nui nga wahine o Nui Tireni kua mate o ratou matua, kaore o ratou tungane, he karati, he papatupu o ratou.
>
> 3. He nui nga wahine mohio o Nui Tireni kei te moe tane, kaore nga tane e mohio ki te whakahaere i o raua whenua.
>
> 4. He nui nga wahine kua koroheketia o ratou matua, he wahine mohio, he karati, he papatupu o ratou.
>
> 5. He nui nga tane Rangatira o te motu nei kua inoi ki te kuini, mo nga mate e pa ara [sic] kia tatou, a kaore tonu tatou i pa ki te ora i runga i ta ratou inoitanga. Na reira ka inoi ahau ki tenei whare kia tu he mema wahine.
> Ma tenei pea e tika ai, a tera ka tika ki te tuku inoi nga mema wahine ki te kuini, mo nga mate kua pa nei kia tatou me o tatou whenua, a tera pea e whakaae mai a te kuini ki te inoi a ona hoa Wahine Maori i te mea he wahine ano hoki a te kuini.

Ākenehi Tomoana: Kia ora nga mema Honore e kimi nei i te ora mo tatou. E tu ake ana ahau ki te tautoko i tenei motini, engari e mea ake ana ahau kia riro rawa mai te Honore i nga tane katahi ano ka pai te korero i tenei motini.

[modern translation]
Meri Mangakāhia: I acknowledge the honourable members sitting, my greetings to you all. The proposal that I move for approval, to the Honourable leader, and the honourable members, is that this house makes a law to empower women to vote for members for themselves to the Māori Parliament.

I will explain the reason I have proposed that Māori women be empowered to vote, and for female members to the Parliament.
1. There are many women in New Zealand whose husbands have died, and who have lands of their own under Crown grant, or native title.
2. There are many women in New Zealand whose parents have died, who have no brothers, and who have lands of their own under Crown grant, or native title.
3. There are many knowledgeable women in New Zealand who are married, but whose husbands are not knowledgeable in managing their land.
4. There are many women whose parents are elderly, who are knowledgeable, and who have lands of their own under Crown grant, or native title.
5. There are many male chiefs of the country who have appealed to the Queen about the ills afflicting us, but we have not been relieved on account of their appeals. Therefore I ask this house that women members may stand.

It may be the best to do the following, that the women members appeal to the Queen about the ills afflicting us and our lands, and perhaps the Queen will agree to the appeal of her Māori women friends because she herself is a woman.

Ākenehi Tomoana: Greetings honourable members seeking our well-being. I stand to support this motion, but I say that the men should have the honour, and then it will be right to speak on this motion.[65]

Ballara is unsure what Ākenehi Tomoana meant, but considers that 'Akenehi may have been responding to [her husband's] wishes to postpone debate on this issue while the various factions attempted to resolve their differences over the limits of Māori delf-determination'.[66] While women did not achieve suffrage within the Māori Parliament until 1897, the chiefs did approve the formation of women's committees in 1894.[67]

The issues that the women's committees dealt with were many. Ballara is right in suggesting that they centred on land issues, which affected men and women.[68]

In 1895 a number of committees met at Te Hauke in Hawke's Bay, in what was dubbed in the Pākehā press a 'Maori Women's Parliament'.[69] Ākenehi Tomoana addressed the assembly.

Taku take i tu ake ai ahau i tenei wa ko te kaha mo tatou i runga i tenei mahi, he mea na aku kia kaha tatou te mahi i tenei mahi i runga i te kaha kua tukua mai kia tatou, kaua hei hoha te ngakau, i te mea kua whakamana tatou nga wahine ki te Pooti mema, a kua to to ia hoki tatou e nga taane ki tera mahi, kia Pooti ki tana mema, ki tana mema, a kua mana hoki tatou i raro i te mana whakatu komiti i Pahitia i te Paremata o te kotahitanga i Pakirikiri, no reira e hara i te hanganoa ta tatou mahi i tenei ra, kia mahi tatou he ora mo tatou, he kore ranei[.] Kua maha nga tau i rapu ai nga taane, nga rangatiratanga, mema nga Kiingitanga, kore noa ake tatou i whiwhi ki te ora, aha koa kua taea a Ingarangi, e nga rangatiratanga e nga Kingitanga, kihai rawa i whiwhi ki tetahi paku ora mo tatou. No reira au ka mahara e kore ano hoki e taea e tatou e nga wahine. He aha koa kote mahi me te tikanga kia rite ia tatou. Engari kaua hoki nga taane hei whakatonga mai kia tatou ki nga wahine, e taea hoki e tatou te aha na tatou hoki i pehea ai, kua Pakeke mai ano a ratou i nga taane. Heoi aku kupu kia ora tatou i roto i te tau hou.

[modern translation]
The reason I stand at this time is to express the courage/commitment we need for this task. I say that we should undertake this with the determination given to us, not as a burden [to ourselves], but because we have the authority to vote for representatives, and we have been drawn to this work by the men, to vote for this representative or that, and we have the mana under the authority to establish committees that was passed at the Kotahitanga parliament at Pākirikiri. Therefore, our activities this day are not unsanctioned. We must strive for the best outcomes, or achieve nothing. For many years men, chiefs, members of parliament, and the Kīngitanga have persevered but have been unsuccessful in achieving even the smallest gain for us. Despite trips to England by the chiefs and the Kīngitanga we have not received even a little benefit for ourselves. And so I think that we women will also not be able to achieve this, despite the fact that we are up to the task and that it is right. But let not the men find fault with us, the women. We are able to achieve whatever, however. They have grown up from the men. Those were my words to you. Greetings in this new year.[70]

The Kotahitanga newspaper, *Huia Tangata Kotahi,* covering the meeting, stated 'Many women members stood to support this uplifting speech for them, and their organising work that they, the women, had started'.[71] This newspaper, in a later issue, printed some of the meeting's discussion in which we can see the women's focus on the retention of the remaining Māori land. Also noticeable is their adherence to a parliamentary-style language.

HANUERE 7, 1895, 2 P. M.
TIAMANA Ka panuitia atu ko te take tuatahi ara whakamutu i te Kooti i roto i nga iwi Maori.

Heke Puhara – E tu ake ana ahau kia waiho tonu i tenei take katoa kia mutu te Kooti.
TE ARAMA – E tutoko[sic] ana ahau i ta te Honore Mema e mea nei kia waiho tonu i runga ... [illegible] Horiana Tiakitai, Pane Te Uruorangi ... Kaitoritori, Raina Mokopuna, Kuini Te Orora Meri Anata, Wharekauri ... tautuko[sic] ana.
HEPINE TE ROHU – E patai ana mehemea ka tu te kooti ki Taupo ka haere ano pea ahau ki reira.
MARAEA PURI – Taku mahara me haere anake te korero i runga ia tatou take kia marama kia oti pai, koia ahau i akiaki ai, e te Tiamana. He tokomaha nga mema i tu ki te tautuku[sic], me te unu unu hoki i nga tono whakawa kua Panuitia i roto i nga [K]ahiti.
TIAMANA – I te mea kua roa koutou e korero ana mo tenei take a kaore he kai whakahe, he aha koa ka tukua atu ano e au te patai ki te whare. Ko nga mea e whakaae ana kia whakamutua te koati [sic] me ki mai a e. Nga mea e whakakore ana me ki Noo riro ana i te ae, Pahitia ana e te Tiamana.

TAKE TUARUA.
Ko te hoko whenua kia whakamutua i roto i nga takiwa maori.
HEKE PUHARA – Taku whakaro e te Tiamana kia waiho tonu i te take e mea nei kia whakamutua te hoko.
HORIANA TIAKITAI – E tautoko ana ahau i tenei take kia whakamutua te hoko koia nei te mate nui kua pa kia tatou ara ki nga iwi maori. A he tokomaha nga mema i Tautoko.
TIAMANA – Ko nga mea e whakaae ana kia whakamutua te hoko whenua me ki mai ae. Nga mea whakakore me ki mai Noo riro ana i te ae, Pahitia ana e te Tiamana.

TAKE TUATORU.
Kia whakamutua te Riihi whenua.
HERE RIPENE – E tautoko ana i tenei take kia mutu te riihi.
HEKE PUHARA – Me tahi atu e tau toko ana.
TIAMANA – Ka tukua te Patai, kite whare, riro ana i te ae Pahitia ana e te Tiamanu.

TAKE TUA WHA.
Ko te whakamutu i te Ruri whenua Maori.
AKENEHI TOMOANA – E tuake ana e te Tiamana ko toku whakaro [sic] kia waiho tonu i runga i te take e mea nei kia whakamutua te ruuri i nga whenua a te Maori, kua oti te whakamarama ngamate i pa kia tatou.
WIKITORIA TE UA – E tautoko ana kia mutu te ruri he tokomaha ngawahine i roto i nga iwi Maori kua whiua e te kawanatanga, ki te herehere mo runga i a ratou ake whenua. He tokomaha nga mema i tautoko.
TIAMANA – Ka tukua te Patai riro ana i te ae. Pahitia ana e te Tiamana.

TAKE TUA RIMA.
Ko te whaina mo te hunga e takahi ana i enei take kua whakaotia e tenei hui i na whakaotia ete Paremata ote kotahitanga.
ARAPERA PANAPA – E whakae [sic] ana au ki tenei take hei whakakaha ia tatou take kua Pahitia ake nei.,
ATANETA KEMARA – E tautoko ana.
MARAEA PURI – E tautoko ana.
HEKE PUHARA – He menemana taku, me haina nga tangata katoa i nga ingoa ki tetahi Tiiti, whakamana i te whaaetanga [sic] ki tenei take.
Ataneta Kemara, Maremare Timu, Te Orama, Akenehi Tomoana, Wikitoria Te Ua, i tautoko me etahi atu.
ATARETA WAIRAKAU – E tautoko ana au ki enei take katoa, me te Menemana kua oti katoa i au enei take i te hui i tu ki [illegible] i te Kirihimete nei, katu ko enei take kua oti noa atu i te hui i Parikino [illegible] ki te hui ki Waitangi me nga hui e rua ki te Waipatu, me te hui ki Turanga[.] Na reira au e mea ai kia . . . hoki ia tatou i [ko]nei.
Horiana Tiakitai, Koka Tongi, Ema Tiakitai, Maraea Ropitoi, Pane Te Uruorangi, Wharekauri Kerei, Arapera Panapa, Hana Puriri, me etahi atu nga kai tautoko.

TIAMANA – Ko nga mea e whakae[sic] ana mo te take whaina me ki mai a e. Nga mea whakakore me kii Noo, riro ana i te ae, Pahitia e te Tiamana.
TIAMANA – Me korero te whare mo te Menemana, a Heke Puhara kia haina tia nga ingoa ki tetaki [sic] Tiiti whakamana whakaae tanga, i raro i nga take mo te whaina.
MARAEA ROPITOI – E tautoko ana.
MERE [ILLEGIBLE]NATA, HANA PURIRI, TE ORAMA – Nga kai tautoko.
HORIANA TIAKITAI – Ki taku whakaro [sic] me waiho te menemana me unu mai ki waiho te haina e meatia nei e te menemana.
HEKE PUHARA – Me waiho te haina i te taha o te whaina, ko te take tenei e tika ai te whaina kua whakaaetia nei e te whare, ki te kore he whaina kaore kau he painga o te whaina.
WIKITORIA TE UA – E tautoko ana ahau i te Menemana a te Honore Mema a te Pakipaki.
Ema TIAKITAI, RAINA TIPUNA, nga kai tautoko.
HORIANA TAIKITAI – E unu ana ahau i taku kupu unu i te Menemana ki waho.
TIAMANA – Ko nga mema e whakae ana ki te Menemana me ki, ae, nga mea whakakore me ki, Noo, kua riro i te a e Pahitia ana e te Tiamana.

TAKE TUA ONO
Ko te haina ki te Kirihipi kia whakahaeretia i tenei tau i runga i nga iwi.
Kuini Te Arora – E whakaeana au ki tenei take kia whakahaerea te Haina[.]
Rongonui Te Wheoro, e tautoko ana i tenei take, Here Ripene, Arihi Hiraka, Irihapeti Kaitoritori, Ema Tiakitai, Merania Hemi, Marara Whitingara, Hepine Te Rohu, Akenehi Tomoaua[sic], Pane Uruorangi[,] Maraea, Puri, Ataneta Kemara, nga kai tautoko.
Tiamana – Ka tukua te Patai ki te whare, riro ana i te ae, Pahitia ana e te Tiamana.

TAKE TUA WHITU
Ko te moni kotahi pauna i runga i te tangata i whakaetia e te ture i te tau 1892 kia kohia.
Ema Tiakitai – He menemana taku. E mea ana au he nui rawa te pauna ma te tangata kotahi engari me nuku iho kaore hoki he moni a etahi.
Ataneta Kemara – E tautoko ana i te Menemana.
Meri Anata – E tautoko ana.

Hepina [sic] Te Rohu – E tautoko ana e rangi kaia tatou nga tikanga mo te Pauna mo te iti iho ranei.
Hana [illegible] – Kanui toku uaua mo tenei take [illegible] au e whakae mo tenei take.
Here Ripene – E tautoko ana au i te take e mea ra me hoatu te pauna he tikanga tera kua oti noa atu.
Pirihira Ngarori – E tautoko ana.
Akenehi Tomoana, Marara – E tautoko ana mo te pauna aha koa tae ki te [illegible]

[modern translation]
7 January, 1895, 2 p.m.
Chair: The first issue will be stated, namely, to stop the [Native Land] Court amongst the Māori tribes.

Heke Pūhara: I stand to support the adjournment of this whole matter until the end of this court session.
Te Arama: I support what the honourable member is saying, let it remain.
[illegible] Hōriana Tiakitai, Pane Te Uruorangi . . . Kaitoritori, Raina Mokopuna, Kuīni Te Orora[,] Meri Anata, Wharekauri . . . in support.
Hepine Te Rohu: I ask that if the court sits in Taupō, whether I should go there.
Maraea Puri: I consider that the discussion should follow the resolution, so that it is clear and is done properly, that is what I am urging, Madam Chair. *Many members supported this and the removal of requests for judgement that have been published in the [Government] Gazette.*
Chair: Because you have been discussing the resolution some time and there has been no one opposing it despite me putting the question to the house. Those who agree that the Court should be stopped say 'aye'. Those who disagree should say 'no', the ayes have it. It is [declared] passed by the Chair.

Second Resolution
That land sales should be stopped in Māori districts.
Heke Pūhara: It is my opinion that this resolution, that sales be stopped, be allowed to stand.
Hōriana Tiakitai: I agree with this resolution that sales be stopped. It is the principal ill afflicting us, the Māori people.
Many members supported this.

Chair: Those who agree that land sales be stopped should say 'aye'. Those disagreeing should say 'no', the ayes have it, passed by the Chair.

Third Resolution

That the leasing of land be stopped.

Here Ripene: I support this resolution that leasing cease.

Heke Pūhara and others supported this.

Chair: The question is put to the House, the ayes have it, passed by the Chair.

Fourth resolution

The cessation of surveys of Māori land.

Ākenehi Tomoana: Madam Chair, I stand [to speak]. I think that the resolution should be left to stand, that says that the surveying of the lands of the Māori should be stopped, the ills that afflict us have been explained.

Wikitōria Te Ua: I support that surveying should stop. There are many women amongst the Māori tribes who have been punished by the government by imprisonment, on account of their own lands.

Many members agreed.

Chair: The question is put; the ayes have it. Passed by the Chair.

Fifth resolution

The fining of people who break these resolutions which have been enacted by this meeting, and enacted by the Kotahitanga Parliament.

Arapera Pānapa: I support this resolution as a means of strengthening the resolutions we have passed.

Ataneta Kēmara: I support it.

Maraea Puri: I support it.

Heke Pūhara: I have an amendment, that all people should sign their names to a deed which sanctions agreement to this resolution.

Ataneta Kēmara, Maremare Timu, Te Orama, Ākenehi Tomoana, Wikitōria Te Ua and some others supported this.

Atareta Wairākau: I support all these issues, and the amendment. I have dealt with all these issues at the meeting at Parikino [illegible], the meeting at Waitangi, and the two at Waipatu, and the one at Tūranga. And so I say [illegible] here.

Horiana Tiakitai, Koka Tongi, Ema Tiakitai, Maraea Ropitoi, Pane Te Uruorangi, Wharekauri Kerei, Arapera Pānapa, Hana Pūriri supported this.

Chair: Those who agree to fines should say yes; those who disagree should say no. The ayes have it; passed by the Chair.

Chair: The house should discuss Heke Pūhara's amendment, that people should sign their names to a deed of agreement relating to the issue of fines.

Maraea Ropitoi: I agree.

Mere [illegible], Hana Pūriri and Te Orama supported this.

Hōriana Tiakitai: In my opinion, the amendment should be left. Take out the reference to signing in the amendment.

Heke Pūhara: We should leave the signing with the fine, which would make the fines agreed to by the house right. if there is no fine [signature?] there is no benefit in the fine.

Wikitōria Te Ua: I support the amendment of the honourable member from Pakipaki.

Ema Tiakitai and Raina Tipuna supported this.

Hōriana Takitai: I withdraw my statement that the amendment be withdrawn.

Chair: Members who agree to the amendments should say aye, those against should say no. The ayes have it; passed by the Chair.

Sixth Resolution

The signing of a covenant to be circulated around the tribes this year.

Kuīni Te Arora: I agree with this resolution that that signatures be organised.

Rongonui Te Wheoro supports this resolution; Here Ripene, Arihi Hiraka, Irihāpeti Kaitoritori, Ema Tiakitai, Merania Hēmi, Marara Whitingara, Hepine Te Rohu, Ākenehi Tomoaua[sic], Pane Uruorangi[,] Maraea [sic], Puri, Ataneta Kēmara support it.

Chair: The question is before the house, the ayes have it; passed by the chair.

Seventh Resolution

That the one pound per person [levy] agreed to by law in 1892 be collected.

Ema Tiakitai: I have an amendment. I think that the pound per person is too much. It should be reduced as some people have no money.

Ataneta Kēmara: [I am] supporting the amendment.

Meri Anata: [I am] supporting it.

Hepine Te Rohu: I am supportive but we may choose to give one pound or less.

Hana [illegible]: I am uncomfortable with this resolution. I [illegible] support this resolution.

Here Ripene: I support the resolution saying that [people] should give the pound; it has already been decided.
Pirihira Ngarori: [I am] supporting it.
Ākenehi Tomoana and Marara: [We] support the pound, although [illegible].[72]

Komiti wāhine also sent in reports to the Māori-language newspapers from a number of regions, and while land matters were a primary concern, the women also discussed wider issues. Te Komiti Wahine o Rotorua, for instance, objected to:

2. Tuarua. E tino whakahe ana matou ou hoa wahine ki le [sic] Taake kuri kia kaua rawa e whai mana ki o matou takiwa ki o matou kainga maori hoki.
3. Tuatoru. He take apiti ko te Ture hou ate kawanatanga, kua whakataua nei ki runga i nga Rori, mo nga kaata wiir [sic] ririki e kitea ana e haere taimaha ana ka whainatia ki ta te Ture i kite ai, na e tino whakahe ana matou no te mea ko nga Rori e takoto nei i o matou takiwa ehara i te mea hoko te kaupapa o nga Rori ete kawanatanga, engari he mea hoatu noa e matou hai painga mo matou mo te ao katoa ano hoki, kaua te kawanatanga e whakawhirinaki ki te moni i utua ai nga tangata mahi o nga Rori, no te mea he utu werawera te tikanga o taua moni.

2. Second. We, your female friends, strongly object to the Dog Tax, that it should not be authorised in our districts, and in our Māori villages.
3. Third. Another issue is the government's new law, which has been applied to the roads, and for small-wheeled carts seen going along laden that are fined on the provisions of the law. We strongly object because the government did not pay for the roads lying in our district, but we provided them for our benefit and that of the whole world. The government should not rely on the money they paid the men who made the roads [as a reason to say they own them] because that money was to pay for their [the workers'] toil.[73]

The women recognised that Māori families, who often had large numbers of dogs, would be hit hard by dog registration. That unlicensed vehicles might be fined rankled given that they saw the roads as their own property, not as belonging to the state.[74] The Heretaunga women's committee, meeting at Pakipaki, discussed the impact of alcohol on their communities.[75]

Tuatoru: Kote whakaaro tenei hui kia whakamutua i nga wahine te kai i nga wai whakahaurangi kia pai ai te whakahaere i nga tikanga e watea ai e pai ai e puta mai ai he ora kia tatou. (Pahiatia ana.)...
Tuarima: E ahei ana hoki i te Komiti te whiu nga wahine taane ranei e whakararuraru aua [sic], e haurangi ana, ki nga moni kaua e hoki iho i te 5s. herengi, mo nga wahine, kinga moni kaua e hoki iho i te 10s. herengi mo nga Taane, a ki te kore e utua ka ahei te Komiti Wahine ki te muru i runga i ta ratou i whakaaro ai, he tika. (Pahitia ana.)

[modern translation]
Third: It is the view of this meeting that women be stopped from consuming intoxicating liquors, so that the procedures may be run properly, so that things may run smoothly and we all reap the benefits. (Passed)...
Fifth. The Committee is able to punish women or men who cause trouble, or get drunk, with a fine of no less than 5 shillings for women, and a fine of no less than 10 shillings for men. And if it is not paid, the Committee is able to seek retribution, to the extent that they believe is proper. (Passed.)[76]

The committee thus combined both modern and traditional forms of punishment, fines, and muru, where a community confiscated an offender's belongings. Women's committees also undertook key organisational and support work, such as catering for the Kotahitanga meetings,[77] and raising money for the movement.

Ko te kohi tenei a te Peka o te Komiti Wahine o Hinehauone, e noho ana ki Waikekeno Flat Point, mo runga i te whakahau ate Tiamana ote Kotahitanga kia kohi mo te Mana Motu Hake...

[modern translation]
This is the collection of the branch of the Women's Committee of Hinehauone living at Waikekeno Flat Point, in response to the directive from the Chairman of the Kotahitanga to collect for [the cause of] Māori autonomy...

The activities of Māori women's committees sometimes extended into the Pākehā world. For example, the *Wanganui Herald* reported in 1897 that the 'Native Women's Committee' in Whanganui, headed by Emma Hīpango, raised £22 17s 'in aid of the sufferers in recent floods', and agreed to 'get up a poi dance' for Queen Victoria's jubilee celebrations.[78]

Niniwa-i-te-rangi and Mahuta

One of the leading women within the Kotahitanga was the wealthy Wairarapa landowner, Niniwa-i-te-rangi.[79] Niniwa of Ngāti Hikawera (Ngāti Kahungunu) descent, possessed a deep knowledge of her tribe's history, and participated actively and successfully in the Native Land Court (see chapter 1).[80] She also won a case against the Government in the Supreme Court over the compulsory acquisition of some of her lands, resulting in changes to land legislation.[81] Niniwa brought the same spirited attitude to her activities within the Kotahitanga. Because Pāpāwai, the eventual home of the Kotahitanga Parliament, was her own marae, her influence was assured to some degree, but she also worked hard to ensure that she was not only seen as a leader within the movement, but that her opinion also counted. For example, she was the only woman named on a Kotahitanga committee in 1898 organising a petition against the Government's proposed land legislation.[82]

Niniwa also led a delegation of Ngāti Kahungunu to a meeting of tribes at Waahi Marae in Huntly in 1898 called by King Mahuta of the Kīngitanga. The Kotahitanga and the Kīngitanga existed as separate entities, groups that shared a desire for greater Māori autonomy and for the retention of Māori lands, but divided by their differing positions in the wars of three decades earlier. Hēnare Kaihau, the Member for the House of Representatives (MHR) for Western Māori had unsuccessfully introduced a bill to create a Māori council with authority over Māori lands, and the Kīngitanga wanted it introduced into Parliament again with wider support. The Kotahitanga wanted backing on their stand for the cessation of any further sales of Māori land.[83] In a letter to *Te Tiupiri*, Niniwa indicated that it was appropriate for women to attend.

> . . . *ka uru nei te taane te wahine ki roto i kotahitanga tu tahi ai, no konei he mea tika kia whiriwhiri nga mema (Ladies) me nga komiti wahine, mo te haere kite Hui a te Kingi ki reira whakarongo ai ki ana kupu.*
>
> [modern translation]
> . . . men and women join the Kotahitanga and stand together. Therefore it is right that Lady members and women's committees should deliberate regarding attendance at the King's meeting, to listen to his words there.[84]

Wikitōria Tūmua of Pūtiki disagreed. She wrote back, countering:

Na ko taku whakaaro mo tenei, i runga i taku ata whiriwhiri i aua kupu a Niniwa.
1. painoatu nga wahine rangatira, kia haere ki taua Hui, Kia kite whenua, kia kite tangata kati i enei.
2. —Ko te whakapuaki kupu i roto i uga [sic] Hui pera o tatau, kaua tera. No te mea kua whiriwhiria nga mema o te kotahi tanga hei minita mo te whare ariki, mete whare o raro ote Paremata maori, ko ratau nga tangata tika mo taua mahi, mo te whakapuaki kupu i nga Hui pera. Ite mea hoki ko ratau te mangai o te iwi nui tonu.

[modern translation]
So, my thought on this on carefully perusing Niniwa's words.
1. It is fine for chiefly women to go to that meeting, to see the land and the people, but leave it at that.
2. Speaking rights at our meetings like that, should not be permitted. Because the members of the Kotahitanga have been chosen as ministers for the Upper House and the Lower House of the Māori Parliament, and they are the right people for that work, speaking publicly at meetings like that. Because they are the representatives of the whole people.

Niniwa attended nevertheless, and was likely the only woman who spoke publicly. She asserted herself as a woman in her speech, while also giving support to the Kīngitanga, through the king, Mahuta.

Karanga e Mahuta, karanga ki o Iwi, kua rupeke mai nei ki to Marae, karanga te reo o Tipuna i tenei waahi, karanga kite ahuatanga o tera waahi, kua ngaro te tangata kite po, me titiro mai e koe, he Wahine tonu au e korero atu nei, e haere nei hoki ki to Marae . . .

[modern translation]
Call out Mahuta, call to your tribes who have assembled here on your marae. Call the voices of your ancestors who are here, call out to the essence of that place where the people have been lost to the night [died]. Look at me, I am just a woman speaking, coming to your marae . . .[85]

Niniwa concluded with asserting her own iwi, and role in advancing the cause.

Homai taku kingitanga kia au homai taku mana, homai kia utaina e ahau ki runga kia Takitimu ite mea kua pakaru nga Waka katoa koia ahau i ki ai kati hoki ki runga i enei Waka tukua mai hoki kia utaina e ahau ki runga i era Waka heoi nei ka huri iho.
Heoi ano.

[modern translation]
Give me my kīngitanga, give me my mana, so I can bestow it on the Tākitimu [canoe] because all the canoes are broken. That is why I say stop affiliating with these canoes [new causes of the day] and allow me to affiliate with these other canoes.
That is all.[86]

Wī Pere, the MHR for Eastern Māori and one of the Ngāti Kahungunu delegation, clarified her words, 'Listen, those of the East, the person who said that Mahuta should come aboard Takitimu is a woman, and I support what Niniwa said', that people should look at new ways of working together.[87]

Niniwa maintained her sympathy for the Kīngitanga. When she heard that the Premier, Richard Seddon, had suggested that Mahuta could be appointed to the Legislative Council, she was not in favour, and spoke to Taingākawa Te Waharoa, one of the leading Kīngitanga figures, about her concerns. As she wrote in *Te Tiupiri*:

Kaati hei konei taaku kupu. Kite whakaae a Mahuta kite tono ate Pirimia ote Koroni o Nui Tireni. Kua taka toona ingoa Kiingi i runga ia ia.
...
I puta atu ano i ahau tenei kupu kia Tainga-a-kawa i tooku tutakinga atu kia ia i Poneke ite tau kua hori ake nei kia puritia tona tamaiti ara mo runga i te kupu a te Pirimia (Hetana) kia tae mai a Mahuta kite Paremata i Poneke he mea titiro naaku ko te hiahia nui o te Pirimia kaua tenei ingoa a te Kiingi e whakahuatia ki runga kite Maori.

[modern translation]
This is what I have to say. If Mahuta agrees to the request of the Premier of the Colony of New Zealand, his name of king would fall away from him.
...
When I met with Taingākawa in Wellington last year, I said to him to hold on to

his child on account of what the Premier (Seddon) said about Mahuta coming to Parliament in Wellington. What I can see is that what the Premier really wants is that is this name of king should not be spoken [used] amongst the Māori.[88]

While she acknowledged that some tribes might consider that Mahuta's participation in Parliament would be beneficial to Māori aspirations, Niniwa saw the role of the Māori king as more valuable when independent of the New Zealand government.

Niniwa-i-te-rangi and the Māori-language newspapers

Niniwa-i-te-rangi was one of the leading Māori public intellectuals of her time. This is not widely acknowledged because she wrote exclusively i roto i te reo Māori, mostly in the Māori-language newspapers that were aligned to the Kotahitanga: *Huia Tangata Kotahi* (1893–1895); *Te Puke ki Hikurangi* (1897–1913); and *Te Tiupiri* (1898–1900). When Hāmiora Mahupuku, the owner of *Te Puke ki Hikurangi* died in 1904, Niniwa took over the running of the niupepa with several of her female relatives.[89] Her writing covered a wide range of issues, but within the time frame of this volume, her most significant journalistic endeavour, together with Meri Mangakāhia, involved editing a ladies' column in *Te Tiupiri*.

> REIRI KARAMU
> E kore e tau te he ki nga Etita, mo nga whakaaro a nga Wahine e tuku mai ana ia ratou reta kia panuitia.
> Niniwa i te Rangi
> Meri H. Mangakahia   Nga Etita
>
> [modern translation]
> LADIES' COLUMN.
> The editors take no responsibility for the thoughts of the women sending their letters in to be published.
> Niniwa-i-te-rangi
> Meri H. Mangakāhia   Editors.[90]

The column was largely political, covering news from the women's committees, and occasionally parliamentary discussion, as seen in the following excerpts.

It appears that Niniwa was the more active editor, and wrote much of the column's material. For example, in early 1899 Turi Wano of Heretaunga wrote to the editors about a number of issues, including her local Māori Member of Parliament, Wī Pere.

> *Ehoa ma tenei kua rongo ake ahau e korerotia ana kua tono a Taare Mete, a Hurinui, a te Heuheu me Mohi Teatahikoia kia pootitia ratou he mema kakari kia Wipere mo te nohoanga i te Paremata o te Koroni a te Tihema e tu mai nei. Kei te rapu noa taku ngakau ki te putake i tono ai enei o tatou tungane kia pootitia ratou kaore ano ahau i kite noa. Tena pea ko korua kei te matau. Ko ahau kaore i te matau ki te putake. Tena pea mo te Pire Poari nei? He aha etahi atu putake? Mo te pire penihana pea? Mo te mahi turaki kawanatanga pea? Mo te Motuhake ranei?*

> [modern translation]
> My friends, this is what I have heard being said, that Taare Mete, Hurinui, Te Heuheu and Mohi Te Ātahīkoia have called that they be elected opposing Wī Pere for the seat in the Parliament of the Colony of New Zealand this December. I am trying to find the reason these of our brothers ask that they be elected, but I haven't been able to see one.
> Perhaps you two know. I do not know the reason. Perhaps because of the Land Board Bill? What are some other causes? Is it about the Pensions Bill? Or being in opposition to the government? Is it about [the issue of Māori] autonomy?

Turi also touched on an issue that caused great anxiety to Māori in the late nineteenth century: that their people might completely disappear.

> *E aku hoa kaore rawa korua i te kore e matau ki tenei, ara ko nga Maori e 39, 000 (toru tekau ma wa mano) inaianei. I mua e 43, 000 wha tekau ma toru mano) te Iwi Maori. Ko te pakeha kei te nui haere tonu. Inaianei ka tata te 800, 000 (waru rau mano) ki taku mahara ko te putake i piki ai te pakeha he pai no ana tikanga. Ko te ora o te pakeha kei roto katoa i ana tuhituhinga me ana korerotanga.*

> [modern translation]
> My friends, you must know about this, that the Māori [number] 39,000 now. Before the Māori race was 43,000. The Pākehā are still increasing, and are now

close to 800,000. I think the reason the Pākehā are climbing is because their practices are good. The health of the Pākehā is in his writings and his talk.[91]

Niniwa responded the following month, backing Wī Pere on account of his long experience within Parliament.

Koia i kau matua tonu ki roto ite Paremata ote koroni me tona mohio ki nga mate e pa mai ana kite iwi maori e mahia mai nei e te Kawanatanga o Nui Tireni Ehoa ko Wi Pere te tangata koia te mema kaha kite mahi i nga mate onga iwi e tae mai ana ki Poneke nei ara nga tangata e kawe atu ana i o ratau mate ki aia, ahakoa tane, wahine he rite tonu me ahau ano Hoki, a me tahi atu o ana mahi i roto i te Whare Paremata; mo te patai mo te Pire.

[Wī Pere] has become a senior figure in the colony's Parliament, with his knowledge of the ills afflicting the Māori people being done by the New Zealand government. Friend, Wī Pere is the person, he is the member active in dealing with the problems of the tribes coming to Wellington, that is, the people bringing their problems to him, whether men or women, and even me, and [he is also proficient with] other workings of the House of Parliament such as questioning bills.

On the matter of the supposed declining Māori population, Niniwa put this down to a Pākehā conspiracy.

Ehoa kaore au nei i te whakapono ki tenei kau te; ae, e tika ana ko te tatau nui tenei, ko te take na te pakeha tenei kaute, e ngari ma tatau ano tatau e kaute katahi ka tika, ko ta te pakeha kaute e rere ke ana kei runga i o tatau whenua te taungia iho, ara, kei te whakaatu kite Kiuni [sic] me tona Kawanatanga ko te nui tenei ote iwi maori ko ratau whenua i nui ke atu ia ratau he mea tika kia puare tonu te hokohoko i o ratau whenua kia rite ano kia ratau te rahi, ehoa kei te penei oku mahara he mea tika rawa me tahuri nga iwi o runga ite motu nei ara oia takiwa oia takiwa kite kaute i to ratau tokomaha tanga, ma o tatau mema ano ote koroni e whakahaere nga tangata hei kaute, kia kitea e tika ana taua kaute[.]

[modern translation]
My friend, I do not believe this figure; yes, you are right that this is the census. The reason [I do not have faith in this figure] is that the Pākehā undertook this

count, but when we count ourselves then it will be correct, the Pākehā's count is different because its reference is to our lands, that is, by showing the Queen and her government that this is the size of the Māori race, and their land is bigger than they need, then it's right that the purchasing of their lands be unrestricted so that the amount [of land] they [Māori] have is in proportion [to their population]. My friend, what I think is that it would be right that the tribes of this country, that is, of each district, should set about counting their own population. Our [Māori] Members of the Colony can organise the enumerators, to see that the count is right.[92]

Part of the problem of Māori undercounting was due to individuals of mixed ancestry being counted as 'half-castes' or Europeans.[93] However, the 1901 census proved predictions of the demise of Māori wrong, showing a small increase in the Māori population.[94]

Conclusion

The issues confronting Māori communities affected both men and women. The realities of colonisation, land loss, and economic and political marginalisation, impacted upon all. Whānau, iwi and hapū thus viewed, and confronted or mitigated these threats collectively. It was chiefly Māori men who undertook much of the interaction with the government; they traditionally assumed leadership roles within tribal structures, and they were more familiar to the patriarchs of the Pākehā world. Māori women, unable to vote for their own parliamentary representatives until 1893 (a right their men had gained in 1867) were effectively cut out of most official political activity. It is therefore not surprising that men's voices predominate in the archives, both within the repositories of public records and the pages of surviving newspapers that recorded the nineteenth-century political arena.

That Māori women's voices are harder to find does not mean that they had no political voice at all. As seen from the texts above, women who possessed mana through illustrious whakapapa felt no qualms about speaking for their people, as in Topeora's denunciation of the Kīngitanga, or Mere Kuru's hostility towards the intrusion of Pākehā gold prospectors. Those who felt the responsibility to use this mana could be influential within their own iwi and often on a wider Māori stage. However, how they represented themselves politically changed over the century, as in the example of Te Paea Tīaho who was an influential voice within the Kīngitanga, but appears to have operated primarily in rūnanga composed mainly of men. As we can see from the Ngāti Maru protest at losing their beach lands in 1869, women could organise themselves within their own komiti, but the archival evidence does not tell us if this was a relatively common or exceptional event at this time. However, by the end of the century, the advent of women's suffrage nationally and the predominance of the Kotahitanga as the primary Māori political voice for many tribes, created an environment in which women could meet and discuss political issues amongst themselves. Women of mana, such as Meri Mangakāhia, Ākenehi Tomoana and Niniwa-i-te-rangi, refused to be excluded from discussions of matters that impacted on all, although their deliberations were often within women's groups rather than together with the men. Niniwa-i-te-rangi also wrote extensively, often on political issues, for the Māori-language newspapers. As in the past, the issues Māori women faced were ones they shared with men. Their activities were thus complementary to men's activities, both genders striving for a common good.

Nevertheless, women's political organising was also undertaken in aid of improving their status and ensuring their political rights. In 1891 two Māori men were prosecuted for illegally taking under-sized trout, using a net, and fishing without a licence. In their defence they claimed they had a right to fish under the Treaty of Waitangi. By the late nineteenth century access to traditional food resources was severely reduced due to the drainage of wetlands and the introduction of trout and other species into waterways. Māori were criminalised for pursuing hunting and fishing practices, and went to court to defend their actions. Witnesses testified to having fished at the river for generations. Katarina Uru, whose testimony was interpreted and summarised in a newspaper report, said she had lived at Kaiapoi since childhood, amounting to over 40 years. She recounted a tribal tradition of netting fish, regardless of species, rights that continued on the basis of native reserves granted under Kemp's Deed. When asked if Ngāi Tahu had been compensated to give up their traditional food gathering sites, the paper stated: 'Witness said she was no man, and could not answer politics, as she had to attend to household duties'.[95] Katarina's suggestion her gender precluded her from participation in political debate might suggest evidence of Māori women's reduced status within the political arena, which some were contesting in the 1890s through active organising for electoral reform. That she was 'no man, and could not answer politics' was certainly accurate, for Māori women did not have the right to vote until 1893 when universal suffrage was enacted. However, her words can equally be interpreted as a critique of Western patriarchal models of femininity, which regarded women's proper sphere to be in the home. This ideology of separate spheres and women's capacity for political participation and debate was subjected to sustained challenge during the final decades of the nineteenth century, by both Pākehā and Māori women, as they argued the case for widening the grounds of political citizenship.[96]

CHAPTER 5.

'I will not desist from writing to you': Māori Women's Petitions

A petition is a form of writing that addresses the public sphere. It is specifically directed to those in authority who have the power to effect positive material change in the lives of the supplicants. As such, petitions are relational, for they call on an established connection with the petitioned, and remind the addressee of their obligation to investigate an injustice, provide redress and relieve the suffering of the writer. Because the right to petition is open to all citizens, they are 'a popular form of political participation' typically utilised to bring public attention to an issue and mobilise support for reform.[1] New Zealand's most well known petitionary actions of the colonial period are the women's suffrage petitions, culminating in the granting of universal suffrage on 19 September 1893.

Māori were early and active petitioners. Northern chiefs appealed to King William for protection and friendship in 1831, while several deputations seeking an audience with Queen Victoria carried petitions to England in the 1880s. At the same time Māori regularly addressed petitions to the governor. Such was the volume of petitionary actions, a dedicated government committee was established to review, investigate, and make recommendations on them in 1871. Many Māori women took the opportunity provided by this official forum to publicise issues of relevance to them, and to engage in political debate and discourse. This chapter examines the petitions sent by Māori women to the Native Affairs Committee during the final three decades of the nineteenth century, at a time when Māori communities and families faced a range of social and economic pressures from which they sought relief.

The Native Affairs Committee

Women were signatories to petitions before the Native Affairs Committee was established, such as Eruea Parirua's 1865 petition concerning a Crown Grant for land she claimed at Wairoa,[2] but it was the Native Affairs Committee that received the bulk of Māori petitions after 1871. In a small number of cases, Māori petitions were sometimes sent to other committees, such as Kenehuru (Eliza) Meurant's 1873 petition for an inquiry into the loss of her lands, which was investigated by the Public Petitions Committee, set up in 1865, and to whom Māori sometimes directed their appeals.[3]

Although routinely drawn upon as sources by historians and legal scholars, the petitions Māori sent to the Native Affairs Committee have not yet been considered as a *body of writing*. This contrasts with a lively and substantial scholarship dedicated to nineteenth-century indigenous petitioning across the British empire and the United States, which stresses the petition both as a form of writing and as a political act. Scholars argue for petitions as a vital source of information about indigenous engagement with the state. For some Australian historians, petitioning is perceived as 'a crucial means by which Aboriginal people made claims and sought redress'.[4] In a context where Aboriginal voices are rare in colonial archives, Australian scholars embrace petitions, regarding them as embodiments of Aboriginal aspirations and a window onto their perspectives on colonial power and authority in the mid-nineteenth century.[5] In Canada, Megan Harvey regards the petitions Coast Salish people sent to colonial and Canadian governments from 1864 to 1874 as protest texts. For Harvey, petitions demonstrate how the Coast Salish 'incorporated textual communication into their expanding vocabulary of political conduct'.[6] Ravi de Costa, drawing on examples of petitionary actions from Australia, New Zealand and North America, claims they 'document the productive links between the moral world in which indigenous people sought co-existence, the governing authority and that realm, and their own identities within it'.[7] That is, petitioners actively reminded colonial officials and imperial figures of their moral obligations, using the vocabulary and ideas of Christian humanitarianism. Emphasis on petitioning as a form of activism is not confined to the British colonies, for indigenous petitioning in the Spanish colonial world is also framed politically as 'a collective process of voicing a complaint'.[8]

Māori petitioning has also been characterised as a form of political protest based on collective action.[9] In contrast, this chapter examines the petitions directed to the Native Affairs Committee, which tended to be appeals from individuals, or families, rather than from large collective entities, although these were received at times. Guy Finny estimates that in the final three decades of the nineteenth century the committee received over 2300 petitions, 'representing tens of thousands of signatures', the majority from Māori, and mostly relating to the subject of land.[10] During those decades, the House of Representatives referred the petitions of around 145 Māori women to the committee. Between them, these 145 women were signatories to a total of 217 petitions investigated by the committee.[11] This number reflects the fact that some women were active petitioners, repeatedly sending appeals for investigation.

Māori women's petitioning peaked in the 1890s. This increased engagement with the state is partially explained by their participation in temperance and suffrage campaigns, in organisations such as the Women's Christian Temperance Union, as well as their own committees within the Kotahitanga movement, but it was also influenced by their lived experience. Women and their families felt the effects of dispossession through confiscation of land and the activities of the Native Land Court, and this was a catalyst for many individual women to petition for redress. Tania Rei identifies the final twenty years of the nineteenth century as two decades of crisis, and this is reflected in women's petitioning. In the ten years from 1886 to 1896, Rei found 'at least forty petitions concerning land issues were presented to Parliament signed by Māori women on their own account or on behalf of iwi'.[12]

Female petitioners, who ranged from chiefly women or large landholders, to widows, the elderly and the impoverished, actively sought to put their claims in writing, for they understood that petitions offered, 'a way of raising the profile of an issue, ensuring that matter was noted in the official records of Parliament and attracting the direct attention of lawmakers, Ministers and government officials.'[13] Common petitionary issues included requests for rehearings before the Native Land Court, payment disputes with the Crown and private sellers, succession issues, surveys and land frauds.[14] Although a large proportion of the 217 petitions from women were concerned with land, a small number petitioned for personal reasons, often relating to a slight against their reputation, or women used the petitionary process to bring attention to the actions of others. For instance, in her 1898 petition Metapere Rōpata: 'complains of having been turned out of her house at Waikanae by Wi Parata, her father.'[15]

Summaries of petitions presented, as well as the committee's decisions, can be accessed through the digitised corpus of the *Appendices to the Journal* of the House of Representatives (*AJHR*).¹⁶ A bilingual report of the committee was published annually in the *AJHR*. Unfortunately, these reports abridged the petitions, and only referred to the supplicants in the third person. For example, petition No. 309 was described as follows:

> No 309. – Petition of Maraea Taunakiwehe.
> PETITIONER complains that her name was omitted from the title to a block of land called Whakapoungakau Pukepoto, in which she alleges she has large claims. She asks that her name may be put in the title to that block.
>   I am directed to report as follows: That this petition should be referred to the Government for favourable consideration.
>   17th August, 1888.
>
> [TRANSLATION.]
>   No. 309. – Pukapuka-inoi a Maraea Taunakiwehe.
> E whai kupu ana te kai-pitihana mo te kapenga o tona ingoa i tetahi poraka whenua e karangatia ana ko Whakapoungakau Pukepoto. E ki ana hoki ia he nui ana take i roto i taua poraka. A e inoi ana ia inaianei kia whakaurua tona ingoa ki te karaati ia ki taua poraka.
>   Kua whakahaua ahau kia ki penei: Me tuku tenei pitihana ki te Kawanatanga kia whiriwhiria e ratou.
>   17 o Akuhata, 1888.¹⁷

The original petitions, held by Archives New Zealand in Wellington, were usually written in the first person, and are accompanied by other correspondence, including letters from the petitioner, their family or supporters, as well as government reports, memos and other documentation that reveals the official response. What these files also reveal is a substantial and rich body of Māori writing, including by women, yet to be investigated in any depth.

The petition: style, structure and tone

As a form of writing, petitions tended to adhere to a formal structure; they drew upon official vocabulary, deployed standard phrases and words, and were often deferential in tone. This likely reflects the fact that Māori made use of intermediaries to compose the texts, possibly relying on lawyers who were familiar with the format and formal language requirements. Maraea's petition (No. 309) follows the formal structure in many respects: it adheres to a standard format in its composition, beginning with an address to a higher authority, followed by a statement detailing the grievance, and closing with a request for relief or prayer for assistance. Unfortunately the original text, submitted in the Māori language, is missing, so we have only the official English-language translation:

Katikati
June 9th 1888.

To His Excellency the Governor and to the House of Representatives in Parliament Assembled.
Your Excellency and Sirs
Greeting

I wish to bring under your notice a serious injustice inflicted upon me in the consequence of the omission of my name from the title of a block of land at Rotorua called the Whakapoungakau Pukepoto block. I have large claims to that block and have no interests in any other lands. My claims through ancestry are admitted by all persons concerned and my name was put into the title at the original hearing of the block but when the subdivision was being made it was omitted and it was known that my name was left out by the Interpreters of the Court in arranging the names alphabetically. My two daughters who derived their claim from me were admitted into the title and my grandchildren, the children of Kaikaramu, who are some of the principal chiefs of the land as well as my great grandchildren were admitted as owners upon the same grounds while, I, the person through whom they claim am excluded.

For the reasons I have advanced I appeal to your Honourable House and to His Excellency the Governor to shew me some consideration after you have considered my letter and devise some means by which my name can be put into the title to my land when the Court sits to complete the subdivision. (The Court was adjourned owing to the Tarawera eruption Mr. Clarke being the presiding judge and it was then that my name was found to have been omitted).

May you be pleased to consider the injustice that has been done me living as I am upon the land of other persons at Katikati and send me a reply to my petition.

From your obedient Servant
(Sd.) Maraea Taunakiwehe.[18]

Translation and interpretation

Of the petitions submitted by Māori in the final three decades of the nineteenth century, the majority were composed in te reo, and then translated by a government official into English. While translators attempted to render te reo into English as accurately as possible, this could obscure the oral elements of the text. As the Abenaki scholar Lisa Brooks notes, while in format, style and rhetoric, petitions generated by indigenous peoples often followed European conventions, they also retained elements common to customary forms of orality such as metaphor and symbolism.[19] It is commonly acknowledged by print-culture scholars that, 'Māori often wrote as they spoke.'[20] This view is based on deep engagement with Māori letters and the corpus of Māori-language newspapers, but Māori-language petitions also share this characteristic. Because they were translating text from te reo Māori, which could draw upon metaphor and other oral forms, into the English language, government officials had to *translate*, and also *explain* the petitioner's meaning.[21]

English-language explanations, expressed in the formal standardised language of government, often failed to replicate the rhetorical and emotive power of a Māori-language petition. An extract from Rīpeka Turipona's 1884 petition concerning her land near Tauranga, which she claimed was sold without her consent, offers one illustration.

Ki a Paranihi Minita Whakahaere o te taha Maori me nga Mema katoa e noho ana i roto i te Paremete tena koutou

He Pitihana tena naku kia tirotirohia mai e koutou aku tono, I te Takiwa i tu ai a Hone Hianga hei Minita

Ka timata taku tuku atu i a aku Pitihana kaore i whakaaetia, mai, Muri iho ka tu ko te Roretana hei Minita ka tukua atu ano aku Pitihana kaore i whakaaetia mai

Muri iho katu ko Paraihe hei Minita katukua atu ano e au aku Pitihana kaore na aku i whakaaetia mai

Ko aua Pitihana aku i tukua atu e au i te tau	1878
I tukua atu e au aku Pitihana i te tau	1879
I tukua atu e au aku Pitihana i te tau	1880
I tukua atu e au aku Pitihana i te tau	1882
I tukua atu e au aku Pitihana i te tau	1883
I tukua atu e au aku Pitihana i te tau	1884

Kua rongo nei au ko koe te Minita whakahaere mo te taha Maori ka ahu atu taku Pitihana kia koe kia whakaritea mai e koe aku tono

[official translation]
This is a petition of mine for you to carefully consider my request. During the time that Mr Sheehan was Native Minister I commenced to forward my petitions, but there was no notice taken of them. After this Mr Rolleston was appointed Native Minister and I sent a petition to him also, but it met with the same fate. Then Mr Bryce was appointed to the same office but my petition met with the same result. I forwarded petitions during the years 1878, 1879, 1880, 1882, 1883 and 1884 and as I have now heard that you are the Minister for Native Affairs, I have sent a petition to you also to see what you will do for me.[22]

There are some slight differences in meaning between the Māori-language petition and the translation. For instance, Rīpeka uses the words 'kaore i whakaaetia, mai' which means 'were not agreed to', and she states this repeatedly, whereas the government translation renders it as 'that there was no notice taken'. Rīpeka also lists every petition she submitted by year, whereas the English translation folds this information into one sentence, effectively minimising the repeated and persistent attempts for redress. Rīpeka also asks that her requests 'kia whakaritea mai e koe' meaning 'to be sorted out by you', whereas the English translation suggests something far softer, removing her direct language and underplaying the urgency of her appeal, not to mention her emphasis on obligation and responsibility. As Jane Caplan notes, in moments where there were competing languages and differential levels of expertise in literacies 'this gap in comprehension or translation could be exploited by those who knew how to use it'.[23]

With a palpable sense of exasperation T. W. Lewis (Under Secretary, Native Department) wrote in a memo to the Native Minister: 'The writer applies to every succeeding Native Minister & nearly every year for land to which she says she is entitled at Tauranga.'[24] Rīpeka had no case, claimed Lewis. She did not give up though, putting into action a statement on her 1882 petition that only her death would stop her from writing. Her government file opens in 1877, and closes in 1899. During those years, Rīpeka's repeated attempts to obtain redress took place against the backdrop of personal loss. Over that time she gave birth to twelve children, none of whom survived infancy. While every petition was ignored or rejected, she was also grieving for a baby, and for the children who would have succeeded to her interests. Rīpeka died in 1905.[25] She is buried next to her husband, Anglican clergyman Wiremu Turipona (d. 1896) who actively supported his wife's land claim. They lie together in the grounds of Holy Trinity Church, Parawai, at the location where they actively served and supported their community.

Collaborative and collective writing

As a body of writing, the petitions might be formulaic, but the messages they contain are not. While they all share a common focus on dispossession, they also demonstrate the variety of ways in which Māori women sought to challenge the state, and the specific strategies they used to articulate their feelings. We can see this more clearly when we look at the original petitions and their associated documentation as the petitions slowly moved their way through official processes. Petitioners' strategies included the use of scribes, persistent and regular petitioning, and a willingness to address their claims to a variety of forums in writing, of which the petition is just one example.

Intermediaries played important roles in the petitioning process. Maraea's petition (No. 309), outlined earlier, was sent to the Native Department, who in turn traded memoranda with Native Land Court officials. Chief Judge William Gilbert Mair acknowledged that he could not 'understand why her name was omitted from the List unless her own people did it intentionally'. However, he asserted that the court was not at fault if the name had not been submitted, and that Maraea's daughter, Hēni Pore (Jane Foley), had been present and should have looked after her mother's interests. The officials debated by what means it might be possible to include her name on the Crown Grant, but given that the subdivision had not been completed, it seemed reasonable that this could be effected. Maraea (or Pihohau or Pikokau) of Te Arawa was an elderly woman; she had been taken captive by Ngāpuhi after the fall of Mokoia in 1823, 65 years earlier.[26] It is doubtful Maraea was familiar with the court's processes.

Nothing happened for several years, until in 1892 Maraea wrote to John Ballance, Premier and Native Minister, requesting that her case be revisited. Although the initial letter was written in Māori, it is clearly influenced in style by formal English correspondence. Maraea signs it with an 'X', so it is likely that her daughter, Hēni Pore, who had had an extensive formal education, composed it for her.

Katikati
Maehe 11 [1892]
To His Honourable the Native Minister

 E Pa, kua whaihonore au inaianei ki te tuhi atu kia koe, i runga i te mana kua whakawhiwhia atu kia koe, no kona ka tukua atu tenei tono aku kia koe hei ata hurihuri mau, notemea kua pa tetehi mate nui noa atu kia hau, ko taku mate tenei, kahore <u>aku</u> <u>whenua</u> e noho nei au i te ao marama. Ko nga whenua o aku tupuna i tika nei kia taka mai kia ahau, he maha, he nui atu hoki, a i runga i nga whakahaere he a te Kooti Whenua Maori, a etehi tangata hoki o te iwi, ka kore atu ena whenua ia hau, ko nga whenua e tika kia taka mai kia hau kei Rotorua. I mahi nui ano taku tamahine a Heni Pore (Jane Foley) ki te whakahaere i taku take, a he roa te taima kahore i tu i te Kooti. Na he tono tenei naku kia koe, kia pai mai koe ki te homai e tetehi whenua moku, he wahine maori hoki au kua kaumatuatia a ko au ano ki te rapu oranga moku i runga i te whenua o te tangata ke, heoi na mau e huri huri mai taku tono.

 Na to pononga   her
  Na Maraea X Taunakiwehe
     mark

Kaituhi titiro hoki Heni Pore K. Raihana
a ka whakarite nei au i taku tamahine ia Heni Pore hei kaiwhakahaere maku i runga i tenei take e mau iho nei mo a muri ake nei.
    her
  Maraea X Taunakiwehe
    mark
Kaituhi Kaititiro hoki
Heni Pore Kai Whakamaori Raihanatia
 Jane Foley Licensed Interpreter.

[official translation]
Katikati
March 11th. 1892
The Hon
    The Native Minister

Sir,
    I have the honor to write to you under the 'mana' of the office you hold. I submit this, my application for your careful consideration. A serious 'mate' has come upon me, that is to say, I have no land in this world. My father possessed much land to which I had the right to succeed. Through the wrong dealing of the court however and of some of the people these lands passed from me. The lands which should fall to me by right are at Rotorua. My daughter, Jane Foley, did much in the conduct of my claim and after a long time the court (?disallowed) it.

    This is an application of mine requesting that you will be pleased to grant me a piece of land. I am a Maori woman and am now getting very old and I work for my own living on land that does not belong to me. Do you carefully consider my application.

    From Your Humble Servant
        her
    Maraea   X   Taunakiwehe
        mark

Witness –
    Heni Pore Licenced Interpreter
I hereby appoint my daughter Heni Pore to act as Kai-whakahaere for the above 'take'.
        her
    Maraea   X   Taunakiwehe
        mark
Witness J. Foley – Licensed Interpreter.[27]

Also in Maraea's file is a letter from her daughter arguing that her mother's case fell under the provisions of section 13 of the Native Land Court Amendment Act 1889. This section provided a process by which a person could claim 'that his interest has been prejudicially affected by any error or omission committed or made in any decision or order of the Court', and allowing the Chief Judge to make an order 'for the purpose of remedying such error or omission', so long as the existing owners had not already sold, leased, mortgaged or otherwise legally bound the land.[28] Judge H. G. Seth-Smith reported back to the Native Department that Judge J. A. Wilson had 'found & reported that the omission of her name was intentional and not the result of any error or omission within the meaning of the section above referred to[.] The application was accordingly dismissed.' The Acting Under Secretary W. J. Morpeth recommended the Native Minister reply that, 'you do not see that you can do anything for her.'

Maraea's employment of an intermediary to help compose her text marks the petition as a collaborative act, or what Martyn Lyons describes as a form of 'delegated writing'.[29] It is often difficult to uncover who these scribes and intermediaries were, but they played a key role in assisting Māori to engage with the colonial system. As Bradford Haami notes, many tribal groups had scribes who attended courts, especially the Native Land Court, and made a written record of the proceedings, so it is not unreasonable to suggest that they may have composed petitions.[30] Colonialism gave people opportunities, offering social and economic mobility to a group of people who supported and fostered petitioning as scribes, interpreters and lawyers, both Māori and Pākehā, for land loss was such a palpable issue within Māori society.[31] Scribes included women; daughters wrote petitions for their mothers, for example, Hēni Pore, a well educated woman, who in her role as a licensed interpreter became familiar with the formal language of government and with legal proceedings, and developed an understanding of the complexities of nineteenth-century native land legislation. Hēni Pore is not the only example. Ruiha Teira petitioned on behalf of her mother in 1881, and Mereana also campaigned in writing for her mother, Jane Maria Phillips.

Letters as petitions

Petitions were the product not only of several hands, but also many voices. In some instances, senior women spoke for their kin, wider community or hapū, expressing the collective view by leading a petitionary appeal. A good example comes from Ngāi Tahu, who hold mana whenua for the South Island, excluding the very north of the island. Ngāi Tahu's experience of land loss is quite different to that of tribes in the North Island where the government, and then settlers, purchased blocks of various sizes, often in a piecemeal fashion. Ngāi Tahu were dispossessed of their territory through a series of ten land sales between 1844 and 1864; apart from the three Banks Peninsula purchases, the blocks sold were massive in scale. Kemp's Purchase (1848) was the largest, incorporating most of Canterbury and Otago, totalling about 20 million acres (over 800,000 hectares), or almost a third of the whole country, for £2000, amounting to about 41.7 acres for every penny received. Henry Tacy Kemp, the government's purchasing officer, among other pledges, had promised Ngāi Tahu ample reserves, but Walter Mantell, who was given the responsibility to draw these up, allowed only 6,359 acres, later admitting that, 'My rule, in calculating what quantity of land I would give the Natives, was that I allowed ten acres to each man, woman, and child. . . . In making the allowance I tried to allow as little as the Natives would agree to take.'[32] By the last decades of the nineteenth century the lack of a sufficient land base had resulted in economic marginalisation and impoverishment for the tribe.

Ngāi Tahu leaders began to pursue their kerēme (claim) in 1871, regularly petitioning for the land sales to be investigated. Well known petitioners include John Tōpi Pātuki, H. K. Taiaroa and Horomona Pōhio, but women were equally involved in the political process, leading petitionary actions and also giving evidence to any resulting commissions of enquiry. Guy Finny argues that because the majority of land-related petitions heard by the Native Affairs Committee (around 85 per cent) concerned private grievances, it was, 'predominately a body at which to direct personal grievances rather than a body in which to direct political protest.'[33] However, Ngāi Tahu leaders used petitions to remind colonial officials of the promises made under Kemp's Purchase and the obligations established by that agreement, which the Crown had failed to address.[34]

The Treaty of Waitangi did not enter the vocabulary of Ngāi Tahu petitions. Instead, their appeals were based on the promises made under Kemp's Deed, and many Ngāi Tahu whānau pursued local claims on this basis. In 1893 Pīpī Kōruarua wrote to Hōri Kerei Taiaroa, Member of the House of Representatives (MHR), Ngāi Tahu chief and parliamentary representative for South Island Māori, about littoral land at Te Waihora (Lake Ellesmere):

Taumutu
Hanuere 16
Kia Hori Kerei Taiaroa
    eta tena koe[.]
Kia mohio mai koe e mate noku me oku hoa koia au i tuhi atu ai mau etuhituhi

ki te Kawanatanga kia whakatapua to matou kaika ara te pa o waikakahi i te taha hau whakarua o te Roto o Waihora. Ko tenei pa, ko Waikakahi e pa tawhito ano. i te tau 1844 i te hoko a te Keepa i te poraka ongaitahu i reira ano a matou e noho ana me o matou whare e tu ana[.] i reira matou i te wa o matara. Ki taku mohio ko Tukupane, Ko tamakeke: ko ipika kote hikawera me tahi atu i reira e noho ana[.] e inoi ana au kia tono koe kia Rahuitia e te Kawana mo matou[.]
Heoi ano naku
na pipi Koruarua
metahi atu

[official translation]
Taumutu
January 16. 1893.
To
Hori Kerei Taiaroa

    Sir, greeting[.] Know you, it is because I and my friends are not well that I write to you. Will you then write to the Government and ask them to have our 'kainga' that is the 'Pa' at Waikakahi on the North East side of the Waihora Lake set apart for us. It is an old pa and was in our occupation and we had houses standing there in the year 1844, when Mr Kemp affected the purchase of the Ngaitahu Block. We were occupying it in Mr Mantell's time, and I think too that Tukupane, Tamakeke, Ipika, Te Hikawera and others were living there. I request you to move that it is reserved by the Governor for us.
Sufficient
Pipi Koruarua &rs[35]

Taiaroa put their request to Alfred Cadman, Minister of Native Affairs, adding: 'I know for a fact that many applications have been made for that Pa, my impression was that it had already been set apart.' The Native Department referred the matter to Judge Alexander Mackay, who was unsure of its location. He thought that Pīpī was wrong about it being inhabited, and that it likely 'had been sold to Europeans long since'.[36] The following year Pīpī Kōruarua and Rōra Tāwhā petitioned Parliament.

Taumutu
8th Aug 1894.
To the Honorable the Speaker and Members of the Legislative Council.

We your Petitioners are Native women living at Wairewa and Taumutu.

There is a Pah called Waikakahi situate on the Eastern side of Waihora Lake in the Provincial District of Canterbury.

Before the arrival of Europeans in this colony the Waikakahi Pa and its adjacent fern grounds and eel weirs were in the occupation of our Ancestors.

T[sic] In the year 1848 your petitioners heard of Mr Kemp who is said to have negotiated the purchase of the Ngaitahu land.

Your petitioners heard at that time that the natives were to retain their Pas and kaingas where they lived. Your petitioners knew this to apply to this particular Pa when Mr Mantell was Commissioner.

Your Petitioners were living there at that time and it was not until your Petitioners married that one went to live at Taumutu and the other at Wairewa. We did not know that our birthplace had been taken by the Govt.

It was not until years afterwards that we knew the Govt had taken Waikakahi Pa.

One of your Petitioners spoke to Mr Alex Mackay Commissioner about Waikakahi Pa but has not received an answer.

Your Petitioners also wrote to the Government last year about the matter and were told that the Waikakahi Pa had been made a reserve for school purposes.

We your Petitioners pray that our Pah and sacred places and eel fisheries and fern workings may be returned to us, or such other relief granted to us as your Honourable D[sic] Council may consider just and equitable.

And your petitioners will ever pray
  -Rew- Pipi Koruarua
   Rora Hupariki Tawha[37]

The Native Affairs Committee requested more information from the government's officers. The Superintendent of the Canterbury Province had set the area aside as a reserve in 1873, but as the paperwork was not at hand little else was known. The women received a letter from C. J. A. Haselden, the Under Secretary for the Justice Department. Three years later they dictated a letter in reply, reactivating their appeal.

Taumutu 16 Oketopa 1897
Ki te Hon Minita Maori
    Tena koe

Kote pukapuka a Te Hekeretini hekeretari o te tari onga Ture ote 2 Nohema 1894 morunga i ta maua pukapuka inoi mo to maua kainga mo te Pa o Waikakahi[.] E tono ana maua kia whakahokia mai kia maua[.] Apiti ki a maua mahinga kai[.]

Kua rongo maua kua hoatu taua pa mo nga mahi kura, me nga mahinga kai tetahi kua hokona ranei, ki nga Pakeha. he mea pai kia whakahokia mai kia maua te kainga tuturu o maua me o maua matua[.] He mate nui rawa tenei no maua[.] Kaore nei maua i hoko i to maua Pa meo maua kainga. Kei ta maua pukapuka tuatahi nga Take o ta maua inoi. Kaore maua i te mohio kite haere kite Tari Komihana ote Karauna i Otautahi[.] ki to maua mohio kataea ano e H. K. Taiaroa te whakaatu te Pa o Waikakahi, i runga i tetahi maapi[.] Ka pai maua kia ohoro tenei mate nui o maua te whakaoti[.]

    Na o korua Pononga
    na Rora Tawha
    Na Pipe Koruarua X
      Tona tohu

[official translation]
Taumutu
October 16th 1897
The Honble Native Minister

Greeting. With reference to the letter from Mr Haselden Under Secretary for the Justice Department and dated the 2nd of November 1894 on the subject of our letter making application in respect of our 'kainga' at the Pa at Waikakahi that we asked be returned to us with our cultivations we have now heard that that 'pa' has been given for school purposes and the cultivations [illegible] or that it has been sold to Pakehas[.] it would be a proper thing to give back (to us) what are our permanent 'kaingas' and which belonged to our parents. This is a very grievous calamity to us because we never sold our 'Pa' & our cultivations. the grounds of our appeal are set forth in our first letter. We do not know we should go to the Commissioner of Crown Lands at Christ Church in this matter. We feel sure that H. K. Taiaroa could indicate the Waikakahi Pa on the plan map. We would be pleased if this great grievance of ours will be speedily settled.
From your humble servants

From Rora Tawha
    Pipe Koruarua X mark[38]

Officials undertook further investigations. The Chief Surveyor asked J. E. March, Superintendent of Village Settlements – responsible for new Pākehā settlements – to enquire into the matter. He spoke to George Robinson, 'a very old resident' who had 'a slight knowledge of the Pa', which he believed local Māori had abandoned thirty years earlier. Although March had been unable to meet the women, he dismissed them as unreliable sources of information, stating 'it is doubtful if either can give any definite information on the subject'.[39]

The problem for officials was that they could not be sure exactly where the pā had been sited. The women state that they resided at the pā in the 1840s when Mantell was Commissioner. Even if they had been living there in the 1860s when, according to Robinson, Māori abandoned it, they should have been able to point out its location. But it appears that there was no real effort to get them there to do so. Instead, officials dismissed the women's knowledge preferring to rely on an archive that did not contain all the information required. The last memorandum attached to this file states that the Canterbury Superintendent had made a reserve but 'through an oversight it was afterwards sold, and the Government afterwards compensated the Natives by making a smaller reserve in the same locality and all offering them a large area elsewhere', and, 'It will very probably be found that the site of the old pa is private property'.[40] It is therefore unlikely that they were successful in their claim.

Pīpī and Rōra exemplify how letter writing was often an important precursor to petitioning. Letters had the advantage of operating at a more personal level, being almost as good as a private interview. Māori MHRs as well as the Native Minister received letters from Māori on a regular basis containing appeals for assistance, redress, or relief. Miriama Huriwai, of Ngāi Tahu, appealed for assistance in 1891.

Kanuihitaone Hurae 30 1891
Ki a Hone Keepamana minita Maori tena koe
Ko au ko Huri Wai e Wahine no te iwi o ngaitahu i noho ki Te Waponamu [sic]
    No oku take katoa iroto o nga wenua o ngaitahu kua maua e te
Kawanantanga me te kore te tahi moni paku nei hei aroha kiau kua
momona te iwi pakeha e noho ana i runga i te oneone i heke nei nga toto oku
tipuna i runga i te ringa kaha ko au kei konei e noho mate ana i te kai kore i

te weruweru kore mo oku tau nga 78 nui atu ranei toku ruruhi metoku mate kai toku haere kirikore toku mate i te hau aitu pai atu kia au me hemea i horo iho ki runga ia au nga hiwi me ngapuke pai atu ho ki mehemea i tahupokia mai au e nga waipuke o tenei o o [sic] penei
Kua kore au e kite i tenei mate
E koro e te minita maori mete kawanatanga e inoi tenei na ku kia tau mai ta koutou manakitanga ki runga i to koutou pononga kamutu ia[.]
    Na Miriama Huriwai Kaipara

Kia Hone Keepamana minita maori kia ora koe mate atua koe e tiaki waitohua

[official translation]
                Canvastown
                July 30th, 1891
To Hon. Mr Cadman
   Native Minister
     Greeting

I, Huriwai, am a woman of the Ngaitahu tribe resident in the South Island. All my interests in the land of the Ngaitahu have been seized by the Government without the payment to me of even the smallest sum of money as an equivalent for them. Europeans are living in affluence upon the lands for which the blood of my ancestors was shed, while I am in want of sufficient food and clothing. Better would it have been for me had the mountains and hills fallen on me or that I had been carried away by the floods, then I would not have been reduced to my present state of poverty.

    Friend, the Native Minister and the Government, I appeal to you to show your servant some consideration.
Ended from
   Sgd. Miriama Huriwai Kaipara[41]

    The official translation collapses some sentences together and excludes some key details. For instance, in the Māori-language petition Miriama specifies she is 78 years of age, and emphasises her suffering from want of warm clothes and food. Repetition of key words and phrases has an important role to play in petitionary appeals, directing emphasis to the supplicants' dire situation. Miriama's letter speaks repeatedly of suffering, but this word does not appear in the official translation. She also asks the minister and government to show 'aroha' or compassion for her, an elderly woman. In phrasing and style, Miriama's letter looks very similar to a formal petition.

In content, Miriama's letter is also political in nature, for she holds the Government responsible for her landlessness and poverty. Because letters are often interpreted as largely personal documents strongly associated with women, they have tended to be discounted as political documents. Jessica Horton, writing about Australian Aboriginal women, argues that their letters are a form of political writing.[42] Normally, says Horton, women's letters have been used by scholars to demonstrate resistance, while men 'critique' and are therefore politically active.[43] Given that Māori women's petitions were supplemented or preceded by 'letters of complaint that contain long, detailed, and original narratives', their petitions should be considered within the context of a longer tradition of written protest and critique of the state.[44]

The fate of petitions

As Pīpī and Rōra's efforts demonstrate, a petition could emerge from letter writing campaigns directed at a wide range of officials, that aimed to draw attention to an injustice. Individuals or collectives often turned to petitioning once all other avenues for redress had been exhausted. Many would not have their cases resolved for decades. So while petitioning was a tool available to assert claims, or to lodge a protest, it relied upon a public sphere willing to listen, investigate and act upon their prayers or protests. The phrase 'I will not desist from writing to you', which provides this chapter with its title, comes from Rīpeka Turipona, who campaigned for two decades to gain redress, without success.

While petitions are exciting sources for gaining access to indigenous perspectives and responses to colonialism, this has to be considered alongside the official responses. The state could ignore a protest, and dismiss the recommendations of the Native Affairs Committee, meaning it was up to the petitioner to keep the issue alive. Gaining government interest in one's case often required persistence on behalf of the petitioner, and also the resources to travel to Wellington to give evidence before the committee. Many petitions that dragged on for decades related to contested decisions of courts in the 1870s and 1880s, and these often centred on the exclusion of individuals from land grants. If individuals were not present when either the Compensation Court or the Native Land Court sat, it was an uphill battle to gain justice.

In 1878 Te Korowhiti Tuataka (Mrs Douglas) petitioned Parliament about her exclusion from a grant of land, previously confiscated, investigated, and returned to its original owners by a compensation court. Her petition, in which she claimed to be a principal owner, was sent to the Native Affairs Committee, which took evidence from witnesses in September 1878. The petition and the minutes of evidence were laid before the House, and subsequently published in the *AJHR*.

> Petition.
> To the Speaker and Members of the House of Representatives assembled at Wellington.
> THE PETITION OF TE KOROWHITI TUATAKA, IN WHICH SHE PRAYS THE ATTENTION OF THE HOUSE OF REPRESENTATIVES TO THE MATTERS HEREINAFTER SET FORTH,
>
> Sheweth,–
> That my lands Pukepoto, Ohauiti, and Te Karai belonged to persons deceased, of whom I am the true representative.
> 2. That these lands were confiscated by the Government and subsequently returned to their original owners, but about that time the principal owner died, and the land fell to me and to my younger sisters (or cousins).
> 3. That Mr. Henry Clarke, Commissioner, chose the persons whose names were to be in the grant for that land. My younger sisters' (or cousins') names were inserted, and mine was left out, notwithstanding that all the Maoris said that I was the principal owner. He (Mr. Clarke) paid no heed to that.
> 4. That, subsequently, the said land was leased to Captain Morris, M.H.R., and then sold, and he is now seeking to have the sale ratified by the Government.
> 5. That Mr. Clarke assisted Captain Morris in obtaining the said land.
> 6. That Captain Morris told my husband, Edward Douglas, that he heard all the Natives admit that I was the principal owner of the said land.
> 7. That I made an application to Mr Fenton (Chief Judge, Native Land Court), in which I asked him to explain how the land stood and he replied that it had not been passed through the Native Land Court.
> 8. That I have made many applications to the Government for redress for my grievance suffered at the hands of Government Office, but nothing has been done.
> Your petitioner therefore prays your Honorable House to take her causes of complaint, as above stated, into your consideration, and afford such relief as to you may seem fit. And your petitioner will ever pray:
> TE KOROWHITI (her x mark) TUATAKA,

Witness : – E. Douglas. Wife of E. Douglas, Ferryman, Te Wairoa. Wairoa, 19th July, 1878.[45]

According to H. T. Clarke, Major Mair was Commissioner in 1869 when the land was investigated. Clarke had taken over in 1871, and in the following year Te Korowhiti Tuataka and her Pākehā husband Edward Douglas visited Clarke's office to discuss her claims. In evidence to the Committee, she stated:

When we went to Mr. Clarke's office we found there Hamiora Tu and others. I do not remember who the others were; I do not know them. We found Hamiora Tu and his friends engaged with Mr. Clarke on some business of their own. We had been there about half an hour waiting, when Hamiora Tu said to Mr. Clarke, 'We will defer our business for the present, because it will take a very long time.' Mr. Clarke agreed to that, and then he asked my husband some questions, which I did not catch, because I was not acquainted with the English language. When he finished talking to my husband in English, he turned to me and said, 'What have you come to talk about?' and I said, 'I have come to talk about the land of my father.' He said, 'What land do you refer to?' I said, 'Pukepoto and Ohauiti.' He said, 'It won't do; you are too late for the Court. Where were you when the Court sat?' I said I was at Mercury Bay at that time. I said to him, 'Knowing, as you did, that the Court was going to sit, why did you not send me a letter informing me of it?' He said, 'Well, it is too late.' He told me to go away that the talk was over about these lands. That is all I have to say about that interview.
183. [The Chairman.] When he told you you were too late, did he admit your claim or deny it?— *He admitted my claim, but told me I was too late.*
184. He said that he was aware you had a claim I should like you to be specially distinct upon that point —*Mr. Clarke admitted that I had a claim, but told me I was too late.*[46]

When testifying, Clarke's memory became decidedly weak. He said, 'I have a very indistinct remembrance of a woman who had married a European coming to see me, and I suggested to her the proper time for her to appear was when the case was opened.' Although he claimed that he had printed notices circulated amongst Tauranga Māori, he had not advertised hearings in newspapers, as would have been done if it had been a Native Land Court case.[47]

The committee's report considered that 'the non-insertion of the petitioner's name in the grant arose probably partly through the forgetfulness of her own people'. However, Te Korowhiti's relatives may have left her name off on purpose. Her husband, Edward Douglas, had fought in engagements during the New Zealand wars, including against Ngāi Te Rangi at the battle of Gate Pā.[48] This may well have been the reason her relatives may not have seen to Te Korowhiti Tuataka's inclusion in the Compensation Court award. It is clear from her testimony that she had a valid claim, although she appears inexperienced, and unfamiliar with the legal processes she was dealing with. In the end the committee determined that no unlawful acts had taken place, but as 'the petitioner had some right to have her name inserted in the grant', it recommended another Commission of Enquiry.[49] It appears the committee's recommendation was not acted upon, for she continued to petition the House on an annual basis, sometimes several times a year. The emotional cost and burden of having to persistently pursue her land rights was belatedly recognised by the committee in its 1890 report on yet another one of her petitions. Her regular petitionary actions caused them to recommend the government, 'inquire as to whether the Native Affairs Committee's reports upon previous petitions in this matter have received due attention, as the restlessness of the evidence and reports, extending over a period of ten years, suggests an indifference that must be very distressing to the petitioner.'[50]

Petitioners needed to be persistent for their cases often wound their way through the political process slowly, and it was incumbent upon the individual concerned to keep their appeal alive in the minds of officials. Cases could take decades to be resolved to the satisfaction of the petitioner, as was the case with Emily Buckworth (Emeri Maraea Mautaranui, see chapter 3). The government file on the case begins in 1865, with a declaration from Emily's aunt, Elizabeth Fulloon, stating that she 'lived with and was dependent upon my late brother James Fulloon who was murdered by Natives on the East Coast of New Zealand on or about the twenty second day of July 1865'.[51] Several decades later, in August 1891, Emily submitted the following petition:

> To the Hon.
> The House of
> In Parliament assembled
> Wellington
> The humble petition of
> Emily Maria Fulloon sheweth.
> That on May 16th 1865 my father James Fulloon, Govt Agent was murdered by Maoris

at Whakatane, while on board the Govt Cutter 'Kate' anchored off Whakatane Heads, I Emily Maria Fulloon being at that time 10 months old. I was born on the 26th July 1864.

My father James Fulloon was a native of Whakatane, & had large claims to land in the District by being closely related to Te Mautaranui a chief of the Ngatiawa and Urewera tribes. My relationship to the said James Fulloon can be proved by all old Maoris here and by subsequent Land Courts held here & in which I as his child have always been admitted.

The Govt in confiscating the land on the East Coast confiscated the greater part of the land in which James Fulloon had claims and in awarding lands at the Confiscation Courts held here afterward none was awarded to James Fulloon or his wife & child.

Neither myself or my mother have ever received any monetary or landed assistance from the Govt.

Wherefore your petitioner humbly prays that your Hon. House will compensate me to the extent of £500 for the loss I have sustained thro the confiscation of my fathers lands and for his murder by Natives here while in the employ of the Government. There is no land in this District now owned by the Govt of equal value to the land confiscated.

I may state that I am James Fulloon's only child.

    Mrs Buckworth
      nee Emily Maria Fulloon
Maori name Maraea Te Mautaranui
Whakatane
  Bay of Plenty
    15th Aug 91[52]

Petition No. 611 was sent to the Native Affairs Committee, which recommended it be, 'referred to the Government for favourable consideration.'[53] Emily's petition was not, however, favourably received, causing her to write a letter to the Native Minister on the matter in December 1891. In style, the handwriting in the letter is different to the August 1891 petition, which suggests that Emily used a lawyer to compose the petition. Her letter, written in a steady and elegant hand, requested further consideration, and provides further evidence that petitions were part of a range of writing strategies and forums for gaining redress which Māori used regularly and persistently. Letter writing offered the petitioner another opportunity to lay out their case, which is what Emily proceeded to do, emphasising the death of her father while in government service as a basis for compensation, which she sought in the form of the resolution of her land claim:

> Whakatane 5th December 1891
>
> To The Honourable
>   The Native Minister
>   Wellington
>
> Sir
>
> I have just received a letter from Wellington dated 21st November, stating that under your instructions, my Petition to the Government has been rejected. I only spoke to you about my claim at Opotiki on the 20th November; I hardly think this letter can have been written with your knowledge on the 21st November.
>
> I will now give you full particulars of my case as follows: –
> In the year 1865 my father James Fulloon, Government Agent, arrived at Whakatane in the Government vessel 'Kate' he was sent to Whakatane to raise a Native Contingent; he was murdered while asleep on board the vessel. My father had large claims to land at Whakatane as he was closely related to Te Mautaranui, an influential chief (now dead) of the Urewera and Ngatiawa tribes. At the time of my father's death I was only a few months old and was brought by my mother on the Government steamer 'Luna' to my father's funeral. The Natives took my mother & shewed her all the lands to which I was entitled to, being the only child of Hemi Te Mautaranui (James Fulloon). My mother then returned with me to Auckland and afterwards married Mr George Brown, Native Interpreter. Some years after my father's death the lands on the East Coast were confiscated, amongst other lands a good deal of that to which my father was entitled.
>
> A Court of Compensation was held at Whakatane of which I think my mother knew nothing, and, at which my aunt Elizabeth Fulloon was awarded 50 acres of arable land here also some sections in the township. I may state that the natives here tell me they knew nothing about Elizabeth Fulloon having been awarded this land & further had they known so, they would have objected as I, as his only child had prior claims to his lands. I have been often asked why I was not receiving a pension from the Government, being the only child of a Government official, killed while serving the Government.
>
> You asked me why I have not put in this claim before, as a girl I did not think of these things, as I was living with my mother, and had no wants.

I am now married and have several children and I think of them. I come back to live at my native place, and find the lands once owned by my father, now owned by Europeans, owing to his lands being confiscated, or awarded to others who have no claim to them. I think when you have read this, you will agree that I have a very strong claim on the Government, not only on the account of the confiscation of my father's lands, but also as the only child of a Government official, killed while on Government Service. I think the reason given in the letter from Wellington for rejecting my claims, viz, that Elizabeth Fulloon was compensated, a very poor one, and the letter I think cannot have been written by your direction, if so, I hope after reading these particulars of my case, you will reconsider your decision.
In conclusion, in putting aside my just claim, as the child of a Government Servant killed while on Public Service, I would only ask that a portion of my ancestral lands be returned to me.

> *I am*
> *Your most obedient Servant*
> *Mrs M. Buckworth*
> *neé Maria Fulloon*

Although written with composure and assurance, the letter had little effect, for it was followed by a second petition, dated 23 August 1892, the content of which followed closely the first petition, but included further details drawn from Emily's December letter to the Native Minister.

The Hon. The House of Representatives
    Wellington
In Parliament Assembled.
    The humble petition of Emily Maria Fulloon showeth.
    That on May 16th 1865 James Fulloon, Government Agent was murdered by the Natives while asleep on board the Government Cutter 'Kate' anchored off the Whakatane Heads.
    My father had been sent to Whakatane by the Government for the purpose of raising a Native Contingent.
    I was at that time about 10 months old. I was born on the 26th July 1864.
    My father James Fulloon was a native of Whakatane, and had large claims to land in the Whakatane District being closely related to Te Mautaranui a leading chief of the Ngatiawa and Urewera Tribes.
    My relationship to the said James Fulloon can be proved by all old Maoris still

alive here, and by subsequent land courts held here, at which my claims as his child, to any lands in which he was interested, have always been admitted.

The Govt. in confiscating the Maori lands on the East Coast confiscated the greater parts of the land in the immediate neighbourhood of Whakatane in which my father held large interests the said lands being owned by the Ngatiawa and Urewera Tribes as the records of the Native Land Courts will show; and in awarding lands at the Compensation Court afterwards held here, none was awarded to James Fulloon's wife and child. Neither my mother or myself have ever received any monetary or landed assistance from the Government.

The old European residents here always thought I was receiving a Pension from the Government and when told I had never received any assistance of any sort I was strongly advised to bring my case before the Government, not only on account of being James Fulloon's child, but also to try and get some compensation for the loss of my fathers lands through confiscation, the said lands being now the most valuable in the District.

Wherefore your Petitioner humbly prays that your Hon. House will compensate me to the extent of £500 for the loss I have sustained thro the confiscation of my father's lands and for his death while in the service of the Government.

Mrs C. Buckworth
neé Emily Maria Fulloon
Maori name Maraea Te Mautaranui
Whakatane 23rd August 1892[54]

Four months later, Emily again wrote to the Native Minister seeking information on the progress of her 1892 petition for: 'I have not heard anything about it.'[55] In March 1893, Native Minister Cadman received an alarming letter claiming Emily was inciting local Māori against the government surveyors. Its author, Oliver Creagh, selectively quoted from a letter he claimed to have received from Emily requesting he pass on her suggestion that she was willing to use her influence to quell resistance at Rūātoki if the Native Minister promised to get her petition recognised by the Government. Cadman immediately telegraphed Creagh to, 'Inform Mrs Buckworth that Government will make no such promise but proceedings will be taken against her if it can hereafter be shewn that she has incited the Natives in any way to break the law by stopping the survey.'[56]

Offended by the words and tone of the telegram, Emily wrote a long and angry letter to Cadman.

'I will not desist from writing to you': Māori Women's Petitions

Whakatane

To the Native Minister, Wellington.

Sir,

From the tenor of a telegram which Mr O.M. Creagh, surveyor, showed me to-day, from yourself, stating that if I incited the Uriwera [sic] Natives to obstruct the 'Survey on which Mr Creagh is engaged I should be arrested' I think you must have been misinformed by Mr Creagh as to what I have done in this matter. Some few days ago in course of conversation with Mr Creagh he mentioned to me that he had spoken to you when in Auckland about my influence and mana in the Uriwera [sic] country, and he told us you had quite altered your opinion with regard to my Petition to the Government as you had been told personally that I lost no land by my father's death, and that he was of opinion that the Government would reconsider their decision with regard to my petition. The following day I sent a letter to Mr Creagh of which I enclose a copy. Mr Creagh told me a few days afterwards that he had sent a telegram to you stating what I had said in my letter to him, and I was very much surprised and annoyed when Mr Creagh showed me your reply to his telegram which almost states that I was inciting Natives to oppose the survey.

On the morning of Monday 6th inst. which was the day on which the Natives were to decide whether or not they would allow the survey to proceed I went to the meeting expecting to see Mr Creagh and learn what was his reply from you to his telegram. No reply had come. I may tell you, and I think Mr Creagh can tell you the same, that one word from me would have decided whether the survey should proceed or not. Not having a reply from you through Mr Creagh and considering the way I have been treated with regard to my Petition, which for two Sessions has been favourably recommended to the Government, I made up my mind to say nothing, for or against the survey, as I did not wish to see trouble amongst my people, but I told the Natives to use their own judgment. I have written this letter, as I wish you to thoroughly understand I have in no way incited the Natives to stop this survey; and I should feel obliged if you would kindly send me a copy of the telegram Mr Creagh sent to you, as I feel you have been misinformed, or otherwise you would not have worded your telegram in the way you did.

I have the honour to be,
Yours faithfully,
M. Buckworth
Maraea Te Mautaranui, Whakatane, March 8 1893.

> Enclosure.
> Copy of my letter to Mr Creagh
>
> Dear Mr Creagh,
> Will you on behalf of Mr Cadman give me in writing a promise that my Petition to the Government shall be recognized, if I come up to Ruatoki on Monday and use my influence with the Natives to allow this survey to proceed without any further trouble. The majority of the Natives who are now against the survey proceeding are my near relations. I should like a reply to this before Monday in writing or perhaps it would be better for you to come and see me. After hearing what Mr Cadman said to you, when you spoke to him, re my Petition to the Government, I would accept a written promise from you on his behalf that the recommendations of my Petition by the Native Affairs Committee to the Government be complied with.

Cadman had received false information from Creagh, who claimed, 'Mrs Buckworth is the chief instigator in opposition. Reported she advised Natives cut telegraph wires if disturbance occurs.'[57]

Emily wrote again on 4 October 1895, this time directing her letter to the Premier Richard Seddon. She sought an answer to her petition, and asked: 'what compensation I may look for and that the same may be granted as soon as possible.'[58] She received a third rejection of her claim for compensation.[59] The final document in her file dates to February 1911, and is Emily's response to a letter from T. W. Fisher, Under Secretary of the Native Department, concerning the final settlement of her claim. With an air of resignation she responded:

> I suppose as this is the best the Government intend to do for me I must accept the amount offered, although it has cost me nearly £200 in expenses during the last 22 years to prove my claim.[60]

Jane Maria Phillips (Ngāti Ruanui) also fought for compensation over several decades. Unlike Emily Buckworth, Jane had support from her family. Born at the Bay of Islands to Kōtiro Hinerangi and Alexander Grey, Jane's two sisters left an imprint on the public imagination and the archival record. Her sister Sophia gained fame as a guide at Rotorua's thermal district, and bore witness to the devastation of the 1886 Tarawera eruption.[61] Another sibling was Lucy Lord, also known as Takiora Dalton, who has left behind a significant documentary trail, having corresponded regularly with Donald McLean during the 1870s about her claims to land in Taranaki (see chapter 4). Jane's petition for redress dates back to the confiscation of land from 'rebels' in Taranaki, specifically to ancestral land called Pōnui to which her sister Lucy Lord had unsuccessfully sought to gain title. As West Coast Commissioner, William Fox had investigated and dismissed Lucy's claim in the 1880s. Nevertheless, Jane continued her sister's claim, staking her rights to the land as Lucy's successor.[62]

> *The Honourable the Speaker, and Members of the House of Representatives of the Colony of New Zealand, in Parliament assembled.*
> *Sir and Gentlemen,*
> *This the petition of Jane Maria Phillips humbly sheweth.*
>
> *Firstly. That I am a halfcast [sic] of the Umutai hapu of Ngatiruanui Tribe, of Taranaki, and a direct descendant of the principal chiefs of the same.*
>
> *Secondly. That I am 55 years of age, and therefore not trying to get claims recognized to which I have only recently become entitled. The claims of which I am about to speak existed long before the war. I have never participated in the slightest degree in any of our Tribal lands. My immediate ancestor Ponui was a non-combatant during wartime, and my sister Takiora was Government guide and interpreter to the forces. I mention this to show that my nearest relatives were not rebels.*
>
> *Thirdly. In 1865 I came to Taranaki to lay my claims to land, but the military authorities would not allow me to come up country to communicate with the Natives. In 1867 I returned, but with the same result. After this I wrote to the Government of the day and Sir Donald McLean assured me that my claims in the Waimate Plains and other blocks near the coast would be remembered, but I never heard any more about them. My husband about this time was appointed to a Native School in the north, and I held the position of assistant teacher. I sent my eldest daughter down to Taranaki but she was told she could not represent her mother and her claims – she being the offspring of a halfcast by a European – were not acknowledged.*
>
> *Fourthly. I came to Taranaki in September last year (1893) at the death of my sister. I found that, though she had had large areas of land she had disposed of them all, but of course that is nothing to do with this petition. What I mean is that I found that the lands in which I am interested had all been confiscated and reserves made*

for the Natives. I was told by the Public Trustee, New Plymouth, Mr Rennell, that it was too late for me to be put in to the Reserve grant as it would be too much trouble to revise it. Though he was aware that there were many in the Deed who should not be there and many left out who should be in. Of course the interests in the blocks that have been confiscated I can see it would be impossible to get as they are so divided by leases to Europeans. The isolated position in which we were placed (School Teaching) among the Natives in the North prevented us hearing anything about the extent of the West Coast land confiscations.

Fifthly. I can clearly show my ancestral rights in the lands of the Waimate Plains: Waihi; Turangatapuwai; Rakuku; Ketemaraea; Howata; Te Aoroa; Kaitawa; Te Ponui-a-Rina; Te Matapu; Akire; Opuora; Te Aratira; Heretoa; Waipa &c. These are all big blocks, but have been confiscated, with the exception of the reserves into which it is too late for me to be admitted. I also have a good interest in 'Te Ngaere' block a proof of which is the fact of my three cousins Onetu, Ngaauta, and Tekenui, being the largest shareholders therein. But the same and my claim could not be considered as it would reopen the whole question. My claims in the abovementioned can easily be proved.

Sixthly. I am not a 'tutuha' [sic] or person of no consequence in the hapu as can be gathered from the claims of my mother's first cousin Te Wharerata being recognized as being first, he has the largest share in the Reserves and my mother's other cousin by a younger branch, 'Wairau' by name is recognized as next to Wharerata, but it is of course easily ascertained that I am no imposter.

Seventhly. Seeing that (notwithstanding that the law now admits the claims of children of halfcastes by Europeans) I am debarred from prosecuting my claims on behalf of myself and my children, I would pray that your Honourable House would be pleased to take my case into favourable consideration, and grant me compensation in land, for the loss of my ancestral and birthrights, if through want of knowledge, I have not complied with some law regarding limit of time for making application. I pray this may be graciously overlooked (for surely a misapprehension cannot obliterate a right) the peculiar position in which I was placed being taken into consideration. Should your Honourable House be graciously pleased to grant me compensation, I would be willing to take an equivalent value in land in the Hokianga district.

Trusting that this my petition, shewing the hardship under which I am placed (for the rebels and disloyal natives have fared better than I) may meet with your favourable consideration. And your petitioner will ever pray.

I have the honour to be,

Gentlemen,

Yours most respectfully,

Jane Maria Phillips[63]

Although the committee recommended the Government 'make full inquiry into the petitioner's case and grant such relief as may appear necessary',[64] Jane's son, John G. Phillips wrote to the Premier Richard Seddon in April 1896 about her petition for 'we have not heard any more about it'.[65] It appears they got no satisfaction because in 1898 Jane sent another petition to the House for consideration, but this time submitted it jointly with her sister Sophia.

To the Honourable the Speaker of the House of Representatives.

Sir,

May it please your Honourable House to take into consideration this, the respectful petition of Jane Maria Phillips on behalf of herself and sister Sophia Taiawhio and which sheweth.

1. That your petitioners are half-castes of the Ngatiruanui tribe of Taranaki.

2. That they are over sixty years of age and therefore contemporaneous with the elders of the tribe.

3. That their joint families number 25 persons sons and daughters.

4. That their immediate ancestors and themselves have always been loyal subjects. Their late younger sister Takiora acted as guide to the troops during the West Coast Campaign and Sophia being guide at the Hot Lakes at Rotorua.

5. That I (Jane) on two occasions endeavoured to reach my people, but was compelled by the Commander of the forces to return to my then home in Auckland, though assured that my land interests would not suffer.

6. That your petitioners have no land for themselves or children from which to make a living, nor were they granted an interest in the West Coast Reserves.

7. That one family in the Umutai, father, sons and daughters descendants from the same family of ancestors as your petitioners have 370 shares in the reserves, while the late Wharerata and Wairau (each descendants from the same family) had ninety shares each and the child of the latter (notwithstanding she already had a large personal interest, as have each of the young children) inherited all her father's shares, while Wharerata's (who died without issue) was shared among the different branches of the tribe the greater part going to his mother's side. This is against all Maori custom and will ultimately tend to divert the interests in these reserves to persons who have inter-married with the tribe.

8. Your petitioners pray that your Hon. House will consider their unfair position, their loyalty, their age and the hardship this state of affairs imposes upon their grown-up sons and daughters and will grant them land as compensation for what they have lost through the rebellion of their people and also their just interests in the reserve.

    I am

        most respectfully

            Jane Maria Phillips[66]

Like Te Korowhiti Douglas, petitioning was Jane's final opportunity for redress, for she had exhausted other avenues. In 1882, her daughter Mereana Paraea, hearing that her aunts had received 200 acres each at Taranaki, requested the claims of her mother and herself be investigated for they were 'equally strong'.[67] She was directed to the West Coast Commission. That year, Jane's husband appealed for consideration in a letter to William Fox, who was then hearing claims for title to confiscated land in the region, to have his wife's claims acknowledged. George Phillips revealed to Fox that 'I have written to the Native Minister and Department several times' on the subject of her claim to lands at Taranaki and, 'was informed an opportunity of bringing them forward would be afforded under the West Coast Settlement Act, and Mr Richard Hobbs, M.H.R. told me that I should write to you and could use his name as a guarantee of the justness of the claim. Mrs Phillips is a sister of Mrs J. Dalton (Takiora) who has received some large amounts both of money and land on account of the family interest in land on the plains, and I should think that her so successfully establishing her claims would only strengthen my wifes [sic].'[68] Fox's note on the letter dismisses Jane's application because, 'Takiora's claims were those of a resident member of a tribe & chiefly for special services <u>supposed</u> to be rendered by her towards the acquisition of lands by the Govt. & otherwise. <u>Mrs Phillips cannot claim on either ground</u>.'[69]

Contesting confiscation

Confiscated land was the subject of a number of women's petitions, often representing the interests of their families (see chapter 3). Early petitioners included Wikitōria Tautawe, who sought compensation in 1871 for the loss of lands at the Bay of Plenty included in confiscations, 'she having been prevented by illness from attending the compensation court'[70] and Martha R. (Keke) Cowell, who petitioned in 1872 for the restoration of confiscated lands in the Waikato.[71] Hārete Hikairo sought the return of her mother's interests in Waikato land in 1873.[72] Rāhera Tiwaia sought 2000 acres in the Waitōtara district, confiscated by the Crown, which should be returned to her on account of her loyalty during the war, and for saving the lives of two Europeans.[73] Loyalty and humanitarian acts were common grounds for seeking return of confiscated lands, which were often taken indiscriminately.

In 1881, Ruiha Teira petitioned the House on behalf of her mother. The official translation of Ruiha's petition is all that remains:

> This Petition
> The Humble Prayer of L. M. Plumbridge (Ruiha Teira)
> This is my Petition to the House to consider the suffering of my mother.
> This is what Sir William Fox said to me when the Commission was appointed with reference to the One hundred acres, on the 13th August 1880, he asked me why I laid claims to land while my mother was still living. My mother appeared before the Commission when here but received no favor from Sir William Fox.
> I now therefore wish the House to look into the grievances of my mother, for the person who has left Parihaka will not return there again.
> The Government ought to consider this matter.
> From
> Your Petitioner
> Ruiha Teira
> (L. M. Plumbridge)
> Opunake[74]

Ruiha and her family 'took no part in the rebellion', yet their land had been swept up in the confiscations.[75] Theirs was 'a substantial grievance', reported the committee, and one that was admitted by the House for a number of years, but 'never dealt with' and therefore ought to be 'finally disposed of without further delay'.[76] Her petition was sent to William Fox, West Coast Commissioner for investigation, who ultimately rejected it.[77]

By the 1880s and 1890s, petitions presented reflected the variety of ways in which dispossession was practised. Increasingly petitions addressed exclusions from lists of owners set out by the Native Land Court, for example, Hōriana Hōne and 33 others, who sought redress in 1883 relating to a Native Land Court adjudication that they believed led to the loss of their land block through sale.[78] Others sought redress from the impact of inaccurate surveys.[79] Land taken by the local council for a road without any compensation was the catalyst that spurred Hāriata Ngāheko into action. She petitioned for redress, and threatened to put up a toll-bridge if the claim was not investigated.[80]

Petitions reflected too, divisions within communities, in addition to the marginal circumstances under which some women lived. Ngāhauporoaki (of Ngāti Ruanui) petitioned in 1884, claiming a man 'who assumes the power of a chief' had turned her off her land awarded to her by the West Coast Commission, and had 'destroyed her house; she now has no land to live on.'[81] By the 1890s, petitioners seeking relief from landlessness and poverty or access to fishing reserves, and protests against passage of legislation appeared with regularity.

Removing land restrictions

At the same time as land loss was taking its toll, women were also petitioning to obtain financial control over their land interests, which were subject to restrictions under Native Land legislation. Emma Rolfe sought the removal of restrictions from land, 'so that she may deal with the land as she thinks proper.'[82] Agnes Simeon (Ākanihi Kurakitoro) wanted to 'be allowed to deal with her lands herself' and prayed for the removal of restrictions on title for they 'prevent her properties being properly and profitably worked'.[83] Inuwaiti de Thierry also sought to gain control over her land and her future, 'so as to enable her to dispose of what is useless, and thus save her home for herself and her family.'[84]

Emma Rolfe brought her case for the removal of restrictions on alienation of 100 acres in the Tikorangi District to the Native Minister, instructing her lawyer to write to him on the matter in April 1886. In support of the application, her lawyer was 'instructed to explain' that, 'about £500 has been spent by Mr Rolfe in buildings and other improvements chiefly on the Eastern half of the section, which is not included in the application but will if it is complied with still remain under the present restrictions. This eastern portion contains the homestead.'[85] Emma's husband had accumulated debt, 'and a little money is also required to add to the livestock on the farm. What is necessary could readily be obtained by a mortgage of the least valuable half of the land which Mrs Rolfe who cannot legally effect a mortgage would make over to her husband for that purpose, the other half of the section being amply sufficient as a provision against distribution from want of enough land to cultivate.'[86] No reply is recorded, but in November 1887, Emma petitioned on the matter. This was a collaborative endeavour, for, as her husband Frederick W. Rolfe noted in the cover letter addressed to their local MHR that accompanied the petition: 'I trust you will present it for us and at the same time do your utmost to carry it through'.[87] There was a great deal riding on this request, for a successful petition would extract them from economic disaster, allowing them to retain their home.

Although the petition was in Emma's name alone, it was likely initiated by her husband and composed with his knowledge and support. Following a pattern of the late nineteenth century, petition No. 260 adopted the third person, which reflected Emma's use of a lawyer to compose the text:

> *To the Honourable the Speaker and Members of the House of Representatives in Parliament assembled.*
>
> *The Memorial of Emma Rolfe wife of Frederick William Rolfe of Tikorangi in the Provincial District of Taranaki, Farmer.*
>
> *Sheweth.*
>
> *That your memorialist is a half-caste, being the daughter of a European father and a Native mother, but was brought up with and educated as a European and in the year 1873 intermarried with her present husband.*
>
> *That by order of the Native Land Court held at New Plymouth on 7th day of August 1887, before John A. Wilson Esq. a Judge of the Native Land Court Two hundred acres of land situated in the Ngatirahiri [sic] Block No.1, in the said Provincial District of Taranaki being the allotment No.103 in Block V on the map of the Waitara Survey Dist. was awarded to your Memorialist and her children, all of whom are under the age of 21 years.*
>
> *That by the said grant the said allotment of land is made inalienable without the consent of the Governor in Council.*
>
> *That at a Native Land Court held New Plymouth on 7th August last your Memorialist was named and appointed guardian of the infant children.*
>
> *That Frederick Wm Rolfe the husband of your memorialist has with your*

memorialist and their family resided on the said land for about ten years & has spent large sums of money amounting in all to over £500 in building, fencing and other improvements.

That your memorialist (having considered the amount of money expended by her husband in cultivating and improving the said allotment of land, and that such monies were spent and improvements made by him on the understanding with the other native owners of the said block, that the said allotment, when the land was partitioned, would be the absolute property of your memorialist and her children, and would be subject to their disposition) is desirous that the restriction on alienation of the said property contained in the Crown Grant to be issued in pursuance of the said order of the Native Land Court should be removed that your memorialist may be enabled to transfer all her right and interest in the same to her husband, and rest in him full control thereof.

That part of the Matarikoriko Reserve, containing twenty five acres or thereabouts, was on the division of the said reserve at the Native Land Court at Waitara on the 19th July 1887 before the said J. A. Wilson Esq. awarded to your memorialist and her infant son Henry G. Rolfe and your memorialist was then appointed trustee for the said son H.G. Rolfe but the said piece of land is subject to the above mentioned restriction as to alienation.

That in the interests of herself and her son the said H.G. Rolfe your memorialist is desirous that the said restrictions as to alienation should be removed from the said land so awarded to them in order that the same may be utilized either by mortgage or by sale to the holders of adjoining lands, as from the position and area of this land (25 acres only) it is practically useless.

Your memorialist therefore humbly prays that Your Honourable House will sanction the removal of the restriction in alienation, on the said 200 acres of land in the Ngatirahira Block so as to permit the transfer of the same and the full control thereof to the said F. W. Rolfe, and that you will further sanction the removal of the like restriction from the 25 acres part of the Matarikoriko Reserve in order that the same may be mortgaged or sold, or grant such other relief as to your Honorable House shall seem fit.

Emma Rolfe

The Native Affairs Committee recommended the Government remove the restrictions, for they appeared 'unnecessary & unjustifiable'.[88] Native Department officials were suspicious, though, and urged caution, fearing, 'if the application was granted that the property would soon be lost, as it is the intention of Mrs Rolfe (in the event of her application being acceded to) to transfer the property to the husband, and it is the latters intention to mortgage it. This I do not think we should allow.'[89] The petition was declined. Emma Rolfe continued to pursue her application, writing numerous letters to the Native Minister, reminding him of previous recommendations, promises and the obligations, but with little success.

Conclusion

Māori women's petitionary appeals addressed the material circumstances of their living conditions. For those at the wealthier end of the spectrum, this amounted to protecting their large land interests, but for those at the other extreme, who were in poor health, elderly and frail, or widows, they petitioned to fend off starvation. Most of the petitions received, though, were from women in between these two extremes: those with small land interests, who sought to regain land lost through a range of colonial mechanisms. Women critiqued colonial institutions in the process of their appeals. Huingapaura Rangihatau's appeal set out in the final paragraph of her 1895 petition regarding her exclusion from the Waihī block sums up the general feeling: 'This is a prayer from me asking you to grant us relief – do not make us paupers and wanderers in New Zealand'.[90]

Women's petitions, it should be noted, were part of a larger corpus of writing that demonstrates their political will to gain redress, dating from the 1850s. One only has to look at the letters Māori women sent to Donald McLean to see these laid the foundations for petitionary appeals. Māori were well versed in writing to political figures, so a petition offered yet another forum for articulating their protest as well as their land rights. Fiona Paisley and Kirsty Reid describe petitions as a formulaic style of writing, which over time took on an increasingly bureaucratic nature, becoming a kind of form-filling exercise, but this does not mean the content of petitionary appeals is unimportant or generic.[91] Because of their bureaucratic nature, forms do not get the same attention as more active writing styles and genres, such as letters and manuscripts. Their deferential tone also lends petitions a passive character, yet the examples offered in this chapter demonstrate that petitioning was an active form of writing; it required the petitioner to locate a scribe or intermediary to translate the claim into the appropriate language, and, most significantly, petitioners actively and tirelessly campaigned to keep their claims alive, often for decades.

As noted, the most well known petitionary action led by New Zealand women were the suffrage petitions, culminating in the Electoral Reform Act 1893, which extended the franchise to all women in the colony. Māori women signed these petitions, and were active in the campaign for voting rights. In expanding our vision to women's petitionary appeals sent to the Native Affairs Committee, the everyday realities of colonial life for a cohort of Māori women, who spoke for their whānau and communities, is brought to the fore. As such petitions are not only an archive of Māori women's political activity, they also 'often articulate the more personal details of their lived relations.'[92]

CHAPTER 6

'I am the prosecutrix in this case': Legal Encounters and Testamentary Acts

Dealing with application forms, contracts, last wills and testaments, attestations and other documents of a legal nature were not uncommon experiences for Māori in the nineteenth century. In their engagement with a variety of legal processes and institutions, Māori women have contributed to a substantial archive that attests to the circumstances under which they participated in the colonial legal system and used legal agents, the degree to which they understood the law, and how the legal system treated their testimony.

Māori women signed legal documents, attended and presented claims before the Native Land Court, and came before the regular courts as victims, defendants and witnesses. Examining records created out of legal acts helps unravel the particular ways in which English law impacted upon and shaped Māori women's lives. Such a project is enhanced by digitisation, which has enabled greater access to a variety of sources that expose the everyday engagements of individuals with the law, and the legal system and its functionaries, as well as the impact of the law upon families and communities.[1] With a corpus of 400,000 nineteenth-century texts, He Pātaka Kupu Ture/The Legal Māori Archive confirms the abundance of Māori-language law-related material available, and the Lost Cases Project Database holds over 4000 Supreme Court and Court of Appeal cases from the 1840s to the 1860s, largely drawn from newspaper reports and judges' notebooks.[2] Settler newspapers, which often recorded courtroom testimonies verbatim, are accessible in digitised form on *Papers Past*, hosted by the National Library of New Zealand. Although *Papers Past* is not comprehensive, digitisation has reinforced the importance of newspapers as the 'main textual record of early colonial law', providing researchers access to the spoken testimonies of indigenous men and women, even if just in translation.[3]

Court records offer an insight into 'everyday social and economic life, a perspective rarely available from personal papers or even other aspects of the public record', but the documents generated by the legal system and its functionaries have limitations.[4] For instance, the legal archive operates on a hierarchy, generating the least information from the more active but low-level courts, but the richest records from the highest courts, and it is cases in these courts that tended to be reported in the newspapers. Māori engagement with the English legal system was uneven, too, for they had their own forums for obtaining justice that did not necessarily generate a legal document, although hints at these practices and punishments imposed can be gleaned from the records of third parties who either experienced or witnessed these forums.

Going to court

Māori participated at all levels of the court system, and in all kinds of cases, from criminal trials through to 'those concerning commerce'.[5] From the 1840s, Māori gave testimony before the courts, but this was usually limited to those who professed Christianity. Their capacity to testify as witnesses in legal forums was widened by the Unsworn Testimony Ordinance 1844, itself enabled by the Colonial Evidence Act 1843, which was passed by the imperial Parliament to 'allow colonial legislatures to pass acts or ordinances to allow their indigenous inhabitants to give unsworn testimony before the courts'.[6] The Ordinance gave those of the 'aboriginal race' (inclusive of individuals with one Māori parent) 'by reason of defect of religious knowledge and belief would be by law incompetent to give evidence in Court' to testify in civil and criminal proceedings, before a Justice of the Peace or a jury, 'upon making an affirmation that he will speak the truth, the whole truth, and nothing but the truth'.[7] Despite the use of the male pronoun, Māori women were not excluded from providing unsworn testimony.

There were pragmatic and ideological reasons for allowing indigenous testimony. According to legal historian Shaunnagh Dorsett, the widespread uptake of Christianity amongst Māori meant they were already testifying in regular courts, while the importance of Māori to commerce in settler society meant they could not be excluded from legal processes.[8] There were also strong ideological reasons to support 'proposals to allow indigenous testimony in colonial courts', says historian Damen Ward.[9] Extending English law into Māori territory had an ideological basis in the philosophy of racial amalgamation, in which Māori were to be eventually brought under the rule of English law. In the courtroom, judges addressed those Māori present on the justice and superiority of English law as part of the amalgamationist goal of encouraging Māori to adhere to the rule of law and legal processes. Pākehā authorities may also have feared that Māori may have resorted to seeking utu in cross-cultural disputes.

Women appeared in court to testify in treason trials (see chapter 2), in domestic assault cases, bigamy cases, and property crimes cases. They also went before the lower courts to defend their resource rights. This chapter looks at how cases of interracial violence, which included sexual assault and rape, heard before the criminal courts, were utilised by judges to assure Māori of British justice. It considers a libel case, and examines legal documents, particularly women's wills, as key sources for investigating women's economic rights.

Sexual violence

Sexual violence marks the colonial experience for some Māori women. In the courtroom the burden of proof lay with the woman, and victims were often subjected to aggressive cross-examination by the defence, who challenged their character and morality. It is likely many cases of rape and attempted rape went unreported and unrecorded, partly because of the public humiliation, loss of respectability, and the cross-examination of character that victims feared they would be subjected to in a courtroom situation.[10] Māori women were treated in a similar way to Pākehā before the court. However, Māori women had other options, for they could choose to seek punishment of their attacker on the basis of customary law, and in Māori-controlled forums. Others brought cases before the civil commissioner or resident magistrate, who sought to work with Māori communities to reach a satisfactory conclusion, in a way that could usefully demonstrate the justice of English law.

In the mid-nineteenth century, sexual violence cases that went before the Supreme Court were reported in full, inclusive of the victim's testimony. In March 1866 Michael Caffrey stood in the dock of the Wellington Supreme Court and entered a plea of not guilty to a charge of assault with intent. His victim was a Māori woman. Justice Johnston, 'anxious that the Maoris should be satisfied that Justice should be done', secured the services of a second interpreter for that purpose. Having a skilled interpreter was a basic requirement in a colony that accepted the evidence of Māori in court. For further insurance, Johnston invited a Māori assessor to sit on the bench, giving him the right to pose questions or make suggestions.

The two main witnesses in the case were Māori women. The victim of the attack was the first to give evidence. She was sworn and said, through an interpreter:

I am the prosecutrix in this case, I do not know my age. I am a widow and have been so for two years, I live at the Taita with Manihera and Mihi, the former, who sits there, is the uncle of my husband, and Mihi is his wife. I was at the Taita on Saturday, the 27th January, Mihi was with me in a garden outside a house close to the public road. There was a post and rail fence with palings and a gate between where we were and the road, people passing on the road could see us. This was before noon, I saw the prisoner on the 27th January, I had never seen him before. Prisoner came to us from the direction of Wellington, he came through the gate. When he came in he picked up a piece of fire and lit his pipe. There was a fire there and we were sitting by it with our backs to the road.

His Honor: How then could you see him come in through the gate[?]
Witness: When we heard him open the gate, we looked round. This was in a small place in front of two houses, there were no people in the garden, or in the houses, only our two selves. When he lit his pipe he went and stood between us. Mihi went to fetch some potatoes, and while she was away, he made use of improper words to me. I said 'Kahori.' [sic] He repeated the words and I said 'Kahori' again, and said 'Karpoi iakoe hire' [sic] (it is good, you go away). He said some words in English, I cannot repeat pakeha words. When he spoke to me he took hold of my hand and dragged me along the ground, from the fire to the peach garden. While he was dragging me I screamed out 'Oh! I am being hurt (mate)' when he got me into the garden, he took me by the throat and put his knee upon my chest, (witness here described the assault, the particulars of which are unfit for publication, but it appeared that the prisoner did not accomplish his purpose.) Mihi then came up and pushed prisoner away from me, Mihi told me to come away, and we both went up toward Buck's public house. Prisoner followed us and struck Mihi in the face with his fist. We told Buck of prisoner's conduct before prisoner came up and struck Mihi, Buck held prisoner while we got away to the cart.

'I am the prosecutrix in this case': Legal Encounters and Testamentary Acts

...

> By the Court: I screamed out when he was dragging me. Mihi went about 200 yards. She came back when I screamed. I screamed when he took hold of my hands. He did not give or promise me anything. He had no drink with him. Mihi did not bring any spirits when she came back. Mihi did not know that there was any wrong in him, she went away for food. He had been there sometime before Mihi went away. He was standing there smoking. We did not speak to him at all. He stood there without speaking as long as I have been standing here giving my evidence. I went to Buck's directly I got up. He followed us quickly. Since my husband's death I have lived at that pa. I have had a child but it is dead. I am supported by my relatives. I have never been to school. The nearest Maoris at the time of the assault were as far as from here to the wharf. There were no persons going along the road. Before prisoner dragged me he caught hold of my hands and tried to kiss me. I turned my head away. He did nothing else. Prisoner was quite sober. Prisoner did not give me or Mihi any money to fetch spirits. I had no conversation with prisoner about running away with him to the Wairarapa. We did not offer the prisoner any food.

The second female witness, niece of the victim, confirmed the details of the evidence of the first witness in every respect.

> On the 22nd Jan. last we were at the Taita. We made a fire in the garden near the whare. I know the prisoner. I saw him on that Saturday. I never saw him before. We were sitting looking towards the road. The fire was between us and the fence. We were both sitting at the same side of the fire. Prisoner came toward us from the road. He came in through the gate. He went and lit his pipe and stopped there smoking it. Sometime after he came I went into the potato field. While I was there he did not speak. While I was in the potato field, a short time after I went there, I heard him call out loud. I came at once and saw [redacted] on her back in the peach garden, and the prisoner was holding her by her throat. Her clothes were torn and he had one foot on one of her hands. I pulled him away. (The evidence here is unfit for publication.) We went into the road and prisoner followed us. We went to Buck's. Buck and the others were standing outside. I spoke to Buck and complained of what prisoner had done. Prisoner came up and struck me in the chest with his fist and knocked me down. Buck saw him strike me.

Caffery claimed he was a victim of the women, who had plied him with liquor. While in a drunken state he was assaulted and attacked 'in a most shameful manner, and his trousers had been torn off', robbed of his money, his watch and clothing. A jury found Caffery guilty of the lesser charge of indecent assault and he was sentenced to 18 months imprisonment. This verdict pleased the judge for 'he would have blushed to think a Maori would not receive the same justice as a settler's daughter, as if the honour and purity of the one were not to be defended and protected as much as the other. He (the prisoner) possibly thought, that because the prosecutrix was dark-skinned, he might commit outrages upon her which he would not dare attempt upon a white woman, but he would find that the arm of justice would punish the offenders equally whether the crime was committed against maori or pakeha.'[11] This is a telling speech for it exposes Māori women's vulnerability to sexual violence, and a court system that accepted widespread colonial attitudes about Māori women's supposed 'natural' promiscuity, what has been described as a 'racialised language of morality'.[12]

In 1862, the Wellington Supreme Court heard a case of criminal assault with intent to commit rape against William Hughes. The victim was the first witness called. She gave her evidence in Māori, which was interpreted for the court by Mr Nairn. She said:

> I am a married woman; I know Hughes the prisoner: I saw him on the 13th March, in the bush, I cannot state the precise time; it was by the side of the road near the Hutt River; I asked him to show me the road to Charles Mabey's; there were two men present, Hughes and another; I did not stay with them, but merely stopped to put the question; Hughes went with me; he showed me the road out for a little distance; he then said to me, '[redacted], I wish to have connection with you'; he spoke to me in Maori; I said 'no, I would rather not'; he offered me £1, but I refused and told him to keep his money; I turned to come out on the road, when he then seized me by the shoulder and tore my clothes; he knocked my hat off my head, and seized me by the hair; I called aloud to the other white man, when Hughes seized me by the throat so tight that I could not speak; I was about falling to the ground; when I fell, he held me down with one hand, and with the other he pulled up my clothes, taking indecent liberties (the details of which are unfit for publication); I asked him why he should try to do me an injury; he tried to unfasten his belt, but I struggled and cried out; he then struck me violently on the nose, making it bleed; I then scratched his face; I still struggled to get free, and I said, 'I will

now tell the police'; he did not effect his purpose; when I told him he would seek the police he cursed the police; I then went towards his companion, and I said, 'This man is a nice sort of fellow'; it was about forty or fifty yards from the road; I said a little to him, and he said, '[redacted], wipe the blood off your face'; the prisoner did not hear him; I came out into the road to return to my own home.

By Mr. Borlase: I was married at the Hutt church; I have seen the prisoner at times, but was not acquainted with him; I have seen him at my own whare; I know McHardie's public-house; our whare is about a mile and a half from McHardie's on this side; we have lived there seven years; I wanted to see a native woman who was living at Mabey's; this was the first time I went to Mabey's; when I came to where the men were working they gave me a bottle with gin in it; I drank a little; it was before the ill-usage; I did not ask him to come and show me the road; I asked him where is the road and he said, 'come here [redacted]'; when he offered me the pound, I did not see the money; I did not ask to see the money, I said 'keep your money'; before I was struck on the nose, I did not kick him; I did not run, I was too weak; the prisoner did not try to stop me; I have been at McHardie's; I go there to fetch provisions for myself and husband; I go but seldom; I have not left McHardie's accompanied by different men at different times; when I came up afterwards to where the two men were working, the other man said he would give me 10s. if I would wipe the blood off my face; I did not see the money; the prisoner was not there at that time.[13]

The emphasis on the woman's marital status, the link suggested between alcohol and moral weakness, and the claim of an exchange of money, which served to suggest she was a willing party to a commercial exchange, were all typical strategies used by the defence in sexual-violence cases.[14] Familiarity between victim and assailant was also often used to undermine the testimony of women. David Wilkie, an associate of Hughes who was present at the scene of the crime, claimed 'she seemed to know the prisoner'. Even though the policeman, David Lyster, saw the victim at McHardie's crying and bleeding, under cross-examination he had 'heard it remarked she was of bad character.' John McHardie, the publican, described her as 'having a very bad name for chastity.' The fact that she cohabited with a white man offered further evidence of her immorality. A conviction was more likely if some physical resistance could be proven and supported by witnesses as was the case here, for the jury found Hughes guilty and he was sentenced to twelve months imprisonment with hard labour.

Even if there were witnesses, and clear evidence of assault and physical resistance, a woman's morality was still questioned, for this was a key defence strategy to undermine the character and reputation of a woman. A Māori woman gave evidence through the interpreter that she was walking with her Pākehā husband when three Māori men on horseback drew up to them. One of these men invited her onto his horse. Under pressure she conceded, but once on board he 'took improper liberties'. Surrounded, she called out for assistance. Her husband attempted to free her from the three men, but he was dragged away, and unable to prevent his wife from being raped. The arrival of a Pākehā man on horseback interrupted the assault and saved the woman from further attacks. In court, the judge and defence lawyer questioned the woman, and this is her response:

> *I resisted Hoani until he got me down; afterwards I had no power or strength to do so. In the struggle my gown was much torn; the rents I shew were then made. My left arm was sprained, and it is still sore. I shewed the rents to the white man who came up. He took my handkerchief and wiped the dust off my face; and took my shawl and tied it around my body.*
>
> *By Mr Lee: I am not married to Jim. I don't know how long I have lived with him. I am not married to any one else. My wedded husband (tane marina [sic]), who was a chief of the Waikato, is dead. [Witness here replied in the negative to several questions touching upon her personal reputation.]*

The questioning of the victim's character and morality continued, despite the details of the assault being confirmed in every respect by her husband, who testified to his wife's determined resistance to the men's advances. George Lee, who interrupted the assault, confirmed her emotional state and torn clothing. Despite this the defendant's counsel, Mr Lee, told the jury that he would provide evidence of the woman's poor character and discredit the evidence of her husband, calling two Māori men to testify to her immorality. This constituted the whole of the defence case. The prisoners, though, were found guilty. Racial amalgamationist philosophy worked against the interests of the female victim in sentencing, though. The judge, citing Māori ignorance of English law, decided to pass, in his words, a comparatively light sentence, of four years imprisonment.

Interpreter James Grindell paused to take a moment to think about how to translate the phrase 'penal servitude', when the judge said 'tell them slavery', the response from those present in the court was astonishment.[15]

The Waka Maori *libel case*

Ārihi Te Nahu (Ngāti Kahungunu) demonstrated the political capacity of women, although in her case it had legal repercussions. In 1876, Henry Russell, a member of both the Hawke's Bay Provincial Council and the parliamentary Legislative Council, sued George Didsbury and James Grindell, the printer and editor respectively of Te Waka Maori o Niu Tirani, for libel.[16] The offending material was a letter from Ārihi Te Nahu and three men, and a letter from Māngai Uhuhu (or Uhuuhu) and others.[17]

Three years earlier, a Parliamentary enquiry, the Hawke's Bay Native Lands Alienation Commission, investigated Māori complaints about a number of land sales in Hawke's Bay, including the Heretaunga Block. Russell was one of the 'Twelve Apostles', members of the wealthy Hawke's Bay elite who purchased the Heretaunga Block comprising 16–17,000 acres in 1870. Ngāti Kahungunu initially leased this land to the 'Apostles' in 1864, and it was the tribe's intention to continue doing so when placing the Block before the Native Land Court in 1867. Karaitiana, a leading chief, had wanted to keep the Block in his name alone, but agreed to allow ten names, representing sixteen hapū, on the grant, but on the understanding that no land could be sold without the agreement of all ten grantees.[18] However the grantees, some of whom were in considerable debt, were entitled to sell their shares without reference to anyone else, and the lessees began working on them individually, so that in 1870 the whole block was acquired.

One of the commissioners, C. W. Richmond, considered that '[m]any natives have not as yet fully realized what pecuniary responsibility is, and fancy themselves wronged when made to pay their just debts', and that no real injustice had occurred.[19] Although the price received, 'about £1 6s. 8d. an acre', was less than half that if the land had been sold in smaller blocks, he still considered it 'fully adequate'.[20] However Wiremu Hikairo, a Māori commissioner, considered that '[t]he land is good, and the area large, but the price is small', and that, given the purchasers' processes, 'I do not think that this was a proper way of making a sale of land'.[21] Purvis Russell (Henry Russell's brother) and the lawyer

Mr J. N. Wilson looked after Ārihi's interests, although the other chiefs had originally allotted her £1,500.[22] Significant legal battles were fought before the deed was finally confirmed in 1881, by which time Ārihi had negotiated £2,500.[23]

Russell set himself up as a protector of Māori interests, and helped fund the Repudiation Movement and their newspaper, *Te Wananga*. Led by Ngāti Kahungunu chiefs Hēnare Matua, Tomoana and Takamoana, the Repudiationists sought to overturn fraudulent land sales. However, Russell's allegiance to the cause, along with the lawyer politician John Sheehan, had more to do with their antipathy, both political and social, towards Donald McLean and his friends, than a genuine concern for Māori land rights.[24] Through the mid 1870s the movement was active in petitioning Parliament and litigating land claims, with its newspaper engaging in extremely robust political debate with *Te Waka Maori o Niu Tirani*,[25] a newspaper run by the Native Department, of which McLean was minister, which had government funding. The Repudiation Movement's greatest success was getting Parliament to call the Hawke's Bay Native Lands Alienation Commission. But by the end of the decade, the Repudiation Movement had run out of steam and Māori were disappointed with the commission's reports. Russell's coffers had run low, and a change of government in 1877, with Sheehan as Native Minister, did not change much for Māori.[26]

Ārihi Te Nahu, the granddaughter of the great chief Te Hāpuku, was one of the Māori whom Russell professed a desire to protect, taking over the management of her financial affairs. However, by 1876, Ārihi was dissatisfied with Russell and vented her frustration in her letter to the government's *Te Waka Maori o Niu Tirani*. Just as Russell and the Repudiation Movement combined due to a common enemy, Ārihi was happy to utilise the tool of Russell's enemy, the government's bilingual newspaper for Māori readers. Ārihi dictated her letter to her husband, and instructed him to append the other names as they were aware of the issues; Māngai also dictated his letter to Ārihi's husband, appending the names of men and women without their knowledge, although most were subsequently happy to be associated with the text.

Although the opening sentence of the letter betrays Ārihi's authorship with 'aku kupu' (my words) it purports to be from the signatories ('we') and discusses her in the third person. It is only half way through the letter that 'nga kupu . . . a Ārihi', supposedly Alice's own words, are introduced.

Ki a te Etita o te Waka Maori
Pakipaki Mei 19, 1876.

E HOA, – Utaina atu aku kupu ki runga i to Waka hei titiro iho ma oku hoa Pakeha, Maori hoki, i nga mahi e mahi nei to matou hoa Pakeha ki a matou, ki nga iwi Maori o Ahuriri.

I te 9 o nga ra o Mei nei ka tu te hui a taua Pakeha ki te Aute; te putake o tana hui, mo nga whenua o nga Maori kia tukuna atu ki a ia. Kaore etahi o nga Maori i pai kia hoatu o ratou whenua ki taua Pakeha, ki a Henare Rata, no te mea kua tino mohio aua Maori ki nga mahi he a taua Pakeha. Na, no te kitenga o taua Henare Rata i etahi o nga Maori kaore i pai ki te hoatu i o ratou whenua ki a ia, katahi ia ka mea atu ki nga Maori, – 'Whakarongo mai koutou. E kore e tika kia pupuri koutou i o koutou whenua, no te mea he nui a koutou nama ki a au; koia au i mea ai me homai a koutou whenua, kia rite ai a koutou nama e takoto nei i roto i taku pukapuka. E kore e tika kia hoatu ki tetahi atu Pakeha, no te mea ko au tonu te hoa pono mo koutou, mo nga Maori. Ki te mea ka tino kore koutou e tuku mai ki a au i o koutou whenua, ka tino mate rawa atu koutou, ka tono hoki au ki a koutou kia homai nga moni e £50 pauna i te marama kotahi, hei whakarite mo nga moni i namaia mai e koutou ki a au. Me homai enei moni i ia marama i ia marama, a rite noa nga mano pauna i ia tangata i ia tangata o koutou.'

Katahi ano matou nga Maori ka mohio e penei ana nga mahi a to matou hoa Pakeha; heoi, katahi matou ka kite i te mahi patipati a tenei Pakeha, a Henare Rata. Na, e nga hoa Pakeha i nga pito e wha o te motu nei, kia marama mai ta koutou titiro mai ki nga mahi e mahi nei to matou hoa Pakeha ki a matou ki nga iwi Maori o Ahuriri. Tana mahi tuatahi, ko te ki mai me tahuri matou ki a ia, ko ia hei matua aroha ki nga Maori, ko matou hei tamariki ki a ia, mana hoki e tiaki o matou whenua kei riro i nga tini Pakeha e noho nei i Nepia, 'Kei tupu ake,' e ai ki tana ki, 'o koutou uri i muri i a koutou kaore he whenua ma ratou i muri i a koutou. Ki te tukuna mai o koutou ki a au, ka tiakina e au mo a koutou tamariki a muri ake nei.'

Na, i naianei kua kite matou i nga mahi tinihanga a taua Pakeha, a Henare Rata; kua tino raru matou i ana mahi patipati. Otira, tera atu ano ana mahi tinihanga o mua atu i tenei. I nga tau maha kua hori ake nei ka mahi ano ia i tetahi mahi penei te ahua me tenei ki tetahi Maori rangatira, ko Hori Nia Nia. Riro katoa nga whenua i a Henare Rata, kei te noho mate taua tangata a Hori Nia Nia i enei ra. No te mutunga o tana mahi ki a Hori Nia Nia ka mahia nei e ia taua mahi ki a matou, ki enei hapu e patipatia nei e ia, kia pera ano matou me Hori Nia Nia e tangi nei ki ona whenua. I naianei e kore rawa atu matou e pai ki nga mahi a Henare Rata.

Muri iho ka tu nei te Paremete, otira kua tu noa atu te Paremete, ka mahia ano e ia taua mahi ki a Arihi te Nahu. Ka ki atu ia ki a Arihi, – 'Me homai o whenua, maku e tiaki kia toe ai hei whenua mou mo a mua ake nei, maku ano hoki e whakahoki mai tou whenua a Heretaunga ki a koe. Ka mahi au ki a koe mou whenua kia hoki mai ki a koe ki runga i te hoko he a etahi Pakeha e noho nei i Nepia.' Muri ihi i tena ka ki mai ano taua Pakeha, a Henare Rata, ki a Arihi kia hoatu tona whare ki a ia, mana e hoatu tetahi whare mona ki te Pakipaki, ka whakaae atu a Arihi kia riro i a ia tona whare. Ko nga kupu enei a Arihi mo taua mea, ara; – 'No te rironga o taku whare i a ia kaore taua Pakeha e homai whare moku, kua mutu te korero mai a taua Pakeha ki a au tae noa mai ki tenei tau 1876, kore rawa taua Pakeha e pai ki te korero mai ki a au, kore rawa atu. Ko toku whare kei runga ano i toku whenua e tu ana. Ko te tangata nana i tino tono mai taua whare ko tana Kai-whakamaori, ko te Waiti; tenei ano nga pukapuka a te Waiti kei a au e tiaki ana. No te rironga mai o taku whare i a Henare Rata, ka whakanohoia e Henare Rata tetahi Pakeha ki roto i taua whare, katahi ka riro katoa te mana o aku mea i taua Pakeha. Ka tono au i tetahi tangata ki te tiki rakau maku ka panaia mai e taua Pakeha. Kaore hoki i tukua atu e au ki a ia te mana o aku rakau, me aku heihei. Heoi ano ta maua i korero ai ko te whare anake, ko nga mea katoa i roto i te whare, i waho hoki, ki a au te tikanga o ena mea katoa; i naianei kua tango katoa taua Pakeha mana katoa aku mea i te whare, i waho hoki. Heoi, katahi te Pakeha kino rawa ko Henare Rata! He nui nga mahi wairaweke a taua Henare Rata ki a au. Ko tetahi mahi a taua Pakeha, ko aku moni i te Peeke i a te Wirihana raua ko Pauihi, kua kiia e taua Pakeha kaore kau aku moni i te Peeke, kua pau. Na, kia mohio koutou, ka nui rawa atu nga mahi kino a tenei Pakeha, a Henare Rata ki a au, ki a Arihi. I mua atu i tenei ko Pauihi raua ko te Wirihana nga kai-tiaki i aku moni i te Peeke, ka nui te pai. I a raua aku moni e tiaki ana, me aku whenua, me aku mea katoa, ka nui te pai; e homai ana e raua nga itareti o aku moni kia kite au i nga tau katoa. No te rironga ki a Henare Rata katahi ka kiia mai e ia kua pau-koia nei te itareti a Henare Rata i homai ki a au, kua pau aku moni.

'Heoi, ka puta atu au ki waho o ana mahi katoa. Katahi au ka mohio koia nei te tikanga o ana kupu e ki nei, "Ko ia hei matua ki a au, ko au hei tamaiti ki a ia, a wehea noatia maua e te mate" – kaore, he patipati kia riro oku whenua i a ia me oku mea katoa. Kaore ano au i kite i te pai o ana mahi i ki nei ia mana e whakahoki mai oku whenua, mana e mahi nga mahi katoa moku. Katahi au ka kite koia nei te "pai" o tana mahi ko te wairaweka i nga Maori kia raru i a ia te patipati. He nui atu nga mahi a taua Pakeha, a Henare Rata. Ko tetahi o ana mahi he tono i nga whenua kia riihitia ki a ia mo nga tau e rua te kau ma tahi; kua nui noa atu nga tau etahi whenua kei a ia, ko nga moni e homai ana mo nga tau e toru, e £5. Ka nui te kino o te mahi a tenei Pakeha, kino rawa atu. E mea ana ahau kua hinga a Pauihi raua ko te Wirihana, me kauaka a Henare Rata e pupuri i aku moni, me homai aku moni ki a au ano te ritenga. Ehara hoki i a au i whakarite ma ratou e whakahaere aku moni, engari na Henare Rata i patipati me tahuri atu au ki ana whakahaere, "kia ora ai au."

'Katahi au ka whakapono ki te kupu a Raka raua ko Tanara i ki mai ai ki a au, "Taihoa nga Maori ka raru i a Henare Rata" – na, i naianei kaore ano i tae ki te tau kua kite au i te he a taua Pakeha, o Henare Rata. Na, i ki ano hoki taua Pakeha, a Henare Rata, e kore ia e pai ki te Kawanatanga, kauaka au e pirangi ki a te Raka raua ko Tanara. Heoi, kua rongo au kua tae atu te tono a taua Pakeha ki tetahi o nga apiha o te Kawanatanga kia haere mai hei whakamana i ana rihi i o matou whenua. Taku kupu, kaore au e pai ki a Henare Rata – kore, kore rawa atu. Taku kupu ki nga apiha a te Kawanatanga, kauaka koutou e haere i runga i te tono a taua Pakeha, na te mea ko tana mahi he tautohe ki te Kawanatanga kia kore matou, nga Maori, e pirangi atu. Ko tana mahi he patipati ki a matou. Ko tetahi hapu o matou nana i whakawehiwehi ki ana nama, a whakaae ana taua hapu i runga i to ratou wehi ki nga mahi a taua Pakeha. Ko tetahi hapu, ko Ngatitekaro te ingoa, kua puta ki waho i nga mahi a taua Henare Rata, a na te nui o ana mahi whakawehiwehi i hoki atu ai ano taua hapu – he wehi no ratou. Ko tetahi hapu, ko Ngati-te-whare-kakahu, kua puta rawa atu ratou ki waho, kaore ratou i mataku i nga mahi a Henare Rata; kua puta hoki te kupu whakawehiwehi a taua Pakeha kia whakahengia aua hapu e te Roia. Heoi, ko au e pai ana ki te putanga o enei hapu ki waho i nga mahi a tenei Pakeha a Henare Rata. Heoi aku kupu.

'E hoa e te KAI TUHI, – Ahakoa kino aku kupu, utaina atu kia kite iho te Kawanatanga i nga mahi e mahia nei e tenei Pakeha; ahakoa kore he tikanga o ena kupu, utaina ki runga i te Waka Maori.'

Na o hoa aroha, na
    ARIHI te NAHU,
    NEPIA te HAPUKU,
    HAPUKU te NAHU,

TIPENE,

      me matou katoa.

[newspaper translation]
To the Editor of the Waka Maori
Pakipaki 19th May, 1876.
FRIEND, – Please take on board your canoe (*Waka*) my words, that the Pakeha and Maori friends might know of the conduct of our Pakeha friend towards us, the Maori people of Ahuriri.

On the 9th of May, he, the said Pakeha, held a meeting at Te Aute, for the purpose of getting the Maoris to let him have their lands. Some of the Maoris, however, were not willing to let their lands go to that Pakeha, Henry Russell, because they were thoroughly aware of his wrong-doings. Well, when this Henry Russell saw some of the Maoris were not willing to let him have their lands, then he said to them, – 'Listen to me. It will not be just for you to withhold your lands, because you are greatly indebted to me; therefore I say, let me have your lands as a means of liquidating the accounts which I have against you in my books. It would not be just to give (your lands) to any other Pakeha, because I am your true friend, the friend of the Maoris. If you persist in refusing me to have your lands, you will come absolutely to grief, for I shall demand of you a sum of £50 per month in liquidation of the money which you have obtained from me. You will have to pay me this sum each month, until the thousands of pounds which you have all received be repaid.'

It was only then that we discovered that our Pakeha friend intended to act in this way – only then that we discovered the deception of this Pakeha, Henry Russell. Now mark, ye Pakehas throughout the island, the conduct of our Pakeha friend towards us, the Maori people of Ahuriri. His first step was to persuade us to attach ourselves to him, saying that he would be a loving father to the Maoris, and that we should be his children; he would take care of our lands lest the many Pakehas who live at Napier should get possession of them, 'and,' said he, 'your children after you be left without any land when they grow up. If you make over your land to me I will preserve it for your children.'

We have now discovered the deceit of this Pakeha, Henry Russell; we are great sufferers by his treachery. But this is not the only instance of his duplicity. In years gone by he acted in the same manner to a Native chieftain named Hori Nia Nia. All his land went to Mr. Henare Russell, and now Hori Nia Nia is landless and living in a state of destitution. Having accomplished his purposes with regard to Hori Nia Nia, he now commences to wheedle our hapus, with the view to placing us in a similar position to that of Hori Nia Nia, who is now grieving for his lands. But we now object to his proceedings; we desire to have nothing whatever to do with him.

After the Parliament (first) met (in Wellington), or rather, some time after, he commenced a similar course of action towards Arihi te Nahu. He said to her, 'You must make over your lands to me, and I will preserve them as a possession for you in time to come; and I will also recover for you your land at Heretaunga. I will also institute proceedings for the recovery of your lands illegally purchased by some of the Pakehas, who live at Napier.' Subsequently, he asked Arihi to let him have her house, promising to provide another one for her at Pakipaki; and she accordingly consented to let him have her house. The following is Arihi's account of the matter: – 'After he got possession of my house he would not provide another one for me, and from that time to the present, 1876, he has ceased to speak to me on the subject-he will not speak to me at all about it. My house (in question) stands upon my own land. The person who was active in bringing about the transfer of the house was his interpreter, Mr. White, and I have now in my possession his letters (or written documents) on the subject. When Mr. Russell got my house he put a Pakeha into it, who immediately took possessiou [sic] of all my goods and chattels, and property (thereabouts). I once sent a man to get some timber for me, but he was driven away by that Pakeha. I did not transfer to him (Mr. Russell) my trees (or timber), and my fowls &c. Our arrangement had reference to the house alone; everything within it and about it was to remain in my possession, but the Pakeha living in the house appropriated to himself everything in the house and everything about it. What a bad man is this Pakeha, Henry Russell! His wide-awake dodges in connection with my affairs have been many. With respect to my money in the bank, in the keeping of Mr. Purvis (Russell) and Mr. Wilson, he informed me that I had no money there – that it was all expended. Know all of you, that the bad doings of this Pakeha, Henry Russell towards me, have been very many indeed. Previous to this Mr. Purvis (Russell) and Mr. Wilson were the trustees of my money in the bank – then everything was satisfactory. They had charge of my money and my lands, and everything that belonged to me, and all was well; they showed me the interest on my money every year. But when the trusteeship was transferred to Henry Russell, he told me my money was all expended. This was the interest which he gave me; he said my money was all spent.

'However, henceforth I shall decline to have anything whatever to do with him; I withdraw from any participation whatever in any of his plans. I know now the meaning of his words, that "he would be my parent and I should be his child until separated by death." They were merely spoken for the purpose of cajoling me to let him have my lands and all my other property. I do not like this Pakeha in any way. I have not seen any good resulting from his assertions that he would get back my lands for me, and that he would manage all my affairs. the only "good" I have seen resulting from his professions has been his wide-awake dodging to deceive and distress the Maoris. The schemes of that Pakeha, Henry Russell, are many. Another thing he is endeavouring to do is to lease the (Maori) lands for twenty-one years. He now holds on lease other lands for very long periods, for which he only pays a rent of £5 for three years. The work of this Pakeha is bad, very bad indeed. Mr. Purvis (Russell) and Mr. Wilson are no longer trustees (of my property), and I desire that Mr. Henry Russell also shall not hold my money. It was not my proposal that they should manage my money, and Mr. Henry Russell coaxed me to let him have charge of my affairs that "I might be safe."

'Now I believe the words of Mr. Locke and Mr. Tanner, who told me that "the Maoris would by-and-by come to grief through Mr. Russell" – and a year had not passed when I discovered the wrong-doings of that Pakeha. He told me that he did not like (was opposed to) the Government, and that I was not to connect myself in any way with Mr. Locke and Mr. Tanner; yet I have heard that he has asked for the presence of an officer of the Government to legalize his leases of our land. I have to say that I do not want anything to do with Mr. Russell – nothing, nothing whatsoever-and to you, officers of the Government, I say, do not assent to his request, because he is a persistent opponent of the Government, and wishes us, the Maoris, also to have no regard for the Government. His conduct towards us is hypocritical and disingenuous. He frightened one of our *hapus* about their indebtedness to him, and, under intimidation, induced them to agree to his proposals. Another *hapu*, Ngatitekaro, withdrew themselves from all connection with him and his proceedings, but overcome with dread of his many threats, they returned and submitted to him. Another *hapu*, Ngati-te-whare-kakahu, withdrew from him altogether; they were afraid of Mr. Henry Russell's devices, and he has told them that his lawyer will proceed against them and bring them into trouble. I approve of these *hapus* withdrawing themselves from Mr. Henry Russell. I have no more to say.

'Mr. EDITOR, – Although I may have spoken strongly and severely, nevertheless receive my words, that the Government may know of the actions of this Pakeha; although my words may be unimportant, take them on board of the *Waka Maori* notwithstanding.'

From your friends,
ARIHI TE NAHU,
NEPIA TE HAPUKU,
TE HAPUKU TE NAHU,
TIPENE,
And all of us.[27]

Ārihi accused Russell of the sort of unethical behaviour that the Repudiation Movement was criticising and accusing other Pākehā of doing. Russell saw an opportunity, as *Te Wananga* proclaimed:

The 'Waka Maori,' in ignorance no doubt, of the criminal proceedings in preparation against the Editor, for publishing the false and calumnious letter by Mangai in a former number against the Honourable H. R. Russell, has, in its last issue, inserted another letter, purporting to be signed by Arihi, and others, of the same libellous character.[28]

In the same issue *Te Wananga* published a letter from Urupeni Pūhara, who came from Pakipaki, the same small settlement where Ārihi resided. His letter attacked Ārihi's account, which he considered a personal criticism of Russell, but an attack on the Repudiation Movement too.[29]

Ārihi considered this letter to be a gross intrusion into her affairs. She immediately wrote back to *Te Wananga*, answering Urupeni's various points, but also angrily denigrating his own personal ethics and behaviour in an attempt to humble him amongst his own people.

RETA I TUKUA MAI.
KI TE ETITA O TE WANANGA

Tukua atu taku reta ki TE WANANGA, he whakautu mo te reta a Urupeni Puhara. E kii nei, e hara i a Henare Rata ki te tahae i oku whenua, taku kupu kia Urupeni, he porangi pea tona mate, kaore pea ia e ata titiro iho ki nga mahi i mahia e Henare Rata ki au, ko au hoki e mohio ana, ko koe e Urupeni kaore koe e mohio, ko au hoki te tino tamaiti a tena Pakeha, e mohio ana i au ana mahi katoa i mahia ai e ia ki au. Tena iana, kia ata titiro mai koe e Urupeni, na Henare Rata tonu i hoko a Heretaunga, kaore ano he moni i riro noa mai i au, e kiia mai nei e Urupeni, ko nga moni e riro mai ana i au, he putake ano tona. He moni o aku kei te Peeke, ko taua Pakeha na kei te pupuri mai. Tuarua, he whenua toku kei a Henare Rata e riihi ana, ko te Rohitu, kaore ano au i tango i nga moni, e kiia mai nei e Urupeni, he kore moni hei hoko rama, na reira au i rere ai ki te Kawanatanga, taku kupu mo tenei, e hara au i te wahine kai rama, kaore ano au i kitea e te Pakeha e haurangi ana i te taone, kaore ano oku whenua i riro hei utu rama, kaore oku whenua i riro i te mokete. Engari tena tangata a Urupeni, kua kitea e te tini Pakeha e noho nei i Nepia e haurangi ana i te rori, nona nga whenua i pau i tena mea i te waipiro, me te mokete, ko au, kaore ano au i mate i tena mate i te mokete, me te haurangi, tena ko koe e Urupeni, kua mate koe i te mate pohara, kua penei tonu koe i te kuri e hongi nei i te haunga tutae, ira tonu te tangata i kitea kei reira e tono ana he moni, i tino mahi rawa ano hoki taua tangata ki te whai-haere i au, kia hoatu he moni maana hei purei werowero, ka hoatu e au te rima hereni maana, katahi au ka kite atu e tangohia ana tona koti e te Pakeha hei uru mo ta raua purei, kaore tahi ana putake moni i au i tono mai ia kia hoatu he moni maana. Tena ko au i kiia nei e ia he Kootimana e tango ana i nga moni a Henare Rata raua ko te Kawanatanga hei hoko rama. E koro kia rongo mai koe he putake moni taku kei a Henare Rata. Ko aku moni katahi, ko oku whenua ka rua, kaore ano, ano i tango i te moni oku whenua, ko Henare Rata kei runga e noho ana, he aha ra koe te ata titiro ai, ina hoki e ki nei koe, he koroheke koe, kanui to mohio, katahi au ka kite, kaore koe e mohio, ina hoki, kua rere noa koe ki te whakahoki i taku panui, kaore nei au i tuhi i te ingoa o Urupeni. Koia kei te tahae i aku moni, me aku whenua hoki, katahi nei au ka mohio ko Henare Rata tetahi o nga ingoa o Urupeni, kaati tenei. Me korero ake hoki au mo tetahi o nga kupu a Urupeni e ki nei, ko toku marena kei te here i oku whenua. Taku kupu mo tenei, e hara i a Hiraka te tangata e korero nei ki oku whenua, kaore a Hiraka i te korero moku whenua. Ko Henare Rata anake te mea kei runga i oku whenua e noho ana, koia hoki te tangata kei te here i oku whenua, kia waiho kia ia, e kiia nei e Urupeni, ko taku marena kei te here. He aha ra a Urupeni te mohio ai he tangata marena ia ki tetehi wahine, kaore he take i mahuetia ai a Urupeni taana wahine marena, kaore a Urupeni e utu ana i tona marena. E koro e Urupeni, nau koa i pokanoa ki te utu i taku panui, koia au i tino korero ai i ou henga, i ou mate. Me korero ake ano e au etahi kupu mo nga kupu a Urupeni e kiia nei e ia, e hara te mahi a Henare Rata i te tahae, ko au ra e mohio ana ki ana mahi katoa, ko au hoki te Maori kua mauria e taua Pakeha ki ana mahi katoa, no muri nei te tini o te Maori i uru ai ki nga mahi a tena Pakeha. Otira, kua korerotia ra hoki e au ana mahi i taku reta i tukua ra ki Te 'Waka Maori,' tenei ake ano etahi kei au ano e mohio ana. Kia ata titiro mai ano nga kai titiro Nupepa ki nga mahi a Urupeni i te tau kua hori ake nei, 1875, ko te marama ko Hepetema 28, i haere taua tangata ki Nepia, ko ana moni i haere ai e 3 hereni e 7 kapa i pau tonu i te utu o tona tikiti, akuanei ka moe atu i Nepia, no tetahi rangi ka hoki mai te taenga ki te Teihana, kaore tahi he moni hei utu tikiti, heoi ano ka mate te tangata nei i konei. Ka tono haere ki tetehi moni hei utu, e tae mai ai ki nga tamariki, ki te wahine hoki. Katahi ka tono atu kia Hamiora Tupaea, kaore nei o tera tangata ona kaainga i konei. Ka ki atu, e hoa, kaore o hereni, he mate toku, kaore tahi oku tikiti, kaore hoki aku hereni, ka ki atu a Hamiora, kaore aku moni, ka rongo a Petera Puiti, ka ui atu, he aha tena, katahi ka tono atu, homai he hereni hei utu moku i te Rerewei, ka hoatu e Petera, katahi ano ka tae mai ki Pakipaki. Ko tenei tangata ko Petera te mutunga mai o nga kauhau a te Maori, nana i utu tenei tamaiti rangatira, he uri no nga kaumatua tino rangatira o mua, no Hawaikirangi, riro ana ia ma te tangata iti rawa e utu ma Petera. E kore au e korero i enei korero, mei kaua koe e rere noa i runga i taku reta tawai mai ai ki taku kainga i nga moni a Henare Rata, e kii ana hoki koe, kia mohio koe, naku tonu aku moni. Kua kite hoki koe, kua korerotia e au i runga ake nei. Kia rongo mai koe, kaore au e pena me koe, kaore aau [sic] putake moni, ka tono noa ki tenei ki tenei, ko au, titiro mareri [sic] ai au he putake moni taku kei a Henare Rata, ka tono au. He putake moni ano hoki taku kei a Te Wiremu, na kona au i tono ai, e kii nei koe he hoko taku i Pukekura. Katahi ano te putake o te porangi ko koe e Urupeni, kua tanumia pea to kanohi, me to ngakau e te whakahi. Te ata titiro koe ki nga korero o taku panui, e takoto marama ana, e hara i te mea e korero ana ahau kia Urupeni. Kaore ano au i tango pokanoa i te mea a te tangata ko Urupeni anake te tangata ewhanako i taku patu pounamu i a Owahanga, no runga i te turanga ki toku papa tera patu, whanakotia ana e Urupeni, whakawakia ana a Urupeni mo tona tahae i taua pata [sic], hinga ana ia i te Komiti nui a Henare Matua, me nga tino rangatira nunui o Wairarapa, na, ko au kaore ano ano [sic] au i penei me ia e whakautu mai nei i taku panui, kia rongo mai koe, kaore au e mataku, me he mehemea ka tonoa mai au kia haere au ki te Hupirimi Kooti mo tenei mea, ka haere au. Kanui toku hiahia kia whakawakia au mo taku panui me ta Mangai, me kii katoa mai naku katoa, ka haere atu au ki te Kooti mo ena panui e rua, ahakoa na Mangai tetehi, me kii e au naku katoa raua, e pai ana au kia whakawa kia mohio ai koe e Urupeni ki toku tamarikitanga, ki tou koroheketanga poauau. Kaore ano au i kai i te pua o te nau, kaore ano au i noho i te ra o Hewa. Ina katahi ano ia ki tenei i kiia mai nei e koe ki te Pakeha, i kii

mai nei hei matua mo nga Maori, te kotahi he mahi maana, ko te matua anake, ara, e whatoro ana ki raro. Otira, e kore au e korero i tenei, kua kitea ra hoki i era i korerotia i runga ake ra. Kaati aku kupu i konei, kaore au e whakahoki i a Te Etita o TE WANANGA, *kaore ana kupu penei me a Urupeni. E hoa e Te Etita o* TE WANANGA, *kei pouri koe mo ena kupu aku, he mahi hoki tena kua whanua kia mahia a koe e te kai ta Nupepa, ahakoa kino tukua atu hei pakinga ma te waihuri whenua he mahi hoki kua whanua kia mahia e koe. E te kai ta Nupepa, ahakoa kino, tukua atu hei pakinga ma te wai huri whenua, he mahi hoki kua whanua kia mahia e koe. Heoi aku kupu whakautu mo nga kupu a Urupeni, na te hoa tautohe.*
NA ARIHI TE NAHU.

Na, e hoa e Te Etita, ki te kore koe e ta i tena reta, me ata whakahoki mai e koe kia au, kei pouri koe, ka makaia e koe.
Pakipaki.[30]

Te Wananga published her letter but chose not to translate it into English. The government, however, translated the letter for the use of the defence's lawyers in the subsequent libel case.

Translated from Wananga of October 21st, 76.

To the
Editor of the Wananga
Insert my letter in the Wananga in answer to the letter of Urupeni Puhara, who says Henry Russell has not stolen my land. I have to say to Urupeni that he is probably afflicted with madness; he could not have carefully considered Henry Russell's dealings with me. I understand them, but you, Urupeni, do not understand them. I am the veritable child of that pakeha, and I know how he has dealt with me in all respects. Now, Urupeni, just consider carefully consider [sic]; it was Henry Russell himself who purchased Heretaunga. I have received no money (from him) without a consideration given, as Urupeni says (I have). For all moneys which I received, a consideration was given. I have money in the Bank, but that pakeha, is withholding it. Secondly – I have land leased to Henry Russell called the 'Rohitu' for which I obtain no money. Urupeni says I had no money to purchase rum, therefore I went over to the Government. In answer to this I say, I am not a woman who drinks rum; the pakehas have never seen me drunk in the town, my lands have not gone for rum, neither have my lands gone by

mortgaging. But that man, Urupeni, has been seen drunk on the road by numbers of the pakehas who live at Napier. His are the lands which have gone for drink and by mortgaging. As for me, I have never suffered from drinking or mortgaging; but you, Urupeni, have been reduced to poverty; you are like a dog sniffing about ordure [*lit*. like a dog smelling the stink of shit]; whenever you see a person you beg money from him. He (i.e, Urupeni) followed me about for money to play at billiards with, and I gave him five shillings; then I saw a pakeha taking his coat from him as payment for the game for which they had been playing. He has no claim whatever upon me that he should ask me for money. But he said of me that I was like a Kootimana (Scotch thistle) getting hold of money from Henry Russell and the Government to purchase rum. My friend, hearken to me; I have claims on Henry Russell for money. First, there is my money; and secondly my lands. I have not received the money on account of my lands which are occupied by Henry Russell. Why do you not consider these things? – for you say you are a man of mature years and experience; but I now perceive that you do not understand, for you have rushed without cause to answer my publication (i.e her letter in the Waka Maori), for I did not write the name of Urupeni that he was robbing me of my money and my lands; I find now, however; that 'Henry Russell' is another name for Urupeni. Enough of this. I will now refer to the assertion of Urupeni that my lands have been kept from me by my marriage, In answer to this I say that Hiraka (her husband) transacts no business in reference to my lands; Hiraka has nothing to say about my lands. Henry Russell alone is occupying my lands, and he is the man who withholds them from me that he may obtain them himself – and yet Urupeni does not consider that he is a man married to another woman, and that there was no cause for his deserting his married wife. Urupeni has not made any compensation for his marriage. Old man, you Urupeni, have taken upon yourself without cause to answer my publication (i e her letter), therefore I expose your faults and your misery. I must refer to the words of Urupeni where he says the acts of Henry Russell are not (acts of) robbery. I know all his works. I am the Maori whom that pakeha has connected with all his transactions; the other Maories, many in number, became connected with him afterwards. But I have already made known his conduct in my letter which I sent to the Waka Maori, and there is still more that I know.

Let the newspaper readers mark the conduct of this man, Urupeni, last year 1875. On the 28th of September he went to Napier, he took with him three shillings and sevenpence, which he paid for a ticket. He slept at Napier, and on another day he started on his return, but when he got to the station he had no money to pay for a ticket, and so he was in a dilemma. He then went about begging money to pay (for a ticket), until he came to some children and a woman. Then he asked (money) of Hamiora Tupaea but that man has no place of residence here. He (Urupeni) said, 'My friend, have you any shillings? I am in a difficulty; I have no ticket and no shillings.' – Hamiora said, 'I have no money.' Petera Puiti overheard them talking and said 'What is that?['] Then he said 'Give me some shillings to pay my railway fare'. Petera gave him some, and so he got back to the Pakipaki. This man Petera is one of the lowest class of the Maori people, and he paid the fare for this scion of nobility, a descendant of grand old chiefs of Hawaikirangi – and his fare was paid by one of the lowest of the Maories, even by Petera. I would not advert to these things had you not rushed upon my letter and jeered me in respect of moneys received by Henry Russell, as you say. I desire you to know that my money is my own, as you know, and as I have said above. Mark me, I am not like you; you have no claim to any money whatever, you beg of any person, but I, having claims upon Henry Russell, asked him for money. I also have claims upon Mr Williams, and therefore I asked (for money), although you say I am selling Pukekura. You are the chief of fools. Your eyes are blinded and your eyes perverted by your rashness. You should have considered that the statements in my publication were perfectly clear, and not intended to apply to Urupeni. I have never taken anything from any person without having a right to it; but Urupeni robbed me of my greenstone mere named 'Owanga' [sic]. That weapon came to me from my father's side, and it was stolen by Urupeni; an enquiry was held over him stealing it and he was condemned by the Great Committee of Henare Matua, and the principal chiefs of Wairarapa. Now, I am not like that man who has answered my letter. Listen to me, I am not afraid. If I should be required to attend the Supreme Court about this matter I shall do so. I am very desirous that I should be proceeded against legally for my publication, and also that of Mangai. I am willing to take all the responsibility upon myself for both letters. I will appear before the Court to answer for both letters; although one was by Mangai, I will acknowledge them both. I should like to be tried so that you, Urupeni, might see my childishness and your own dotage and stupidity. I was never under the necessity of living upon the berries of the <u>Nau</u>, or starving in a parched land. Now, however, I am affected by what you have said to the pakeha who is called the Parent of the Maories – he should be kept to the proper duties of a parent, but his hands are stretched out below (towards the land). But I shall say nothing about this; it can be seen in what I have stated above. Let what I have said be sufficient. I shall not answer the Editor of the Wananga as he has not spoken in the same way as Urupeni.

> My friend, the Editor of the Wananga, do not be annoyed at the words which
> I have spoken. It is a work which is the duty of a publisher of a newspaper
> to perform; although they may be evil (words) publish them nevertheless,
> and let the flood overwhelm them. I have nothing more to say about Urupeni,
> my opponent.
>   By Arihi te Nahu
> Friend, the Editor. If you do not print this letter, send it back to me. Do not be
> annoyed and throw it away.[31]

Ārihi demonstrates her bravado in taking all responsibility for both letters as well as her destruction of Urupeni's character. She also points to the social changes that were impacting on Māori communities at the time, such as railways, alcohol and gambling. The letter shows that elements of more traditional thinking and tikanga remained: Urupeni's begging is made worse in that he is reduced to getting money from a low-born individual; and when he steals Ārihi's greenstone heirloom, it is to a Māori rūnanga that she goes for recompense rather than the Pākehā justice system.

Henry Russell chose to sue James Grindell, the editor, and George Didsbury, the printer of *Te Waka Maori* for defamation rather than the authors of the libellous letters, Ārihi Te Nahu and Māngai Uhuhu. Russell's motivations were most likely political: the government, his political enemies, operated the offending newspaper. But his aims were also realistic – as his lawyer suggested, suing Ārihi and Māngai for libel was 'practically impossible',[32] and Russell no doubt saw his best chance of gaining damages was from the public purse.[33] In November 1876 the Parliamentary opposition had managed to get the vote of £400 cut; the paper continued with funding from Donald McLean, the Native Minister, the Premier, Harry Atkinson, and several others, still under McLean's watchful eye.[34] Notwithstanding the newspaper's 'grey' official status,[35] *Te Waka Maori* had published the letters when still officially financed, and the Government took responsibility for the defence, an 'unjust and unconstitutional' act decried by its foes in Parliament and the press.[36]

The main trial was held in Wellington, but the Supreme Court appointed a lawyer, George Sainsbury, as a commissioner to take evidence from Māori witnesses at Napier to be used at the subsequent trial. In July 1877 Ārihi Te Nahu, the first defence witness, was subjected to four days of 'examination, cross-examination, and re-examination' by Walter Buller for the defendant (in effect, the Crown) and by the plaintiff's lawyers, including Wilson, her former trustee.[37]

The court went over her assertions against Russell in great detail, but also why she had written the letter.

> *My reason for writing what has been quoted, was that I might get my money back. When I wrote my letter I wrote it from feelings of irritation in consequence of all these matters. I fully believed all the statements in the letter. They were quite correct so far as my personal knowledge went, and so far as I could learn from others.*[38]

The collective nature of mana, and of 'knowing' things, can be seen in other statements. Her letter had also followed a meeting between Sheehan and some of her relatives: Ārihi had missed it due to illness.

> *After the meeting I talked to Nepia Te Hapuku [her father's younger brother] and Hapuku Te Nahu [her brother].... I do not know how long after the meeting it was that this talk took place. It was soon after at Pakipaki in his own house. The finish of the talk was that it was decided I should publish. We were all decided that I should word the letter. It was arranged that I should put in the names of all the people who objected to Henry Russell's conduct.*[39]

Her view of shared understandings and responsibilities, and the importance of orality within Māori society, can also be seen in the following discussion about her letter.

> Q. – What did you mean by the expression in your letter. 'But when the trusteeship was transferred to Henry Russell, he told me my money was all expended?'
> A. – *I did not say in the letter that he told me with his own mouth, but according to our Maori ideas his saying so to Hapuku is the same as saying it to myself in that he and I are one.*[40]

As Ārihi was a key witness for the defence, Buller's questioning was relatively gentle. Under cross-examination the atmosphere was more combatant, and her responses were brief.

> Q. – Did any pakeha suggest the writing of this letter?
> A. – *No. I am the pakeha. I have sufficient knowledge to know when evil deeds are done to me, and to speak.*

Q. – Did any pakeha suggest it before hand?
A. – No.

...

Q. – Did any pakeha tell you to repudiate the memorandum of charge?
A. – *I will not answer that question as I was not allowed to finish my last answer.*
      Question repeated
A. – *Who is this pakeha? Perhaps you know who he is.*

...

Q. – What was the conversation between you and the Heretaunga people of which you told Mr. Sheehan?
A. – *That they had been offering me money to complete the purchase of Heretaunga.*
Q. – What was the amount?
A. – *Why don't you produce the money belonging to me in your hands?*
Q. – Do you decline to say what the amount was?
A. – *Why should I disclose it?*
Q. – Have you been offered £6000 to settle the Heretaunga purchase?
A. – *I decline to answer the question.*[41]

Notwithstanding that Ārihi had 'sufficient knowledge to know when evil deeds are done', and stood up to the questioning, other evidence suggests that she was sometimes out of her depth when dealing with land issues. When Buller asked her about a meeting she had with Russell and his lawyers in Wellington to give her affairs over to him to protect, she said:

> When the deed was read over to me by the Interpreter it appeared to me that the contents were different to the understanding arrived at between Mr. Russell and me the night before. . . . I asked questions about the money. This was after I made the mark to the deed. . . . I objected some time to sign the paper. I was afraid of Mr. Henry Russell, I was afraid he was deceiving me. I then considered that as he professed to be a great friend of mine I ought to repose confidence in him, and I accordingly signed.[42]

One can imagine her concern and apprehension at trusting Russell, but doubt about what else she could do. Buller revisited this meeting in his re-examination.

Q. – Why did you first object to sign the deed at Wellington when Mr. Davis [an interpreter] was there?

A. – I was afraid I would be entrapped by Mr. Russell, my reason for being afraid was that I had seen some of his deceitful works before. I don't remember exactly, but I think the amount in the charge was over £1000. I objected about the money because I was afraid of his wide-awake tricks. I was the only Maori there. I do not know what amounts I owed to make it up to £1700. I asked Mr. Russell 'what are all these items?' His reply was 'It is as much to protect your lands from the pakehas.' This was before I signed. I thought this was true, and therefore I agreed to sign.[43]

Ārihi Te Nahu's evidence, in the end, was not good enough. Soon after an Auckland newspaper reported rumours that she 'broke down in her statements, which are said to be of a contradictory nature'.[44]

Hemaima, Māngai's Uhuuhu's wife, the other woman to give evidence at the hearing appears to be even less sure of the legal processes than Ārihi.

It was then in reply to what Mangai said that Henry Russell made use of heavy expressions that he [Māngai] sets out in his letter, that is making us pay our debts at once or he would take us into the Supreme Court. I then became frightened and sad. He then told us to return and sign our names to the deeds. We told him that we were not prepared to sign because neither the rents for the land nor the number of years were agreed upon, what we wished was that everything be fairly arranged before signing. Henry Russell insisted on our coming to sign.
Q. – Was there anything that induced you to sign?
A. – Henry told me and Mangai that if we would come and sign he would give us some money. 50l for Mangai and I was to get 30l. That was for our signing. We then thought about signing. We then came to Napier the next morning. He did not pay us the money before we came to sign. He told us that after we had signed he would give it to us. We requested him to pay us beforehand but he would not. We came to town and went to the Wananga office, myself, Mangai, Kingi, Ihakara, Hone and other Waikareao grantees, not all of them. We went to Mr. Locke's office, the deed was interpreted to us there. I did not approve of the contents. I signed it, my reason for doing so was that Mr. Russell said if we would sign he would give us the money. Another reason was the expressions made use of by Mr. Russell with respect to our debts (as stated in Mangai's letter) because Mangai was in debt to him. The debts were mine and Mangai's, I used to ask Mangai to get whatever I required. The things I asked Mangai to get for me was a plough and harrow.[45]

Russell sought to project himself as morally superior to other Hawke's Bay capitalists, and as looking after Māori interests. While Māori were sometimes suspicious of him, his methods led Māori to believe they could trust him (at least more than other Pākehā) and that they had a relationship with him that was more than just financial. Unfortunately Pākehā land purchasers considered Māori with a lack of financial acumen as 'fair game', and Russell was no exception.

The case proved expensive for the Government. Russell won, and was awarded £500 plus costs, which the *Evening Post* estimated as nearly £4,000.[46] Buller charged the Government £2,369 for his services, not including taxes, and the expenses for Māori called as defence witnesses were also paid from the public purse.[47] According to the *Evening Post*, both sides tried to get these witnesses on side and 'were treating them liberally'.[48] John Sheehan consequently sued the editor and printer for libel, and the government rather wisely agreed to read out an apology to him in Parliament and to provide him £100 to give to charity.[49] This was not the end of legal battles involving Ārihi Te Nahu and Henry Russell: in 1881 Russell successfully sued Ārihi for £2,746 owing to him.[50]

By 1878 the Repudiation Movement, as it was known, was a spent force, in debt and with little to show for its efforts.[51] In that year William Rees, a politician and lawyer who had acted for the movement, teamed up with Wī Pere, a Rongowhakaata and Te Aitanga-a-Māhaki leader who had carried the Repudiation flag in Poverty Bay, to form a trust to administer remaining Māori lands in that district. Māori, including women, entrusted over 200,000 acres of their land to the new trustees, who had extensive managerial powers. Unfortunately within a couple of years it was foundering; no support from Parliament, delays in the Native Land Court, and large debts from buying out Pākehā owners all contributed to the failure. A series of trusts followed in an attempt to salvage the wreckage but large amounts of land were later sold to cover the losses.[52] In August 1880, Atereta Ruru, concerned about her land published the following notice in Māori in the *Poverty Bay Herald*.

Turanganui,
19 Akuhata, 1880.
Kia WIREMU RII RIIHI, roia, raua ko WIREMU PERE, o Papati Pei, he tangata Maori, nga Kaitiak i [sic] whatatutia mo Pakake-a-whiri Koka, me etahi atu Poraka roto i e takiwa o Turanga.
Kia mohio Korua ko aua kai tiaki he whakaatu tenei kia korua ko ahau ko

ATERETA RURU, he tangata Maori, o Niu Tireni, e mea ana ahau i konei kia whaka kore kia whakamutu, nga mana nga tikanga whakahaere i tukuna atu e au kia korua i roto i etahi pukapuka tiaki naku na etahi tangata Maori hoki o nga karaati nga tangata no ratu[sic] nga whenua i whakahuatia i runga ake e tetahi taha, me WIREMU RII RIIHI, roia, raua ko WIREMU PERE, o tetahi taha. E tuku atu ana ahau tenei whakaatu kia korua no te mea kaore i marama ki au nga painga e puta ana kiau i runga i taku whakatutunga i a korua hei kiatiaki moku. Kahore ano i puta tetahi painga ki au.
    ATERETA RURU.

Kaititiro:
    M. J. Gannon.

[modern translation]
Gisborne
19 August, 1880.
To WILLIAM LEE REES, lawyer, and WIREMU PERE, a Māori person of Poverty Bay, Trustees appointed for Pakake-a-whiri Koka and some other blocks in the Gisborne district.

    Let you, those trustees, know that this is a statement to you that I, ATERETA RURU, a Māori person of New Zealand, state here that I cancel and stop the authority and management given by me to you in trustee documents [signed] by myself and other Māori people of [Crown] grants, in which the people whose land it is are named on one side, and WILLIAM LEE REES, lawyer, and WIREMU PERE, on the other side. I furnish this notice to you because the benefits coming to me through your appointment as trustees are not clear to me. I have not yet received any benefit.
Atereta Ruru
Witness: M. J. Gannon.[53]

This notice appeared with two others, identical except for the blocks named, one by a man, Īhaka Ngakangioue, the other by a woman, Āreta Te Apatū. We do not know how they fared in extracting their lands, but the notice is interesting in its construction. It is written in legalistic Māori, and was possibly composed first in English and then translated. The witness, Michael Joseph Gannon, formerly a parliamentary interpreter and in 1880 a clerk in the Native Land Court, certainly had experience with legal terminology and may have assisted in writing the notice.[54]

Testamentary declarations

Māori women could be the victims of fraud executed by those they trusted, including by professionals they hired to assist them to negotiate legal processes. Sometimes women got bad advice. Although we know little about the circumstances, Rongopāmamao had to tell her friend Mahora, who was married to a Native Department employee George Thomas Wilkinson, that their suit could not go ahead.

Ototoika
12 Akuhata 1895

Kia Mahora
*   E hoa tena koe korua ko to Rangatira me a korua tamariki i te nohoanga mai i to koutou kainga.*
*   Kua tae mai tau reta kiau. Kua tae ahau kia Parehuiroro e ki ana ia kua mutu noa atu tana whakaaro ki tatatou tono.*
*   Kua tukua atu tana tono wawahi mo ona hea i roto o Pakeho[.]*

*   he oi e Hora ka nui rawa nga tangata kua tono kia unuhia [?] ta taua kehi[.]*

Kua korero hoki maua ko te Wirihana mo ta tatou tono. e ki ana ia he nui rawa taku ruihi i taku whiwhi ki tana mohio no konei e hora i runga hoki i te ngoikore o nga take tupuna. Kua tau aku whakaaro me kore hoki taku kehi kei pouri mai koe ki au e taea hoki te aha tetehi take ko taku ano i whaki atu na ki a koe ma te mohi hoki ka tika[.]
Kaore au e tae atu kei te mate au[.]
he oi ano na to hoa
na te Rongopamamao

[modern translation]
Ototoika
12 August 1895

Dear Mahora
    My friend, greetings to you and your husband, and your children, living there at your place.

> I have received your letter. I have been to see Parehuiroro and she says she has made up her mind regarding our submission.
>
> She has issued her own submission to split off her shares from within Pakeho.
>
> well, [Ma]hora, there are many people who have asked that our case be dropped.
>
> Wirihana [Wilkinson] and I have also spoken about our bid. He says, my loss is greater than my gain, from what he knows of the area, Hora, and the weak position of ancestral matters. I have decided to drop my case. Don't be upset at me. What can be done [it is fruitless], another reason is that which I disclosed to you [before]. Te Mohi will put it right.
>
> I won't be going as I am sick.
>
> Concluding,
>
> from your friend,
>
> Rongopāmamao[55]

Use of interpreters, legal agents, and even family and friends, did not always guarantee inheritance of assets, which prompted some government officials to encourage Māori to make wills to secure their interests. According to Tai Ahu, because there was uncertainty over the rules of succession under custom as applied within the Native Land Court, the 'making of wills was actively encouraged by colonial governments'.[56] There is very little known about Māori uptake of testamentary practices in the nineteenth century. We have found at least 23 examples of wills made by Māori women between 1863 and 1900, but we have no doubt there are more in existence.

As other chapters in this volume demonstrate, Māori women participated in many legal forums, such as the Compensation Court and the Native Land Court, and they appeared before commissions of inquiry as witnesses. This participation generated a significant archive worthy of examination. Women took part in court proceedings as witnesses, claimants on an individual basis, or they appeared to advance and represent their family or iwi interests. In a few cases, they acted as interpreters, for example, Hēni Pore (Jane Foley) and Marian Stewart. The most significant institution dealing with testamentary declarations was the Native Land Court, which dealt with title investigations, partition orders and issues relating to succession.

Women's freedom to control land interests was constrained by the Native Land Court at times. Whilst in their communities women were used to exerting authority over land and resources, in the court they were subject to native land legislation that set processes of investigation and ownership based on the patriarchal nuclear family, in which the male breadwinner exerted total financial control. Customarily, upon marriage Māori women retained rights over land. In contrast, under the English law of coverture any property or money belonging to a woman became her husband's upon marriage.[57] In addition, upon marriage a woman's legal identity was folded into her husband's, as was her real property, although a husband was not able to sell real property or bequeath it without his wife's permission.[58] In the Native Land Court, Māori women's customary rights to manage land were acknowledged under clause 22 of the Native Lands Act 1869, which gave Māori women the legal status of single women, but over time their rights to convey and bequeath their lands were subject to restrictions.[59]

As written documents, wills are formulaic texts created out of a collaboration between a testator and a legal representative, but because this transfer of property moves from the oral to the written and involves cross-cultural communication, like petitions, the creation of wills relies on acts of translation and interpretation. Traditionally, Māori wills took the form of ōhākī, and these were recognised by the court until 1895, when they were abolished under section 33 of the Native Land Laws Amendment Act.[60] An ōhākī is an oral declaration or 'announcement of testamentary wishes to individuals gathered around [a deathbed] in a public performance'.[61] A feature of an ōhākī was its breadth in that it could encompass land and personal property, 'political and social arrangements also, as well as instructions on the burial of the deceased.'[62] Will making, then, drew upon an oral tradition of testamentary declaration. Formal written wills, though, had to adhere to certain formalities and conventions set out in the Wills Act 1837. This involved a proscribed format, composition and language, that it be in writing, signed by the testator and in front of witnesses, who had to attest to the document.[63]

Under the Native Succession Act 1881 the Land Court was empowered to recognise 'informal wills or writing in the nature of a will'.[64] Often these informal wills involved the use of scribes from within the community. In a succession case heard before the South Island Native Land Court in February 1887, Mere Kui testified that a will had been drawn up at the direction of Heremaia Tahitu and written by Mātene Kōrako:

> Deceased died in '71. There was a will leaving the property to Mere Kui, Peti Crane and Hannah Campbell. I purchased H. Campbell's share but it was lost. There are persons in the Court who were present at the time the will was made.

Matene Korako wrote the will. The persons present are Mere Hinehou Korako, Tini Brown and Sarah Palmer.[65]

Mere Hinehou Kōrako confirmed Mere Kui's claim.

I knew the deceased. I saw [the] will written. I know what the contents were. My husband wrote the will.

Hannah Campbell, sister of Mere Kui, also testified.

I am one of the persons mentioned in the will. It is perfectly correct as to my selling my share to Kui. I have nothing to say against the land being given to two.

Wills, as Victoria R. Bricker notes, are rich sources for studies of kinship, inheritance patterns, wealth, land ownership and material possessions.[66] The earliest extant written will of a Māori woman belonged to Etara Jillet, the widow of hotel-keeper Robert Jillet. Robert had died in 1860, and Etara was one of the beneficiaries of his estate. Under his will, he directed his four executors to sell his estate and hold the proceeds in trust to be divided equally 'between the Native woman Te Tara who is now and has been for many years living with me as my wife and my five reputed children by such Native woman namely Charlotte, John, Susan, William, and Sarah'. The trustees were directed to ensure the maintenance and education of the children, and were appointed guardians of those aged under 21.[67] Etara's will, devised in April 1863, is written in English, and signed with her mark. In it she bequeathed her share of her husband's estate, as well as 'any landed estate at Otaki and Kawhia in the colony of New Zealand that I may be entitled to to my children to share and share alike'.[68] It is possible Etara hoped to secure her children's interests in tribal land because she may have been uncertain of their rights as children of mixed ancestry who lived at a distance from their Māori kin. At least in making a testamentary declaration she could feel secure that she was protecting her children's economic future, as well as ensuring their tribal connections were maintained. This is a very different future from what Robert envisioned for the children as specified in his will.

In 1881, women lost the right to bequeath property as they wished. Under section 3 of the Native Succession Act, in cases where an individual died without making 'hereditary disposition', the court was to be guided in its judgements on succession by native custom, but where a couple was married by custom, the court was to be 'guided by the law of New Zealand'.[69] This meant that Māori women were subject to the same restrictions as Pākehā women under New Zealand law, and a woman could not make a will without the consent of her husband.[70] Rai Watt's will was 'made with the consent' of her husband, Isaac Newton Watt, in April 1885, even though a year earlier married women gained legal capacity as *feme sole* under the Married Women's Property Act, giving them the freedom to dispose of their real or personal property by deed or will as if they were single women.[71] Given the restrictions on married women's property rights under New Zealand law prior to 1884, it was through testamentary declarations that women could ensure the financial security of daughters and nieces. In her will, Rai Watt made land over to her married daughters as tenants in common with the right to dispose of the land as they pleased. She specified the land was to be held separately from their husbands.[72] In other cases, Ria Tutereiao made Rūhia Pōrutu her sole beneficiary, while Mere Pawa made Ani and Atarete Enoka equal beneficiaries of her estate.[73] This type of inheritance was particularly important for married women, for in this way they obtained property in their own name. Meri Taki was the sole beneficiary of Maata Kuiatu's estate, which was, 'for her own use and separate use free from the debts and control of her present or any future husband.'[74]

While at times New Zealand laws restricted Māori women's capacity to manage their property, they did take advantage of legislation that provided them with some level of property protection. Deserted wives could apply to a magistrate for an order protecting their earnings from their husband, and any debts he may accumulate in his name. In such cases, the order enabled a deserted wife to act with the legal capacity of a single woman. Ani Parata obtained a married woman's protection order against her husband in August 1873, declaring he had 'been guilty of repeated acts of cruelty' and 'had habitually failed to provide a maintenance' for her.

> And the said Ani Parata Ngauru then and there applied to me [James Coutts Crawford, Resident Magistrate] for an order to protect any money or property she might acquire by her own lawful industry and property which she might become possessed of after her desertion against her husband or his creditors or any person claiming under him.
>
> Now I the said Resident Magistrate having heard the matter of the said complaint and being satisfied of the fact of such desertion and that the said Ani Parata

Ngauru is maintaining herself by her own lawful industry and that such desertion was without reasonable cause do hereby adjudge and order that the earnings and property acquired by the said Ani Parata Ngauru since said Thirteenth day of December one thousand eight hundred and fifty nine being on or about the day on which the said Ani Parata Ngauru was so deserted as aforesaid shall be protected against the said Hemi and all creditors and persons claiming under him.[75]

Ani Parata devised her estate by will in 1875, and did so as if a single woman. She bequeathed her land at Pipitea pā and Ōrangikaupapa to her nieces, Mere and Ana, leaving the remainder of her real property to her mother and brother as tenants in common.[76]

In her will a woman could articulate complaints and assert authority. In 1875 Mary Toro bequeathed her real and personal property to her husband absolutely, as well as two quarter-acre sections in Havelock (Marlborough) 'known as land belonging to Paora te Riki the said Paora te Riki having unlawfully come by the same at the oath of my Uncle Hura'.[77] In 1875, Matire Piripi specified in her will that 'any titles [that] may be discovered, and defined by processes of law in Native Lands here in New Zealand must go' to her beneficiaries in equal shares.[78] Wills were also a way to place certain restrictions on use of land into the future. In 1877 Hana Te Kaewa, a widow, specified that her sections at Ōtākou must not be sold.[79] Ria Moheko had extensive land interests in Otago. 'I bequeath unto my adopted children namely Patuki Topi of Ruapuke and Hone Wiwi Taiaroa of Otago Heads the whole of my land in the Otago Heads Reserve', to be divided equally between them. These lands were 'not to be mortgaged or sold to any European or Native other than a Native of the Ngaitahu tribe.'[80] Women were willing to go to higher courts to contest wishes of a testator: Airini Tōnore and Mary Ann Rhodes both took their cases to London's Privy Council.[81] Such instances were rare, for it was an option only available to women of great wealth.

Of the 23 wills sighted, just over half were signed with a mark, but this did not necessarily equate with a lack of understanding of legal processes or the content of the text. Understanding the texts was supposed to be enhanced by accurate translation, for the practice was that interpreters usually read out wills in Māori to the testators. Ebenezer Baker, for instance, interpreted the English-language will of Ria Tutereiao. Baker attested 'she properly understood' it and 'being unable to write she made her mark' before witnesses.[82] Such attestations are a common part of the documentation attached to probate files, reflecting the existence and creation of the testamentary declaration within a cross-cultural context.

Generally, the signature is 'not understood as a piece of writing intended to convey a meaning but as a graphic symbol or device, with names signified by a mark or stamp used as and regarded as signatures.'[83] In his work on northern India, Christopher Bayly uses the phrase 'literacy aware' to describe a society familiar with commercial and property transactions.[84] Māori were a 'literacy aware' society, for legal transactions were common, and a range of marks were recognised as a record of one's legal identity and accepted as legal signatures. As Hilary E. Wyss notes, a mark is a record of authority, 'symbolic of presence rather than an inability to write out one's name.'[85]

Conclusion

Māori women did seek to use the law to protect their interests, taking up the opportunity to devise and bequeath their property in wills, and turning to the court to obtain protection orders against husbands. However, women tended to be the victims of the legal system, as the cases presented in this chapter show. Māori women's experience of sexual violence during the nineteenth century reveals the powerful hierarchies of power and race that operated within the courts, which tended to follow characterisations of Māori women as 'naturally' promiscuous. Such depictions of the sexually available 'native woman' have long histories; they were popularised in European contact narratives, and became embedded within settler colonial mindsets. Such views filtered into the courts, influencing the decisions of all-male juries who tended to find the accused guilty on a lesser charge.

There is some debate over the degree to which Māori levels of literacy enabled them to negotiate an ever-expanding and complex legal system, particularly native land laws. According to Bradford Haami, missionaries, who instructed their pupils in religious texts, poorly prepared Māori to cope with 'cumbersome English legal jargon'.[86] Māori capacity to present petitions and devise wills, and to make use of intermediaries, suggests a far more complex picture that is more in keeping with the findings of Māmari Stephens and Tai Ahu, who argue te reo Māori had a high civic status in the mid-nineteenth century. This sitation owed much to the amalgamationist views of leading colonial officials, who sought to, 'institute English law in New Zealand by persuading Māori communities of its merits.'[87] In using te reo Māori in a range of official publications, the government's aim was to educate and inculcate amongst Māori an understanding of official and legal institutions and processes, with the ultimate goal of supplanting Māori institutions and concepts with English models.[88] Use of te reo Māori was also borne of pragmatic need: in order to engage with Māori, officials and public servants employed in the Native Department required a working knowledge of the language. Because te reo Māori was used in creating legal documents and contracts, as well as in legislation, 'engagement between private individuals and the legal system' was enhanced and encouraged.[89] Nevertheless, only a small number of women used the law to manage and protect their interests. In the end, the law was a powerful tool of colonialism; it underwrote dispossession in the Native Land Court, regarded Māori women's bodies as property, and failed to fully acknowledge the violence perpetrated against them.

CHAPTER 7

'If I die, I am dying for the Lord': Religion

Although Anglican Church Missionary Society (CMS) missionaries arrived in New Zealand in 1814, they had little success until the latter half of the 1820s. From the missionary side, this may be put down to their increased economic independence from their Bay of Islands hosts, better leadership, better linguists amongst their ranks, and a shift in policy from promoting 'civilisation' first to a greater emphasis on conversion. Māori, who had tended to use the missionaries as conduits for European goods, were also seeking new ways in which to gain knowledge of, and engage with, the outside world. We can perhaps discount Kendall's baptism of Maria Ringa in 1823 so she could marry Philip Tapsell (see chapter 8) – she ran off after a day – but the mission claimed its first genuine believer, a deathbed conversion, in 1825.[1] Wesleyan missionaries arrived in 1822, with French Catholic priests following in 1838. What began as a trickle of conversions soon became a flood as Māori sought out the new spiritual knowledge of the Pākehā.

It is surprising that there are relatively few surviving accounts from Māori women on religious matters. Literacy and religious texts were of especial importance to the spread of missionary Christianity, and Māori came to prize scriptural knowledge, which was included as part of the intellectual armory employed by chiefs in formal speeches. This lacuna, at least in governmental archives, may be partly due to New Zealand's lack of an 'official' religion. Although a few officials may have had evangelical impulses, the government was less concerned about what Māori believed than how their religious practices might impact on general peace and the processes of colonisation. This is not to say that women may not have written about their religious beliefs and experiences, but that their writing may now be lost, held privately, or waiting for future discovery.

Yate's letters

Reverend William Yate joined the CMS Mission in 1828 just as Northland Māori were becoming enthusiastic for the missionary faith. Yate is perhaps best known for sexual scandal: when returning from a visit to England in 1836, allegations arose of a relationship with the third mate of the ship he was travelling in, and his fellow missionaries also gathered testimony from young Māori men detailing his involvement in homosexual activity. Yate did not get back to New Zealand, returning to England from Sydney after an unsuccessful attempt to rescue his reputation.[2]

On his initial return to England, before scandal erupted, Yate published a book, *An Account of New Zealand*, on CMS activities, in which he included a number of letters from Māori in which they attested to their Christian faith. Letter writing was a practice that he actively encouraged.

> In order both to cultivate, and to draw out, the feelings of those among whom I was labouring, it appeared to be one very useful plan to induce them to commit their ideas to writing. In pursuance of this method, the Christian Natives, and those desirous of becoming Christians, have at different times, during the last four or five years, addressed Letters to me; which have accumulated at length to a somewhat bulky mass of correspondence.[3]

From this 'bulky mass', Yate selected those which best suited his purposes, including some from women. In 'reading' the letters we need to be aware of Yate's motivations. Although a religious man, he was of fairly humble origins, and his book gave him a short period of relative fame in polite society while he was in London.[4] His fellow missionaries were less impressed. Quite apart from his alleged sexual transgressions, they believed the book to be inaccurate, and 'resented what they considered to be an assertion of self throughout the volume'.[5]

Although Yate acknowledges his encouragement of Māori writing, he does not explain his methods. The letters are in English, so are almost certainly translations. Yate states that they 'addressed Letters to me', something he may have encouraged. He does not indicate if the authors wrote their own letters, or dictated them to him or another person, or whether he assisted them in crafting their words. Whatever his degree of input, it is clear it is Yate's message being projected. As Judith Binney notes, 'Yate's relationship with his pupils was one charged with emotionalism, but an emotionalism derived from religious preoccupation. It is clear that the primary basis of his teaching was to awaken the neophytes to the omnipotence of sin.'[6] This can be seen in the letter of Wāhanga, a 'married native [man] living in Mr. Kemp's family' who wrote, 'Who can bear the pain of the fire which burns for ever? I want to make haste to Jesus Christ, that I may be saved from it.'

Wāhanga's wife, Pāhuia, also wrote:

> LETTER II. FROM PAHUIA, WIFE OF WAHANGA. *Mr. Yate It is true, it is very true, that it is good to tell to Jehovah all that is in our heart, whether it is good, or whether it is evil. My desire is, that my soul may be saved in the Day of Judgment. It will not be long before Jesus Christ appears to judge mankind; and I also shall be judged. It is right that I should be judged, and that I should be condemned; for my heart is very wicked, and will not do one good thing not one, not one, not one, that Jesus Christ, and God, and the Holy Spirit say is good: if I am angered by them, it will be just. But will not the Son of God save me? You say he will; and I believe it. You say that, bad as it is, he will wash my soul in His blood, and make it good and clean. That is what I want. I want to be admitted into His Church, and to be made His Child, and to be taught His lessons out of His Book; and to be taken care of by Him, and to be done what with, done what with, done what with Thou, O Lord Jesus, say what! Mr. Yate, listen: this is all from me, from PAHUIA.*[7]

Pāhuia's letter states that she 'want[s] to be admitted into His Church', most likely indicating that she is yet to be baptised. The CMS missionaries applied stricter criteria in admitting Māori for baptism as full members of the church mission than their Wesleyan counterparts, and it was missionaries who decided whether individuals were sufficiently transformed.[8] The following letter from another woman, Raru, recounts various sins that she has committed.

> LETTER VIII. *Mr. Yate If you are willing to permit me to enter the sacred Church of Christ by baptism, my heart is very desirous to be baptized. I altogether believe that Jesus Christ is the Son of God; and that he died for my sins, and for the sins of the world. Here I am: and have been, of old, a very wicked woman; but now my heart is sore on account thereof. I have been thinking of Jesus Christ's love for me, though I am such a sinful woman; and that makes me sorrowful. It is my desire, for the future, to act as the Bible*

says, and to forsake all my sins, and to repent before God, for all I have done wrong; and to love Jesus Christ, because he loved me. These are my thoughts to you, Mr. Yate, from me, from Raru, who was so bad a woman as to be always quarrelling with her husband Paru, and teazing him; and who twice beat her mother for scolding her child; and who once stole things out of Mrs. Hamlin's place for food. It is not a desire to have a new name, but because I love the Saviour, makes me wish to be baptized. This is all. RARU.[9]

Her words 'It is not a desire to have a new name' also point to the missionary practice of bestowing 'Christian names' upon their communicants. That she mentions it shows that possessing the new name had some novelty or cachet, and perhaps marked the owner out as more fashionable or sophisticated. The author of the following letter sports a Christian name, although she would have been known by a Māori version, such as 'Hēra Wātikini' or something similar.

LETTER XXVI. SARAH WATKINS WARU TO THE REV. W. YATE; FROM THE WAIMATE, NOV. 1834. To Mr. Yate Sir, Mr. Yate, how do you do you, who permitted us to enter the Church of Christ? This is the thing, Sir if, from our baptism, we walk uprightly before you, then the words of God will spring up within us: for you desire us to live as in the presence of God. But I am writing to you that you may hear my thoughts. If the grace of God should cause us, the evil, the deaf, the hard-hearted people, to hear and obey the callings of God, then all will be well; but we are more inclined to listen to evil than to good: perhaps this is the reason, perhaps it is not, that we have not in truth received the things of Jesus Christ. Ah, Sir, we are not yet jealous enough of the deceitfulness of our hearts, which are yet native and ignorant, and blind and deaf, and hard and covered over with sin; and the sinfulness of our hearts confuses all the words of everlasting life, which we hear with our ears, and read out of the Word of God. The thoughts of our native heart sometimes say, 'By and bye listen: do not listen to-day: to-morrow will do for you to be thoughtful about the soul to-morrow, or by and bye.' How is it to be? and how am I to be rid of this distracting native heart? Think you about it and do you say. Sir, Mr. Yate, listen to my speech. I am very well, as I am writing this book to you; but before you return here again, perhaps I shall be returned to dust, perhaps I shall not; for God has said, that every man who lives in this world must die; but he has not said when. Sir, Mr. Yate, listen to me, and I will tell you all about those who have died since you left New Zealand. Many who believe in Christ have died; and it is well that his believing people should go to Him, and not sit here for ever. Kape Kohine's younger sister was one: Tuwakawaha's daughter was another; the elder brother of Mere Hemara, Tangiwai; the wife of your boy Toa-taua, and Toa has been crying ever since she died; Kohine Rangi her name was Mere, for she was baptized, and she partook of the sacrament of the Lord's Supper; and Mr. Henry Williams is come up from Paihia for the purpose; Mr. Clarke sent a messenger for him she died; and she died believing, and she is gone to heaven. Another also, as I am writing this book, is dying Koihuru, the wife of your good boy Henare; one at the village of Ngai-te-wiu, a believing woman; another, Pekapeka, the wife of Hako; all these are dead; and before you come back we shall be all swept away. Hurry back again altogether; hurry back again to this native land! Mr. Yate, how do you do? Waru and I are to go to the Lord's Supper next week: pray for us, that God would cause us rightly to go. Mr. Yate, health to you, and to all your friends. I am well, and George; and Caroline and Cosmo are well: and I am thinking, that though, before you come back here, my body may die, my spirit will live, and it will live happy with God for ever. This is all my speech to you, Sir, mine, SARAH WATKINS WARU.[10]

Yate had already left New Zealand about five months earlier, and Hēra was fully expecting him to return. Her letter betrays either her own preoccupation with death and the danger of sin, or that this was a discourse expected by Yate. Several times she refers to her 'native heart', which is most likely a translation of the term 'ngākau māori'. As in English, Māori emotions may emanate from bodily organs, but the term 'māori' in this context has a variety of meanings, including 'freely' or 'without restraint'.[11] Missionaries in the nineteenth century considered Christianity and civilisation as curbs to impulsive 'savagery'. The 'native heart' might therefore refer to a propensity to excess or violence, to a lack of civilisation, or in the context of this text, to superstition and lingering pagan influence.[12] It appears that Hēra was sincere in a desire for transformation, but she was also aware that this was appropriate language for missionaries and converts.

Deathbed scenes

Untimely death was always a possibility in the nineteenth century, and Hēra's letter refers to dead and dying people. Deathbed utterances were powerful concepts in both Māori and Pākehā cultures. Within Western culture, '[c]hildren were encouraged to think about death, their own deaths and the edifying or cautionary death-beds of others',[13] and the deathbed scene was a convention prevalent in Victorian fiction, and used as Christian propaganda.[14] Some Christians also believed that 'spiritual phenomena [were] exhibited while in the dying state', and righteous Christian deaths were 'the portable evidence of Christianity'.[15] For missionaries and their supporters, deathbed utterances by Māori also vindicated the work of proselytising indigenous peoples, and they were seen as a genuine expression of conversion (with apostasy unlikely). For Māori, death is a particularly tapu state, and the ōhākī of a dying chief carried great weight.[16] It is thus not surprising that some deathbed scenes involving Māori women appear in the archive. However, because the dying person was unlikely to be a position to record their own last words, such voices were generally relayed by third parties.

Yate's *Account* presents an obituary to 'a converted native', Ann (Ani) Waiapu, in which her deathbed utterances are recorded. This was also published in the *Missionary Register* on October 1834, and an almost identical handwritten version sits in the Yate Correspondence in the Alexander Turnbull Library.[17] Ani died in 1832. According to the obituary, Ani lived for many years with the Kemps, a missionary family, although she 'clung to her native superstitions with a frightful eagerness'.[18] She then married Waiapu, who was employed at the mission, and they had two children. After her husband's conversion and taking on of the name of James (Hēmi) in 1830, Ani's attitudes slowly changed. 'The convictions of sin in the mind of his wife had been very gradual: it was only as she discovered the fallacy, one by one, of her native superstitious observances, that she gave them up, and embraced the doctrines of the Gospel.'[19] Unfortunately she was afflicted with consumption, which led to an early death.

Naturally, Ani's concerns are for her children. She instructs her husband, 'James, do not keep my children from going to heaven. I think now I must die; but do not keep Sarah and William from going to heaven. Take them to church: never take my girl on board ship; but let them both go to God, the great and the good.'[20] The reference to the ship concerns sexual relations with visiting sailors, an activity the missionaries termed as prostitution. The main focus, however, is her realisation of her impending death and her ascent to heaven.

'Ah. Mrs. Kemp,' said she, as that kind woman was smoothing her pillow, 'alas! Mrs. Kemp, good bye. I am going to Jesus Christ, who loves me. I shall see him now.

I have seen him with my heart; and now I love him with my heart. It is not my lips only that believe, but belief is firmly fixed within me.'[21]

Ani, at this time, had not been baptised. Perhaps, by virtue of her upbringing with the Kemps or her husband's conversion, she was already known as 'Ann'.[22] But she had been a candidate for some time, and Yate was keen that she be christened before her death. To his explanation of the Sacrament she replied:

'Yes, Jesus did indeed die upon the cross for me and but for Him, I should now die a native death, and go to a place of darkness and punishment.' 'Mr. Yate, do you tell me, Shall I be carried up to the House of Prayer on the next sacred day? and will you let me and James eat of the bread and drink of the cup, concerning which the Saviour said, "Do this in remembrance of me?"' She then added, 'What are we to remember?' I replied, 'That Christ loved us, and died for our sins.' 'Ah! I shall never forget that,' was her quick reply. 'But,' I said, 'Jesus sometimes, at his Supper, reveals Himself more clearly to his children; they see more of his love; he is set forth crucified among them; and when they see this, they love him more, and try to serve him better.' 'Then, James,' was Ann's expression, 'get a litter ready, that I may be carried up to the House of God on Sunday; for I desire to try his love.'[23]

On the Sabbath she was brought to the service, where Yate 'healed [her] of the worst malady that ever affected human beings the malady of sin'.[24] The account is deliberately emotive, and the obituary includes Ani's words for effect.

'Jesus Christ is mine, Mr. Yate,' she said, 'and I am Jesus Christ's. I know him now; I know him now: he is come here' fixing her hand upon her heart 'and he will not go away again any more.' I asked her if she wished to return to the world, and be restored to health: 'What!' was her reply, 'and Jesus Christ sometimes with me, and sometimes not; and I sometimes thinking evil, and sometimes thinking good! No, no, no! Mrs. Kemp will be a better mother to my babies than I shall be. I will go.'
...
She said much about her Husband, and Saviour and Friend in heaven: her last words were, 'James, I am going. I am full of pain: I am going above, away from pain;'[25]

Yate was able to insert himself within the narrative, as her spiritual saviour upon earth: death 'bare towards her no frowning countenance; he was no unwelcome guest. He arrived, and was acknowledged as a long-expected friend; a friend, who came to break the fetters that had bound her soul to earth'.[26] But the text was also designed to appeal to English donors, who should know that their money had saved an unknown Māori woman from damnation. Unfortunately Ani's infant son soon after succumbed to the same disease, but readers could be assured that: '[h]er surviving daughter is under the care of Mrs. Kemp; and will be brought up by her in that holy religion, whose ways, from the experience of the lamented mother, have been proved to be "pleasantness and peace."'

For missionaries, as in the Ann Waiapu account, the woman's voice was part of a wider discourse. A similar, although briefer, account can be found in a speech by the Wesleyan missionary, Reverend James Wallis of Whāingaroa. In 1845, Wesleyan missionaries and male Māori converts (through interpreters) spoke at a meeting in Auckland. Māori women may have been present, as Weretā, 'a converted native, from the Taranaki (south) district' included a reference in his greeting to 'My Brethren and Sisters', although there is no evidence that they spoke publicly. When Wallis addressed the crowd, he recounted another deathbed scene in support of a motion that although any success came from God, men should be active in spreading the word of God. His speech included a reference to 'the wife of a chief of rank' who 'died under very encouraging circumstances'.[27] The chief was identified as Wiremu Nēra Te Awaitaia (of Ngāti Māhanga) so the unnamed woman was probably Rōra Tūrori, a high-ranking woman of Ngāti Tūwharetoa.[28]

> I asked her if she had any thing to communicate, or any final directions to give. She answered 'No, excepting to thank you for all your kindnesses towards me.' ... Casting her arms upwards, she exclaimed – 'Now I am going to the kingdom of Glory,' and sinking into the attitude of death, without a struggle, she expired.[29]

While Yate's account of Ann Waiapu was particularly directed at readers in England, Wallis's retelling of Rōra's words were aimed at the Māori and Pākehā listening at the meeting. Both women, however, were exemplars of righteous death, and their words employed to proclaim missionary success.

The accounts above show the dying Christian thinking of heaven on her deathbed; for Māori the ōhākī was an opportunity for a dying chief to proffer more temporal advice and instructions. In 1865 the Christchurch *Press* stated that it had 'been requested to publish the following notice respecting the death of Priscilla Panepane, a Native woman of rank among the tribe residing at Kaiapoi'.[30]

Kaiapoi, 29 Mei, 1865.

E hoa ma, kia roko Koutou, kua mate a Pirihira Panepane, he wahine rakatira no roto i te hapu i a Tuahuriri, no roto i a Tuteahuka, no roto i a Maru. Na, e hoa ma, kia roko Koutou ki tana kupu poroporoki i penei i kona ra e koro ma, e kui ma, e tama ma, e hine ma, i kona ra ki te ao, kia atawhai hoki i te ao nei ki to tatou taoka nui ko te pakeha. Ka mutu tana poroporoki.

[newspaper translation]
Kaiapoi, May 29, 1865.
Let all our friends be informed that Priscilla Panepane is dead. She was a woman of rank of the family of Tuahuriri, which is related to Tuteahuka and descended from Maru. Hear, friends, her last words, which were these: – 'Farewell all of you, ye mothers, ye brothers, ye sisters; I leave you in the world; be ye obliging towards our great source of riches, the white people.' Thus ended her words.[31]

Pirihira's death occurred during a period of tension and war, when it was not unusual for some ōhākī at this time to express loyalty to the Crown or friendship to Pākehā, or instruct the tribe to adhere to the law and Christianity.[32] Ngāi Tahu never fought the Crown militarily; more sparsely populated than northern iwi, they were demographically swamped before the start of wars in Taranaki in 1860. Pirihira's instruction to atawhai (be kind to) the Pākehā should be seen in the context of the tribe's expressions of support for the Crown at a number of public meetings, including several at Kaiapoi.[33] The sentiments she expressed were popular amongst Pākehā, and were reprinted in some other settler newspapers around the country (in several cases more than once).[34]

Other deathbed scenes recounted by Māori adhered to more Christian themes. In 1858 Hākopa Te Pātūtū, most likely of Te Āti Awa,[35] wrote an account of the death of his wife Rāhira who was suffering from a throat disease.

Ka tata ia ki te mate, katahi ka puaki ake tona whakaaro, ki au 'E pai ana au, e haere ana ki ta taua tamaiti. Kia rongo mai koe, ki te mate au e mate ana au mo te Ariki, ki te ora au e ora ana au mo te Ariki.'

[modern translation]
When she was close to death, then she revealed her thoughts to me, 'I am fine, and going to our child. Listen to me, if I die, I am dying for the Lord. If I live, I am living for the Lord.'[36]

Another Māori account of a deathbed scene appeared in an article printed in the religious niupepa, *Te Korimako*, in 1887, although the text states that the death occurred in 1855. Hōhepa Parāone Hūkiki's account described the death of his daughter, Hiraina Parāone, a pupil at Thomas Chapman's mission school. Although not stated, Maketū was the likely location of the story, as the missionary Chapman lived at the Bay of Plenty settlement between 1851 and 1861.[37] It starts with Hōhepa, his wife Pirihira and others beside Hiraina's bed.

Na Pirihira tenei i ui iho. E Hine e pehea ana koe? Ka kii ake a Hiraina, e pouri ana ahau kia Te Hapimana raua ko Mata Hapimana, kia korua hoki, ki a korua tamariki hoki, ka kii ake ano ki au E Hepa, kia kaha te whiu i o tamariki i muri i au nei, kaua ratou e tukua kia tutu. Mehemea ka tutu ratou kia kaha te whiu, kia ahua pai, kei kite mai au, ka nui toku pouri. Muri iho, ka kii ake ano a Hiraina, kua tae atu toku aroha, kia Te Mete raua ko Mata Mete, ka ui iho ano a Pirihira. E Hine, e mohio ana koe ki te wahi e haere ai koe? Ka kii ake a Hiraina. E hara i au te whakaaro, na te Atua te whakaaro ki te mate ranei ki te ora ranei . . .

. . .

tikina a Ruihi Hauiti, he hoa tera nona i te oranga, he tino hoa, ka tae mai a Ruihi ka totoro atu te ringa, ka kii atu hei konei e Rui, ka haere au kia Miriama, kua mate tera, i mua tata i a ia.

[modern translation, quotation marks added]
Pirihira asked this, 'Girl, how are you?' Hiraina said 'I am sad for Mr Chapman and Mother [Mrs] Chapman, for you and your children.' She said to me 'E Hepa [Hōhepa], make sure you chastise your children after I am gone, don't let them be unruly. If they are, really chastise them, so they are good, lest I see it and become very sad.'

    Afterwards, Hiraina also said 'My love goes out to Mr Smith, and Mother Smith' and Pirihira said 'Girl, do you know the place you are going?' Hiraina said 'I don't know, God knows about life and death . . .'

. . .

she said, 'Fetch Ruihi Hauiti,' she was a friend of hers during her life, a real friend. When Ruihi came she stretched out her hand and said 'Farewell, Rui, I am going to Miriama.' She had died, just before her.[38]

It appears that Hōhepa believed that Hiraina's near-death state gave her insights that others lacked. Whether this derived from missionary teaching or Māori concepts of tapu (or both) is unclear.

Na ka ui iho ano ahau. Kia Hiraina Paraone. E Hine, ka pehea nga tangata katoa i te hokinga mai o te Karaiti, a muri ake nei. Na ka kii ake a Hiraina, ka puta mai ia a mua ka ara ake nga tangata katoa me o ratou tinana, a ka korerotia te ritenga o a ratou mahi, a ka haere te hunga i mahi i te pai ki te ora tonu, ko te hunga hoki i mahi i te kino ki te ahi ka tonu, ka mutu i konei te korero ake kia matou . . .

Then I questioned her, Hiraina Parāone, again, 'Girl, how will the people be when Christ returns in the future?' Hiraina said, 'he will appear in the future, and all the people and their bodies will rise up, their actions will be judged and the people who did good will go to eternal life, those who did evil will go to the eternal fire,' and she stopped speaking to us . . .[39]

Six days later it was clear her death was imminent. Hōhepa asked Hiraina:

E Hine, ko wai tau e tatari nei? Ka kii ake ia, ko Te Hapimana. Na ha haere a Aporo Naihi, ki te tiki i a Te Hapimana, a ka tae mai a Te Hapimana. Ko tona reo tuatahi tenei i patai iho ai. E Hiraina, e haere ana koe, ka kii ake, ae. Ka ui iho ano Te Hapimana, ko te patai tuarua. E Hiraina, e haere ana koe ki to Matua, ki runga ki te Rangi; ka mea a Hiraina. Ae. Ka ui iho ano a Te Hapimana, ko te patai tua toru. Ae. Haere i runga i te kaha o te Matua, o te Tamaiti, o te Wairua Tapu, ne? Ka mea ake ano. Ae.

'Girl, who are you waiting for?' She said, 'Mr Chapman.' So Āporo Naihi went to fetch Mr Chapman who came. This is what he said first, 'Hiraina, you are going,' she said 'yes.' Mr Chapman asked his second question, 'Hiraina, you are going to your Father in heaven' and Hiraina said 'yes.' Mr Chapman asked again, his third question, 'Yes, go with the strength of the Father, the Son and the Holy Spirit, eh?' She said again 'Yes.'[40]

Hiraina died soon afterwards. The article does not give much detail about the individuals, or when and why it was written. Hōhepa may have written the account soon after the death. He expressed both his and his wife's sadness at their daughter's passing, and their joy that her soul would go to heaven, something he was convinced would happen. *Te Korimako* was edited by the evangelist philo-Māori Charles Davis and funded by American Baptist philanthropists, so Hōhepa's account, with considerable religious content including scriptural quotations, fitted well with the overall kaupapa of the niupepa.

The Institute of Nazareth

Sister Mary Joseph (Suzanne) Aubert is New Zealand's most famous Catholic nun. Having been recruited by Bishop Pompallier in France, she arrived in Auckland in 1860, and in 1862 helped form the small congregation of the Holy Congregation. This order took over a boarding school for Māori girls, the Nazareth Institute at Mount St Mary's near Freemans Bay.[41] Peata, the first Māori nun, also taught at the school. Formerly known as Hoki, Peata was a daughter of the Ngāpuhi chief Rewa, and was one of Pompallier's earliest converts. She entered Catholic folklore as having faced off a Māori war party at the Catholic mission at the sack of Kororāreka in 1845,[42] and remained a staunch adherent of the church until her death. On 24 June 1867, Pompallier celebrated the feast of the nativity of St John the Baptist at the Auckland Cathedral, which 'afforded another opportunity to the Catholic children of this city and neighbourhood of wishing his Lordship many happy returns of his patron's feast-day', and where the various schools presented addresses. Peata and Hēra (Sarah) signed the address 'on behalf' of the students of the school.

> *Feast of St. John the Baptist, 1867*
> *From the Native pupils of the Nazereth Institution.*
> *(Translated from the Maori.)*
>
> Father and beloved Bishop, – We wish to convey to you, on this your patron feast, our affectionate congratulations. We give thanks to Almighty God for all the edifying works performed by your Lordship with so much Christian abnegation for the salvation of souls. You, beloved Bishop, have conveyed to us the knowledge of the true faith. We rejoice that all your works are blessed by the hand of God. Your spiritual labours for the salvation of the Maori people

have been, very great. Yes, my Lord, the great trials and hardships which, your Lordship has endured in planting the seed of our holy faith in this island will be remembered with the deepest sense of gratitude by generations yet unborn.

You have, my Lord, caused that branch of the Church in New Zealand to flourish and bring forth an hundredfold.

We take this most pleasing opportunity of expressing to your Lordship our deepest sense of gratitude for the blessings of the Christian education which we now receive in this Institution. In these sentiments of filial gratitude we humbly request your Lordship's holy benediction. – We have, &c.,

    (Signed) Hera.

    Peata.

(On behalf of the pupils of the Institution of Nazareth.)[43]

Although it was originally given in Māori, it is difficult to know how much input the students had, or whether any of the French nuns also helped compose the address. In *Letters on the Go*, Jessie Munro provides another example of an English-language text created to celebrate Pompallier's birthday in late 1868 that 'promote[d] bicultural unity as still the primary mission goal, despite a context of increasing Irish monoculturalism'. Although also from 'The pupils of the Nazareth Institute', Munro asserts that the text 'show[s] ... Suzanne's command of English'.[44]

The increasing Irishification of the Catholic Church in New Zealand was the least of Sister Aubert's worries. By 1868, she and Peata were running the school on their own, and they had few funds to operate with. Pompallier's diocese had little money to give, and with the passing of the Native Schools Act 1867, the government had taken effective control of Māori education, and was more interested in creating its own village schools than funding the church boarding schools.[45] The school's two-and-a-half acres of orchards and gardens no doubt supplemented the pupils' diet, but money was scarce.[46] An official visit by the new Governor, Sir George Bowen, and his wife in May 1868 to the two Catholic schools, Māori and Pākehā, at Mount St Mary's was therefore an opportunity not to be missed. Sister Aubert composed a special song in their honour,[47] and various addresses were read out to the vice-regal couple, such as the following for Lady Bowen.

Ki te Wahine Rangatira tino nui ko Perekehana Poene, te hoa wahine tino aroha o Kawana Perekehana Poene.
'*E kui tino nui i Nuitireni, tena ra ko koe. E kui aroha, haere mai, haere mai ki a matou nga kotiro Maori o te Kura Kaweneti o Nahareta; haere mai, haere mai, ka nui to matou rongo ki to mahi tino matua ki nga iwi no Ateraria. Ka nui hoki to matou mohio ki tou aroha me tou hiahia pai mo nga Maori. No reira ka hari rawa matou ki a kite i a koe. E whaea atawhai, ka nui to matou whakawetai ki a koe mo tou haerenga mai tino atawhai ki a matou. E hari ana matou ki a kite i te hoa wahine tino aroha o to matou Kawana tino pai te tino Kaiwhakarite o tona Nuinga Rawatanga ko Wikitoria Kuini kororia. E matau ana matou, e kui aroha, kua puta mai koe i Nuitireni, ka puta tetahi whaea mo nga iwi o tenei motu. Kia hari koe, e kui, kia hari te kawanatanga o tou hoa tane tino nui. Kia hari korua i o korua tamariki, kia ora roa koe, kia hari korua i tenei whenua.*
'*Heoiano, e kui tino aroha, tino atawhai. Na nga kotiro akonga o te Kura Kaweneti o Nahareta.*
'*Akarana, Mai 2, 1868.*'

[newspaper translation]
'To her Ladyship Lady Bowen, the beloved wife of his Excellency the Governor, Sir G. Ferguson Bowen. O thou, the great lady of New Zealand, be welcome. Beloved lady, come to us, the Maori girls of the school of Nazareth Institution. Come, come. We have heard of all that thou hast done for the people of Australia. We know also that thou lovest and desirest the welfare of the Maori, and therefore we are most happy to see thee. We feel most thankful towards thee for thy most honourable and benevolent visit to us. We are happy to see the beloved lady of our great Governor, the high representative of her Gracious Majesty Queen Victoria and we understand, beloved lady, that the inhabitants of New Zealand will have in you a most amiable and tender mother. Be happy, dearest lady. May the government of your very distinguished husband be prosperous and glorious. Be happy in your dear family, and may you with them enjoy every blessing in New Zealand.
'From the Maori girls of the Nazareth Institution, Mount St. Mary's, Auckland, New Zealand.
'May 2, 1868.'[48]

Again, we do not know to what extent this address was composed by the girls themselves, perhaps assisted by Peata. Given the importance of the event, it is likely Sister Aubert also had some input. She also ensured that a full account was provided to the newspapers.[49] Unfortunately, the church sold the land in 1869, and the Institute had to move to smaller premises. In 1871 it closed, and Sister Aubert moved to Hawke's Bay to undertake missionary work there. Sister Peata, who was now blind, moved in with the Irish nuns of the Sisters of Mercy. Soon after she returned to Te Tai Tokerau where '[s]he wandered into the bush, and her body was found eight days later'.[50]

Te Mōmona

Although members of the Church of Jesus Christ of the Latter-day Saints arrived in New Zealand in the 1850s,[51] serious missionary endeavours began in the 1880s, with Māori the most responsive to the Mormon message. By 1885, there were sixteen Māori branches of the church and four Pākehā ones. Elders Alma Greenwood and Ira Noble Hinckley Jr. worked in New Zealand in 1883–84, especially in the Wairarapa and East Coast regions, with considerable success, and they were responsible for thirteen of the branches established.[52] Robert Joseph argues that the Mormon openness to Māori expressions of spirituality, and fortuitous interpretation of earlier Māori prophecies, contributed to the church's success.[53] The missionaries may appear patronising at times: in 1883 Greenwood wrote that '[t]he natives are anxious to learn and they are like clay in the hands of the potter ready to be moulded into any shape', but they also appear to have been able to relate to, and form friendships with, Māori.[54]

Greenwood and Hinckley also sought converts in South Taranaki, where they formed a friendship with Hōriana Whakamairu, almost certainly related to the influential Mormon convert Īhaia Whakamairu of Ngāti Kahungunu.[55] There are several letters written to Hinckley, held in the Huntington Library, California, attributed to Hōriana. These show the warmth of her feelings for Hinckley, and her familiarity even to the point of making fun of him. She also addresses him as 'Nowetini' (Norwegian). Both Māori and Mormons have a keen interest in whakapapa and, although 'Hinckley' is originally an English name, the Norwegian reference may relate to one of his forebears, or it might just be a nickname. The first letter is in Māori.

From Horiana Whakamairu
1884

Mangaia hurae 14
Kia hingeri nowetini e tamatenara kou tou katoa, ku atae mai tau reta aroha kia matou katoa[.] Kanui tomatou aroha kia koutou katoa[.] etama nui atu teti ka otau kupu momaua kotaku tu akana ikimai nei koe mehe me a maua iuru kiro to ite hahi kua karanga tia maua he tu a hine mokoutou ae ena pea au euru atai ho a emohio ana no au kote meano ia temea tika kotaua kupu itu hi mainei koe
  heoi kia Nowetini
    hingeri
me mutu tou kaha kitekai
koi nui tononona
kore nga katiro [sic] epirangi kia koe ito taenga kiuta kakore to kotiro epirangi kia koe[.] kanui te pai[.] heoiano na
  to hoa aroha nui kia Nowitini[.]
Kia hingeri Nopera

[modern translation]
From Hōriana Whakamairu
1884
Mangaia, 14 July.
To Hinkley [the] Norwegian. Young man, greetings to all of you. Your loving letter has come to all of us. Great is our love for all of you. Young man, what you said about us my older sister and I is correct, if we had joined the Church we would have been called 'sisters' for you. Yes, perhaps I will join, and wait a bit. I now know that the thing that is right is what you wrote.
    Well. To [the] Norwegian, Hinkley.
You had better stop eating so much or your backside will get big and the girls won't want you when you get back to [America], your girl won't want you. That will be good. Enough of that.
From your loving friend, to [the] Norwegian.
To Hinckley Noble.[56]

The second letter is in English, after Hinckley has left to return home. It is headed with the dates that Hinckley received and answered it while still in Auckland in handwriting that matches the rest of the letter, and is quite different to the handwriting of the Māori letter. This suggests that Hinckley received a letter from Hōriana in Māori, and the surviving document is his translation written in his own hand. The letter is just as affectionate as the earlier item, with references that may have made sense only to them, such as the 'Babies', but also betrays the emotion felt, when a friend departs and is unlikely to be seen again.

From Horiana Whakamairu (A Maori)

Received Oct 22/84   )
Answered Nov 6/84   )   at Auckland.

Manaia, Oct 1st 1884.
Mr. I. N. Hinkley
   Dear Brother:
   Before you leave the land where you have sojourned for the last two years (or more) I wish to pen a few lines as a farewell letter.
   Friendship, such as we formed with you, is lasting. It cannot be erased in a day, month, nor a year. In fact, while memory lasts we will ever think of you, and the many enjoyable times I had with you.
   You have had times of trouble, of persecution and hardship, and on the other hand, this has been intermingled with joy and happiness. Not only earthly happiness, but that peaceful and comforting influence which cometh from above.
   While you have these vicissitudes to pass through you have ever enjoyed yourself. You have tasted of the bitter, which enabled you to better appreciate the sweet.
   Your name will ever be held in kind remembrance by me, trusting at the same time your pleasant times you will have at home, will not be of such a nature to forget Manaia, and your friends at that place.
   Many times have I thought about the Norwegian and the time spent with you.
   You have numerous enemies in New Zealand, as well as friends. Friends that would stand by you in adversity as well as prosperity. In times when trouble brooded over you, I know they would not forsake you.
   When you get home don't let that 'kotiro' [girl] of yours make you forget New Zealand.
   I presume you will be joining the Matrimonial train as soon as you can. As a writer says 'Get into the Matrimonial car, And ride along without a jar.' Oh! then for the good times, too numerous to mention. Well Old Friend, Old Granny is well, digging away in the garden. She is putting in potatoes, melons &c. &c. She is troubled by the Spirits as ever. Change the subject again, I am taking care of the

'Babies' you gave me: (Wahs [illegible] Best crop) giving them[illegible] food, clothes & everything to make them comfortable.

They are very peaceable children, never complaining about anything. Never crying, never singing, in short never doing anything, except staying just where they are put.

This is what I like about them, for if otherwise I should have to let them out to the neighbors. (Don't forget it.)

Homai taku awha [awhi] ki Greenwood, mo Nopera ka nui, ka nui awha.
Ka mutu te kupu. [Give my embrace to Greenwood, and many embraces for Noble. That's all on that.]

I hope you have a pleasant voyage home; also trust you will have a 'Kapai' [good] time, then 'haere hoki mai' [come back] again. If they would only send you back here it would please me, as well as many others.

When you get to Utah, (the 'Queen of the West') don't forget to write to us. I presume you will be like all the rest of those 'Mormons,' when you get to Zion you will forget there are any Mormons in New Zealand. If you do, just look at my 'Ahua' [likeness] take a 'Hongi' [physical greeting] then send me a letter. Don't forget this. Put it down in your memoranda. The time is coming when you will cross the old Pacific again. God bless you on your voyage.

May you have a pleasant voyage, & a good time at home which I know you will.

With kind love for Bro. Greenwood, also yourself[.] I am as ever your friend and sister in the Gospel.
Horiana Whakamairu
Write to us[,] let us know how you get home.

Good bye, Goodbye.
All the folks here send love to you. Pine, Robert, Sister Ihaia & Katoa [everyone]. We wish you well.

When missionaries are sometimes portrayed in two-dimensional terms, as dogmatic and inflexible, it pays to remember that they could not be successful in their work without some intimacy with their flocks.

Te Ope Whakaora: the Salvation Army

The Salvation Army established itself in New Zealand in 1883, just five years after the movement was founded in London. As Cyril Bradwell and Harold Hill note, the Army began in New Zealand as a largely urban phenomenon, at a time when Māori were largely rural, and they did not undertake missionary work with Māori until 1888 along the Whanganui River. A few Māori, such as Maraea Moreti (Maria Morris), who were exposed to Army activities in urban areas, did join the movement in towns.[57] Extracts of Maraea's account of her capture by Te Kooti, and her witnessing of a number of violent deaths, including that of her husband, are included in chapter 2. These events were traumatic, and obviously had a lasting impression on her.

Maraea encountered the Salvation Army in Gisborne in October 1886, and a year later the movement's newspaper the *War Cry* published an account of her conversion. The article is a mixture of third-person commentary linking her own first-person 'testimony', and is graced with an engraving of Maraea in uniform, taken from a photograph, labelled 'Colour-Sergt. Maria, the Saved Half-Caste'. It begins with the Salvation Army holding a meeting on Gladstone Street, Gisborne's main thoroughfare. Maraea stood beside a crowd of people, 'listening to the far from complimentary remarks about the Army which were being freely bandied about to and fro', until gaining the courage to enter. The texts reads, 'The Captain was reading from the last chapter of Revelations, and here we must let Maria speak for herself'.

'The Word Shot Home.
I felt it, and I went back to my house and said, "These people are not mad, like so many people tell me."'[58]

The article provided a potted story of her life, included her experiences as a captive of Te Kooti's group. She mixed with both Māori and Pākehā, attended various churches, and read the Bible.

A few days after the first Army meeting I met a Cadet in the street selling 'War Crys,' and I asked him in Maori to 'sell me a 'Cry' for nothing' (Maori expression for asking). He gave me a 'Cry,' and I said in English 'Got no money.' he smiled and said, 'God bless you!' I next saw the Captain go into my neighbour's house – she was a good woman. I shrinked in to hear them talk. The Captain asked me if I was saved? Was I a Christian? Did I love God? I kept answering in Maori, and at last I said in English,

'I am a Heathen!'
Then he bombarded me properly, and told me all about Salvation. After this I used to go to the Army meetings. I was very 'pouri' (sad), and my Maori

friends used to say, 'Maria is getting bewitched by the Army.' At last a light came out of the darkness, and I felt I was wicked. One Friday night, twenty-six days after the officers opened fire, I came out at the Holiness Meeting and knelt at the table. They all prayed for me, but it was no good, my heart was stubborn. I went home and prayed. Oh what a miserable week I had. I wrestled with great wrestlings. I couldn't get rid of the devil, and God wouldn't have anything to do with me. Then the Captain came and talked with me, and I told him some of my history and about my husband's death, and when I told him this part he saw I was angry, and he asked me could I forgive Te Kooti for Jesus' sake? and I said 'No!' Then he prayed with me to have power to forgive my enemies, and all at once the light broke in upon me, and I cried for forgiveness.

I pardoned Te Kooti,

and I felt my sins were forgiven from that moment, and I knew I was saved. After this I was so happy; I began to understand my Bible. I used to read the hymns, especially 'There is a Fountain filled with Blood,' and I resorted to constant prayer. Before this I seldom prayed.[59]

Maraea's account localised her conversion story. Not only was she a 'saved half-caste' from Gisborne, but she had suffered at the hands of Te Kooti, a religious prophet who was then still alive and very much in the public imagination. At the time this article appeared in 1887, he had been pardoned by the government four years earlier, and had recently made trips to Napier and Wairoa. He was also planning to visit Poverty Bay, the scene of many of his killings, something the authorities barred him from doing in 1889 on account of the raw feelings held by both Māori and Pākehā communities there.[60]

The narrative also explained that Maraea found the public aspects of Salvationist work difficult, such as wearing the uniform. She also became angry when people laughed at her when speaking in the community.

Then there was another fight for me, a big struggle, to overcome my temper; it was a bad one. The Captain and Cadet would talk and pray, and the devil would pull, and I was miserable again. I got 'quite mixed' (Maori for 'bewildered'). At last Major Barritt came to Gisborne, and we had a Holiness meeting on the first morning (Sunday), and he talked about sanctification, and I listened and prayed, and all at once the light came like before. I got the victory;

The Devil was Beaten,

and ran away. Then I felt my heart was washed white as snow; all my sins were

> *gone and I knew I was sanctified through the blood of Jesus. I was washed clean, no spots left. I soon began to grow bold to speak for my Saviour – to testify, to speak in open-airs, to march, and to pray aloud. Now I want to do everything or go anywhere for Jesus, because I am sanctified to His service.*
>
> ...
>
> *I know ... that I have done wicked things, but the past is forgotten, God has forgiven my sins. The Salvation Officers were the first ever to speak to me about my soul. They touched my heart and brought me to God, and that's why*
>   **I Love the Salvation Army**
> *and I want to be a real Blood-and-Fire Soldier for Jesus and go forth and fight the devil.*[61]

Maraea's use of words also aligned with the Salvationist world she now inhabited and loved. She was an early Māori convert to the Army, and her narrative was printed not for a Māori audience, but a Pākehā one. We do not know whether she wrote her words or was interviewed, whether the newspaper or fellow church members encouraged her to engage in this discourse, or if she did it on her own initiative. She remained a fervent member of the Army until her death in 1907, and participated in some of its Māori events, so we can assume that her text reflects the kind of message that she would have wanted broadcast.

Despite its work on the Whanganui River, and the establishment of a corps at the predominantly Māori community at Ōtaki, a certain ambivalence existed in the Salvation Army towards proselytising Māori; a 'Maori Division' was started in 1889, disbanded in 1894, was reconstituted in 1896, and disbanded again in 1899.[62] The Army attracted some Māori followers in urban settings, such as Emare Poroumati, a Te Arawa woman from Rotorua. Emare first wrote to the *War Cry* in 1894. As with Maraea's account, she discusses her conversion, but she chose to direct her story to Māori members of the church in their own language.

> *Ki te Etita o te Reo Tana [Taua] ara ('War Cry') a te Ope Whakaora.*
>
>   *Tena Koe, – Me pai koe ke [ki] te ta i aku kupu ke [ki] to pepa ne? (A e tino pai ana au ki te ta i nga korero pai katoa, kia tere rawa koe ki te tuku mai i etahi atu.) No maehe i mauhe [mahue] ake nei ka kotahi ai toku tau ki roto i to koutou whakapono. A he wa ano i whakaarotia ai, he wa ano i mahia ana, a katahi nei ka oti, ara toku hiahia kia tuhi atu ki ta koutou 'Reo Tana [Taua],' whakaatu i toku koa mo te mea nui, mea ngaro rawa kua kitea nei e ahau. Pupu tonu te koa i toku ngakau, tiaho tonu toku wairua i te hari*

mo tenei manakohanga mai a Ihowa ki a au. Ka mea atu nei hoki ahau, 'e te Ope Whakaora, kei a koe te mana o Ihowa. (Koianei tetahi o nga mea kua whakakitea mai ki a au.) I ngaro hoki ahau a na koutou i kimi, ka kitea, i mate, a na koutou i whakaora.' Ko te Karaiti te rata, ko ana kupu nga rongoa; a ko te Wairua Tapu te kai mahi: a ko enei e toru i mahia katoatia mai i roto i a koutou. Koia taku whakanui mo to koutou ingoa irunga ake nei, katahi ano ahau ka kite i te tikanga o taua ingoa, ka whakapou hoki na te Atua tenei Ope Whakaora. Ka rite ki te matapo i whakaorangia ra e te Karaiti, i mea ra 'i kapotia ahau, heoi kua kite: a ka whakapono nei hoki, he tama tenei na te Atua.' Ka rua te kau ma ono (26) oku tau i whanau mai ai ki nga hara ki nga mate o te ao, heoi ka kotahi tau tonu me te hawhe o toku whanau houtanga i te Wairua Tapu, ki te ora. Kei te 3, o Hoani Rongo Pai, te whaka maramatanga mo tenei te 3, me te 7, o nga rarangi. E hoa ma, kua kite koutou i te tiaho o toku maramatanga, na, whakakororia tahi tatou. He utu hoki ahau mo a koutou mauiuiranga maha i roto i te Ariki.   NA EMARE POROUMATI.

[newspaper translation]
To the Editor of the 'War Cry' of the Salvation Army.

   Greetings. Would you be so kind as to print my words in your paper? (And I am happy to print all good stories, and you should be quick at sending in some more.) Last May I had been one year in your faith. I thought about it for a while, more time doing it, and then it was done, that is, my desire to write to your 'War Cry' to show my joy at this big, hidden thing that I have found. The joy bubbles up in my heart, my spirit shines with happiness from God's consideration for me. And I say, 'Salvation Army, you have the mana of Jehovah. (This is one of things shown to me.) I was lost, and you looked for me and found me, I was suffering, and you saved me.' Christ is the doctor, his words are the medicine, and the Holy Spirit is the means. These three things all worked within you. And so I praise your name above, and I saw for the first time the meaning of that name, and I declared that this Salvation Army came from God. I was like the blind man who was healed by Christ, and said 'I was blind, and now I see, and I believe that this is the son of God.' It is 26 years since I was born into the sins and pains of this world, and it is one and a half years since my being born again in the Holy Spirit, to life. The explanation for this is in the third [chapter] of St. John's Gospel of John, verses 3 and 7. friends, you have seen the shining of my light, so, let us all give glory together. I am payment for your many ills within the Lord   From Emare Poroumati.[63]

Early the following year the *War Cry* published the second of Emare's letters, printed only in Māori.

'KI TE ETITA.'
'Kia ora koe i te manaaki a to tatou Ariki a Ihu Karaiti. Amine.'
Kua kite iho ahau i aku kupu i tuku atu na ki to pepa, a kanui taku whakawhetai mo to tono kia tuhi atu ano.
E hoa ma, tenei ahau te whakawhetai atu nei ki to tatou Matua i te rangi. Mona i manako mai ki ahau hei hoa mo koutou ki te kauwhau i te Rongo Pai. Tangohia ana e Ta te wahangutanga o toku mangai; whakanekehia atu ana te ruaruatanga o toku ngakau. Meingatia iho ahao [sic] e Ta kia ngohengohe rawa kia rite ki te pepi whanau hou. Kati ko to koutou pononga i naianei i roto i te Ariki i tana mahi tohu hoki. Kua meinga kia pakari. Koia ra tenei ka totoro a wairua atu nei ki te ru ki a koutou kei roto i a te Karaiti toku korerorero me toku hari kia koutou. Ka mea atu nei hoki whakaatu mai ki a matou i tou ahua i nga pakanga hoki e whawhaitia ana e koutou ki ena takiwa. A ko ahau ka pena tahi. E mahara ana ahau kaore ano he kupu Maori ki te Reo Tana i muri mai i taaku. A e mohio ana ahau he tokomaha noa atu nga tangata wahine o roto o Whanganui me Otaki e ahei ana mo te tuku korero mai.
Mo te mea e hoa ma e whakapono ana ahau ara ki te penei ta tatou mahi ka tautoko tatou etahi i etahi a he pono hoki ki te huihui o tatou whakaaro kia kotahi ka tino pakaru i a tatou te mahunga o te Rewera.
Kia mana te tono a to koutou hoa pononga.
Kia tau te rangimarie a te Karaiti ki o koutou wairua. Amine.
E. POROUMATI, Panaera, Akarana.[64]

[modern translation]
To the Editor
'Greetings to you in the love of our Lord Jesus Christ. Amen.'
I have seen my words that I sent to your paper, and I am pleased at your request for me to write again.
 Friends, Here I give thanks to our Father in heaven, for his blessing that I may be your friend and preach the Gospel. Sir, remove the silence from my mouth, and shift the doubts from my heart. Sir, make me as malleable as a newborn baby. And so, I am your [plural] servant in the Lord and in his work of witness. I have been made strong. And so I reach out in spirit to you to shake hands with you in Christ, with my words and my happiness to you. And I say, tell us about how you

are going, and the battles you are fighting in your areas. And I will do the same. I am thinking that there were no Māori words in the War Cry before mine. And I know there are many women in Whanganui and Ōtaki capable of sending stories in.

    Friends, because I believe if we all do this, and support each other, and faithfully combine our thought as one, then we will truly smash the Devil's head.

    Let the request of your servant be fulfilled.

    May Christ's peace rest upon your souls. Amen.

    E. Poroumati, Parnell, Auckland.

The language of Emare's second letter reflects her desire to preach. Her letter moves from addressing the editor, to 'friends', to God, and back to the Māori readers again in a manner reminiscent of oral discourse. Emare was fluent in English, but she preferred working with Māori people, including for a time as a missionary for the Presbyterian and then the Methodist Māori Missions in the early twentieth century, before returning back to the Salvation Army.[65]

Conclusion

Religion can be both a public and a personal concern. As with other public matters, it was more often Māori men who took on leadership roles, or represented the community, regarding religious issues. Expressions of personal faith from women that may have been recorded on paper, like other private texts, were less likely to be included in the public archive. Like some other aspects of Māori women's lives, the archival record of their religious experiences is patchy. In particular, we know of women's leadership in the various syncretic religious responses[66] (which from the 1860s were generally lumped together by Pākehā as 'Hauhau' movements) and faith healing ('tohunga-ism'), but the primary sources available were written by others, rather than the women themselves.

    As the texts in this chapter show (and those in chapter 2), Maraea Moreti's description of her willing participation in Pai Mārire ceremonies, then her more reluctant observance of religious practices when a prisoner of Te Kooti, demonstrate how religion could have a significant impact on Māori women. At times we need to read texts in which women proclaim their faith with an eye to the motives of those who reproduced or helped create them. For example, how much of the voices in Yate's letters belong to the women concerned, or to their missionary who sought ongoing support from Britain? To what degree is Maraea

Moreti's account of her conversion to Salvationism her own, and how much was constructed by the newspaper for its readership? Notwithstanding these issues, it is clear that religion and faith are important factors in understanding the lives of Māori women of the nineteenth century.

CHAPTER 8

'I am burning like fire': Private Matters

I am burning like fire from the pain caused by [you]'. Anger and shame inspired these words, written by a Māori woman to her unfaithful husband who had recently deserted her. She then carefully placed the letter, along with one addressed to her brother, in a bedroom drawer. A few weeks later, on 6 April 1884, she committed suicide, an act that led to a coroner's inquest, and the creation of a government file held at Archives New Zealand in Wellington, where those letters now reside.[1] Suicide was not unknown in Māori society, but individuals were likely to have expressed their feelings in other ways, such as whakamā (withdrawing emotionally), or through waiata (sung poetry).

Even though letters to the government 'are seldom emotional' or 'ever betray intimate, personal feelings', sometimes records associated with the business of state inadvertently reveal glimmers of the personal lives of Māori women, as well as their more collective and public engagement in the historical experience of the colonial era, when significant social, economic and political transformations took place in Māori society.[2] In writing to the state, sometimes Māori women's 'formalised dialogue' reveals fragments of their life histories, such as when they articulated the difficulties of managing resource depletion, the anxieties and concern caused by family illness, as well as the joy or grief associated with personal relationships.[3] In letters to government officials they requested money, food or clothing, often in a direct and transactional tone. In these instances women's writing entered government archives because they pressed their claims. In seeking relief or justice, their requests were designed for a wide audience.

This chapter explores the potential of public records for examining private lives and emotional expression. Although the material available is patchy, the topic of private lives is nevertheless broad. Much of the material in the preceding chapters is relevant to this topic, but the texts that we explore here are quite clearly very personal in nature. This chapter focuses in particular on correspondence conducted by letter, a genre that was versatile, and could be used to express a variety of information and emotions. Examples presented here include expressions of love, joy, sorrow, grief or pleasure that appear in items in government archives, often in personal letters addressed to officials which were not originally envisioned as public documents.[4] In letters addressed to government officials, who were often friends of the family, women articulated their fears about family illness, revealed family shame generated by bankruptcy, and expressed concern about their economic livelihoods. While documents generated by the state tend to be pragmatic and functional, the names and signatures attached to documents, such as a marriage certificate, register not just an important moment in life, but can act as a window onto histories of intimacy and relationships as they form, evolve, mature or break down. Outside government archives, Māori continued to register their emotions in traditional genre, as the expression of grief in a waiata tangi for a recently deceased husband published in a Māori-language newspaper, illustrates.

Hinemoa's letters

Hinemoa's words open this chapter, but this was not the name by which she was known. However, it is the name she used to sign her letters. Family may have addressed her by that name, or it may have been a term of endearment used by her husband. Nevertheless in signing as Hinemoa, she drew upon a well known Māori metaphor for forbidden love. The Hinemoa of legend was the beautiful daughter of a chief, widely admired and desired, especially by a young man of lesser rank. Our Hinemoa, though, did not live happily ever after with her lover, Hawke.

Although widely respected, and noted especially for being committed to the welfare of her people, at 40 years of age, Hinemoa had already experienced two failed relationships by the time Hawke walked out on her, leaving her with two young sons aged nine and seven, and pregnant with another child. Abandoned, she took her life by strychnine poisoning, which she also administered to her young sons, who both died in agonising pain.[5] The circumstances surrounding their deaths, and her role in them, were widely reported in the settler press, which printed the letters she addressed to the man who had 'caused pain to my heart'. Written in Māori, they were translated for the coroner's inquest, and the English-language versions widely published.[6]

While the 'personal records kept as government archives are unembellished official logs of moments in an individual life story' and 'often procedural or transactional' in nature, records of the state can sometimes bring the 'unwelcome judgment of the judicial system' to bear on sensitive matters.[7] Hinemoa's letters were created out of private anguish, and she addressed her feelings and thoughts to particular individuals; they were not designed for public consumption, but entered the official record and the archive because she committed a crime, in which her actions were subjected to judgment. After her death, Hinemoa's words, and her private shame, were made public by an inquiring settler press that had little interest in protecting her reputation, nor that of her whānau.

Murder-suicide is a tragic and extreme result of a relationship breakdown, signalling the emotional and psychological turmoil induced by the shame of a very public act of abandonment. According to her brother, who testified at the inquest, during the preceding three months Hinemoa was, 'much grieved . . . through Hawke having left her, and refusing to live with her again.'[8] In a letter she explained that: 'Perhaps now he will know the truth of my love for him.'[9]

Hinemoa was responding to her husband's adultery, which was the subject of gossip and rumour amongst the community, and her actions were modelled on examples from the past. Traditionally a woman might compose a waiata aroha as a response to gossip, or to shame a 'neglectful husband or lover'.[10] Sometimes this was followed by whakamomori (suicide), which was, according to Margaret Orbell, 'fairly common in traditional Maori society. Often it happened when a person had been shamed, even if they were not to blame; in this situation, removing oneself with tragic finality from one's large and very close kinship group was a way of restoring honour and redeeming a lost reputation.'[11]

Pūremu

Adultery or pūremu was a serious offence; it was a crime against marriage, an institution that served to create political, economic and social bonds between whānau. Committing pūremu broke those bonds, and it was punished with severity. A married woman who committed pūremu, for instance, might be punished with the loss of her life, but compensation would also involve a payment to the aggrieved party, usually with taonga of great value, such as greenstone, weapons and cloaks, in order to restore the honour of both families.[12] By the 1850s, items of great value included stock, particularly farm animals. When Meri Te Waiheke's son committed adultery with the married daughters of chiefs, it disgraced his whānau. A rūnanga was held to discuss an appropriate punishment. It was agreed that Meri was responsible for compensating the families her son had dishonoured. It is not known how the young women were punished. In this letter Meri accepts her son's crime, outlines the financial burden the requirement for compensation placed upon her, and expresses her immense disappointment in him:

> Rangiohia, Hurae 27-/59
> *Kia Piripi Terangiatahua, kia Tamihana, kia Kutia, e hoa ma tena koutou, tenei taku korero kia koutou, kua hara taku tamaiti a Karipa, kua puremu ki nga wahine ma rena tapu o nga tamariki rangatira o Waikato, kotahi te wahine kua o ti te he £50 te utu, toko toru nga wahine marena i puremu nei a Karipa ko te kotiro mero iti takahau te tokowha te tehi he ana ko tana rungawaitanga ki te whakamoe i tetahi atu wahine marena ki te teina o karamo takirau, huia taua kohuru tanga i taua kotiro, me tana hungawaitanga nei puta ana te utu a Karipa, kotahi hoiho puta ana i te tahi o nga wahine marena nei, e 2 hoiho naku te tehi na Karipa ano te tehi, he ana, e 2, wahine kaore i utu a, he kare no te moni ia au, e £75 te utu a Karipa kei muri, e 50 o te tehi 25 huia ka 75, he tika tona tenei hara he mea ata runanga marire na Waikato karanga ano taua runanga, e Ripa me pehea enei o wahine, ka ki mai a Karipa, me utu kei runga aku kau, whakae ana taua runanga, tenei te tihi i whakaritea e te runanga kotahi hoiho wahine, kotahi kau, ma Karipa enei i homai hei utu mo taku, whakae ana ia*
>   *E hoa ma kei*
>
> *Ki mai koutou kaore au e ako ki taku tamaiti, te taenga mai o Tuhourangi ki konei ka whakahoki i a ia, me au ka kiatu kia haere, kare epai, ka nui taku ako kaore e rongo, ne, 26, i runangatia ai taua haranei*
>   *Ka tika atu ia i te kaipuke*
>   *heoi ano*
>   *Na Meri Tewaiheke*

[modern translation]
    Rangiohia, July 27-/59
To Piripi Te Rangiatahua, Tāmihana, and Kutia. My friends, greetings.

This is what I have to tell you, my child Karipa has sinned, and has committed adultery with the married wives of young Waikato chiefs. There is one woman, for which he was fined £50. Karipa fornicated with three married women, a young unmarried woman is the fourth. One of his wrongs was his act of sleeping with another married woman, the younger sister of Karamo Takirau, together with his mistreatment of that girl, and his sins, Karipa's cost [fine] is one horse on account of each of the married women. Two of the horses belong to me, one is Karipa's. There are two women for whom reparations have not been paid, as I have no money. Karipa owes £75, 50 for one and another 25 makes 75. His guilt is plain, it was carefully discussed in council by Waikato, and that council asked, Ripa [Karipa], what should be done about these women? Karipa replied, that my cows be used as payment, to which that council agreed. This was their final ruling. One mare and one cow. Karipa gave me these to pay for mine. He agreed to this.

My friends, do not say that I do not teach my son. When Tūhourangi came here, they returned him, and I said for him to go, it is not right. I have given him ample instruction but he does not obey. Twenty-six people deliberated over those crimes.

He has gone off in the ship.

That is all.

From Meri Te Waiheke[13]

Marriage

Pūremu, once appropriately compensated, also marked the end of a marriage. Early missionaries regarded with distaste the practice of utu, viewing it as a marker of 'savagery', while the freedom associated with divorce was viewed as a sign of immorality, which they sought to replace with Christian models of family and controlled sexuality. As part of their 'civilising' project, early missionaries sought to encourage Māori to take up Christian marriage. This was bound up with practices of record keeping, particularly documentation of the event in the form of a marriage certificate. When speaking to one Māori couple about their impending marriage in 1828, Anglican missionary Henry Williams told them 'it was much more proper that these things should be written on paper, than to follow their native customs. I therefore prepared pen, ink, and paper, in due form'.[14]

Marriage certificates were a necessary part of the bundle of paperwork associated with formalising relationships in the European world, as illustrated by the marriage of Maria Ringa and Philip Tapsell, understood to be the first Christian wedding performed in the country. It took place several months after Anglican lay missionary Thomas Kendall baptised Maria, daughter of chief Te Ape, on 4 March 1823. In June 1823, Kendall read the banns of marriage three times on the request of Tapsell, and presided over the wedding on 23 June.[15]

Missionary House at Mata Hui
Bay of Islands New Zealand

Marriage solemnized at Mata Hui in the Bay of Islands New Zealand in the year 1823.

Phillip Tapsell First Officer of the Ship Asp now at anchor in the Bay, and Maria Dinga a Baptized native female of the Bay were married in this place by Banns with consent of Guardians this twenty third day of June in the year one thousand eight hundred and twenty three by me Thomas Kendall Minister and Missionary.

This Marriage was . . .   ) Phillip Tapsell
solemnized between us   ) The mark of X Maria Dinga

In the presence of Mr. [illegible] Wilson Commander Royal Sovereign
    Mr. D. Brind Commander Ship Asp[16]

Kendall certified that the marriage took place 'according to the Form contained in the Common Prayer Book of the Church of England and that the nature of the contract was clearly explained to the Bride and her native friends in the presence of several respectable witnesses and fully understood by them', with signatures of nine European witnesses.[17] Maria famously left her husband almost immediately after their wedding. Her dismissive attitude to the sacrament of Christian marriage, but particularly Kendall's involvement in sanctifying the relationship of a couple who were clearly unsuited for the responsibility marriage entailed, embarrassed the Church Missionary Society leader, Samuel Marsden. Under his leadership the missionaries often refused to marry interracial couples, whose relationships they regarded as born of convenience, rather than affection. By the 1830s, the Anglicans softened their approach, recognising that Pākehā traders had some influence amongst tribes. With increasing competition for conversions amongst rival mission organisations, missionaries also became more willing to accept interracial couples in an effort to inculcate and spread Christianity amongst Māori.[18]

Messages of affection

A marriage certificate registers the formal recognition of a relationship, but these documents are devoid of emotional expression. When it comes to declarations of affection it is to love letters that we must turn, and while there are few extant examples in public collections, those that do exist draw upon customary forms of expressing emotion through metaphor, allusion and rhetoric regularly found in proverbs, poetry and song.[19] By the 1840s, missionaries noted Māori enthusiasm for letter writing, especially love letters, which were 'the chief use of their literacy skills'.[20]

William Speer collected samples of Māori writing while travelling through the southern region of the country in the early 1860s. The son of an Anglican minister, Speer visited a number of British colonies and on his travels collected mementoes to commemorate the places he saw and the people he met, which he pasted into an album, now held by the Alexander Turnbull Library in Wellington. Speer's album opens with the signature of southern Ngāi Tahu chief Tōpi Pātuki, pasted on the inside cover. Also contained in the album are two waiata Speer collected from Ruapuke, and two short letters signed by Māori women and addressed to Speer, both dated August 1863. The first letter, written in pencil and signed by several hands is difficult to decipher, as the text in the right hand bottom corner is smudged, while the handwriting is also hard to read. Nevertheless, it is possible to detect the signatures of three women: Hēra, Peti Mata, also known as Elizabeth (Betsy) Moss, and Ellen Kihau. Peti Mata also features in a pencil sketch drawn by Here Wete. In it she is depicted dancing with Mr Piata (Mr Speer), the album's creator.[21] Hēra Tieri, of whom little is known, wrote the second letter, perhaps just as a piece of innocent fun, which Speer annotated as a 'Maori love message'.

Ruapuke Akuhata 17/1863
Haere ra e taku aroha kia Mitipi e ta tena ra koe ka nui toku aroha kia koe /
He mihi atu taku kia koe te noho maina i kona / Ka mutu ia Matou hoa aroha /
Na hera tieri

[modern translation]
Ruapuke, August 17/1863
Go my love to Mr Speer. Sir, greetings. Great is my love for you. / I greet you who is living there. / Ended, by our loving friends. / From Sarah Tieri[22]

In writing their greetings of affection on paper Ellen Kihau, Hēra Tieri and Peti Mata were participating in an already well established social practice within their community. Ruapuke residents had learnt to write without the aid of a missionary, probably through the instruction of white men married into the community, and through informal instruction amongst Māori themselves. On his second visit to the island in 1844, only a few weeks after the arrival of the island's first resident missionary Johannes Wohlers, local Māori gave the surveyor John Barnicoat a letter, sealed with wax, for delivery to Ōtaki, a coastal town north of Wellington. Barnicoat noted the 'practice of communicating with one another in this manner is common among the natives, who perhaps are delighted in making use of their newly acquired faculty of communicating their thoughts by writing'.[23] By 1863, Ngāi Tahu wrote for a variety of purposes, ranging from personal pleasure, to the instrumental and pragmatic.

Although most letters were exchanged between Māori, such as the one Barnicoat was instructed to deliver, these do not appear in archival collections in great numbers. Examples of writing between Māori correspondents do exist in private manuscript collections, for many Pākehā, such as William Speer, collected samples of Māori writing, which they regarded as curios. Arthur S. Atkinson, for instance, opportunistically collected letters in war-torn Taranaki from Māori villages where the residents had been forced to quickly evacuate, leaving tangible and evocative evidence of recent occupation behind them.[24]

Moments of great stress and anxiety activated letters, particularly during the wars of the 1860s. Amongst the Atkinson letters is one from Mere Paea Kōkiri to Hairuha and Rāwinia communicating her concern for her friends.

Aperill [Aperira] 19 1860
Haere atu ra e taku reta ki te kawe atu i toku aroha kia Hairuha e hoa tena koe[.] Ka nui toku aroha atu kia koe ia au e noho atu nei[.] E hoa ma tena koutou[.] Kia rongo mai koutou ko te mamae ia au kia koutou i te po i te ra e kore e mutu he roimata taku kai i te ra i te po kia koutou i te putanga mai o tena He kia koutou[.]
E hoa e Rawinia tena korua ko to Tungaane[.] Heoi ano[.]

Na Mere Paea Kokiri
Taupiri i Waikato

[modern translation]
19 April, 1860.
Go, my letter, to carry my affection to Hairuha, my friend, greetings. My love for you is great as I am sitting here. My friends, greetings. Let you hear that the pain I have for you in the night and day will never end, tears for you are my food night and day from that wrong having happened to you. My friend, Rāwinia greetings to you and your brother. That is all.
From Mere Paea Kōkiri.
Taupiri in Waikato.[25]

In sending news of family, including communicating good or bad news to relatives and friends, letter writing served to help maintain kinship connections by making words mobile. In the words of Abenaki scholar Lisa Brooks, 'Writing not only travelled among communities but mapped the ties between them.'[26] Words were carried short distances, but also across countries. Alison Jones and Kuni Jenkins relate the story of chief Te Koki (Ngāpuhi), who when he heard of his son's death in Sydney in 1820, news of which was carried by letter, requested his child's name be pointed out so that he could hongi it: 'his son's name on paper, like a signature, held the wairua of the child, and touching noses – in a hongi, exchange of breath – with the name that stood in his place would have brought the family as close to the boy as they could get at that moment.'[27] As this moment of heightened grief illustrates, 'writing brings people close', for as a 'material object, the written document is a surrogate for the writer's body.'[28]

A number of letters of farewell addressed to George Grey and Lady Eliza Grey, written by Ngāti Raukawa women of mana in the 1850s, express grief at the departure of the governor and his wife. Before leaving, Grey gave a series of speeches at a number of venues across the country in 1853, which prompted Māori speeches in reply, and these often formed the basis for letters.[29] In their compositions, Pīpī Te Whiwhi, her daughter Jane, and Ruta Te Rauparaha, 'employed customary oral forms of expression in the written compositions that they modelled on the English letter form'.[30] Drawing from the public world of speech, these farewell letters were written as public documents, not to a single individual. Indeed, composers had a wide audience in mind, as this extract from Jane's letter to George and Eliza demonstrates, for it also contained a message to

Mākere, daughter of Kahe Te Rau-o-te-rangi and Jock Nicol, who travelled with the Greys to the Cape Colony.

> Otaki
> 20 September 1853
>
> My dear father, the Governor, and my dear mother, Lady Grey.
> . . .
>   This is a salutation to you all, including your girl, my young relative, Makere. I am still crying because I didn't see your departure. My crying for you, and my sadness, is indeed great.
>   I don't know how to compose words in my letter [as] I am a child. However, I have a lament for my father, my mother and my sister. Go to your homeland. Give my love to my dear sister, Makere.[31]

In contrast, Ruta Te Rauparaha and Pīpī Te Whiwhi's letters show a variation in writing style and skill, indicating they did not write them. Rather, it was their command as orators on display.[32] Pīpī and Ruth did not need the skills of writing, for they had scribes who could turn their oratory into words upon paper. Pīpī's daughter, Jane, was of a generation expected to obtain the skills of reading and writing, and to use them for the benefit of their families.

Learning composition

Most of the letters collected for *He Reo Wāhine* were addressed to colonial officials.[33] These are of interest to the historian seeking evidence of women's changing social, material and emotional circumstances. They range from letters of farewell, to requests for equipment or financial assistance due to impoverishment or ill health, requests for information about land claims, and letters of complaint. As will be seen in the material from this section, some of these letter writers were educated in mission schools, or sent by their parents to live with Pākehā kin in Australia specifically to obtain an education.

    Emily Russell (d. 1887), daughter of Kohukohu timber trader and mercantile elite, George Frederick Russell, was sent to Melbourne to be privately educated, befitting the increasing economic status and respectability of her father. She regularly wrote letters to her family.[34] In her evidence to the West Coast Commission in 1880, Ākanihi Kurakitoro (Agnes Simeon) regarded education as essential to her children's future.

> *I want to protect my children; I brought them into the world, and I must provide for them. I wish to be certain that, if anything happens to me, they will be supported until they are old enough to take care of themselves. There are four girls and five boys; the eldest, who is a boy, is fourteen years of age. I have sent my eldest daughter to Melbourne to be educated. She is staying with my husband's mother, who has a governess for her. She will come back again in about two years' time, when she has finished her education.*[35]

Education equated with care, which was often expressed as securing the future social and economic opportunities of children. Recognising that success lay in an ability to negotiate the Pākehā world of commerce, some parents sought to obtain an education in English for their children, giving them a skill set that might enhance their future prospects. Young women also desired to learn these skills, for writing offered the possibility of freedom from parental or community control.

Learning to write encompassed a wide range of genres, including creative expression. In the papers of Joseph Mathews, held at the Alexander Turnbull Library, are samples of children's writing in English from Awanui and Kaitāia Schools, where his son and son-in-law taught, respectively.

> *A boy was one day sitting on the steps of a door. He had a broom in one hand, and in the other a large piece of bread and butter which somebody had kindly given him. While he was eating it and merrily humming a tune he saw a poor little dog quietly sleeping not far from him. He called out to him to Come here poor fellow.*
>
> Annie Catherine Boyes
Awanui School
December 7th 1875
>
> The Spider
> *Do you see the spider in the picture. He has just got his web done; and there he sits in the very middle of it, ready to pounce upon a fly. The spider loves work.*

He begins to work as soon as he begins to live. Every spider is born a weaver. Even the youngest spider knows how to weave his web just as well as the oldest. The spider never has to go to school to learn his task. So, the little duck can swim as soon as it is hatched. And the little bird can build its nest, and the bee can make the honey without any teaching. God has given the creatures the power to do their work. And that is why they never make any blunders.
Eliza Colenso, Kaitaia School, April 12th 1876[36]

Before the 1867 Native Schools Act, missionaries were the key providers of education in Māori communities. While English was emphasised, it was not necessarily the lingua franca of choice for everyday conversation, or even writing. The letters of Matire (Matilda) Moncur illustrate this. She was a foundation pupil of Reverend John Morgan's school at Ōtāwhao established in 1849, with the financial support of George Grey. Morgan proposed to offer all lessons in English, and specifically targeted 'half-caste' children like Matire, whose parents:

> are generally anxious for their education but their small means will not allow of their being sent to private schools. The mothers of these children are generally the daughters of the leading chiefs, and as they are with their Parents living amongst the various tribes along the coast, and in the interior, these children will no doubt in future years exercise great influence amongst their respective tribes, either for good or for evil. How important then that they should receive a Christian education, that hereafter they may not stand in the way to retard the advancement of the Aborigines, but on the contrary some of them may be employed as schoolmasters and schoolmistresses amongst them.[37]

By the end of 1850, Morgan had 40 boarders, 36 of them 'half-castes'.[38] As he had hoped, his school offered instruction in the English language and by October 1852, Morgan reported that of the 38 pupils, all, bar one, could read and write in English.[39]

The daughter of Kāwhia trader James Moncur (d. 1845) and Rewa Te Rārangi Pouaka (Ngāti Hikairo), Matire married John Morgan's nephew, Samuel, in 1855. Although educated in English, she was clearly more comfortable with the Māori language, which is reflected in her correspondence with Donald McLean. In 1871 she wrote from Alexandra (now Pirongia) of the impoverished state of her family, her husband having left numerous debts, which she was struggling to pay. Her request for relief is written in a standard letter format, with rhetorical embellishments from Māori oral conventions absent, likely reflecting the use of a scribe familiar with formal letter writing.

> Alexandra
> 15 June 1871
>
> Dear Sir,
>   I regret being in a position compelled to trouble you, but having no other remedy, you will I trust excuse this liberty. My circumstances being such as to completely break down any hope of maintenance for my children, without your kind assistance. Owing to the mental derangement of mind of my husband who has not been in a good state since your last visit to Alexandra. In addition to my affliction in respect of my husband, I have been sued for debts contracted by him before his illness, which I have to meet, it amounted to £13-4-6, and another summons from Auckland for £24- in what manner to meet it I do not know, further I am from necessity, obliged to get credit from the Stores for food &c which cannot be done without. I blame my having to leave 'Kawhia' four years last April, which thoroughly broke up my house and destroyed my property, together with repeated raids since and losses attending them, is the cause of my present position and distress.
>   Dear Sir. If you would please take these facts into your kind consideration and help me over my difficulties, you will confer a boon on my children and an everlasting gratitude from your
>   very & Obedient Servant
>   Matilda Morgan
>
> Honble. D. McLean
>   Auckland
>
> P.S. I have never received any compensation for the losses sustained at Kawhia.
>   M. M.[40]

A second letter to McLean is written in Māori. It is highly likely Matire composed the letter, as the handwriting style and signature match. In it she warns McLean against listening to or believing the words of Hāmi Mōkena, her husband, Samuel Morgan.

> *Arekahanara*
> *Mei 30th 1873*
> Kia te Makarini
> *Kei whakakarongo koe ki nga korero a Hami Mokena kua porangi i te kainga waipiro*
> *Na Matire Te Rarangi*
> Matilda Morgan
> To Mr McLean

[modern translation]
> Alexandra
> May 30 1873
> To Mr McLean
> Do not listen to the stories of Hāmi Mōkena who is mad from drinking alcohol.
> From Matire Te Rārangi
> Matilda Morgan
> To Mr McLean[41]

Matire, Samuel and their children struggled to regain their stability and prosperity after they were forced to leave Kāwhia. As Matire explained, it was this event that was the cause of all their problems, being the catalyst for Samuel's indebtedness, his failing health and struggles with mental illness.

Many Māori women corresponded with Donald McLean. He was, after all, second only to the governor in the control and authority he exerted in Māori land purchasing and race relations until his death in January 1877. Over his career McLean cultivated close relationships with leading Māori men, and acted as patron for the mixed-descent sons of white fathers of respectable standing, such as Henry Balneavis and Native Land Court Judge, Frederick Maning. McLean welcomed correspondence from white men married to Māori women, because with their close ties to Māori communities, they could be of use to him and the government as translators and intermediaries. One of his correspondents was Samuel Morgan.

Samuel Morgan wrote to McLean in July 1871, requesting assistance to gain compensation for his family's property at Kāwhia. Their loss was 'heavy', which was made harder by having such a 'large family'. Others had their losses compensated, but he was still waiting, he noted.[42] Two months later, Morgan again requested McLean's assistance to obtain compensation 'which you kindly promised to see about', and asked for employment as 'I have as you know a large family and I am anxious to get a situation if possible'.[43] By 1873, Morgan's claim had not yet been actioned. Recognising that it was information McLean wanted, Morgan became a member of McLean's network of informants when he offered news of the 'hauhau', and Māori views about road construction and surveys from a source who 'doesn't wish his name mentioned'.[44] This exchange of information may have prompted Matire's 1873 letter warning McLean that Hāmi was not to be trusted, for Hāmi was suffering psychologically because of his drinking. His debt continued to increase, placing further stress upon Matire and their twelve children.

Morgan had a poor reputation amongst Waikato Māori, but the reduced position of his wife, a relative of King Tāwhiao, caused by his 'intemperate habits' marginalised him further from the Tainui tribes, who had little sympathy for him. When Matire, then separated from Morgan, sold her Pirongia land in early 1877 in order to pay his debts, Morgan turned the new owner's surveyors away. Fearing violence, and angry at Morgan's role in causing disturbances in the King Country, Ngāti Maniapoto leader Rewi Maniapoto ordered him out of the region, sending twelve men to escort him across the border, where he was taken into the care of Te Wheoro. Not long after this, Morgan was imprisoned at Ngāruawāhia for vagrancy.[45] Morgan's life ended in dramatic and tragic circumstances, when he died at the hands of a fellow prisoner on 20 February 1877. Although Matire requested his body be released to her after the police investigation, when Morgan was buried on 22 February, few came to pay their last respects, and his wife and children did not attend.[46]

Ties of friendship

McLean operated through direct personal contact in order to carry out policy. In cultivating the friendship of men of influence and social standing, such as Henry Balneavis, who McLean referred to affectionately as 'My Dear Bal', he created obligations for families. This association was of value to Balneavis, who hoped he could count on McLean's support in obtaining justice for his children, whose land interests he had been struggling to establish. When Balneavis's daughter Jemima (c.1848–1907), who married John Shera in 1873, wrote to McLean after the death of her father, she did so based upon long established ties of friendship and association.

October 18th [1876]

My Dear Sir Donald

    I write to you as one of my father's oldest friends to ask you to use your influence to get a year's salary for us. My dear father left what little he had to be divided equally among his five children. A Memorial has been sent to the Governor through the Minister of Justice and no reply has been received as yet. I am sorry to trouble you during the Session, but I hope that you will see that the Memorial is not forgotten. I am sure you will try all you can for your old friend Bal's children.

    Believe me,
    Yours sincerely
    Jemima Shera[47]

Maria Maning, daughter of Frederick Maning, also corresponded with McLean. In the following letter she gently pokes fun at the correspondence McLean often received, mimicking the style of a 'complaining' letter. Its content articulates the close ties between the Maning family and McLean, who likely helped obtain employment for Maria's brother, Hauraki Maning, in the Native Department.

Auckland
June 20th/70

My Dear Mr. McLean

    It is nothing new for you to get petitions & requests from all sorts & conditions of men & so it gives me courage to do a little in that line on my own behalf. I have just come to town & it seems a dreadful 'sell' Hau being ordered off to Wellington as soon as I arrived. It is like a lady to be unreasonable of course & you may think so – but I am sure affairs of State can be disposed of without his aid so do please be the best of Defence Ministers as you always are and send him back speedily. It is not simply as an escort & all that sort of thing that I want him but for other matters. I'll call it 'business' to give it its proper importance in your eyes.

    I saw your son yesterday. He would like to go down to the 'Empire City' [Wellington] I think & Hau not at all – so we sat over the fire talking mutinously & left much better after it.

    I regretted so much His Excellency's absence it would have been 'so delightful' had he not taken his departure also. He or you or somebody must have taken the sun away with you. It is miserable here & the rain is something dismal to contemplate.

Please (if possible) do let Hau return and 'Your Petitioner will ever pray & c & c...'

Believe me
In all humility
Yours truly
M. A. Maning[48]

Her next letter to McLean, though, was far more serious in tone. Playful references to pleading petitioners are replaced by anxiety about Hauraki's bankruptcy, and its financial impact upon her and others, not to mention the impact on the family's reputation.

Thursday March 6th

My dear Mr. Maclean [sic]

I have been so troubled that I made up my mind this morning to write to you & try if you would help me. It is such hard work this asking favors & it is my first attempt & were it for my own benefit especially it would still be harder but as it is I take heart of grace and enter into my catalogue of troubles.

My brother Hau is the beginning and the ending of it. I have been so ashamed of all I have heard of his doings since my return to town that it were useless to try and palliate his conduct & in this case there is no excuse to be made. I being his sister I cannot bear it with his calm indifference. He has lived with people of the name of Sharpe – & during my stay in town I have also. He is in their debt to the amount of £35. He had kept them waiting & hoping with one story or another until they saw his name in the paper as Bankrupt & since then he has been leading them to believe that through your influence he would get his pay & return to his situation.

It was through his representations & through a sort of belief in him that seems to have been their general delusion they entered into such an occupation that of Board & Residence & they were poor but living comfortably enough – but through this debt of his they are with greatest difficulty – with every prospect of being left homeless in a few days. Mrs Sharpe is a lady unfortunately & feels her position in consequence most keenly & being in both poorly health & elderly it is most hard. Mr Sharpe has been out of employment for many months. I am more unhappy about them because of my inability to help them

– brothers who go the pace – do not spare their female relations & my purse has suffered quite as much as his fathers, only I cannot afford it quite as well but that is my own affair & would not be mentioned here but to show that it is only because I am unable myself to do anything that I write to you now. Papa will do nothing for anybody whom Hau has laid under contribution – but I thought that if you had any intention of retaining him in his office that you might stretch a point by advancing his pay or do something somehow or other that these poor folk should not be utterly ruined through him. I know not how unreasonable ladies requests are supposed to go & this of mine I know to be something most unusual but I do believe in your great kindness & also in your power to do as you like in most things & if you only knew how grateful I should feel for a load off my mind I think you would believe in it being a rather jolly thing to be the Honble Native Minister & everything else that you are. I am in a better humour already than I have been since I came back & found how many there were who had reason to think Manings were capable of doing selfish & untruthful things & I cannot help feeling better when I think of it but as I said I am in better humour & more hopeful since I started this epistle.

Remember too that this style of correspondence is new to me so if there is anything lacking in proper respectful phraseology that I send from ignorance – not wilfully & you must excuse me.

I write on my own thought without signifying any intention beforehand of doing so – but Hau had made use of your name so often of late that Mrs Sharpe asked my advice about calling upon you to ascertain the truth – & the worst also for her upon that hint I speak myself & hope to get an answer for against as soon as convenient. I am so disgusted with things in general & brothers in particular – my experience of them being people who take the pleasantest road to themselves & leave the rough path to others. I suppose I shall feel more amicably taihoa but at present I can only pin my faith upon you – and hope to remain

          Yours very sincerely
          Maria A. Maning

Grafton Road[49]

As a single woman, Maria's ability to help financially support her brother was limited, but nevertheless she endeavoured to do her family duty.

Seeking assistance

Women without access to land or resources relied on seasonal work. Single women's opportunities ranged from seasonal labour to factory work or domestic service. Rihi Huanga wanted her daughter to obtain a government job and applied to George Thomas Wilkinson, the local native officer, for assistance in 1898. He forwarded the letter to the Under Secretary of the Justice Department, which had oversight of 'native affairs' in the 1890s.

Kihikihi
    Oketopa 9th 1898
Kia Hori Wirikihana
    Kai whaka haere a Te Kawanatanga e hoa tena koe
He inoi atu tenei naku kia korua koto taua matua ko Te Kawanatanga
Mo tetehi mahi ma taku kotiro kia homai e korua ara nga mahi e rite ana mana he whaka ako kura he poutapeta me etahi atu mahi a Te Kawanatanga.
E rima ona tau e whaka ako ana i nga kura ka tahi ano ka mutu ka rua tekau ona tau i naia nei
        Heoi ano
    Na Rihi Huanga
Ko tonu ingoa ko Ema Erena
Ko tana mahi kura kua whaka mutua koia nei te take i tuhi atu ai au kia koe kia homai tetehi mahi ma ana
        Heoi ano

[Wilkinson's translation]
    Kihikihi 9th October 1898
To Mr George Wilkinson
    Government Agent
Friend, greeting. This is an application of mine to you and our parent, the Government, for some suitable employment for my daughter, such as teacher in a school or post office work, or any other Government work. She has been engaged school teaching during the past five years. She is 20 years old. That is all, from
            Rihi Huanga
Her name is Ema Ellen. It is because she has ceased to act as a school teacher that I apply to you for some employment for her. That is all.[50]

For his part, Wilkinson advised that Ema was a 'respectable, intelligent, and well behaved young woman', who would, in his estimation, 'carry out satisfactorily the duties belonging to any Government situation if she were successful in obtaining one.'[51]

Teaching was a precarious labour market though, for Māori women were often employed at a lower rank, as teacher aides or assistants, and paid at much lower rates. Many hoped to establish their own schools, but only a handful succeeded in the decades before 1900.[52] The first to do so was Mary Tautari (d. 1906), who established a native school at Taumārere in 1875, which also catered for boarders. Her pupils were mainly Māori girls, who got an education in English and were trained in the arts of instrumental music, singing and household management along European lines.[53] Her main supporter was Sir Donald McLean, who promised he 'would get the government to pay for their board with you' if she was able to attract significant numbers of Māori girls to the school.[54] However she got into financial trouble, and when her key supporter died, Mary turned to McLean's son, Douglas, for help in 1877.

Taumarere, Bay of Islands
March 29th 1877

Dear Sir

On the occasion of the death of your lamented father I felt strongly inclined to make some attempt at expressing my deep sympathy in your trouble, but feared my letter would be an intrusion, therefore remained silent.

At present I am forced to write and ask your kind sympathy for I feel now in great want of a sincere friend and trust that your interest in this school will enable you to kindly overlook my boldness in addressing you on the painful subject on which I am about to speak, namely a certain unpleasant business transaction which if not arranged by your too kind consideration, I shall no doubt be forced to break up this native school founded by your never to be forgotten father and this would be a greater misfortune and pity as the girls are now over their first difficulties and promise to be not only well educated but even accomplished and nice girls.

The business to which I refer to is this. That some time ago (as the enclosed will more fully explain) a money transaction was as far as I knew settled in a satisfactory manner and to my astonishment I received the enclosed by last mail and as I have no possibility of managing the matter in a state of *desperation I apply to your good feelings to act as I believe in my heart your dear father would do in this matter. I wish very much that you could conveniently let me hear from you by next mail and I earnestly beg of you to kindly excuse the liberty I am taking and to which I am <u>actually</u> <u>driven</u> by present state of affairs. With very best and kind wishes*

   I remain yours most sincerely
     Mary Tautari[55]

Although she received 'a kind note' and some advice, in the end her brother-in-law stepped in, paying the debt, and relieving her of anxiety.[56] Although Mary encouraged 'Europeanisation' at her school, this was not to be at the expense of Māori culture, language and ways of life, which she demonstrated her commitment to in her work as a Licensed Native Interpreter in the Land Court. Amongst her cohort in 1888, was Matire (Matilda) Morgan.[57] No doubt their education in the English language, and familiarity with colonial institutions, as well as their personal connections with officials, gave them an advantage in the court, which they could use for the benefit of their whānau and friends.

By the late nineteenth century, many women experienced increasing difficulties in maintaining families from an ever-reducing resource base, as Meri Matimati's letter illustrates.

Kupape 1 Tihema
E hoa e Temakarini
tena koe kia rongo mai koe i taku korero ma matou te tehi kai mau e homai kia rua peke riwai kia ko tahi pihi poaka kia ko tahi peke pihikete
Kia ko tahi topai [illegible] huka ta temea hoki ituhituhi atu ai ahau kia koe he mate rawa no matou i te kai mei kore to matou hemo i te kai e kore ahau e tuhituhi atu kia koe Kite tehi kai nate mate rawa o matou i te kai i tuhituhi ai ahau e Te Makarini kia ma na mai tenei pukapuka

Na ku tena puka puka
Na To Waea na Meri Matimati
Kia Te Makarini

[modern translation]
Coopers Bay 1 December
Friend, Mr McLean. Greetings.

Listen to what I say, about some food for us. Please give us two bags of potatoes, a side of pork, and one bag of biscuits and one [illegible] of sugar because I wrote to you because we are starving. If we weren't starving, I wouldn't write to you for some food. It is due to us starving, that I have written. Mr McLean, please give effect to this letter.

This letter is from me,
From your mother, Meri Matimati.
To Mr McLean.[58]

Others wrote to officials to draw their attention to the burdens of widowhood, old age or illness, which they sought to remedy by gaining a pension, or social assistance. George Thomas Wilkinson forwarded Ani Waiwhakarewa's request to the Native Department in 1895.

Tepaina   Akuhata 22 1895
He Tuhi atu tena naaku ki te kawanantanga kia mahara tia mai te nei wahine e mau nei ta tana ingoa iraro nei a Ani Tewaiwhakarewa
67 no nei ona tau ko taana taane kua mate kaore kau ana tamariki koia ahau ituhi atu ai kia tukua mai i te kawana tanga heoranga mo tenei 'wahinei' e mau nei tona ingoa ituhi atu ai ahau kaore kau ia e kahakite mahi kai maana kaore ano hoki he tangata mahi kai ma ana i te mea kia kua mate nei hoki taana taane i te 16 o akuhata 1892 tetau kaore nei he tangata hei ata whai i aia monga tau imua atu otana matenga
Koia ahau ituhi ai ko toona oranga me homai kia ia e te kawanatanga ara nga mea i hiahia tia eia Heoi ano
     Ani Tewaiwhakarewa

Kia mana mai i akoe taaku reta mehe mea kite mana mai ia koe me tuku mai ki Waingaro i te 28 o Ngara o Akuhata 1895 ko taku iwi ko Nga ti Tahinga

[Wilkinson's translation]
     Mercer, August 22nd 1895
This is a written application of mine to the Government in the hope that it will consider the case of this woman whose name is signed below viz Ani Waiwhakarewa. She is 67 years old. Her husband is dead. She has no children that is why I write asking Government to grant her some relief. She is not strong

enough to grow food for herself and there is no one to grow food for her because her husband died on the 16th August, 1892. There is no one to provide for her now until her death. That is why I write asking that some Government relief, such as she desires, may be granted to her.

    Ani te Waiwhakarewa

Give effect to the request in my letter. If it is granted send (the reply) to Waingaro on the 28th August, 1895.
My tribe is Ngatitahinga[59]

Maangi Pōtae requested support so her husband could access medical care. She also wanted his government pension raised to a level appropriate to his years of service and loyalty to the Crown.

Papawai
Greytown North
31 March 1891

The Honorable
    The Minister of Native Affairs,
      Wellington,
Sir,
    I wish to bring to your notice the case of my husband Henare Potae, who is at present suffering very much from rheumatism.
    When Mr Mitchelson was Native Minister he promised to give my husband a free passage from Gisborne to the Hot Springs, and also an order for admission to the Hospital there.
    It would be of great benefit to my husband if you would kindly grant him the passage & the admission to the Hospital promised by Mr Mitchelson.
    All his ailment was contracted while in service of the Government.
    My husband also had a pension of £100 from the Government but it was reduced to £40, and then it was raised to £75.
    My husband wishes me to ask you to ask the Government to raise his pension again to £100 as he is now an old man & very sick and not able to do anything for himself.
    If you will look in the books of the Government you will see that my husband was always on the side of the Government & was of great service to them during the wars.

This is all I have to say at present.
Please send the answer soon to

Yours truly
Maangi Potae[60]

Widowhood placed women in precarious financial positions. Mākere Tāwhai wrote to the Native Minister in 1894 seeking financial relief. Her original letter no longer exists, so we have only the English translation.

[official translation]

Waima

October 6 1894

The Honourable
  Minister for Native Affairs
  This is a letter of mine to you and the other members of your Government.
  Salutations to you all, great indeed is my love for you in the remembrance of the death of my husband the late Honi [sic] Mohi Tawhai, who died in grief at the action of the Maoris in abandoning the Government of New Zealand.
  This is an application of mine to you and the members of your Government to have pity on us and continue his pension to me and my children for he was a person who loyally supported government measures up to the time of his death and my children will I trust follow in the footsteps of their father, and should have pity on me and continue that pension for our support. I could have them both taught to follow the footsteps of their grandfather Mohi Tawhai and their father Hone Mohi Tawhai for I and my children are as orphans and I am physically unable to provide food for our maintenance.
  That is all, ended
  From
  Makere H. M. Tawhai[61]

These are not begging letters, but instead critique the state. Mākere, for instance, as the widow of a loyal servant of the government, views the government as having a duty and a responsibility for her welfare. Mākere Tāwhai, like many women who appear in this book, sought to hold the state to account.

Remembrance

Financial constraint shaped the lives of many women, but this was not the case for all. Histories of consumption and commerce in colonial New Zealand have yet to track the purchasing power of Māori women. Catherine Bishop has highlighted their role as colonial businesswomen, but women were also consumers of a range of goods and services, notably fabrics and dressmaking services, reflected in the advertising targeted at them.[62] They were also interested in photography, regularly going to studios to have their likenesses recorded on camera for posterity. Some had their portraits painted, which were the cause for joy and happiness. On seeing Gottfried Lindauer's portrait depicting her likeness, Rōra Hakaraia expressed her pleasure in writing to Walter Buller.

>   *Putiki*
>   *Hune 28th 1895*
>   *Kia Te Pura*
>   *Tena koe e rua aku wiki ki Waikanae ka hoki mai au ki Whanganui nei katahi ahau ka kite i te whakaahua i tukua mai nei e koe. Ka nui te koa o to ku ngakau, i rangi nui atu te pai o taua whakaahua. Kia ora tonu koe ma te Atua koe e tiaki i runga i te pai o taua whakaahua.*
>   *Heoi ano*
>   *Rora Hakaraia*

>   [modern translation]
>   Pūtiki
>   June 28 1895
>   To Buller
>   Greetings. I have been in Waikanae for two weeks, and have returned here to Whanganui. I have just seen the likeness that you sent to me. I am really happy with it and I am pleased at the quality of that picture. Thank you. May God protect you on account of the quality of that picture.
>   That is all
>   Rōra Hakaraia.[63]

Rōra's brother was the military leader Te Keepa (Major Kemp). In 1911 she revived the idea of a memorial erected in her brother's memory, first proposed in 1898. She was successful in arranging financial support, and commissioned a statue based on a Lindauer portrait depicting a youthful Te Keepa in military uniform, wearing his medals and holding a sword of honour gifted to him by Queen Victoria.[64] It was unveiled at Pākaitore/Moutoa Gardens in September 1912. On seeing it, Rōra rejected it as a poor likeness of her brother, and refused to pay the remainder of the costs. Several panels of text adorn the plinth, one of which is in Māori alone. Ewan Morris suggests that Rōra arranged this panel, and in it she 'speaks in her own voice' about her brother, emphasising his many contributions to the community, but particularly his status as a peacemaker.[65] In this panel she sought to elaborate on the depiction of Te Keepa in his military finery, by drawing attention to his leadership in many sectors of the community. This is how she wanted him remembered.

Expressions of grief continued to be composed as mōteatea (sung poetry), notably waiata tangi, or laments. In the July 1856 issue of the Māori-language newspaper, *Te Karere Maori* sits the following waiata tangi with an accompanying English translation.

HE TANGI NA TE PAEA MO TONA HOA.
Mo EPIHA PUTINI TE RANGIATAAHUA

Tera Kopu hapai o te ata
Me he mea ko te hoa tenei ka hoki mai.
E mihi ana au taku kahui Tara
I tukua iho ai, ka hinga ki raro e!
Tu ke mai Taupiri i te tonga
Karekare kau ana te tai ki Manuka.
I haere rangitahi ko te rangi ki te mate
Kihai i ponaia te hua i Motutara
Hoki mai pa! to moenga i te whare.
E pupuri nei au te tau o taku ate
Ka ngaro ra e taku manu kohe ata.
Tena ka tiu, ka wehe i a au, i.

[newspaper translation]
LAMENT FOR JABEZ BUNTING RANGIATAAHUA.
BY HIS WIFE, TE PAEA.

The star Kopu harbinger of morn
Appears in view, an emblem this of the beloved,

Methinks returning to me.
My flock of tiny birds, left here to droop
Without a father, o'er you I mourn.
Lo, distant in the south, Taupiri rears its head
In solitude, while the waters of the Manukau
Are rippling onward.
Death has severed thee from us; and thou
Wast borne to heaven, we had time
To fasten in thine ear thy heir loom Motutara.
Come back O father and betake thyself
To thy accustomed slumbers in thy dwelling.
The cord that gives vitality to this frail heart,
I hold, and fain would cut asunder;
For he who was my talking bird, that sung.
So sweetly at the dawn of day, has
Disappeared for ever from my gaze.[66]

It was composed by Te Paea (Sophia) for her husband Ēpiha Pūtini Te Rangiataahua, an important rangatira of the Māungaunga hapū of Ngāti Tīpā, but who had taken up the leadership of his uncle's tribe, Ngāti Tamaoho. Both tribes were part of the wider Tainui confederation, under the ariki, Pōtatau Te Wherowhero. Ēpiha Pūtini's wife, Tīaho Te Paea, was the ariki's daughter (see chapter 4). Although high-born women more commonly composed love songs and men songs of lament, neither genre was limited to one particular gender.[67] The Māori text is rather terse (quite unlike the more florid Victorian verse translation in English), utilising a form of presentation, metaphors and geographical references that would have been familiar to those who heard the song sung, or who read the newspaper; Taupiri, a mountain, and Manukau, a harbour, clearly locate the mōteatea as belonging to the Tainui tribes of Waikato and South Auckland. Mōteatea began to appear in Māori-language newspapers from the mid-nineteenth century to communicate widely the death of a significant person, and to enable shared grief.

Conclusion

Women wrote for private reasons, for pleasure, and for creative expression. Of all genres of writing, though, the letter was the most popular due to its versatility.

In a letter one was able to communicate all kinds of information ranging from the political to the deeply personal. Because letters travelled and made words move, they carried messages that ensured kinship connections were maintained across large distances. Letters were also popular modes of writing because the genre easily encompassed Māori oral expression, in the form of waiata and laments, compositions in which Māori women were highly skilled. Many of the letters featured in this chapter derive from government records, and although they are often framed as appeals for assistance, it is because they were at times addressed to government officials who were regarded as friends and supporters that these items of correspondence offer windows onto private life and emotional states.

EPILOGUE:

'I am writing to you for you to hear'

In 1861 Rīria Hōhepa composed a letter to her husband Hōhepa Tamaihenga, informing him that 'I am writing to you for you to hear'.[1] *He Reo Wāhine* has followed Rīria's lead: it has brought together a selection of Māori women's words so that you may hear them speak about the issues that mattered to them.

Unsurprisingly, land is at the centre of Māori women's writing, and is central to their testimony before official commissions of enquiry or in the Native Land Court, as well as in their many petitions. In their concern for land, theirs was an experience shared with their wider family and community, but in setting out their claims in writing, they testified to ways land loss affected them as women. As Pat Hohepa and David V. Williams note of the Native Land Court, women's experiences in that institution have yet to be fully investigated by historians, but they suspect that it eroded women's succession rights and economic independence, which they had customarily enjoyed. They assert that, 'Maori customary dealings in land were not only subject to assimilationist practices but also gendered views on Mana Wahine. What assisted this was the fact that the Native Land Court was a colonially defined patriarchal institution both in the way it was organised and in its operations.'[2]

As examples from *He Reo Wāhine* demonstrate, some women did very well in the court, eventually acquiring large estates. Even so, as their petitioning demonstrates, most women did not gain advantage from the operations of the court, instead they experienced land loss, but unlike their male relatives, women's economic freedoms relating to land and property, particularly if they were married, were severely constrained because of their gender. Some women tried to protect their interests, and those of their children, by making wills directing the future of their property. Women's wills are valuable sources for shining light on their concerns, and deserve far greater attention than New Zealand historians have hitherto given them, for through the details of the accumulation and distribution of family wealth and property, they reveal insights into family relationships as well as their views about the Native Land Court itself.[3]

Although *He Reo Wāhine* does not focus on the intricacies by which the Native Land Court and related machinery of state undermined women's status, we can see its reach and effects, in particular the dispossession of Māori lands, and the resulting marginalisation, poverty and vulnerability. As the state grew in size through the nineteenth century, Māori women were increasingly required to adhere to its dictates and requirements. In tracing women's correspondence with politicians and public servants, and following cases as they wound through the system, we have brought to light the depth of the difficulties women faced in having their appeals for justice investigated. It is hard to comprehend the state's reach and power in women's lives, without viewing their words and testimonies, for these bring us close to their experiences, thoughts and feelings. As Bryony Cosgrove, writing about the Australian context, notes, 'while literacy played a role in the loss of much Indigenous culture and language, it also equipped Indigenous communities with the means to negotiate with white authorities, albeit on an unequal footing.'[4]

This book is certainly not designed to be the final word on Māori women's experiences, but it offers a few examples of what lies in some of New Zealand's manuscript and archival collections, and perhaps opens the door to further historical research on individuals' lives. It has been constrained somewhat by the limits we have set for ourselves, in terms of the period covered, and also that the women should be heard in their own first-person voices, however filtered or modified that voice might be. More broad topics would lend themselves to more liberal sweeps of archival and manuscript holdings.

In particular, the telling of Māori women's history could benefit from more biographical work on tūpuna wahine. While there are short accounts of various Māori women in the *Dictionary of New Zealand Biography*, and *The Book of New Zealand Women* (many contributed by descendants), a number of women of mana, such as Te Paea Tīaho of Tainui, Takiora Dalton of Ngāti Ruanui, and Niniwa-i-te-rangi and Ārihi Te Nahu of Ngāti Kahungunu, left sufficient historical traces to allow much more expansive stories of their lives to be uncovered, and their imprint on the wider world to be assessed.[5] Niniwa, in particular, was earnestly involved in writing for, and managing, Māori-language newspapers, although much of this activity occurred in the early twentieth century.

As Charlotte Macdonald has noted, Māori possessed a vigorous newspaper culture, and she speculates that: 'the press was a way of women speaking in public that was less possible in the formal protocol of the marae or of the Paremata Māori sessions. Further investigation is needed of their columns.'[6] We agree with Macdonald – work is needed to assess what Māori women's contributions to this lively newspaper culture can reveal about their participation in political as well as intellectual debates. Niupepa also offer windows through which to see other aspects of Māori women's lives. These discourses, including those of Māori and Pākehā males, not only cast light on how women lived, loved, laboured and passed away, but also illustrate the writers' own attitudes to Māori women's place within society. Advertisements tell little known histories of Māori women as consumers of colonial products, and as producers of their own pānuitanga.

Some women, as the material in *He Reo Wāhine* indicates, left a far greater imprint on the public record through sustained letter writing, petitioning campaigns, and engagement with newspapers, but the majority entered the written archive only fleetingly when they encountered the state, or its functionaries. Because of this, the written record is only one of many viable sources for examining Māori women's colonial experience. Throughout *He Reo Wāhine* we have stressed the interconnection between Māori orality and textuality, or voice and text, because for much of the period covered by this volume, the metaphors and allusions common to the oral world were also present in women's writing, especially their letters. Māori took up print for their own reasons, many in order to put their histories and whakapapa on paper. Women's oral compositions, notably waiata, were an area in which they were expert. Capacity and willingness to use both Māori oral sources, such as waiata, and to read textual sources in light of oral conventions, is required if historians are to produce fully textured and nuanced accounts of Māori women's experiences.

Just as importantly, historians should engage more with te reo Māori, either by improving their language ability, or by collaborating with scholars with the necessary skills. For most nineteenth-century Māori, te reo was their primary and often only means of communication, and this is reflected in *He Reo Wāhine*. Government forms women completed and signed were printed in Māori, and their correspondence as well as their oral testimony was largely provided in te reo. Although contemporary officials rendered much of this material into English, and a small number of scholars today have continued translating texts, a massive number of documents remain untranslated to this day, a valuable resource that historians ignore at their peril.

New Zealand scholarship draws heavily upon the public collections of manuscript materials, and especially records of the state, but historians have not always paid close attention to wāhine Māori, even though their writings are numerous. Paying attention to Māori women's words, wherever they might appear – in waiata, archival collections or on public monuments – enriches and broadens New Zealand's historical scholarship.[7] For instance, being attentive to women's words brings different experiences to light: Hinemoa's words, and her fateful decision, for example. Hers is not the kind of experience that usually appears in historical treatments of the Māori past or colonial history, nor used by scholars interested in Māori engagement in writing. A suicide note does not fit in with the argument that Māori wrote mainly for political purposes, or to express tribal identity. As this volume shows, women wrote, and spoke, for a variety of reasons, on war, land, love and sorrow, whakapapa, for their own benefit or for their children, whānau, hapū or iwi. Writing was used for creative expression, and women corresponded in order to maintain familial ties. In their petitions, letters and testimonies, women's imprint on the colonial archives is significant, and attests to the many strategies they took to manage their interests, care for whānau, and give voice to their political views.

NOTES

Abbreviations

ACL	Sir George Grey Special Colletions, Auckland City Libraries
AJHR	*Appendices to the Journals of the House of Representatives*
ANZA	Archives New Zealand, Auckland
ANZC	Archives New Zealand, Christchurch
ANZD	Archives New Zealand, Dunedin
ANZW	Archives New Zealand, Wellington
ATL	Alexander Turnbull Library, National Library of New Zealand
AWM	Auckland War Memorial Museum
HC	Hocken Collections
NZPD	New Zealand Parliamentary Debates

Introduction. Voice, Text and the Colonial Archive

1. Adele Perry, *Colonial Relations*, pp. 8, 10. Also see Antoinette Burton (ed.), *Archive Stories*.
2. A point noted by Arini M. Loader, 'Tau mai e Kapiti te whare wananga o ia, o te nui, o te wehi, o te toa: Reclaiming Early Raukawa-Toarangatira Writing from Otaki', p. 22.
3. Notable examples include Berys Heuer, *Maori Women*; Angela Ballara, 'Wāhine Rangatira: Māori Women of Rank and their Role in the Women's Kotahitanga Movement of the 1890s', pp. 127–139; Tania Rei, *Māori Women and the Vote*. Anne Else (ed.), *Women Together* includes entries on Māori women's organisations, and Māori women feature in Sandra Coney (ed.), *Standing in the Sunshine*, and in Barbara Brookes, *A History of New Zealand Women*.
4. Charlotte Macdonald, Merimeri Penfold and Bridget Williams (eds), *The Book of New Zealand Women*. Ngahuia Te Awekotuku's *Mana Wahine Maori* is an essential and pioneering work on Māori women's history. Some key biographies include: Pei Te Hurinui Jones, *Puhiwahine*, and Paul Diamond, *Makereti*.
5. Patricia Grimshaw, 'Maori Agriculturalists and Aboriginal Hunter-Gatherers' in Ruth Roach Pierson, Nupur Chaudhuri and Beth McAuley (eds), *Nation, Empire, Colony*, p. 22. On intermarriage and mixed-descent families see: Atholl Anderson, *Race Against Time*; Damon I. Salesa, *Racial Crossings*; Angela Wanhalla, *In/visible Sight*; Angela Wanhalla, *Matters of the Heart*; David Haines, 'In Search of the "Waheen": Ngai Tahu Women, Shore Whalers, and the Meaning of Sex in Early New Zealand' in Tony Ballantye and Antoinette Burton (eds), *Moving Subjects*, pp. 49–66.
6. Judith Binney, *Stories Without End: Essays*, p. 165.
7. Exceptions are: Yvonne Sutherland, 'Nineteenth-century Māori Letters of Emotion: Orality, Literacy and Context'; Lyndsay Head, 'The Abduction of Hinemare's Children', pp. 20–22.
8. An exception is Lyndsay Head, 'Land, Authority and the Forgetting of Being in Early Colonial Maori History'.
9. There is a rich and exciting scholarship on indigenous writing in colonial contexts, particularly in Canada, Hawaii, Australia and the United States: Robert Warrior, *The People and the Word*; Lisa Brooks, *The Common Pot*; Rick Monture, *We Share Our Matters*; Niigaanwewidam James Sinclair and Warren Cariou (eds), *Manitowapow*; Noenoe K. Silva, *Aloha Betrayed*; Penny van Toorn, *Writing Never Arrives Naked*. The writings of indigenous women are explored by a range of scholars, including: Elizabeth Nelson, Sandra Smith and Patricia Grimshaw (eds), *Letters From Aboriginal Women of Victoria, 1867–1926*; Virginia Moore Carney, *Eastern Band Cherokee Women*; Cari M. Carpenter and Carolyn Soriso (eds), *The Newspaper Warrior*. For a particularly innovative and thoughtful approach to recovering and interpreting indigenous women's voice and agency see: Noelani Arista, 'Listening to Leoiki: Engaging Sources in Hawaiian History', pp. 66–73.

10 Loader, p. 24.
11 For example, see Kerry Howe, 'Two Worlds?', pp. 50–61.
12 Naomi Simmonds, 'Mana Wahine: Decolonising Politics', p. 13
13 Waiata are a significant source for historians interested in Māori women's expression and experience during the nineteenth century, of which Margaret Orbell's work offers ample evidence.
14 Paul Meredith and Alice Te Punga Somerville, '"Kia Rongo Mai Koutou Ki Taku Whakaaro": Māori Voices in the Alexander Turnbull Library', p. 101.
15 Diana Meads, Philip Rainer and Kay Sanderson, compilers, *Women's Words*. Sue Loughlin and Carolyn M. Morris, compilers, *Womanscripts*. Phil G. Parkinson and Penelope Griffith, *Books in Māori, 1815–1900*.
16 A. T. Ngata and Pei Te Hurinui Jones, *Nga Moteatea*, 4 vols. (various dates, 1928–1990); John Caselberg, *Maori is My Name*.
17 Frances Porter and Charlotte Macdonald (eds), *My Hand Will Write What My Heart Dictates* includes 13 waiata, 34 letters, a petition, two extracts from reminiscences and the evidence of two women (both from 1906) given before a government enquiry. Amongst the 34 letters, some writers appear more than once, including Lucy Takiora Dalton, Ruta Te Rauparaha, Matara Tetere, Mere Paea and Ruta Manuahura.
18 Porter and Macdonald, p. 17.
19 Meredith and Te Punga Somerville, p. 99.
20 The quote is from Noenoe K. Silva, 'Nā Hulu Kupana: To Honor Our Intellectual Ancestors', p. 49.
21 Tony Ballantyne, *Webs of Empire*, p. 185.
22 *Ibid.*, p. 187.
23 Christopher J. Lee, 'Gender Without Groups: Confession, Resistance and Selfhood in the Colonial Archive', p. 714. On critical approaches to colonial archives see: Ann Laura Stoler, *Along the Archival Grain*; Nigel Worden, 'Cape Slaves in the Paper Empire of the VOC', pp. 23–44; Clare Anderson, 'Subaltern Lives: History, Identity and Memory in the Indian Ocean World', pp. 503–507; Clare Anderson, *Subaltern Lives*.
24 Ballantyne, *Webs of Empire*, pp. 177–78.
25 Bradford Haami, *Pūtea Whakairo*.
26 Bettina Bradbury, 'From Civil Death to Separate Property: Changes in the Legal Rights of Married Women in Nineteenth-Century New Zealand', *New Zealand Journal of History*, pp. 40–66.
27 For example, George Grey, *Polynesian Mythology, and Ancient Traditional History of the New Zealand Race, as Furnished by their Priests and Chiefs*; John White, *Ancient History of the Maori*.
28 In *He Kōrero* Alison Jones and Kuni Jenkins note it was men who collected the phrases for Kendall's *Grammar* (1820). Evidence of this is seen in the phrases themselves, none of which refer to women's activities, such as weaving or gardening (p. 167). Later collectors did gather information from women, notably the southern ethnograper Herries Beattie who worked mainly in the first half of the twentieth century: J. H. Beattie, *Traditional Lifeways of the Southern Maori*, Atholl Anderson (ed.). The Carrington manuscript, which records Ngāi Tahu migration traditions, was created in the 1930s by journalist Hugh Carrington, who worked closely with Hariata Beaton-Morel: Te Maire Tau and Atholl Anderson (eds), *Ngāi Tahu*, p. 12.
29 Māori text in George Grey, *Nga Mahi a nga Tupuna*, p. 198. English text from *Te Ao Hou*, 10 April 1955, p. 8.
30 Maui Pomare, *Legends of the Maori* vol. 2, James Cowan (ed.), pp. 109–111; J. M. McEwen, *Rangitāne*, pp. 48–50.
31 Takaanui Tarakawa, 'Ko te Rerenga Mai o Mata-atua, me Kurahaupo me Era Atu Waka, i Hawaiki', *Journal of the Polynesian Society*, vol. 3, no. 2, June 1894, pp. 59–64, translation 'The Coming of Mata-atua, Kurahaupo and Other Canoes from Hawaiki to New Zealand' by S. Percy Smith, pp. 65–71.
32 *New Zealand Herald*, 10 September 1866, p. 5.
33 Waikato Confiscations, Proceedings of Compensation Court, File NO 2/8, Onewhero Block (1866), Waitangi Tribunal, Raupatu Document Bank vol. 103, pp. 39598, 39606.

34 'Evidence Taken in Napier before Commissioner George Edward Sainsbury, Esquire, Commissioner Appointed by the Supreme Court for the Purpose', Russell v. Grindell & Didsbury Libel Case, pp. 1, 4, MA 24 1/3, ANZW.
35 *Te Manuhiri Tuarangi*, 15 May 1861, p. 4.
36 William Yate, *An Account of New Zealand, and of the Formation and Progress of the Church Missionary Sociey's Mission in the Northern Island*, pp. 258–59.
37 Opotiki Confiscation, Minutes of Compensation Court: Opotiki sitting 7 March 1867, Waitangi Tribunal, Raupatu Document Bank, vol. 120, p. 46194.
38 Angela Middleton, *Pēwhairangi*, p. 75.
39 Freda Rankin Kawharu, 'Heke Pokai, Hone Wiremu', from the Dictionary of New Zealand Biography *Te Ara – the Encyclopedia of New Zealand*, http://www.TeAra.govt.nz/en/biographies/1h16/heke-pokai-hone-wiremu; Angela Ballara, 'Turikatuku', from the Dictionary of New Zealand Biography *Te Ara – the Encyclopedia of New Zealand*, http://www.TeAra.govt.nz/en/biographies/1t114/turikatuku; Hariata Te Pouaru to Grey, 3 February 1851, GNZ MA 379, ACL; Letter from Hariata Arama Karaka Pī, 31 October 1867 in McDonnell Papers, Folder 11, MS-Copy-Micro-0651-2, ATL; *Wairarapa Daily Times*, 13 January 1894.
40 This is stressed by Gabriela Ramos and Yanna Yannakakis (eds), *Indigenous Intellectuals*, pp. 3–4.
41 *AJHR*, 1862, E-13.
42 *Wanganui Herald*, 7 December 1867, p. 3. Hēni Pore (Jane Foley) and Marian Stewart both worked as licensed interpreters.
43 *AJHR*, 1899, B-07.
44 Lawrence Venuti, 'Introduction' in Lawrence Venuti (ed.), *Rethinking Translation*, p. 5.
45 NZPD, 1861–63, pp. 518–522. Colenso was referring to *Te Manuhiri Tuarangi*, 15 November 1861, p. 2, but also discussed articles in *Te Karere Maori*, 1 May 1862 and 1 July 1862.
46 *AJHR*, 1860, E-4, p. 6.
47 In this approach we are following Kirsty Reid and Fiona Paisley (eds), *Critical Perspectives on Colonialism*.
48 Jones and Jenkins, pp. 45–46.
49 Girls were present at Parramatta, although there are few extant examples of their writing. Jones and Jenkins note that Tuai's wife was with him at Marsden's Parramatta seminary in 1817 (p. 135).
50 Jones and Jenkins, pp. 108–9.
51 Angela Middleton, *Te Puna – a New Zealand Mission Station*, p. 62. See Jones and Jenkins, pp. 108–9.
52 J. L. Nicholas, *Narrative of a Voyage to New Zealand*, vol. 2, pp. 330, 333, 341.
53 Judith Binney, *A Legacy of Guilt*, Second Ed., pp. 175–179; Parkinson and Griffith, pp. 28–31.
54 Carolyn Fitzgerald (ed.), *Letters from the Bay of Islands*, pp. 107–9.
55 *Ibid.*, p. 146.
56 *Ibid.*, pp. 222–24.
57 Jones and Jenkins, pp. 180–82; Kuni Jenkins, 'Te Ihi, Te Mana, Te Wehi o te Ao Tuhi: Māori Print Literacy from 1814–55: Literacy, Power and Colonisation', pp. 12–13, 134, 137; J. M. R. Owens, 'New Zealand Before Annexation', in Geoffrey W. Rice (ed.), *The Oxford History of New Zealand*, Second Ed., p. 39. See Ranginui Walker, *Liberating Maori from Educational Subjection*, pp. 3–4.
58 *Native Trust Ordinance* 1844, quoted by C. J. Parr, 'Maori Literacy, 1843–1867', p. 215.
59 H. T. Purchas, *A History of the English Church in New Zealand*, p. 73; Parr, p. 211; Walker, *Liberating Maori*, p. 4.
60 T. S. Grace, *A Pioneer Missionary Among the Maoris 1850–1879*, pp. 79–80.
61 For example, Frances Porter (ed.), *The Turanga Journals 1840–1850*, pp. 73–74.
62 *The Missionary Register*, [Sections relating to New Zealand.] 1846, p. 405, http://www.enzb.auckland.ac.nz/
63 William Richard Wade, *A Journey in the Northern Island of New Zealand*, p. 98.
64 Mark Derby, 'Māori–Pākehā relations – Missions and Māori', *Te Ara – the Encyclopedia of New Zealand*, http://www.TeAra.govt.nz/en/maori-pakeha-relations/page-2

65 An estimate of 90 per cent Māori literacy by 1856 is made in Pat Hohepa, 'Current Issues in Promoting Maori Language Use', p. 1. See also, Claudia Orange, 'The Māori and the Crown' in Keith Sinclair (ed.), *The Oxford Illustrated History of New Zealand*, p. 34; M. P. K. Sorrenson, 'Māori and Pākehā' in Geoffrey W. Rice (ed.), *The Oxford History of New Zealand*, Second Ed., pp. 143–44; Ranginui Walker, *Ka Whawhai Tonu Matou. Struggle Without End*, pp. 85–86; Buddy Mikaere, 'Musket Wars, Migrations, New Tribal Alignments' in Danny Keenan (ed.), *Huia Histories of Māori*, p. 119; Bradford Haami, 'Tā te Ao Māori: Writing the Māori World' in Keenan (ed.), *Huia Histories of Māori*, p. 175; Hana O'Regan, 'The Fate of Customary Language: Te Reo Māori 1900 to the Present' in Keenan (ed.), *Huia Histories of Māori*, p. 300.
66 For example, see James Belich, *Making Peoples*, p. 165; Danny Keenan, 'Separating Them From That Common Influence: The Dissolution of Customary Authority 1840–1890', in Keenan (ed.), *Huia Histories of Māori*, p. 137.
67 Parr, 'Maori Literacy', p. 213.
68 D. F. McKenzie, *Oral Culture, Literacy and Print in Early New Zealand*, p. 9.
69 Lyndsay Head and Buddy Mikaere, 'How Literate Were Maori?', pp. 17–20.
70 Note 60, Richard Boast, 'Bringing the New Philology to Pacific Legal History', p. 256.
71 Jones and Jenkins, p. 102.
72 On the integration of writing into many aspects of Māori society see Haami, 'Tā Te Ao Māori', pp. 172–73.
73 Sarah K. J. Gallagher, '"A Curious Document": Ta Moko as Evidence of Pre-European Textual Culture in New Zealand', pp. 44–47.
74 Ngārino Ellis, 'Ki tō Ringa ki ngā Rākau a te Pākehā?: Drawings and Signatures of Moko by Māori in the Early 19th Century', p. 30.
75 Jones and Jenkins, p. 102.
76 Jane McRae, 'From Māori Oral Traditions to Print', in Penny Griffith, Ross Harvey and Keith Maslen (eds), *Book and Print in New Zealand*, p. 29.
77 Lachy Paterson, *Colonial Discourses*, pp. 38–39; J. C. Crawford, *Recollections of Travel in New Zealand and Australia*, p. 103.
78 'Evidence Taken in Napier', p. 24.
79 *Ibid.*, pp. 1, 4.
80 *Ibid.*, p. 1.
81 *Hawkes Bay Herald*, 15 March 1877, p. 3; 10 September 1879, p. 4.
82 Grace, p. 176.
83 *AJHR*, 1879, I-4, p. 27.
84 Dufaur, Lusk, Biss & Fawcett, Legal documents (Maori Clients), Folder 35: Leases, MS 93/67, AWM.
85 *Auckland Star*, 9 December 1901, p. 5.
86 Wade, p. 184; G. F. Angas, *Savage Life and Scenes*, vol. 2, pp. 55–56, 133; Porter (ed.), *Turanga Journals*, p. 103.
87 G. B. Earp, *New Zealand*, p. 131. See Sydney Shep, 'The Paper Record: Phormium Tenax and New Zealand Papermaking', who says New Zealand had a 'scarce paper economy'.
88 G. F. Angas, *The New Zealanders Illustrated*, p. 25.
89 Tony Gee, 'Schoolgirl's slate links back to the deeds of Hone Heke', *New Zealand Herald*, 16 March 2000, http://www.nzherald.co.nz/nz/news/article.cfm?c_id=1&objectid=125342; Middleton, *Pēwhairangi*, pp. 117, 132.
90 The 308 letters in our collection constitute 61 per cent of the total texts, with 49 from the 1850s, 70 dated to the 1860s and 59 in the 1870s. There were 58 in the 1880s and 68 in the final decade of the nineteenth century. The 1850s and 1860s total 119 letters, or 39 per cent of the total number of letters we collected.
91 See Reid and Paisley.
92 Māmari Stephens, 'A House With Many Rooms: Rediscovering Māori as a Civic Language in the Wake of the Māori Language Act (1987)', in Rawinia Higgins, Poia Rewi and Vincent Olsen-Reeder (eds), *The Value of the Māori Language*, vol. 2, p. 53.
93 Tony Ballantyne, 'Contesting the Empire of Paper: Cultures of Print and Anti-Colonialism', in Jane Carey and Jane Lydon (eds), *Indigenous Networks*, p. 219.
94 Boast, 'Bringing the New Philology to Pacific Legal History', p. 257.

Chapter 1. 'I am a woman who wrote this letter': Land Sales

1. William Fox, *The Six Colonies of New Zealand*, pp. 89–90, 98.
2. Raymond Firth, *The Economics of the New Zealand Maori*, pp. 380–82; I. H. Kawharu, *Maori Land Tenure*, pp. 37, 60–63.
3. Land Claims Settlement Act, 1856, section 50 and section 54.
4. D. Moore, B. Rigby and M. Russell, *Rangahaua Whanui National Theme A*, pp. 41–42.
5. Waitangi Tribunal, *Turanga Tangata Turanga Whenua*, vol. 1 (Wai 814), p. 376.
6. Elspeth M. Simpson, 'Halbert, Thomas', from the Dictionary of New Zealand Biography *Te Ara – the Encyclopedia of New Zealand*, http://www.TeAra.govt.nz/en/biographies/1h4/halbert-thomas
7. Old Land Claims Case Files: Thomas Halbert, OLC 1/9 OLC 210, ANZW.
8. Ibid.
9. W. Williams to F. D. Bell, 27 May 1869, Inward Letters – Bishop William Williams, MS-Papers-0032-0640, Donald McLean Papers, ATL.
10. Waitangi Tribunal, *Turanga Tangata Turanga Whenua*, pp. 377–78.
11. Moore, Rigby and Russell, p. 330.
12. Waitangi Tribunal, *Turanga Tangata Turanga Whenua*, pp. 378–79.
13. Angela Wanhalla, *Matters of the Heart*, pp. 52–56.
14. *AJHR*, 1891, G-01, p. vi.
15. Governor Fitzroy allowed direct sales in 1844. This move was reversed by his successor, George Grey in 1846.
16. Kawharu, p. 8.
17. Ani Matenga to Donald McLean, 16 April 1851, Correspondence and other Papers in Maori, McLean Papers, MS-Papers-0032-1010, Object #1007900 (http://mp.natlib.govt.nz/detail/?id=1007900), ATL.
18. Ani Matenga to Donald McLean, 4 June 1851[?], Inward Letters in Maori, McLean Papers, MS-Papers-0032-0702A-04, Object #1031671 (http://mp.natlib.govt.nz/detail/?id=1031671), ATL.
19. Meri Te Aokauai and Tapatu Rutu to Donald McLean, 20 October 1864, Inward Letters in Maori, McLean Papers, MS-Papers-0032-0688E-06, Object #1031154 (http://mp.natlib.govt.nz/detail/?id=1031154), ATL.
20. Paul Goldsmith, *The Rise and Fall of Te Hemara Tauhia*, p. 49.
21. *Te Waka o te Iwi*, October 1857, p. 4.
22. Alan Ward, 'Davis, Charles Oliver Bond', from the Dictionary of New Zealand Biography *Te Ara – the Encyclopedia of New Zealand*, http://www.TeAra.govt.nz/en/biographies/1d3/davis-charles-oliver-bond
23. Harata Panga to Donald McLean, 15 September 1853, Inward Letters in Maori, McLean Papers, MS-Papers-0032-0677B-07, Object #1030245 (http://mp.natlib.govt.nz/detail/?id=1030245), ATL. The modern translation for this item comes from the McLean Papers website.
24. Miriama Neinukua to Donald McLean, 7 July 1857, Inward Letters in Maori, McLean Papers, MS-Papers-0032-0681B-03, Object #1032318 (http://mp.natlib.govt.nz/detail/?id=1032318), ATL.
25. Hana Te Unuhi to Donald McLean, 4 August 1857, Inward Letters in Maori, McLean Papers, MS-Papers-0032-0681b-14, Object #1032370 (http://mp.natlib.govt.nz/detail/?id=1032370), ATL.
26. Metīria Matara to Donald McLean, 13 September 1852, Inward Letters in Maori, McLean Papers, MS-Papers-0032-0676D-18, Object #1032137 (http://mp.natlib.govt.nz/detail/?id=1032137), ATL. The modern translation for this item comes from the McLean Papers website.
27. Grey Māori Autograph Series, vol. 12, pp. 27–29, GNZ MA, ACL.
28. Ibid.
29. Paerau Warbrick, 'Minute Books: An Integral Part of the Māori Land Court' in Annabel Cooper, Lachy Paterson and Angela Wanhalla (eds), *The Lives of Colonial Objects*, pp. 129–33. See also Ann Parsonson, 'Stories for the Land: Oral Narratives in the Maori Land Court' in Bain Attwood and Fiona Magowan (eds), *Telling Stories*, p. 21.

30 For example, Te Naere Tauwehe published a notice in *Takitimu* in 1883 saying he disagreed with his wife, Maraea Harua, selling her shares in land at Pāpatu, Gisborne, and would continue to work that land: *Takitimu*, 22 May 1883, p. 8.
31 Parsonson, p. 24.
32 Personal conversation, Paerau Warbrick.
33 *AJHR*, 1891, G-01, p. vii.
34 *Ibid*, p. viii.
35 *Ibid*, p. 154.
36 Native Land Court, Wairarapa Minute Book 19, pp. 33–34.
37 *Ibid*., pp. 126–27.
38 R. De Z. Hall, 'Kahutia, Riperata', from the Dictionary of New Zealand Biography *Te Ara – the Encyclopedia of New Zealand*, http://www.TeAra.govt.nz/en/biographies/2k2/kahutia-riperata
39 Native Land Court, Gisborne Minute Book 10, 1883, p. 117, cited in Shelley Nikora, 'Riperata Kahutia: A Woman of Mana', pp. 46–47.
40 Gisborne Native Land Court, vol. 9, 1883, p. 156, cited in Nikora, p. 68.
41 Native Lands Act 1865, section 22.
42 Ihapera Hinuere and two others to Fenton, 31 August 1868, BAIE/4309 1/b-34 1868/1754, ANZA.
43 Amiria Kihi and others to Native Minister, 4 March 1892, MA1 842 1892/391, ANZW.
44 Harete Tamihana and another to J. E. Macdonald, 22 July 1883, BBOP/4309 11/a-231 1883/2898, ANZW.
45 Ripeka Tiria Hihina and another to F. D. Fenton, 29 May 1877, BBOP/4309 8/a-488 1877/1563, ANZW.
46 Miriama Tamatera to J. D. Fenton, 25 March 1872, BBOP/4309 3/d-128 1872/455, ANZA.
47 Miriama Rewe to J. D. Fenton, 29 October 1877, BBOP/4309 8/a-117 1877/3116, ANZA.
48 *AJHR*, 1872, C-02, pp. 4–5.
49 Maraea Hepara to J. D. Fenton, 28 March 1876, BBOP/4309 6/a-523 1876/587, ANZA.
50 Maraea Hepara to J. D. Fenton, 17 May 1876, BBOP/4309 6/a-509 1876/931, ANZA.
51 Raiha Puaha to A. J. Dickey, 3 August 1882, BBOP/4309 10/a-265 1882/4460, ANZA.
52 T. W. Porter to Donald McLean, 21 November 1874, Inward Letters, McLean Papers, MS-Papers-0032-0510, Object #1005243 (http://mp.natlib.govt.nz/detail/?id=1005243), ATL.
53 *AJHR*, 1896, G-02, p. 4.
54 See Native Land Court evidence from Otaki Minute Book 1G in '5th February 1869', *Kete Horowhenua*, Horowhenua Library Trust, http://horowhenua.kete.net.nz/site/documents/show/1478-5-february-1869
55 See Native Land Court evidence from Otaki Minute Book 1G in '6th July 1866', *Kete Horowhenua*, Horowhenua Library Trust, http://horowhenua.kete.net.nz/site/documents/show/1248-6-july-1866
56 5th February 1869, *Kete Horowhenua*, http://horowhenua.kete.net.nz/en/site/documents/1478-5-february-1869
57 For information on the Nicholson family see Neville Hurworth, 'About Rhodes Tudor and Albert Henry Nicholson, Two Remarkable Sons of William Nicholson Nicholson of Roundhay Park'.
58 '6th February 1869', *Kete Horowhenua*, http://horowhenua.kete.net.nz/site/documents/show/1479-6-february-1869
59 *AJHR*, 1871, F-08, p. 3.
60 *Ibid*.
61 Angela Ballara, 'Te Whatanui', from the Dictionary of New Zealand Biography *Te Ara – the Encyclopedia of New Zealand*, http://www.TeAra.govt.nz/en/biographies/1t86/te-whatanui.
62 *AJHR*, 1871, F-08, p. 3.
63 *Ibid*., p. 4.
64 *AJHR*, 1871, F-08.
65 *Ibid*.
66 *Ibid*.

67 *AJHR*, 1871, F-08, p. 5.
68 *Ibid.*
69 *Ibid.*
70 *Ibid.*, pp. 6–33.
71 *AJHR*, 1896, G-02, p. 4.
72 The wider case relating to Joshua Jones and the Mokau-Mohakatino No. 1 Block are discussed in: Cathy Marr, *The Alienation of Maori Land in the Rohe Potae (Aotea Block), 1840–1920*, pp. 12–14; Evelyn Stokes, 'Mokau: Maori Cultural and Historical Perspectives', pp. 141–48; and Giselle Byrnes, 'Ngati Tama Ancillary Claims'.
73 DNZB, 'Te Rerenga, Hone Wetere', from the Dictionary of New Zealand Biography *Te Ara – the Encyclopedia of New Zealand*, http://www.TeAra.govt.nz/en/biographies/2t29/te-rerenga-hone-wetere; Marr, p. 13.
74 *AJHR*, 1888, G-04c, p. 4.
75 *Ibid.*, p. 20.
76 *Ibid.*, p. 22.
77 *Ibid.*, p. 2.
78 *AJHR*, 1888, G-04c, p. 4.
79 Mokau-Mohakatino Act 1888.
80 Marr, pp. 13–14.
81 *Huia Tangata Kotahi*, 1 December 1894, p. 4.
82 *AJHR*, 1891, G-01, p. 75.
83 *Ibid.*, p. 76.
84 *Ibid.*
85 *Ibid.*
86 This bill was designed to establish regional Native Land Boards to administer Māori land. It was dropped the following year, but some of its provisions reemerged in the Maori Lands Administration Act 1900. See Donald M. Loveridge, *Maori Land Councils and Land Boards*, pp. 13–17.
87 *AJHR*, 1891, G-01b.
88 *Te Puke ki Hikurangi*, 27 December 1898, p. 2.
89 *AJHR*, 1898, I-03a, pp. 54–55.
90 *Te Puke ki Hikurangi*, 27 December 1898, p. 2.
91 *AJHR*, 1898, I-03a, p. 55.
92 *Te Puke ki Hikurangi*, 27 December 1898, p. 2.
93 *AJHR*, 1898, I-03a, pp. 55–56.
94 *Te Puke ki Hikurangi*, 27 December 1898, p. 3.
95 *AJHR*, 1898, I-03a, p. 56.

Chapter 2. 'I am pierced by war's alarms': Accounts of War

1 *New Zealand Spectator and Cook's Strait Guardian*, 19 August 1848, p. 2. The article identifies her as the sister of 'Etako', most likely Wī Tako Ngātata of Te Āti Awa.
2 Angela Ballara, *Taua: 'Musket Wars', 'Land Wars', or Tikanga? Warfare in Māori Society in the Early Nineteenth Century*, p. 165.
3 'Brief of Evidence of Te Waari Carkeek', (9 June 2003), Waitangi Tribunal Claims 207 & 785. http://www.ngatitoa.iwi.nz/wp-content/uploads/PhotoGallery/2011/10/Te-Waari-Carkeek.pdf
4 'History and Traditions of the Taranaki Coast: Ch. XIII. Te Rau-paraha and his Doings at Kawhia', *Journal of the Polynesian Society*, vol. 18, no. 2, 1909, pp. 52–53. The Māori version of this song was originally published in George Grey's, *Nga Moteatea, me nga Hakirara o nga Maori*, p. 300. A more modern translation and notes can be found in A. T. Ngata and Pei Te Hurinui Jones, *Ngā Mōteatea*, Part III.
5 Patricia Burns, *Te Rauparaha*, pp. 145–47.
6 W. T. L. Travers, *The Stirring Times of Te Rauparaha*, p. 131.
7 'Narrative of the Battle of Omihi, as Related By Ema Turumeke to her Daughter, Mrs. C. J.

Harden, and Translated by the Latter', *Journal of the Polynesian Society*, vol. 3, no. 2, 1894, pp. 107–109.
8   Jenifer Curnow, 'Tohi Te Ururangi', from the Dictionary of New Zealand Biography *Te Ara – the Encyclopedia of New Zealand*, http://www.TeAra.govt.nz/en/biographies/1t102/tohi-te-ururangi; 'Brief of Evidence of Richard Peter Boast', 11 June 2003, Waitangi Tribunal (Wai 207 & 785), http://www.ngatitoa.iwi.nz/wp-content/uploads/PhotoGallery/2011/10/Richard-Boast-Part-3.pdf; Vincent O'Malley and David Armstrong, *The Beating Heart*, p. 14.
9   *Te Manuhiri Tuarangi*, 15 October 1861, pp. 11–12.
10 Edward Shortland, *Traditions and Superstitions of the New Zealanders*, 1854, pp. 178–80.
11 R. Parris to C. W. Richmond, 21 June 1859 in Guy H. Scholefield (ed.), *The Richmond-Atkinson Papers*, vol. 1, p. 472.
12 *Te Karere Maori*, 30 April 1860, pp. 4–5.
13 *Ibid.*, 31 July 1860, p. 50.
14 *Colonist*, 30 April 1861, p. 4.
15 *Te Manuhiri Tuarangi*, 15 May 1861, p. 4. 'Ko au ko Hapurona e korero nei moku mo enei tangata katoa e mau nei nga ingoa ki raro nei, mo nga wahine, mo nga tamariki.' Also *AJHR*, 1861, E-01b, p. 5.
16 John Gorst, *The Maori King*, p. 120.
17 James Belich, *The New Zealand Wars and the Victorian Interpretation of Racial Conflict*, p. 133.
18 *Ibid.*, pp. 133–35.
19 *Daily Southern Cross*, 15 October 1863, p. 3.
20 *AJHR*, 1864, E-02, pp. 96–97.
21 *New Zealand Herald*, 31 May 1865, p. 4.
22 *Daily Southern Cross*, 5 June 1865, p. 4; *New Zealand Herald*, 20 June 1865, p. 5.
23 *Daily Southern Cross*, 20 June 1865, p. 4.
24 *New Zealand Herald*, 20 June 1865, p. 5.
25 *Ibid.*
26 *Daily Southern Cross*, 2 September 1865, p. 5.
27 *New Zealand Herald*, 19 September 1865, p. 4.
28 *Evening Post*, 6 September 1865, p. 2.
29 *Daily Southern Cross*, 26 October 1865, p. 4.
30 An account of this raid is described in Tony Sole, *Ngāti Ruanui*, pp. 283–291. For a breakdown of the government force, see *New Zealand Herald*, 13 August 1866, p. 6.
31 Thomas W. Gudgeon, *Reminiscences of the War in New Zealand*, p. 123.
32 *AJHR*, 1868, A-03, p. 20.
33 *Ibid.*, p. 22.
34 *Ibid.*, pp. 21–22.
35 *Ibid.*, pp. 10–12.
36 *Ibid.*, p. 17.
37 James Belich, *'I Shall Not Die'*, Second Ed., p. n42.
38 James Belich, 'McDonnell, Thomas', from the Dictionary of New Zealand Biography *Te Ara – the Encyclopedia of New Zealand*, http://www.TeAra.govt.nz/en/biographies/1m33/mcdonnell-thomas. Similarly the Ministry for Culture and Heritage's nz.history.net.nz website suggests that, 'His drunken troops behaved appallingly; it seems that a wounded woman was raped several times'. MCH, 'The Year of the Lamb – Tītokowaru's War', Ministry for Culture and Heritage, http://www.nzhistory.net.nz/war/titokowarus-war/year-of-the-lamb
39 *AJHR*, 1868, A-03, pp. 21–22.
40 *Ibid.*, p. ii.
41 *Ibid.*, p. 10.
42 *Ibid.*, p. 5.
43 *Ibid.*, pp. 10, 13, 16, 18.
44 *Ibid.*, p. 10.
45 *Ibid.*, p. 20.
46 *Wanganui Herald*, 27 March 1868, p. 2.
47 *Wellington Independent*, 28 March 1868, p. 6.
48 *AJHR*, 1868, A-03, p. 26.

49 *AJHR*, 1880, G-02, p. 13.
50 Waitangi Tribunal, *The Taranaki Report – Kaupapa Tuatahi*, Wai 143, p. 105; *Deed of Settlement of the Historic Claims of Ngaati Ruanui* (12 May 2001), http://nz01.terabyte.co.nz/ots/DocumentLibrary%5CRuanuiDeed12May2001.pdf
51 *Taranaki Herald*, 22 June 1867, p. 2; 14 September 1867, p. 3.
52 Bettie Howarth, 'Field Day Notes' (18 January 1973) in Brian Herlihy, *The Pakakohi Tribe* (1992), http://repository.digitalnz.org/system/uploads/record/attachment/513/_the_pakakohi_tribe_.pdf
53 See Belich, *'I Shall Not Die'*.
54 Waitangi Tribunal, 'Chapter 4: The Taranaki Wars', *Taranaki Report: Kaupapa Tuatahi*, http://www.justice.govt.nz/tribunals/waitangi-tribunal/Reports/wai0143/chapt04
55 Bill Dacker, 'Truths Far Greater Than Myths', *Otago Daily Times*, 13 August 2012.
56 *Wellington Independent*, 18 August 1862, p. 3; *Daily Southern Cross*, 1 September 1863, p. 3; *Evening Star*, 22 October 1869, p. 2; *Taranaki Herald*, 11 September 1886, p. 2.
57 G. S. Cooper to I. N. Watt, 8 September 1870, CD 1870/3152, ANZW.
58 Pakakohi women to Native Minister, 12 September 1870, CD 1870/3152, ANZW.
59 Pakakohi women to Native Mininster, 30 October 1870, CD1870/3386, ANZW.
60 *AJHR*, 1873, C-04a, pp. 1–2.
61 Also spelled Maraea Morete.
62 Judith Binney, *Stories Without End*, p. 315.
63 Maria Morris, MS2296, ATL.
64 Bronwyn Elsmore, *Mana From Heaven*, p. 170.
65 Morris, MS2296, ATL.
66 Jane Foley to W. F. Gordon, 6 September 1897, W. F. Gordon Collection, Folder 9, CA0001b2/001/0009/0001-0004, Museum of New Zealand Te Papa Tongarewa Archives, Wellington.
67 Alan Ward, *A Show of Justice*, p. 178.
68 Morris, MS2296, ATL.
69 Binney, *Stories Without End*, p. 316; Judith Binney, *Redemption Songs*, pp. 55, 121.
70 See Binney, *Redemption Songs*, pp. 59–60, and fn22, p. 586.
71 *AJHR*, 1868, A-15e, pp. 10–11.
72 *Wellington Independent*, 23 September 1869, p. 3.
73 *AJHR*, 1868, A-15e, pp. 24–25.
74 *Wellington Independent*, 23 September 1869, p. 3.
75 *AJHR*, 1868, A-15, p. 1.
76 *Wellington Independent*, 23 September 1869, p. 3.
77 Belich estimates the whole party at 300 people, of whom up to 200 were men. 'Te Kooti took thirty-two rifles, eight shotguns, and one carbine, with about 100 rounds per gun, from the Chathams.' He acquired another six guns at Whareongaonga, and another ten rifles at Pāparatū. As his campaign progressed, other Māori, with weapons, joined him. Belich, *The New Zealand Wars*, pp. 221–22.
78 *Wellington Independent*, 21 September 1869, p. 3.
79 *Ibid.*, 23 September 1869, p. 3.
80 *Ibid.*, 23 September 1869, p. 3.
81 *Ibid.*, 21 September 1869, p. 3.
82 Belich, *The New Zealand Wars*, pp. 224–45; Binney, *Redemption Songs*, pp. 100–101.
83 Binney, *Redemption Songs*, p. 128.
84 Morris, MS Papers 2296, ATL.
85 Miriama Whakahira, Statement about Renata Hamuhamu, 10 February 1871, AGG-HB1/4 5 75/7, ANZW. Miriama Whakahira, who gave evidence in 1869, may be the same person. See *Wellington Independent*, 23 September 1869, p. 3.
86 Morris, MS Papers 2296, ATL.
87 *Wellington Independent*, 23 September 1869, p. 3.
88 Morris, MS Papers 2296, ATL.
89 *Wellington Independent*, 23 September 1869, p. 3.
90 *Ibid.*

91 *Wellington Independent*, 23 September 1869, p. 3.
92 Morris, MS Papers 2296, ATL.
93 *Wellington Independent*, 23 September 1869, p. 3.
94 *Ibid.*
95 *Ibid.*
96 *Ibid.*
97 Belich, *The New Zealand Wars*, p. 230.
98 Morris, MS Papers 2296, ATL.
99 Belich, *The New Zealand Wars*, pp. 230–31.
100 *Wellington Independent*, 23 September 1869, p. 3.
101 Morris, MS Papers 2296, ATL.
102 *Wellington Independent*, 23 September 1869, p. 3.
103 *Ibid.*
104 Belich, *The New Zealand Wars*, pp. 232–34, 264–67, 275.
105 James Cowan, *The New Zealand Wars*, p. 263.
106 Belich, *The New Zealand Wars*, pp. 228–30.
107 Binney, *Redemption Songs*, pp. 105–24.
108 *Ibid*, pp. 129–30.

Chapter 3. 'I am living here a Stranger on this land': Raupatu and Compensation

1 Waitangi Tribunal, *The Taranaki Report – Kaupapa Tuatahi*, section 1.5, https://forms.justice.govt.nz/search/WT/reports/reportSummary.html?reportId=wt_DOC_68453721
2 Richard Boast, *Native Land Court 1862–1887*, p. 26.
3 *AJHR*, 1928, G-07, p. 15.
4 *Daily Southern Cross*, 10 September 1864, p. 5.
5 *Otago Daily Times*, 18 October 1864, p. 9.
6 Petition of Timata Tetoko claiming a portion of the Township of Ngaruawahia and compensation for its sale by the Government, submitted by John Williamson, and referred to the Government for resolution of the House, 3 December 1864, *AJHR*, 1864, p. ix.
7 *Press* (Christchurch), 12 February 1866, p. 2.
8 *Daily Southern Cross*, 27 February 1867, p. 6.
9 Dean Cowie, *Hawke's Bay*, p. 101.
10 J. A. Mackay, *Historic Poverty Bay and the East Coast, N. I., N. Z.*, p. 309.
11 Boast, *Native Land Court*, pp. 39–42.
12 Boast, *Native Land Court*, pp. 34, 41. For a discussion on the Compensation Court in Waikato, see Vincent O'Malley, *The Great War for New Zealand*, pp. 471–91.
13 John Gorst, *The Maori King*, p. 99.
14 *Daily Southern Cross*, 25 April 1865, p. 5.
15 *New Zealand Herald*, 27 April 1865, p. 5.
16 *Ibid.*, 17 May 1865, p. 5.
17 *Ibid.*, 16 May 1865, p. 6.
18 *Ibid.*, 18 May 1865, p. 5.
19 *Ibid.*, 19 May 1865, p. 5.
20 *Ibid.*, 23 May 1865, p. 6.
21 *Ibid.*, 29 May 1865, p. 5.
22 Boast, *Native Land Court*, p. 30.
23 Waikato Confiscations: Proceedings of the Compensation Court, Box 2, Folder 12: Ngatitipa Claims. Raupatu Document Bank, vol. 104, pp. 39812–4.
24 Boast, *Native Land Court*, p. 33.
25 Ana Paora Te Iwi to Frederick Weld, 21 June 1865, ACFL/8170 1/dx 65/326, ANZA.
26 Ana Paora Te Iwi to Fenton and Mackay, 26 August 1865, ACFL/8170 1/dx 65/326, ANZA.
27 Ana Paora Te Iwi to Frederick Weld, 21 June 1865, ACFL/8170 1/dx 65/326, ANZA.
28 *New Zealand Herald*, 19 May 1865, p. 5.
29 Ana Paora Te Iwi to Fenton and Mackay, 26 August 1865, ACFL/8170 1/dx 65/326, ANZA.

30 Ana Paora Te Iwi to Weld, 21 June 1865, ACFL/8170 1/dx 65/326, ANZA.
31 Opotiki Confiscation, Minutes of Compensation Court: Opotiki sitting 7 March 1867, Raupatu Document Bank, vol. 120, pp. 46195–6.
32 Ibid., p. 46194.
33 Ibid., p. 46159.
34 Ibid., p. 46158.
35 *New Zealand Herald*, 5 July 1867, p. 3.
36 Opotiki Confiscation, Minutes of Compensation Court: Opotiki sitting 7 March 1867, p. 33, Raupatu Document Bank, vol. 120, p. 46086.
37 W. T. Parham, 'Fulloon, James Francis', from the Dictionary of New Zealand Biography *Te Ara – the Encyclopedia of New Zealand*, http://www.TeAra.govt.nz/en/biographies/1f18/fulloon-james-francis
38 *AJHR*, 1866, D-03, p. 75.
39 Judith Binney, '"In-Between Lives": Studies from Within a Colonial Society', in Tony Ballantyne and Brian Moloughney (eds), *Disputed Histories*, pp. 239–42.
40 *Auckland Star*, 29 April 1878, p. 2.
41 Opotiki Confiscations, Proceedings of Compensation Court, Maketu, Raupatu Document Bank, vol. 120, p. 46454.
42 Ibid., p. 46456.
43 Ibid., p. 46457.
44 Ibid., p. 46455.
45 Ibid., pp. 46452–3.
46 *AJHR*, 1892, I-03, p. 15. '… kia tukuna tetahi ora ki aia kia tae ki te £500 mo tona mate i runga i te raupatutanga o nga whenua o tona matua me tona kohurutanga i Whakatane i aia e mahi ana i nga mahi Kawanatanga.'
47 *Bay of Plenty Times*, 24 February 1913, p. 2.
48 Ruta Te Manuahura to Donald McLean, 31 July 1876, Maori Affairs/Series 13/Tapsell Family Claim Waikato/1876–86, Raupatu Document Bank, vol. 73, pp. 28483, 28486.
49 Ruta Te Manuahura to Donald McLean, 22 October 1876, Maori Affairs/Series 13/Tapsell Family Claim Waikato/1876–86, Raupatu Document Bank, vol. 73, pp. 28484, 28487.
50 *Auckland Star*, 28 November 1873, p. 3; 8 June 1876, p. 2.
51 Maori Affairs/Series 13/Tapsell Family Claim Waikato/1876–86, Raupatu Document Bank, vol. 73, p. 28118.
52 *AJHR*, 1882, I-02, pp. 1–2.
53 Ruta Te Manuahura to John Bryce, 4 October 1883, Maori Affairs/Series 13/Tapsell Family Claim Waikato/1876–86, Raupatu Document Bank, vol. 73, p. 28205.
54 Ruta Te Manuahuru to John Ballance, 29 September 1885, Maori Affairs/Series 13/Tapsell Family Claim Waikato/1876–86, Raupatu Document Bank, vol. 73, pp. 28122–3.
55 Ibid., pp. 28118–9.
56 Waitangi Tribunal, *The Taranaki Report,* sections 7.2 and 7.3.
57 *AJHR*, 1872, C-04, pp. 16–17.
58 *Wanganui Herald*, 10 December 1872, p. 2.
59 Taranaki Confiscation, Minutes of Compensation Court: Whanganui sitting 5 March 1881, Raupatu Document Bank, vol. 34, pp. 13155–6.
60 *AJHR*, 1881, G-05, pp. 8–9.
61 Taranaki Confiscation, Minutes of Compensation Court: Whanganui sitting 5 March 1881, Raupatu Document Bank, vol. 34, pp. 13152–4.
62 *AJHR*, 1881, G-05, p. 9.
63 Grey Māori Autograph Series, vol. 2, pp. 89–91, GNZ MA, ACL.
64 *AJHR*, 1880, G-02, p. 24.
65 Ibid., p. 26.
66 Ibid.
67 *Daily Southern Cross*, 1 May 1865, p. 4.
68 Boast, *Native Land Court*, p. 31.
69 *New Zealand Herald*, 2 September 1865, p. 4.
70 Ibid., 11 October 1872, p. 2.

71 *New Zealand Herald*, 19 December 1867, p. 4.
72 Compensation Claim from Hera Pounara, 24 May 1865, ACFL/8170 4/cl 67/861, ANZA.
73 *Daily Southern Cross*, 17 May 1865, p. 5.
74 See *Daily Southern Cross*, 24 July 1863, p. 2.
75 *Daily Southern Cross*, 17 December 1867, p. 4.
76 *Ibid.*, 8 February 1868, p. 3.
77 *New Zealand Herald*, 18 December 1867, p. 4.
78 *Ibid.*, 18 December 1867, p. 4.
79 *Ibid.*, 19 December 1867, p. 4.
80 *Ibid.*, 21 December 1867, p. 4.
81 *Ibid.*, 15 May 1865, p. 5.
82 *Daily Southern Cross*, 29 May 1865, p. 5.
83 *AJHR*, 1878, I-03, p. 25.
84 Waitangi Tribunal, *The Taranaki Report*, section 5.9.
85 Waikato Raupatu Claims Settlement Act 1995, section 5, *New Zealand Legislation*, accessed 7 April 2017, http://www.legislation.govt.nz/act/public/1995/0058/latest/DLM370505.html. Official Translation [section 5] 'E whakaae ana Te Karauna teeraa ko ngaa raupatutanga o ngaa whenua me ngaa rawa i whakamanahia e te Ture Mo Te Whakanoho i Te Hunga Maarie, ara, te Iwi Paakeha 1863, a Te Paaremata o Niu Tireni he mahi tino hee, e peehi kino nei i a Waikato mai raano. E noho pani tonu nei raatou i roto i te rawakoretanga me to hauwareatanga [sic] o ngaa mahi toko i te ora, o ngaa mahi whanaketanga mo ngaa Iwi o Waikato.'

Chapter 4. 'Look at me, I am just a woman speaking': Politics and Mana

1 Te Rangi Hiroa, *The Coming of the Maori*, p. 344.
2 Api Mahuika, 'Leadership: Inherited and Achieved', in M. King (ed.), *Te Ao Hurihuri*, pp. 91–101.
3 The Dictionary of New Zealand Biography is available online through *Te Ara – the Encyclopedia of New Zealand*; Patricia Grimshaw, 'Settler Anxieties, Indigenous Peoples, and Women's Suffrage in the Colonies of Australia, New Zealand and Hawai'i, 1888–1902', pp. 553–72; Charlotte Macdonald, *The Vote, the Pill and the Demon Drink*; Charlotte Macdonald, Merimeri Penfold and Bridget Williams (eds), *The Book of New Zealand Women*; Sandra Coney (ed.), *Standing in the Sunshine*; Tania Rei, *Māori Women and the Vote*; Angela Ballara, 'Wāhine Rangatira: Māori Women of Rank and their Role in the Women's Kotahitanga Movement of the 1890s', pp. 127–139; Miranda Johnson, 'Chiefly Women: Queen Victoria, Meri Mangakahia, and the Māori Parliament', in Maria Nugent and Sarah Carter (eds), *Mistress of Everything*, pp. 228–47; Charlotte Macdonald, 'People of the Land, Voting Citizens in the Nation, Subjects of the Crown: Historical Perspectives on Gender and the Law in Nineteenth-Century New Zealand', pp. 32–59; Barbara Brookes, *A History of New Zealand Women*. Also see Atholl Anderson, Judith Binney and Aroha Harris, *Tangata Whenua*.
4 Rawinia Higgins and John C. Moorfield, 'Marae Practices', in Tania M. Ka'ai, John C. Moorfield, Michael P. J. Reilly and S. Mosely (eds), *Ki Te Whaiao*, pp. 79–80.
5 For example, in 'The Correspondence between the Government and Maori Chiefs', *AJHR*, 1870, A-21, none of the correspondents are women.
6 Kathryn Rountree, 'Re-making the Maori Female Body: Marianne Williams's Mission in the Bay of Islands', p. 52. Also see Angela Middleton, 'Silent Voices, Hidden Lives: Archaeology, Class and Gender in the CMS Missions, Bay of Islands, New Zealand, 1814–1845', p. 4.
7 Although all women, Pākehā and Māori, gained the vote in 1893, women could not stand as representatives until 1919, and the first Māori woman MP, Iriaka Rātana, was not elected until 1949.
8 Angela Ballara, 'Te Paea Tiaho', from the Dictionary of New Zealand Biography *Te Ara – the Encyclopedia of New Zealand*, http://www.TeAra.govt.nz/en/biographies/2t24/te-paea-tiaho
9 *Ibid.*
10 John E. Gorst, *The Maori King*, p. 149.
11 Lachy Paterson, *Colonial Discourses*, pp. 152–53.

12. Te Kuini Topeora to McLean, 21 June 1861, Inward Letters in Maori, McLean Papers, MS-Papers-0032-0685D-10, Object #1032852 (http://mp.natlib.govt.nz/detail/?id=1032852), ATL.
13. Gorst, *The Maori King*, pp. 10, 279–80.
14. Ibid., pp. 313–14.
15. Lachy Paterson, '"A Sparrow Alone Upon the House Top": The *Te Pihoihoi* Press', in Annabel Cooper, Lachy Paterson and Angela Wanhalla (eds), *The Lives of Colonial Objects*, pp. 117–21.
16. *Daily Southern Cross*, 9 February 1863, p. 3.
17. *Hokioi*, 26 April 1863, p. 2.
18. *AJHR*, 1863, E-01, p. 22.
19. Gorst, *The Maori King*, p. 351.
20. Memoranda from James Fulloon, 24 May 1863, MA1 834 1863/144, ANZW.
21. *Daily Southern Cross*, 28 July 1863, p. 3.
22. Ibid., 6 April 1867, p. 5.
23. *New Zealand Herald*, 7 June 1869, p. 3.
24. *Daily Southern Cross*, 28 October 1868, p. 4.
25. Ibid., 22 December 1868, p. 5.
26. *New Zealand Herald*, 24 November 1868, p. 4.
27. Ibid., 10 February 1870, p. 4.
28. Ibid., 11 June 1869, p. 3.
29. *AJHR*, 1870, A-21, p. 26.
30. *Daily Southern Cross*, 12 August 1869, p. 5.
31. Ibid., 18 August 1869, p. 6.
32. Paterson, *Colonial Discourses*, pp. 56–58.
33. James Belich, *'I Shall Not Die'*, Second Ed., p. 12.
34. It is unclear why the Māori forces abandoned fighting when in a relatively strong position. According to the deserter, Kimble Bent, they withdrew their support for Tītokowaru after he was discovered in an adulterous relationship. Ruka Broughton disputes this, and suggests that they were weary of fighting: Ruka Alan Broughton, *Ngaa Mahi Whakaari a Tiitokowaru*, pp. 126–45.
35. She was also known as Takiora Grey (or Gray), Takihora, Ruihi Rihipete Takiora, Bloody Mary, Mrs Blake, Louisa Grey, Lucy D'Alton: Mary Donald, 'Lord, Lucy Takiora', from the Dictionary of New Zealand Biography *Te Ara – the Encyclopedia of New Zealand*, http://www.TeAra.govt.nz/en/biographies/1l9/lord-lucy-takiora
36. Tony Sole, *Ngāti Ruanui*, p. 324.
37. Belich, *'I Shall Not Die'*, p. 66.
38. Sole, *Ngāti Ruanui*, p. 349.
39. Ibid., p. 345.
40. *AJHR*, 1871, F-06b, p. 8.
41. Ibid., p. 6.
42. *AJHR*, 1871, A-01, p. 50.
43. Lucy Grey to Donald McLean (with translation), 26 September 1870, Inward Letters in Maori, McLean Papers, MS-Papers-0032-0694D-12, Object #1032109 (http://mp.natlib.govt.nz/detail/?id=1032109), ATL. The McLean Papers include a number of letters from Takiora, but written in different hands. It is possible that the archived document is a transcription of her original letter. A typewritten translation accompanies the archived document. While much of it is true to the original, the translation provided here is new.
44. *AJHR*, 1871, D-01, p. v.
45. Ibid., F-06b, p. 7.
46. Lucy Grey to Donald McLean, 6 December 1870, Inward Letters in Maori, McLean Papers, MS-Papers-0032-0694G-03, Object #1031544 (http://mp.natlib.govt.nz/detail/?id=1031544), ATL.
47. *AJHR*, 1882, G-05, pp. 16–17; Brian Herlihy, 'The Pakakohi Tribe: Submission to the Waitangi Tribunal' (17 February 1992). http://repository.digitalnz.org/system/uploads/record/attachment/513/_the_pakakohi_tribe_.pdf. The Waitangi Tribunal has determined that Pakakohi are a hapū of the Ngāti Ruanui tribe, although some argue that they are an iwi in their own right. See Office of Treaty Settlements, 'Settlement of Pakakohi and Tangahoe Historical Claims: Presentation to Maori Affairs Committee', http://www.parliament.nz/resource/0000158500.

Notes to pages 168–85

48 Takiora to Donald McLean, 19 July 1872, Inward Letters in Maori, McLean Papers, MS-Papers-0032-0696C-14, Object #1031048 (http://mp.natlib.govt.nz/detail/?id=1031048), ATL.
49 Takiora to Donald McLean, 23 August 1872, Inward Letters in Maori, McLean Papers, MS-Papers-0032-0696D-09, Object #1032404 (http://mp.natlib.govt.nz/detail/?id=1032404), ATL.
50 Lucy Grey to Donald McLean, 12 January 1871, Inward Letters in Maori, McLean Papers, MS-Papers-0032-0695A-08, Object #1031142 (http://mp.natlib.govt.nz/detail/?id=1031142), ATL.
51 *AJHR*, 1871, F-06b, p. 15.
52 Grey to McLean, 12 January 1871.
53 *AJHR*, 1880, G-02, p. 19.
54 Ruihi Rihipete Takiora to Donald McLean (Translation), 19 January 1873, Inward Letters in Maori, McLean Papers, MS-Papers-0032-0697A-07, Object #1030698, (http://mp.natlib.govt.nz/detail/?id=1030698), ATL.
55 *AJHR*, 1879, G-01, p. 26; 1881, H-37, p. 2.
56 *Ibid.*, 1880, G-02, p. 74.
57 *Star*, 23 September 1881, p. 3.
58 *Hawera & Normanby Star*, 31 August 1881, p. 2.
59 *Ibid.*, 13 December 1887, p. 2.
60 Vincent O'Malley, 'Reinventing Tribal Mechanisms of Governance: The Emergence of Maori Runanga and Komiti in New Zealand before 1900', p. 70.
61 *Hawke's Bay Times*, 21 July 1874, p. 295; *Te Wananga*, 31 March 1877, p. 120; *Te Korimako*, 20 November 1886, p. 3; 19 April 1887, p. 4. See also Rei, pp. 14, 25–29. Also see Jane Foley to W. F. Gordon, 10 May 1898, W. F. Gordon Collection, Folder 10, CA000162/001/0010, Museum of New Zealand Te Papa Tongarewa Archives, Wellington. She briefly describes some of her work for the local branch of the WCTU.
62 Ballara, p. 136. See also Rei, pp. 15–24.
63 See Lindsay Cox, *Kotahitanga*.
64 Rei, pp. 26–28.
65 *Paremata Maori o Niu Tireni*, Waipatu, 18 May 1893, pp. 62–63. This is also available at the Electronic Text Centre, http://nzetc.victoria.ac.nz/tm/scholarly/tei-BIM1359Pare-t1-body1-d7-d13.html
66 Ballara, p. 136.
67 *Ibid.*, p. 136, 138.
68 *Ibid.*, p. 129.
69 For example, *Nelson Evening Mail*, 14 January 1895, p. 2.
70 *Huia Tangata Kotahi*, 12 January 1895, p. 1.
71 *Ibid.*, 12 January 1895, p. 1. 'He tokomaha nga mema wahine i tu ake ki te tautoko i te kupu whakakaha mo ratou, i te mahi whakahaere kua timataria ki runga i a ratou i nga wahine . . .'
72 *Ibid.*, 26 January 1895, pp. 2–3.
73 *Ibid.*, 25 August 1894, p. 3.
74 The legislation referred to is the Dog Registration Act 1880 (amended in 1882 and 1890), and the Counties Vehicle Licensing Act 1893.
75 Another example is the Whanganui Native Women's Committee. See *Wanganui Herald*, 28 May 1897, p. 2.
76 *Huia Tangata Kotahi*, 25 August 1894, p. 3.
77 *Te Puke ki Hikurangi*, 21 December 1987, p. 3.
78 *Wanganui Herald*, 27 May 1897, p. 2; 3 June 1897, p. 2.
79 Also known as Niniwa-ki-te-rangi, and Niniwa Heremia.
80 See discussions on the Ngā-waka-a-Kupe Block, Native Land Court Minute Book, Wairarapa, 1892.
81 See *Evening Post*, 20 August 1902, p. 6; *Star*, 19 September 1902, p. 3.
82 *Te Tiupiri*, 23 August 1898, p. 4.
83 See *Auckland Star*, 25 March 1898, p. 2.
84 *Te Tiupiri*, 1 February 1898, p. 8.
85 *Puke ki Hikurangi*, 21 June 1898, p. 1.
86 *Ibid.*, p. 2.
87 *Ibid.*

88 *Te Tiupiri*, 27 April 1899, p. 8.
89 Angela Ballara, 'Niniwa-i-te-rangi', from the Dictionary of New Zealand Biography *Te Ara – the Encyclopedia of New Zealand,* http://www.TeAra.govt.nz/en/biographies/2n15/niniwa-i-te-rangi
90 *Te Tiupiri*, 9 March 1899, p. 14.
91 *Ibid.*, 2 February 1899, p. 13.
92 *Ibid.*, 9 March 1899, p. 14.
93 Kate Riddell, '"Improving" the Maori: Counting the Ideology of Intermarriage', pp. 80, 84, 92, 94.
94 *AJHR*, 1901, H-26b, p. 1. On Māori concerns about inaccurate census counts, and their resistance to the census, see Angela Wanhalla, 'The Politics of "Periodical Counting": Race, Place and Identity in Southern New Zealand' in Penelope Edmonds and Tracey Banivanua Mar (eds), *Making Space*, pp. 198–217.
95 *Press*, 10 March 1891, p. 3.
96 See Brookes, *A History of New Zealand Women*.

Chapter 5. 'I will not desist from writing to you': Māori Women's Petitions

1 Karen O'Brien, 'Boots, Blankets, and Bomb Tests: First Australian Petitioning and Resistance to Colonisation', p. 361.
2 This petition was submitted on 9 August and sponsored by Mr. Graham: Schedule of Petitions presented to the House of Representatives, *AJHR*, 1865, p. ii.
3 Schedule of Petitions presented to the House of Representatives, *AJHR*, 1873, p. xviii. For more on this case see Angela Wanhalla, *Matters of the Heart*, pp. 62–67.
4 Ann Curthoys and Jessie Mitchell, '"Bring this paper to the Good Governor": Aboriginal Petitioning in Britain's Australian Colonies', in Saliha Belmessous (ed.), *Native Claims*, p. 182.
5 Curthoys and Mitchell, p. 183. Also see: O'Brien; Tracey Banivanua Mar, 'Imperial Literacy and Indigenous Rights: Tracing Transoceanic Circuits of a Modern Discourse', pp. 1–28.
6 Megan Harvey, 'Story People: Stó:lō-State Relations and their Indigenous Literacies in British Columbia, 1864–1874', p. 63.
7 Ravi de Costa, 'Identity, Authority, and the Moral Worlds of Indigenous Petitions', p. 674. Also see: Susan Pedersen, 'Samoa on the World Stage: Petitions and Peoples before the Mandates Commission of the League of Nations', pp. 231–61.
8 Gabriela Ramos and Yanna Yannakakis, 'Introduction', in Gabriela Ramos and Yanna Yannakakis (eds), *Indigenous Intellectuals*, p. 4.
9 Māmari Stephens, 'A House With Many Rooms: Rediscovering Māori as a Civic Language in the Wake of the Māori Language Act (1987)', in Rawinia Higgins, Poia Rewi and Vincent Olseen-Reeder (eds), *The Value of the Māori Language*, vol. 2, quote on p. 66 and also drawing on p. 67.
10 Guy Finny, 'New Zealand's Forgotten Appellate Court? The Native Affairs Committee, Petitions and Maori Land: 1871 to 1900', p. 9. Finny's source for this data is the summaries of petitions in the *AJHR*.
11 These numbers are based on the summaries of petitions assessed by the committee listed in the *AJHR*, 1872–1900.
12 Tania Rei, *Māori Women and the Vote*, pp. 12–13.
13 Finny, p. 7.
14 Finny, p. 13.
15 *AJHR*, 1898, I-03, p. 16.
16 The AtoJs Online is hosted by the National Library of New Zealand on its *Papers Past* site: https://paperspast.natlib.govt.nz
17 *AJHR*, 1888, I-03, p. 25.
18 Petition of Maraea Taunakiwehe, 9 June 1888, MA1 843 1892/448, ANZW.
19 Lisa Brooks, *The Common Pot*, p. 224.
20 Yvonne Sutherland, 'Nineteenth-Century Māori letters of Emotion: Orality, Literacy and Context', p. 68.

21 These acts of interpretation are explored in the Hawaiian context by Noenoe K. Silva, 'Nā Hulu Kupana: To Honor Our Intellectual Ancestors', p. 49.
22 Petition of Ripeka Turipona, 10 October 1884, J1 618 1899/613, ANZW.
23 Jane Caplan, 'Illegibility: Reading and Insecurity in History, Law and Government', p. 112.
24 T. W. Lewis, memo to Native Minister, 19 October 1884, J1/618 1899/613, ANZW.
25 *Thames Star*, 2 October 1905, p. 2.
26 Steven Oliver, 'Te Kiri Karamu, Heni', from the Dictionary of New Zealand Biography *Te Ara – the Encyclopedia of New Zealand*, http://www.TeAra.govt.nz/en/biographies/1t43/te-kiri-karamu-heni
27 Maraea Taunakiwehe to Native Minister, 11 March 1892, MA1 843 1892/448, ANZW.
28 Native Land Court Amendment Act 1889.
29 Martyn Lyons, 'Writing Upwards: How the Weak Wrote to the Powerful', p. 7.
30 Bradford Haami, 'Tā Te Ao Māori: Writing the Māori Word' in Danny Keenan (ed.), *Huia Histories of Māori*, p. 177.
31 Ramos and Yannakakis (p. 7) discuss the ways colonialism and the structures that underpinned it lessened the authority of some groups and individuals, while simultaeously raising the status of others.
32 *AJHR*, 1888, G-01, pp. 2–3.
33 Finny, p. 13.
34 For instance, *AJHR*, 1884, I-02, p. 24.
35 Pipi Koruarua to H. K. Taiaroa, 16 January 1893, MA1 908 1906/1412, ANZW.
36 McKay to Hazelden, 8 February 1893, MA1 908 1906/1412, ANZW.
37 Petition of Pipi Koruarua and Rora Tawha, 8 August 1894, MA1 908 1906/1412, ANZW.
38 Rora Tawha and Pipi Koruarua to the Native Minister, 16 October 1897, MA1 908 1906/1412, ANZW.
39 J. E. March to Sidney Weetman, Commissioner of Crown Lands, Christchurch, 14 December 1897, MA1 908 1906/1412, ANZW.
40 Memo to the Under-Secretary of the Justice Department, 5 November 1897, MA1 908 1906/1412, ANZW.
41 Miriama Huriwai Kaipara to Native Minister, 30 July 1891, J1 508 1893/1499, ANZW.
42 Jessica Horton, 'Rewriting Political History: Letters from Aboriginal People in Victoria, 1886–1919', p. 161.
43 Horton, pp. 168, 170.
44 O'Brien, p. 369.
45 *AJHR*, 1879, I-04, p. 27.
46 Ibid., p. 9.
47 Ibid., pp. 4–5.
48 *Bay of Plenty Times*, 10 January 1917, p. 2. See Wanhalla, *Matters of the Heart*, pp. 89–90.
49 *AJHR*, 1879, I-04, p. 1.
50 Ibid., 1890, I-03, p. 7.
51 Declaration of Elizabeth Fulloon, 27 September 1865 in MA1 1029 1910/4655, ANZW.
52 Petition of Emily Buckworth, 15 August 1891, MA1 1029 1910/4655, ANZW.
53 Native Affairs Committee Report on Petition No. 611, MA1 1029 1910/4655, ANZW.
54 Petition of Emily Buckworth, 23 August 1892, MA1 1029 1910/4655, ANZW.
55 Buckworth to Cadman, 3 November 1892, MA1 1029 1910/4655, ANZW.
56 Letter, Oliver M. Creagh (typed copy) to Cadman, 4 March 1893; Telegram (typed copy) Cadman to Creagh, 4 March 1893, MA1 1029 1910/4655, ANZW.
57 This information was revealed in a letter from C. J. A. Haselden, Under-Secretary of Justice, to Buckworth, 20 March 1893, MA1 1029 1910/4655, ANZW.
58 Buckworth to Premier, 4 October 1895, MA1 1029 1910/4655, ANZW.
59 Haselden to Buckworth, 3 January 1896, MA1 1029 1910/4655, ANZW.
60 Mrs E. M. Buckworth to Fisher, 7 February 1911. She was offered £200 as final settlement.
61 See Sophia's Story, MS-Papers-1208, ATL.
62 J. Waldegrave to Jane Phillips, 21 September [?]9, Petition No. 139/98, MA1 1535 1930/380, ANZW. Also R. J. Seddon, Native Minister, to R. M. Houston, 9 September 1899, stating the claim was disallowed by Fox and he cannot reopen 'questions that the Commission was set up to settle'.

63 Petition No. 425, submitted by Mr McGuire, MA1 1535 1930/380, ANZW.
64 *AJHR*, 1895, I-03, p. 12.
65 John G. Phillips to the Premier, 12 April 1896. George Phillips also wrote to the Premier on the same matter, 23 April 1896, MA1 1535 1930/380, ANZW.
66 Petition No. 139/98, MA1 1535 1930/380, ANZW.
67 *AJHR*, 1882, I-02, p. 11.
68 George W. Phillips to William Fox, Commissioner, 22 April 1882, MA1 1535 1930/380, ANZW.
69 Fox's note on the bottom of Phillips letter, dated 22 April 1882, MA1 1535 1930/380, ANZW.
70 *AJHR*, 1871, p. xxiv.
71 *Ibid.*, 1872, H-11, p. 4.
72 *Ibid.*, 1873, p. xv.
73 *Ibid.*, 1876, I-04, p. 10.
74 Petition No. 334, IA1 461 [36] 1881/3845, ANZW.
75 *AJHR*, 1876, I-04, p. 26.
76 *Ibid.*, 1877, I-03, p. 19.
77 Native Affairs Committee Report on Petition No. 334, 5 September 1881, IA1 461 [36] 1881/3845, ANZW.
78 *AJHR*, 1883, I-02, p. 30.
79 *Ibid.*, 1878, I-03, p. 10.
80 *Ibid.*, 1881, I-02, p. 21.
81 *Ibid.*, 1884, I-02, p. 17.
82 *Ibid.*, 1887, I-03, p. 10.
83 *Ibid.*, 1888, I-03, p. 5.
84 *Ibid.*, 1890, I-03, p. 6.
85 H. R. Richmond to Native Minister, 1 April 1886, MA1/845 1892/708, ANZW.
86 *Ibid.*
87 Frederick Rolfe to G. A. Marchant, MHR, 1 November 1887, MA1/845 1892/708, ANZW.
88 Native Affairs Committee Report on the Petition of Emma Rolfe, 8 December 1887, MA1/845 1892/708, ANZW.
89 Note to Premier, 20 January 1888, MA1/845 1892/708, ANZW.
90 Petition of Huingapaura Rangihatau, J1/541 1895/968, ANZW.
91 Paisley and Reid, 'Introduction', p. 10.
92 O'Brien, p. 363.

Chapter 6. 'I am the prosecutrix in this case': Legal Encounters and Testamentary Acts

1 Richard Boast, 'Bringing the New Philology to Pacific Legal History', p. 257.
2 He Pātaka Kupu Ture/The Legal Māori Archive: http://nzetc.victoria.ac.nz/tm/scholarly/tei-corpus-legalMaori.html; Lost Cases Database: http://www.victoria.ac.nz/law/nzlostcases/
3 Anna Johnston, *The Paper War*, p. 181.
4 Charlotte Macdonald, 'Land, Death and Dower in the Settler Empire: The Lost Cause of "The Widow's Third" in Nineteenth-Century New Zealand', p. 494.
5 Shaunnagh Dorsett, '"Destitute of the knowledge of God": Māori Testimony Before the New Zealand Courts in the Early Crown Period', in Diane Kirkby (ed.), *Past Law, Present Histories*, p. 48.
6 Dorsett, p. 39.
7 Unsworn Testimony Ordinance 1844.
8 See Dorsett.
9 Damen Ward, 'Imperial Policy, Colonial Government, and Indigenous Testimony in South Australia and New Zealand in the 1840s', in Shaunnagh Dorsett and Ian Hunter (eds), *Law and Politics in British Colonial Thought*, p. 229.
10 See Karen Dubinsky, *Improper Advances*.
11 *Wellington Independent*, 6 March 1866, p. 5.
12 Angela Wanhalla, 'Interracial Sexual Violence in 1860s New Zealand', p. 72.

13 *Wellington Independent*, 6 June 1862, p. 3.
14 See Wanhalla for further discussion.
15 *Hawke's Bay Herald*, 4 February 1865, p. 1.
16 *Evening Post*, 8 December 1876, p. 2.
17 *Te Waka Maori o Niu Tirani*, 11 July 1876, pp. 167–70; 8 August 1876, pp. 192–93. For a detailed analysis of the libel case see: Lachy Paterson, 'The *Te Waka Maori* Libel Case: A Discussion', pp. 88–112.
18 *AJHR*, 1873, G-07, pp. 18–19.
19 *Ibid.*, p. 26.
20 *Ibid.*, p. 28.
21 *Ibid.*, p. 64.
22 *Ibid.*, p. 26.
23 Miria Simpson, *Ngā Taumata*, p. 56.
24 Alan Ward, *A Show of Justice*, pp. 272–73.
25 Lyn Waymouth, 'Parliamentary Representation for Maori: Debate and Ideology in *Te Wananga* and *Te Waka Maori o Niu Tireni*, 1874–8', in Jenifer Curnow, Ngapare Hopa and Jane McRae (eds), *Rere Atu Taku Manu!*, pp. 153–73.
26 Ward, *Show of Justice*, p. 277; Mary Boyd, 'Russell, Henry Robert', from the Dictionary of New Zealand Biography *Te Ara – the Encyclopedia of New Zealand*, http://www.TeAra.govt.nz/en/biographies/2r32/russell-henry-robert
27 *Te Waka Maori o Niu Tirani*, 8 August 1876, pp. 192–94.
28 *Te Wananga*, 26 August 1876, pp. 314–15. 'He kore pea ki ano te Etita o TE "WAKA MAORI," i rongo noa, ka whakawakia aia mo tana taanga i te reta a Mangai Uhuuhu ma, i taia ai ano eia tetahi reta ano a Arihi Te Nahu ma. E kiia ana e te rongo korero, kua mea atu ano a Henare Rata ki ana Roia, kia whakawakia ano te ETITA o TE WAKA MAORI mo tenei reta ano, ka rua ai whakawa mo te Etita o TE WAKA MAORI.'
29 *Te Wananga*, 26 August 1876, pp. 319–20. 'Na, e hoa ma, me mutu ta koutou mahi i te ingoa o Henare Rata raua ko Henare Matua, no raua hoki taua ingoa kino, e ai ta koutou panui. Na, mehemea ka haere atu a Henare Rata ki to ratou taha Pakeha, ka pehea tatou, ina hoki, kua kinongia e koutou, e hara ianei i a Henare tatou i puta ai i enei ra . . .'
30 *Te Wananga*, 21 October 1876, pp. 387–88.
31 Arihi Te Nahu to Editor, *Te Wananga*, MA 24 1/3, ANZW.
32 *Evening Post*, 27 August 1877, p. 2.
33 We are indebted to Paerau Warbrick for assisting with his knowledge of nineteenth-century defamation law.
34 Jenifer Curnow, 'A Brief History of Maori-Language Newspapers', in Jenifer Curnow, Ngapare Hopa and Jane McRae (eds), *Rere Atu Taku Manu!*, p. 23.
35 In August 1877, William Rees raised the issue of whether the government was still supporting *Te Waka Māori*. See *New Zealand Herald*, 1 August 1877, p. 2. The paper continued to sport the official coat of arms, and to state that it was 'Printed under the authority of the New Zealand Government by GEORGE DIDSBURY, Government Printer, Wellington'.
36 *Evening Post*, 1 August 1877, p. 2; 3 August 1877, p. 2; 7 September 1877, p. 2.
37 *Ibid.*, 25 July 1877, p. 2.
38 Evidence Taken at Napier Before George Edward Sainsbury, Commissioner Appointed by the Supreme Court for the Purpose, p. 5, MA24 1/3, ANZW.
39 Evidence Taken at Napier, p. 1, MA24 1/3, ANZW.
40 Evidence Taken at Napier, p. 5, MA24 1/3, ANZW.
41 Evidence Taken at Napier, pp. 6–7, MA24 1/3, ANZW.
42 Evidence Taken at Napier, pp. 1–2, MA24 1/3, ANZW.
43 Evidence Taken at Napier, p. 9, MA24 1/3, ANZW.
44 *Auckland Star*, 24 July 1877, p. 3.
45 Evidence Taken at Napier, p. 25, MA24 1/3, ANZW.
46 *Evening Post*, 7 September 1877, p. 2.
47 *AJHR*, 1880, H-12; 1895, H-35, p. 1.
48 *Evening Post*, 27 July 1877, p. 2.
49 *Ibid.*, 18 September 1877, p. 2. Boyd, 'Russell, Henry Robert'.

50 *Hawke's Bay Herald*, 17 June 1881, p. 3.
51 Vincent O'Malley, *Agents of Autonomy*, pp. 69–74.
52 Richard Boast, *Buying the Land, Selling the Land*, pp. 384–86; Joseph Anaru Te Kani Pere, *Wiremu Pere*, pp. 399–400; Tom Brooking, 'Rees, William Lee', from the Dictionary of New Zealand Biography *Te Ara – the Encyclopedia of New Zealand*, http://www.TeAra.govt.nz/en/biographies/2r9/rees-william-lee; Alan Ward, 'Pere, Wiremu', from the Dictionary of New Zealand Biography *Te Ara – the Encyclopedia of New Zealand*, http://www.TeAra.govt.nz/en/biographies/2p11/pere-wiremu
53 *Poverty Bay Herald*, 20 August 1880, p. 2.
54 A year later, in 1881, Gannon married Keita Wylie, Wī Pere's sister: Steven Oliver, 'Wyllie, Kate', from the Dictionary of New Zealand Biography *Te Ara – the Encyclopedia of New Zealand*, http://www.TeAra.govt.nz/en/biographies/2w36/wyllie-kate
55 George T. Wilkinson Papers, Folder 1, MS 613, AWM.
56 Tai Ahu, 'Te Reo Māori as a Language of New Zealand Law: The Attainment of Civic Status', p. 57.
57 Barbara Brookes, *A History of New Zealand Women*, p. 57.
58 *Ibid.*, p. 78.
59 *Ibid.*
60 Nicola Peart, 'Where There is a Will, There is a Way – A New Will Act for New Zealand', p. 28, note 19.
61 Alex Frame and Paul Meredith, 'Performance and Māori Customary Legal Process', p. 142.
62 Tom Bennion and Judi Boyd, *Succession to Maori Land, 1900–52*, p. 11.
63 Peart, pp. 30–31.
64 Bennion and Boyd, p. 7.
65 South Island Minute Book 5, 28 February 1887, p. 124.
66 Victoria R. Bricker, 'Where There's a Will, There's a Way: The Significance of Scribal Variation in Colonial Maya Testaments', p. 421.
67 Last Will and Testament of Robert Jillett, AAOM/6029 4/133, ANZW.
68 Last Will and Testament of Etara Jillett (1863), AAOM/6029 5/177, ANZW.
69 Native Succession Act 1881, section 3.
70 Brookes, p. 106.
71 Married Women's Property Act 1884, section 3(1).
72 Last Will and Testament of Rai Watt (1885), DAAC/D239/9073/56/1238, ANZD.
73 Last Will and Testament of Ria Tutereiao (1886), AAOM/6029 51, ANZW. Last Will and Testament of Mere Pawa (1892), AAOM/6029 72/3917, ANZW.
74 Last Will and Testament of Maata Kuiatu (1876), AAOW/22760 736/142, ANZA.
75 Order for the Protection of a Married Woman's Property, 21 August 1873, in Probate File of Ani Parata (1875) AAOM/6029 19/840, ANZW.
76 Last Will and Testament of Ani Parata, 20 July 1875, AAOM/6029 19/840, ANZW.
77 Last Will and Testament of Mary Toro, 27 March 1875, Jean Gadd Papers, MS-Papers-4899, ATL.
78 Last Will and Testament of Matire Piripi (1875), AAOM/6029 21/977, ANZW.
79 Her will was in English and Māori, Will of Hana Te Kaewa (1880), DAAC/D239 9073, Box 37, 806, ANZD.
80 Last Will and Testament of Ria Moheko (1889), CAHX CH171 CH1755/1889, ANZC.
81 Richard P. Boast, 'The Omahu Affair, the Law of Succession and the Native Land Court', pp. 841–74; Bettina Bradbury, 'Troubling Inheritances: An Illegitimate, Māori Daughter Contests her Father's Will in the New Zealand Courts and the Judicial Review Committee of the Privy Council', pp. 126–64.
82 Declaration of Ebenezer Baker, 2 March 1886, AAOM/6029 51, ANZW.
83 Jane Caplan, 'Illegibility: Reading and Insecurity in History, Law and Government', p. 110.
84 Bayly cited by Caplan, p. 111.
85 Hilary E. Wyss, 'Native Women Writing: Reading Between the Lines', p. 122.
86 Bradford Haami, 'Tā Te Ao Māori: Writing the Māori Word', in Danny Keenan (ed.), *Huia Histories of Māori*, p. 176.
87 Ahu, p. 10.

88 Ibid.
89 Māmari Stephens, 'A House With Many Rooms: Rediscovering Māori as a Civic Language in the Wake of the Māori Language Act (1987)', in Rawinia Higgins, Poia Rewi and Vincent Olseen-Reeder (eds), *The Value of the Māori Language*, vol. 2, pp. 56–57. (Quote from p. 57.)

Chapter 7. 'If I die, I am dying for the Lord': Religion

1 J. M. R. Owens, 'Christianity and the Maoris to 1840', p. 18; R. Davis, *A Memoir of the Rev. Richard Davis*, pp. 69–71.
2 Judith Binney, 'Whatever Happened to Poor Mr Yate? An Exercise in Voyeurism', pp. 154–68. For an alternative interpretation of Yate see: Tony Ballantyne, *Entanglements of Empire*.
3 William Yate, *An Account of New Zealand, and of the Formation and Progress of the Church Missionary's Mission in the Northern Island*, pp. 249–50.
4 Judith Binney, 'Yate, William', from the Dictionary of New Zealand Biography *Te Ara – the Encyclopedia of New Zealand*, http://www.TeAra.govt.nz/en/biographies/1y1/yate-william
5 Binney, 'Whatever Happened', p. 162.
6 *Ibid.*, p. 156.
7 Yate, *An Account*, p. 251.
8 Owens, p. 23; Peter Lineham and Allan Davidson, 'Chapter One: The Age of Missions 1814–1850', in *Transplanted Christianity*, Second Ed.
9 Yate, *An Account*, p. 256.
10 *Ibid.*, pp. 273–75.
11 H. W. Williams, *Dictionary of the Maori Language*, Seventh Ed., s.v. "Māori".
12 Lachy Paterson, 'Kiri Mā, Kiri Mangu: The Terminology of Race and Civilisation in the Mid-Nineteenth-Century Māori-language Newspapers', in Jenifer Curnow, Ngapare Hopa and Jane McRae (eds), *Rere Atu, Taku Manu!*, pp. 81–82.
13 Geoffrey Gorer, 'The Pornography of Death', p. 50.
14 Margarete Holubetz, 'Death-bed Scenes in Victorian Fiction', *English Studies*, p. 14; Davis W. Clark, *Death-Bed Scenes, or Dying With and Without Religion*.
15 Clark, *Death-Bed Scenes*, pp. 20, 22.
16 Te Rangi Hīroa, *The Coming of the Maori*, p. 415; Rawinia Higgins and John C. Moorfield, 'Tangihanga: Death Customs', in Tania M. Ka'ai, John C. Moorfield, Michael J. P. Reilly and S. Mosely (eds), *Ki Te Whaiao*, p. 86.
17 Yate Correspondence, fMS-264, ATL.
18 Yate, *An Account*, p. 297.
19 *Ibid.*, p. 298.
20 *Ibid.*, p. 299.
21 *Ibid.*
22 *Missionary Register* (1832), p. 468.
23 Yate, *An Account*, p. 300.
24 *Ibid.*, p. 301.
25 *Ibid.*, pp. 301–2.
26 *Ibid.*, p. 303.
27 *New Zealander*, 27 September 1845, p. 2.
28 Gary Scott, 'Te Awa-i-taia, Wiremu Nera', from the Dictionary of New Zealand Biography *Te Ara – the Encyclopedia of New Zealand*, http://www.TeAra.govt.nz/en/biographies/1t26/te-awa-i-taia-wiremu-nera
29 *New Zealander*, 27 September 1845, p. 2.
30 *Press*, 12 June 1865, p. 3. She is also listed in the Ngāi Tahu 'Blue Book' as Pirihira Panepane, residing in Canterbury. See 'Ngaitahu Kaumatua Alive in the [sic] 1848 As Established by the Maori Land Court in 1925 and the Ngaitahu Census Committee in 1929', Ngai Tahu Maori Trust Board, (1 January 1967, reprinted 1 January 2002), http://ngaitahu.iwi.nz/wp-content/uploads/2013/06/Ngai-Tahu-1848-Census.pdf.
31 *Press*, 12 June 1865, p. 3.
32 For example, *Te Karere Maori*, 1 December 1855, pp. 11–14; *Ko Aotearoa*, 1861, p. 17; *Te Manuhiri*

Tuarangi, 1 August 1861, pp. 13–14; 1 October 1861, p. 12; *Te Karere Maori*, 1 July 1862, p. 14; 20 July 1862, pp. 4–5; 16 December 1862, pp. 6–7; 16 December 1862, pp. 9–11.

33 *Te Haeata*, 1 July 1860, p. 2; *Te Karere Maori*, 31 July 1860, pp. 2–3; *Te Manuhiri Tuarangi*, 1 March 1861, pp. 7–8; 15 March 1861, pp. 2–12.
34 *Wellington Independent*, 20 June 1865, p. 3; *Daily Southern Cross*, 26 June 1865, p. 5; 30 June 1865, p. 7; *Colonist*, 27 June 1865, p. 3; 11 July 1865, p. 6.
35 Hākopa Te Pātūtū is likely to have been a member of one of the Taranaki tribes living in the Wellington area. In 1863 he is recorded as having been wounded while fighting in a skirmish against government forces. *Taranaki Herald*, 26 September 1863, p. 2.
36 *Te Karere o Poneke*, 1 November 1858, p. 3.
37 Philip Andrews, 'Chapman, Anne Maria and Chapman, Thomas', from the Dictionary of New Zealand Biography *Te Ara – the Encyclopedia of New Zealand*, http://www.TeAra.govt.nz/en/biographies/1c13/chapman-anne-maria
38 *Te Korimako*, 22 February 1877, p. 4.
39 Ibid.
40 Ibid., p. 5.
41 Jessie Munro, *Letters on the Go*, pp. 24–25.
42 Jessie Munro, *The Story of Suzanne Aubert*, pp. 85–86.
43 *New Zealand Herald*, 6 July 1867, p. 5.
44 Munro, *Letters*, pp. 27–28.
45 Munro, *Story of Suzanne Aubert*, pp. 90–91; Judith Simon and Linda Tuhiwai Smith, *A Civilising Mission?*, p. 8.
46 *New Zealand Herald*, 1 January 1869, p. 4.
47 Ibid.
48 *Daily Southern Cross*, 7 May 1868, p. 4.
49 Munro, *Story of Suzanne Aubert*, p. 95.
50 Ibid., pp. 110–11.
51 Robert L. Simpson, 'The Church in New Zealand', in Daniel H. Ludlow (ed.), *The Encyclopedia of Mormonism*, p. 1015.
52 Simpson, p. 1016; Robert Joseph, 'Intercultural Exchange: Matakite Māori and the Mormon Church', in Hugh Morrison, Lachy Paterson, Brett Knowles and Murray Rae (eds), *Mana Māori and Christianity*, pp. 50–51.
53 Joseph, pp. 46, 52.
54 *Deseret News*, 19 March 1884, p. 6.
55 Peter Lineham, 'The Mormon Message in Maori Culture', p. 73.
56 Papers of Ira N. Hinckley, (bulk 1882–1884), mssHM 56927–57020, Huntington Library, San Marino, California, United States.
57 Cyril Bradwell and Harold Hill, 'New Zealand History and Salvation Army History: How Do They Interact?' in Harold Hill (ed.), *Te Ope Whakaora*, pp. 27–28.
58 *War Cry*, 1 October 1887, p. 1.
59 Ibid., pp. 1, 3.
60 Judith Binney, 'Te Kooti Arikirangi Te Turuki', from the Dictionary of New Zealand Biography *Te Ara – the Encyclopedia of New Zealand*, http://www.TeAra.govt.nz/en/biographies/1t45/te-kooti-arikirangi-te-turuki
61 *War Cry*, 1 October 1887, p. 3.
62 Hill, *Te Ope Whakaora*, pp. 19–20.
63 *War Cry*, 20 October 1894, p. 2.
64 Ibid., 19 January 1895, p. 5.
65 Hill, *Te Ope Whakaora*, pp. 408–9.
66 For example, Bronwyn Elsmore, *Mana From Heaven*, pp. 268–85; *Te Wananga*, 29 June 1878, p. 329; *Press*, 26 March 1885, p. 2; *Auckland Star*, 14 January 1893, p. 5; *Huia Tangata Kotahi*, 3 March 1894, p. 3.

Chapter 8. 'I am burning like fire': Private Matters

1. Coroner's Inquest File, J1/353 1884/741, ANZW.
2. Ray Waru, *Secrets and Treasures*, p. 234.
3. The phrase 'formalised dialogue' is borrowed from Penny van Toorn; she uses it to describe the formal and structured narratives missionaries, ethnographers and commissions of enquiry require of Aboriginal people: Penny van Toorn, 'Indigenous Life Writing: Tactics and Transformations', in Bain Attwood and Fiona Magowan (eds), *Telling Stories*, p. 2.
4. On state archives and private records see: Christopher J. Lee, 'Gender Without Groups: Confession, Resistance and Selfhood in the Colonial Archive', pp. 701–17; Margaret Critchlow Rodman, 'The Heart in the Archives: Colonial Contestation of Desire and Fear in the New Hebrides, 1933', pp. 291–312.
5. *Star*, 7 April 1884, p. 2.
6. Translations appeared in: the *Taranaki Herald*, 12 April 1884; *Hawera and Normanby Star*, 16 April 1884; *Evening Post*, 23 April 1884; *Hawke's Bay Herald*, 29 April 1884. One letter was reproduced in the *Wairarapa Daily Times*, 29 April 1884, and in the *Manawatu Standard*, 18 July 1884.
7. Waru, *Secrets and Treasures*, p. 234.
8. *Hawera and Normanby Star*, 9 April 1884, p. 2.
9. *Hawke's Bay Herald*, 29 April 1884, p. 4.
10. Margaret Orbell, *Waiata*, Second Ed., p. 2.
11. Margaret Orbell, 'Tikawe's Last Song', p. 23.
12. See Makereti, *The Old-Time Maori*, collected and edited by T. K. Penniman.
13. Meri Te Waiheke to Piripi Terangiatahua, Tamihana and Kutia, 27 July 1859, Letters in Maori, McLean Papers, MS-Papers-0032-0683B-09, Object #1032112 (http://mp.natlib.govt.nz/detail/?id=1032112), ATL.
14. 25 February 1828, in Carolyn Fitzgerald, *Te Wiremu – Henry Williams*, p. 97.
15. Marriage banns between Phillip Tapsell and Maria Dinga, 7 June 1823, Thomas Kendall, letters &c. 1816–1827, MS-0071/055, HC.
16. Marriage certificate of Phillip Tapsell and Maria Dinga, 23 June 1823, MS-0071/058, HC.
17. Marriage banns MS-0071/055, HC.
18. See Angela Wanhalla, *Matters of the Heart*, pp. 25–26.
19. See Yvonne Sutherland, 'Nineteenth-Century Māori Letters of Emotion: Orality, Literacy and Context'; Orbell, *Waiata*, p. 2.
20. Sutherland, p. 84.
21. Angela Wanhalla, 'William Speer's Album: A Scrapbook of Colonial Travel' in Annabel Cooper, Lachy Paterson and Angela Wanhalla (eds), *The Lives of Colonial Objects*, pp. 104–9.
22. 'Maori love message', Speer Album, E-395, ATL.
23. Barnicoat cited in Michael Stevens, 'Kāi Tahu Writing and Cross-cultural Communication', p. 134.
24. Penelope Goode, 'The Kaingarara Letters: The Correspondence of Tamati Te Ito Ngamoke in the A. S. Atkinson Papers, 1857–1863'.
25. Letter to Hairuha and Rawinia from Mere Paea Kokiri, 19 April 1860, Maori Letters from Taranaki, A. S. Atkinson Papers, MSI-Papers-2327-07-11, ATL.
26. Lisa Brooks, *The Common Pot*, p. 226.
27. Alison Jones and Kuni Jenkins, *He Kōrero*, p. 140.
28. Penny van Toorn, *Writing Never Arrives Naked*, p. 198.
29. Sutherland, p. 104.
30. *Ibid.*, p. 2.
31. *Ibid.*, Appendix: Letter 4, unpaginated. The translation is Sutherland's.
32. *Ibid.*, p. 112.
33. Jenny Lee, 'Nga Mahi a Ringa', p. 24.
34. Jane Wordsworth, *Women of the North*, p. 183.
35. *AJHR*, 1880, G-02, p. 27.
36. Joseph Matthews to Christopher C. Fenn, 12 July 1876, Joseph Matthews Letters, MS-Papers-4085, ATL.

37 Morgan's Journal, 23 February 1849 in Jan Pilditch (ed.), *The Letters and Journals of Reverend John Morgan*, vol. 1, p. 309. A view he repeated in a letter to mission authorities, 5 July 1849: Pilditch, *The Letters*, vol. 1, p. 315.
38 Annual Report for 1850, Pilditch (ed.), *The Letters*, vol. 2, p. 440.
39 Morgan to Sinclair and Ligar, Government Inspectors of Schools, 20 October 1852 in Pilditch, *The Letters*, vol. 2, p. 497.
40 Matilda Morgan to McLean, Inward Letters, McLean Papers, MS-Papers-0032-0460, Object #1004782 (http://mp.natlib.govt.nz/detail/?id=1004782), ATL.
41 Matire Te Rarangi to McLean, Inward Letters in Maori, McLean Papers, MS-Papers-0032-0697B-11, Object #1031827 (http://mp.natlib.govt.nz/detail/?id=1031827), ATL.
42 Samuel Morgan to McLean, 28 July 1871, Inward Letters, McLean Papers, MS-Papers-0032-0460, Object #1005447 (http://mp.natlib.govt.nz/detail/?id=1005447), ATL.
43 Samuel Morgan to McLean, 2 September 1871, Inward Letters, McLean Papers, MS-Papers-0032-0460, Object #1013034 (http://mp.natlib.govt.nz/detail/?id=1013034), ATL.
44 Samuel Morgan to McLean, 14 April 1873, Inward Telegrams, McLean Papers, MS-Papers-0032-0086, Object #1009968 (http://mp.natlib.govt.nz/detail/?id=1009968), ATL.
45 Details from: *New Zealand Herald*, 12 March 1877, p. 3; *Thames Advertiser*, 22 February 1877, p. 3. The case was also reported in the Māori-language newspaper *Te Wananga*, 28 April 1877, pp. 162–63 [Māori version], pp. 164–65 [English version].
46 *New Zealand Herald*, 12 March 1877, p. 3.
47 Jemima Shera to McLean, 18 October [1876], Inward Letters, McLean Papers, MS-Papers-0032-0571, Object #1010015 (http://mp.natlib.govt.nz/detail/?id=1010015), ATL.
48 M. A. Maning to McLean, 20 June 1870, Inward Letters, McLean Papers, MS-Papers-0032-0446, Object #1016210 (http://mp.natlib.govt.nz/detail/?id=1016210), ATL.
49 Maria A. Maning to McLean, 6 March [?], Inward Letters, McLean Papers, MS-Papers-0032-0446, Object #1024488 (http://mp.natlib.govt.nz/detail/?id=1024488), ATL.
50 Rihi Huanga to George Wilkinson, 9 October 1898, J1/605 1898/1284, ANZW.
51 George T. Wilkinson to Under Secretary, Justice, 19 October 1898, J1/605 1898/1284, ANZW.
52 See Kuni Jenkins and Kay Morris Matthews, 'Mana Wahine: Māori Women and Leadership of Māori Schools in Aotearoa/New Zealand', pp. 45–59.
53 Steven Oliver, 'Tautari, Hemi and Tautari, Mary', from the Dictionary of New Zealand Biography *Te Ara – the Encyclopedia of New Zealand*, http://www.TeAra.govt.nz/en/biographies/2t12/tautari-hemi
54 Jenkins and Matthews, p. 48.
55 Mary Tautari to Douglas McLean, 29 March 1877, McLean Family: Papers, MS-Papers-0032-0870, ATL.
56 Mary Tautari to Douglas McLean, 20 April 1877, McLean Family: Papers, MS-Papers-0032-0870, ATL.
57 *Auckland Star*, 28 December 1888, p. 3. According to *Waka Maori*, Mary Tautari was appointed an interpreter by the Governor under the Native Lands Act in 1877: 8 May 1877, p. 126. Morgan died in 1895: *New Zealand Herald*, 17 May 1895, p. 4.
58 Meri Matimati to McLean, Inward Letters in Maori, McLean Papers, MS-Papers-0032-0702P-10, Object #1030799 (http://mp.natlib.govt.nz/detail/?id=1030799), ATL.
59 Application of Ani Waiwhakarewa to G. T. Wilkinson, 22 August 1895, AGCS J1 600/af 1898/922, ANZW.
60 Maangi Potae to Minister of Native Affairs, 31 March 1891, J1/545 1895/1245, ANZW.
61 Makere H. M. Tawhai to Minister for Native Affairs, 6 October 1894, MA1 952 1908/409, ANZW.
62 Catherine Bishop, 'Commerce was a Woman: Women in Business in Colonial Sydney and Wellington'.
63 Rora Hakaraia to Walter Buller, 28 June 1895, Lindauer Family: papers relating to Gottfried Lindauer, MS-Papers-9383, ATL.
64 Ewan Morris, 'Māori Monument or Pākehā Propaganda? The Memorial to Keepa Te Rangihiwinui, Whanganui' in Annabel Cooper, Lachy Paterson and Angela Wanhalla (eds), *The Lives of Colonial Objects*, p. 231.
65 Morris, p. 234.

66 *Te Karere Maori*, 31 July 1856, p. 11.
67 Jane McRae, *Ngā Mōteatea*, p. 91; Orbell, *Waiata*, p. 2.

Epilogue. 'I am writing to you for you to hear'

1 Riria Hohepa to Hohepa Tamaihenga, 11 April 1861, McLean Papers, MS-Papers-0032-0685C-04, Object #1030115 (http://mp.natlib.govt.nz/detail/?id=1030115), ATL.
2 Pat Hohepa and David V. Williams, *The Taking into Account of Te Ao Maori in Relation to Reform of the Law of Succession*, p. 29.
3 On the importance of probate records as historical sources for the study of family, gender and property, see Jim McAloon, 'Family, Wealth and Inheritance in a Settler Society: The South Island of New Zealand, c. 1865–c. 1930', pp. 201–15.
4 Bryony Cosgrove, 'Archives, Cultural Sensitivity and Copyright: The Publishing of *Letters from Aboriginal Women of Victoria 1867–1926*', p. 241.
5 Clare Anderson, 'Subaltern Lives: History, Identity and Memory in the Indian Ocean World', pp. 503–7.
6 Charlotte Macdonald, 'People of the Land, Voting Citizens in the Nation, Subjects of the Crown: Historical Perspectives on Gender and the Law in Nineteenth-Century New Zealand', p. 57.
7 Tony Ballantyne, *Archives, Public Memory and the Work of History*. For a broad reading on indigenous textuality see: Crystal McKinnon, '"From Scar Trees to a Bouquet of Words": Aboriginal Text is Everywhere', in Timothy Neale, Crystal McKinnon and Eve Vincent (eds), *History, Power, Text*, pp. 371–83.

NOTE ON SOURCES

One aim of this volume is to show that there is indeed a large and diverse set of sources pertaining to nineteenth-century Māori women's experiences. As we have collated over 500 individual items, but only draw upon a selection of that material for publication in *He Reo Wāhine*, and because there are far too many items to list in a bibliography, we felt it would be useful to provide a brief note on where we sourced the material that underpins this book. For specific details about individual items refer to Notes.

He Reo Wāhine has benefitted from the investment in digitisation of sources made by heritage institutions. Digitisation has meant that not only many catalogues are now online, but also the documents themselves as images, and sometimes as transcriptions. These not only offer access to a wide range of sources without the expense associated with travel, but have often sped up data gathering, and provided new methods for searching and collating material. Searching requires patience and perseverance, though. Personal and place names, for example, may be spelled differently.

Key sites include *Papers Past*, managed by the National Library of New Zealand, which hosts a selection of digitised newspapers from across the country, as well as a small number from the Pacific. *Papers Past* also includes the Māori-language newspapers (1842–1932), which we have made use of extensively. Do note that the early Māori-language newspapers were published by the government, but later, Māori political organisations, iwi groupings and churches also established their own publications. An alternative site where these newspapers can be accessed is the University of Waikato's *Niupepa: Māori Newspapers* website. We also used the *Appendices to the Journals of the House of Representatives (AJHR)*, which can be found on *Papers Past*, and cover the period 1858 to 1931. Colloquially referred to as the 'A to Js', the *Appendices* are a record of government activities, reported annually by each department, and include extensive correspondence from Māori on land matters, as well as reports of enquiries and official investigations into matters relating to native affairs, and summaries of petitions submitted. New material is always being added to *Papers Past*, so it is worth checking the site on a regular basis.

Although digitisation has made access to primary sources much easier, it has not replaced traditional historical research in archival and manuscript collections. Occasionally, information may not be clearly reproduced on an online version, so there is real value in viewing actual documents when possible. Not all online databases are equal, in terms of search capability and what they display. There is a danger in over-reliance on online material in that more pertinent or useful sources may be missed, which means that visiting archives is still essential for historical research. What follows is a brief description of materials gathered for our project held in public archives, organised by institution. There are, of course, still many documents held by whānau, hapū and iwi concerning their own tūpuna.

Archives New Zealand has three regional offices, in Auckland, Christchurch and Dunedin, in addition to the central office in Wellington. At this stage most of their holdings are not digitised. However their catalogue, Archway, is searchable online. As the main repository for government records, Archives New Zealand holds a rich and extensive set of materials of relevance to Māori whānau and individuals. Of most interest are the probate files, and these are now freely accessible and searchable online through familysearch.com. We researched probate files at each archive facility, but in following up these documents online discovered not all were available. If you cannot find a probate file online, then contact the archive where it is held, as it is likely it has not yet been digitised, or has yet to be uploaded. The Maori Affairs (MA) record group holds a large set of material, which includes correspondence from Māori women and men on land matters, as well as issues relating to the operation of the Native Land Court. This group also contains the individual and collective petitions Māori sent to the government. The Maori Trustee (MA-MT) record group includes correspondence on land matters, particularly correspondence relating to Māori desires to control financial benefits arising from rents. In the 1890s, jurisdiction over Maori Affairs was transferred to the Justice Department (J), and we drew on material from that era, as well as coroners files, and correspondence with the governor.

Notes on Sources

Alexander Turnbull Library, National Library of New Zealand, holds papers from prominent individuals, including early missionaries, notably the Yate Correspondence and Colenso Papers, as well as the papers of colonial politicians. During the mid-nineteenth century Donald McLean was one of New Zealand's leading politicians, whose influence was second only to the governor, and many Māori corresponded with him. The McLean Papers are vast, and many items are freely available online as images, transcriptions and translations, including the over 3000 letters written by Māori in te reo. We drew extensively on the McLean Papers, but also examined the records of his son, Douglas McLean, as well as the holdings relating to notable government officials who worked in native affairs, such as Walter Mantell and John White. We accessed the records of colonists, soldiers, ethnographers and journalists who collected Māori writing or corresponded with Māori, such as A. S. Atkinson and W. F. Gordon. In addition, the Alexander Turnbull Library holds material relating specifically to named Māori women, such as the Josephine Love Papers, which contain records relating to legal matters, Maria Morris's autobiography, and an interview with Guide Sophia recalling the 1886 Tarawera eruption.

The Museum of New Zealand Te Papa Tongarewa has archival holdings pertinent to Māori history. Most notable is the W. F. Gordon Collection, which includes his correspondence with Hēni Pore (Jane Foley). Her twelve letters to him touch on her participation in the Women's Christian Temperance Union, matters of whakapapa, as well as her involvement in the battle of Gate Pā (Pukehinahina) during the Tauranga campaign of the New Zealand wars.

The Auckland War Memorial Museum holds the personal papers of George Thomas Wilkinson, who was employed by the Native Department in the Waikato and Thames regions, and was also connected to Waikato Māori through marriage. His papers are a mixture of personal records and correspondence relating to his employment in the public service. We also accessed the records of the Dufaur, Lusk, Biss and Fawcett law firm held at the museum; the firm had many Māori clients. Most of these records relate to land matters, and include powers of attorney, conveyances, probates and wills, agreements, and mortgages.

At the Sir George Grey Special Collections, Auckland City Libraries, we accessed the Grey Māori manuscript holdings containing mōteatea, waiata and details about customary knowledge, as well as commissioned manuscripts. In addition these holdings include letters Māori addressed to Grey, both in an official and private capacity. Amongst those letters are many from Māori women.

In addition to the above institutions, we made use of material in Puke Ariki, Taranaki, and the Christchurch City Library archives, which hold the Ritchie Papers relating to the Chatham Islands; we accessed the Maria Maning Papers at the Hocken Collections, Dunedin, and obtained material from the Huntington Library, California, relating to Mormon missionaries who worked in Māori communities during the late nineteenth century. We made use of the Raupatu Document Bank, a collection of texts from a number of sources, at the Waitangi Tribunal Library, Wellington. An important resource for our project was the Native Land Court minute books, one of the richest sources of information about Māori land and whakapapa. Now known as the Māori Land Court, copies of its minute books are on microfilm and extensively held by libraries across the country.

We did not access the holdings of every public institution in New Zealand, preferring to concentrate on metropolitan and regional institutions with large collections of material, but we are certain that much more exists in the smaller local museums, libraries and archival repositories.

BIBLIOGRAPHY

Ahu, Tai, 'Te Reo Māori as a Language of New Zealand Law: The Attainment of Civic Status', LLM dissertation, Victoria University of Wellington, 2012.
Anderson, Atholl, *Race Against Time*, Hocken Library, Dunedin, 1991.
Anderson, Atholl, Judith Binney and Aroha Harris, *Tangata Whenua: An Illustrated History*, Bridget Williams Books, Wellington, 2015.
Anderson, Clare, *Subaltern Lives: Biographies of Colonialism in the Indian Ocean World, 1790–1920*, Cambridge University Press, Cambridge, 2012.
——, 'Subaltern Lives: History, Identity and Memory in the Indian Ocean World', *History Compass*, vol. 11, issue 7, 2013, pp. 503–7.
Andrews, Philip, 'Chapman, Anne Maria and Chapman, Thomas', from the Dictionary of New Zealand Biography. *Te Ara – the Encyclopedia of New Zealand*, www.TeAra.govt.nz/en/biographies/1c13/chapman-anne-maria (accessed 11 January 2017).
Angas, G. F., *Savage Life and Scenes: Australia and New Zealand: Being an Artist's Impressions of Countries and People at the Antipodes*, vol. 2, Smith, Elder, London, 1847.
——, *The New Zealanders Illustrated*, London, 1847; facsimile edition, Reed, Auckland, 1967.
Arista, Noelani, 'Listening to Leoiki: Engaging Sources in Hawaiian History', *Biography*, vol. 32, no. 1, 2009, pp. 66–73.
Ballantyne, Tony, *Archives, Public Memory and the Work of History*, Hocken Collections, Dunedin, 2015.
——, 'Contesting the Empire of Paper: Cultures of Print and Anti-Colonialism', in Jane Carey and Jane Lydon (eds), *Indigenous Networks: Mobility, Connections and Exchange*, Routledge, New York, 2014, pp. 219–40.
——, *Entanglements of Empire: Missionaries, Māori, and the Question of the Body*, Auckland University Press, Auckland, 2015.
——, *Webs of Empire: Locating New Zealand's Colonial Past*, Bridget Williams Books, Wellington, 2012.
Ballantyne, Tony and Antoinette Burton (eds), *Moving Subjects: Gender, Mobility, and Intimacy in an Age of Global Empire*, University of Illinois Press, Urbana, 2009.
Ballara, Angela, 'Niniwa-i-te-rangi', from the Dictionary of New Zealand Biography. *Te Ara – the Encyclopedia of New Zealand*, www.TeAra.govt.nz/en/biographies/2n15/niniwa-i-te-rangi (accessed 11 January 2017).
——, *Taua: 'Musket Wars', 'Land Wars', or Tikanga? Warfare in Māori Society in the Early Nineteenth Century*, Penguin, Auckland, 2003.
——, 'Te Paea Tiaho', from the Dictionary of New Zealand Biography. *Te Ara – the Encyclopedia of New Zealand*, www.TeAra.govt.nz/en/biographies/2t24/te-paea-tiaho (accessed 19 December 2016).
——, 'Te Whatanui', from the Dictionary of New Zealand Biography. *Te Ara – the Encyclopedia of New Zealand*, www.TeAra.govt.nz/en/biographies/1t86/te-whatanui (accessed 11 January 2017).
——, 'Turikatuku', from the Dictionary of New Zealand Biography. *Te Ara – the Encyclopedia of New Zealand*, www.TeAra.govt.nz/en/biographies/1t114/turikatuku (accessed 11 January 2017).
——, 'Wāhine Rangatira: Māori Women of Rank and their Role in the Women's Kotahitanga Movement of the 1890s', *New Zealand Journal of History*, vol. 27, no. 2, 1993, pp. 127–39.
Banivanua Mar, Tracey, 'Imperial Literacy and Indigenous Rights: Tracing Transoceanic Circuits of a Modern Discourse', *Aboriginal History*, vol. 37, 2013, pp. 1–28.
Beattie, J. H., *Traditional Lifeways of the Southern Maori*, Atholl Anderson (ed.), Otago University Press, Dunedin, 2009.
Belich, James, *'I Shall Not Die': Titokowaru's War, 1868–1869*, Second Ed., Bridget Williams Books, Wellington, 2010.
——, *Making Peoples: A History of the New Zealanders from Polynesian Settlement to the End of the Nineteenth Century*, Penguin, Auckland, 1996.

——, 'McDonnell, Thomas', from the Dictionary of New Zealand Biography. *Te Ara – the Encyclopedia of New Zealand*, www.TeAra.govt.nz/en/biographies/1m33/mcdonnell-thomas (accessed 11 January 2017).

——, *The New Zealand Wars and the Victorian Interpretation of Racial Conflict*, Penguin, Auckland, 1989.

Bennion, Tom and Judi Boyd, *Succession to Maori Land, 1900–52*, Waitangi Tribunal, Wellington, 1997.

Binney, Judith, *A Legacy of Guilt: A Life of Thomas Kendall*, Second Ed., Bridget Williams Books, Wellington, 2005.

——, '"In-Between" Lives: Studies from Within a Colonial Society', in Tony Ballantyne and Brian Moloughney (eds), *Disputed Histories: Imagining New Zealand's Pasts*, Otago University Press, Dunedin, 2006, pp. 93–118.

——, *Redemption Songs: A Life of Te Kooti Arikirangi Te Turuki*, Auckland University Press, Auckland, 1996.

——, *Stories Without End: Essays, 1975–2010*, Bridget Williams Books, Wellington, 2010.

——, 'Whatever Happened to Poor Mr Yate? An Exercise in Voyeurism', *New Zealand Journal of History*, vol. 38, no. 2, 2004, pp. 154–68.

——, 'Yate, William', from the Dictionary of New Zealand Biography. *Te Ara – the Encyclopedia of New Zealand*, www.TeAra.govt.nz/en/biographies/1y1/yate-william (accessed 11 January 2017).

Bishop, Catherine, 'Commerce was a Woman: Women in Business in Colonial Sydney and Wellington', PhD, Australian National University, 2012.

Boast, Richard, 'Bringing the New Philology to Pacific Legal History', *Victoria University of Wellington Law Review*, vol. 42, 2011, pp. 399–416.

——, *Buying the Land, Selling the Land: Governments and Māori Land in the North Island, 1865–1921*, Victoria University Press, Wellington, 2008.

——, *Native Land Court, 1862–1887: A Historical Study, Cases and Commentary*, Brookers, Wellington, 2013.

——, 'The Omahu Affair, the Law of Succession and the Native Land Court', *Victoria University of Wellington Law Review*, vol. 46, 2015, pp. 841–74.

Boyd, Mary, 'Russell, Henry Robert', from the Dictionary of New Zealand Biography. *Te Ara – the Encyclopedia of New Zealand*, www.TeAra.govt.nz/en/biographies/2r32/russell-henry-robert (accessed 11 January 2017).

Bradbury, Bettina, 'From Civil Death to Separate Property: Changes in the Legal Rights of Married Women in Nineteenth-Century New Zealand', *New Zealand Journal of History*, vol. 29, no. 1, 1995, pp. 40–66.

——, 'Troubling Inheritances: An Illegitimate, Māori daughter Contests her Father's Will in the New Zealand Courts and the Judicial Review Committee of the Privy Council', *Australia and New Zealand Law and History E-Journal*, Refereed Paper no. 5, 2012, pp. 126–64.

Bradwell, Cyril and Harold Hill, 'New Zealand History and Salvation Army History: How Do They Interact?', in Harold Hill (ed.), *Te Ope Whakaora: The Army that Brings Life: A Collection of Documents on the Salvation Army & Maori, 1884–2007*, Flag Publications, Wellington, 2007, pp. 23–34.

Bricker, Victoria R., 'Where There's a Will, There's a Way: The Significance of Scribal Variation in Colonial Maya Testaments', *Ethnohistory*, vol. 62, no. 3, 2015, pp. 421–44.

Brookes, Barbara, *A History of New Zealand Women*, Bridget Williams Books, Wellington, 2016.

Brooking, Tom, 'Rees, William Lee', from the Dictionary of New Zealand Biography. *Te Ara – the Encyclopedia of New Zealand*, www.TeAra.govt.nz/en/biographies/2r9/rees-william-lee (accessed 11 January 2017).

Brooks, Lisa, *The Common Pot: The Recovery of Native Space in the Northeast*, University of Minnesota Press, Minneapolis, 2008.

Broughton, Ruka Alan, *Ngaa Mahi Whakaari a Titokowaru*, Victoria University Press, Wellington, 1993.

Burns, Patricia, *Te Rauparaha: A New Perspective*, Penguin, Auckland, 1983.

Burton, Antoinette (ed.), *Archive Stories: Facts, Fictions, and the Writing of History*, Duke University Press, Durham, 2005.

Butterworth, Graham and H. R. Young, *Maori Affairs: A Department and the People Who Made It*, Government Print, Wellington, 1990.
Byrnes, Giselle, 'Ngati Tama Ancillary Claims' (Wai 143), Waitangi Tribunal, Wellington, 1995.
Caplan, Jane, 'Illegibility: Reading and Insecurity in History, Law and Government', *History Workshop Journal*, vol. 68, no. 1, 2009, pp. 99–121.
Carney, Virginia Moore, *Eastern Band Cherokee Women: Cultural Persistence in Their Letters and Speeches*, The University of Tennessee Press, Knoxville, 2005.
Carpenter, Cari M. and Carolyn Soriso (eds), *The Newspaper Warrior: Sarah Winnemucca Hopkins's Campaign for American Indian Rights, 1864–1891*, University of Nebraska Press, Lincoln, 2015.
Caselberg, John, *Maori is My Name: Historical Maori Writings in Translation*, J. McIndoe, Dunedin, 1975.
Clark, Davis W., *Death-Bed Scenes, or Dying With and Without Religion: Designed to Illustrate the Truth and Power of Christianity*, Land and Scott, New York, 1851.
Coney, Sandra, *Standing in the Sunshine: A New History of New Zealand Women Since they Won the Vote*, Viking, Auckland, 1993.
——, *Stroppy Sheilas and Gutsy Girls: New Zealand Women of Dash and Daring*, Tandem Press, Auckland, 1998.
Cosgrove, Bryony, 'Archives, Cultural Sensitivity and Copyright: The Publishing of *Letters from Aboriginal Women of Victoria 1867–1926*', *Melbourne Historical Journal*, vol. 42, no. 1, 2014, pp. 229–55.
Cowan, James, *The New Zealand Wars: A History of Maori Campaigns and the Pioneering Period: Volume II, The Hauhau Wars, 1864–1872*, Government Printer, Wellington, 1956.
Cowie, Dean, *Hawke's Bay: Rangahaua Whanui District 11B Working Paper*, Waitangi Tribunal, Wellington, 1996.
Cox, Lindsay, *Kotahitanga: The Search for Māori Political Unity*, Oxford University Press, Auckland, 1993.
Crawford, J. C., *Recollections of Travel in New Zealand and Australia*, Ballantyne, Hanson & Co., Edinburgh and London, 1880.
Curnow, Jenifer, 'A Brief History of Maori-Language Newspapers', in Jenifer Curnow, Ngapare Hope and Jane McRae (eds), *Rere Atu, Taku Manu! Discovering History, Language and Politics in the Maori-language Newspapers*, Auckland University Press, Auckland, 2002, pp. 17–41.
Curthoys, Ann and Jessie Mitchell, '"Bring this paper to the Good Governor": Aboriginal Petitioning in Britain's Australian Colonies', in Saliha Belmessous (ed.), *Native Claims: Indigenous Law Against Empire*, Oxford University Press, Oxford, 2012, pp. 182–203.
Davis, R., *A Memoir of the Rev. Richard Davis: For Thirty Nine Years a Missionary in New Zealand*, James Nisbet and Co., London, 1865.
de Costa, Ravi, 'Identity, Authority, and the Moral Worlds of Indigenous Petitions', *Comparative Studies in Society and History*, vol. 48, no. 3, 2006, pp. 669–98.
Derby, Mark, 'Māori–Pākehā relations – Missions and Māori', *Te Ara – the Encyclopedia of New Zealand*, www.TeAra.govt.nz/en/maori-pakeha-relations/ (accessed 11 January 2017).
Diamond, Paul, *Makereti: Taking Māori to the World*, Random House, Auckland, 2007.
DNZB, 'Te Rerenga, Hone Wetere', from the Dictionary of New Zealand Biography. *Te Ara – the Encyclopedia of New Zealand*, www.TeAra.govt.nz/en/biographies/2t29/te-rerenga-hone-wetere (accessed 11 January 2017).
Donald, Mary, 'Lord, Lucy Takiora', from the Dictionary of New Zealand Biography. *Te Ara – the Encyclopedia of New Zealand*, www.TeAra.govt.nz/en/biographies/1l9/lord-lucy-takiora (accessed 11 January 2017).
Dorsett, Shaunnagh, '"Destitute of the Knowledge of God": Māori Testimony Before the New Zealand Courts in the Early Crown Period', in Diane Kirkby (ed.), *Past Law, Present Histories*, Australian National University Press, Canberra, 2012, pp. 39–57.
——, 'Sworn on the Dirt of Graves: Sovereignty, Jurisdiction and the Judicial Abrogation of "Barbarous" Customs in New Zealand in the 1840s', *Journal of Legal History*, vol. 30, no. 2, 2009, pp. 175–97.
Drummond, Alison (ed.), *The Thames Journals of Vicesimus Lush, 1868–82*, Pegasus Press, Christchurch, 1975.

Dubinsky, Karen, *Improper Advances: Rape and Heterosexual Conflict in Ontario, 1880–1929*, University of Chicago Press, Chicago, 1993.
Earp, G. B., *New Zealand: Its Emigration and Gold Fields*, George Routledge, London, 1853.
Ellis, Ngārino, 'Ki tō ringa ki ngā rākau ā te Pākehā: Drawings and Signatures of Moko by Māori in the Early 19th Century', *Journal of the Polynesian Society*, vol. 123, no. 1, 2014, pp. 29–67.
Else, Anne (ed.), *Women Together: A History of Women's Organisations in New Zealand: Ngā Rōpū Wāhine o te Motu*, Historical Branch, Department of Internal Affairs/Daphne Brasell Associates Press, Wellington, 1993.
Elsmore, Bronwyn, *Mana from Heaven: A Century of Maori Prophets in New Zealand*, Reed Books, Auckland, 1999.
Finny, Guy, 'New Zealand's Forgotten Appellate Court? The Native Affairs Committee, Petitions and Maori Land: 1871 to 1900', LLB (Hons) thesis, Victoria University of Wellington, 2013.
Firth, Raymond, *The Economics of the New Zealand Maori*, Government Printer, Wellington, 1972.
Fitzgerald, Carolyn (ed.), *Letters From the Bay of Islands: The Story of Marianne Williams*, Penguin Books, Auckland, 2004.
——, *Te Wiremu – Henry Williams: Early Years in the North*, Huia, Wellington, 2011.
Fox, William, *The Six Colonies of New Zealand*, John W. Parker and Son, London, 1851.
Frame, Alex and Paul Meredith, 'Performance and Māori Customary Legal Process', *Journal of the Polynesian Society*, vol. 114, no. 2, 2005, pp. 135–55.
Gallagher, Sarah K. J., '"A Curious Document": Ta Moko as Evidence of Pre-European Textual Culture in New Zealand', *BSANZ Bulletin*, vol. 27, nos. 3/4, 2003, pp. 39–47.
Goldsmith, Paul, *The Rise and Fall of Te Hemara Tauhia*, Reed, Auckland, 2013.
Goode, Penelope, 'The Kaingarara Letters: The Correspondence of Tamati Te Ito Ngamoke in the A. S. Atkinson Papers, 1857–1863', MA thesis, University of Canterbury, 2001.
Gorer, Geoffrey, 'The Pornography of Death', *Encounter*, October 1955, pp. 49–52.
Gorst, John E., *The Maori King, or, The Story of Our Quarrel with the Natives of New Zealand*, Paul's Book Arcade, Hamilton, 1959 (first published London, 1864).
Grace, T. S., *A Pioneer Missionary Among the Maoris 1850–1879*, Bennett & Co., Palmerston North, 1928.
Grey, George, *Nga Mahi a nga Tupuna*, A. H. & A. W. Reed, Wellington, 1971 (first published 1854).
——, *Nga Moteatea, me nga Hakirara o nga Maori*, R. Stokes, Wellington, 1853.
——, *Polynesian Mythology, and Ancient Traditional History of the New Zealand Race, as Furnished by their Priests and Chiefs*, John Murray, London, 1855.
Grimshaw, Patricia, 'Maori Agriculturalists and Aboriginal Hunter-Gatherers', in Ruth Roach Pierson, Nupur Chaudhuri and Beth McAuley (eds), *Nation, Empire, Colony: Historicizing Gender and Race*, Indiana University Press, Bloomington, 1998, pp. 21–40.
——, 'Settler Anxieties, Indigenous Peoples, and Women's Suffrage in the Colonies of Australia, New Zealand and Hawai'i, 1888–1902', *Pacific Historical Review*, vol. 69, no. 2, 2000, pp. 553–72.
Gudgeon, Thomas W., *Reminiscences of the War in New Zealand*, Sampson Law, Marston, Searle & Rivington, London, 1879.
Haami, Bradford, *Pūtea Whakairo: Māori and the Written Word*, Huia, Wellington, 2004.
——, 'Tā Te Ao Māori: Writing the Māori Word', in Danny Keenan (ed.), *Huia Histories of Māori: Ngā Tāhuhu Kōrero*, Huia, Wellington, 2012, pp. 163–98.
Haines, David, 'In Search of the "Waheen": Ngai Tahu Women, Shore Whalers, and the Meaning of Sex in Early New Zealand', in Tony Ballantye and Antoinette Burton (eds), *Moving Subjects: Gender, Mobility, and Intimacy in an Age of Global Empire*, University of Illinois Press, Urbana, 2009, pp. 49–66.
Hall, R. De Z. and Steven Oliver, 'Kahutia, Riperata', from the Dictionary of New Zealand Biography. Te Ara – the Encyclopedia of New Zealand, www.TeAra.govt.nz/en/biographies/2k2/kahutia-riperata (accessed 11 January 2017).
Harvey, Megan, 'Story People: Stó:lō-State Relations and their Indigenous Literacies in British Columbia, 1864–1874', *Journal of the Canadian Historical Association*, vol. 24, no. 1, 2013, pp. 51–88.
Head, Lyndsay, 'Land, Authority and the Forgetting of Being in Early Colonial Maori History', PhD, University of Canterbury, 2006.

——, 'The Abduction of Hinemare's Children', *History Now*, vol. 8, no. 4, November 2002, pp. 20–22.
Head, Lyndsay and Buddy Mikaere, 'How Literate Were Maori?', *Archifacts*, no. 2, 1988, pp. 17–20.
Heuer, Berys, *Maori Women*, Polynesian Society, Wellington, 1972.
Higgins, Rawinia and John C. Moorfield, 'Marae Practices', in Tania M. Ka'ai, John C. Moorfield, Michael P. J. Reilly and S. Mosely (eds), *Ki Te Whaiao: An Introduction to Māori Culture and Society*, Pearson Education, Auckland, 2004, pp. 73–84.
——, 'Tangihanga: Death Customs', in Tania M. Ka'ai, John C. Moorfield, Michael P. J. Reilly and S. Mosely (eds), *Ki Te Whaiao: An Introduction to Māori Culture and Society*, Pearson Education, Auckland, 2004, pp. 85–90.
Higgins, Rawinia, Poia Rewi and Vincent Olsen-Reeder (eds), *The Value of the Māori Language: Te Hua o te Reo Māori*, vol. 2, Huia, Wellington, 2014.
Hill, Harold (ed.), *Te Ope Whakaora: The Army that Brings Life: A Collection of Documents on the Salvation Army & Maori, 1884–2007*, Flag Publications, Wellington, 2007.
Hohepa, Pat, 'Current Issues in Promoting Maori Language Use', *Language Planning Newsletter*, vol. 10, no. 3, 1984, pp. 1–4.
Hohepa, Pat and David V. Williams, *The Taking into Account of Te Ao Maori in Relation to Reform of the Law of Succession*, Law Commission, Wellington, 1996.
Holubetz, Margaret, 'Death-bed Scenes in Victorian Fiction', *English Studies*, vol. 67, no. 1, 1986, pp. 14–34.
Horton, Jessica, 'Rewriting Political History: Letters From Aboriginal People in Victoria, 1886–1919', *History Australia*, vol. 9, no. 2, 2012, pp. 157–81.
Howarth, Bettie, 'Field Day Notes' (18 January 1973) in Brian Herlihy, *The Pakakohi Tribe: Submission to the Waitangi Tribunal* (1992), http://repository.digitalnz.org/system/uploads/record/attachment/513/_the_pakakohi_tribe_.pdf (accessed 26 January 2017).
Howe, Kerry, 'Two Worlds?', *New Zealand Journal of History*, vol. 37, no. 1, 2003, pp. 50–61.
Hubbard, Eleanor, 'Reading, Writing, and Initialing: Female Literacy in Early Modern London', *Journal of British Studies*, vol. 54, no. 3, 2015, pp. 553–77.
Hurworth, Neville, 'About Rhodes Tudor and Albert Henry Nicholson, Two Remarkable Sons of William Nicholson Nicholson of Roundhay Park', *Oak Leaves*, vol. 13, Autumn 2013.
Jenkins, Kuni, 'Te Ihi, Te Mana, Te Wehi o te Ao Tuhi: Māori Print Literacy from 1814–55: Literacy, Power and Colonisation', MA thesis, University of Auckland, 1991.
Jenkins, Kuni and Kay Morris Matthews, 'Mana Wahine: Māori Women and Leadership of Māori Schools in Aotearoa/New Zealand', *New Zealand Journal of Educational Studies*, vol. 40, nos. 1/2, 2005, pp. 45–59.
Johnson, Miranda, 'Chiefly Women: Queen Victoria, Meri Mangakahia, and the Māori Parliament', in Maria Nugent and Sarah Carter (eds), *Mistress of Everything: Queen Victoria in Indigenous Worlds*, Manchester University Press, Manchester, 2016, pp. 228–47.
Johnston, Anna, *The Paper War: Morality, Print Culture and Power in Colonial New South Wales*, University of Western Australia Publishing, Perth, 2011.
Jones, Alison and Kuni Jenkins, *He Kōrero. Words Between Us: First Māori–Pākehā Conversations on Paper*, Huia, Wellington, 2011.
Jones, Pei Te Hurinui, *Puhiwahine: Maori Poetess*, Pegasus Press, Christchurch, 1961.
Joseph, Robert, 'Intercultural Exchange: Matakite Māori and the Mormon Church', in Hugh Morrison, Lachy Paterson, Brett Knowles and Murray Rae (eds), *Mana Māori and Christianity*, Huia, Wellington, 2012, pp. 43–72.
Kawharu, Freda Rankin, 'Heke Pokai, Hone Wiremu', from the Dictionary of New Zealand Biography. *Te Ara – the Encyclopedia of New Zealand*, www.TeAra.govt.nz/en/biographies/1h16/heke-pokai-hone-wiremu (accessed 11 January 2017).
Kawharu, I. H., *Maori Land Tenure: Studies of a Changing Institution*, Oxford University Press, Oxford, 1977.
Keenan, Danny, 'Separating Them From That Common Influence: The Dissolution of Customary Authority 1840–1890' in Danny Keenan (ed.), *Huia Histories of Māori: Ngā Tāhuhu Kōrero*, Huia, Wellington, 2012, pp. 131–62.
Lee, Christopher J., 'Gender Without Groups: Confession, Resistance and Selfhood in the Colonial Archive', *Gender & History*, vol. 24, no. 3, 2012, pp. 701–17.
Lee, Jenny, 'Nga Mahi a Ringa', *Tu Tangata*, vol. 22, 1985, pp. 24–27.

Lineham, Peter, 'The Mormon Message in Maori Culture', *Journal of Mormon History*, vol. 17, 1991, pp. 62–93.

Lineham, Peter and Allan Davidson, *Transplanted Christianity: Documents Illustrating Aspects of New Zealand Church History*, Second Ed., Dunmore Press, Palmerston North, 1989.

Loader, Arini M., 'Tau mai e Kapiti te whare wananga o ia, o te nui, o te wehi, o te toa: Reclaiming Early Raukawa–Toarangatira Writing from Otaki', PhD, Victoria University of Wellington, 2013.

Loughlin, Sue and Carolyn M. Morris, compilers, *Womanscripts: A Guide to Manuscripts in the Auckland Institute and Museum Library Relating to Women*, Auckland Institute and Museum, Auckland, 1995.

Loveridge, Donald M., *Maori Land Councils and Land Boards: A Historical Overview, 1900–1952*, Waitangi Tribunal, Wellington, 1996.

Lyons, Martyn, 'Writing Upwards: How the Weak Wrote to the Powerful', *Journal of Social History*, vol. 49, no. 2, 2015, pp. 317–30.

Macdonald, Charlotte, 'Land, Death and Dower in the Settler Empire: The Lost Cause of "The Widow's Third" in Nineteenth-Century New Zealand', *Victoria University of Wellington Law Review*, vol. 41, 2010, pp. 493–518.

——, 'People of the Land, Voting Citizens in the Nation, Subjects of the Crown: Historical Perspectives on Gender and the Law in Nineteenth-Century New Zealand', *law&history*, vol. 2, 2015, pp. 32–59.

——, *The Vote, the Pill and the Demon Drink: A History of Feminist Writing in New Zealand, 1860–1993*, Bridget Williams Books, Wellington, 1993.

Macdonald, Charlotte, Merimeri Penfold and Bridget Williams (eds), *The Book of New Zealand Women: Ko Kui Ma Te Kaupapa*, Bridget Williams Books, Wellington, 1991.

Mackay, J. A., *Historic Poverty Bay and the East Coast, N. I., N. Z.*, J. A. Mackay, Gisborne, 1949.

Mahuika, Api, 'Leadership: Inherited and Achieved', in Michael King (ed.), *Te Ao Hurihuri: The World Moves On. Aspects of Maoritanga*, Hicks Smith & Sons, Wellington, 1975, pp. 43–64.

Makereti, *The Old-Time Maori*, collected and edited by T. K. Penniman, Gollancz, London, 1938.

Marr, Cathy, *The Alienation of Maori Land in the Rohe Potae (Aotea Block), 1840–1920: Rangahaua Whanui District 8*, Waitangi Tribunal, Wellington, 1996.

McAloon, Jim, 'Family, Wealth and Inheritance in a Settler Society: The South Island of New Zealand, c. 1865–c. 1930', *Journal of Historical Geography*, vol. 25, no. 2, 1999, pp. 201–15.

McEwen, J. M., *Rangitāne: A Tribal History*, Reed Methuen, Auckland, 1987.

McKenzie, D. F., *Oral Culture, Literacy and Print in Early New Zealand: The Treaty of Waitangi*, Victoria University Press, Wellington, 1985.

McKinnon, Crystal, '"From Scar Trees to a Bouquet of Words": Aboriginal Text is Everywhere', in Timothy Neale, Crystal McKinnon and Eve Vincent (eds), *History, Power, Text: Cultural Studies and Indigenous Studies*, UTS ePress, Sydney, 2014, pp. 371–83.

McRae, Jane, '"E manu, tena koe!" "O bird, greetings to you": The Oral Tradition in Newspaper Writing', in Jenifer Curnow, Ngapare Hopa and Jane McRae (eds), *Rere Atu, Taku Manu! Discovering History, Language and Politics in the Maori-language Newspapers*, Auckland University Press, Auckland, 2002, pp. 42–59.

——, 'From Māori Oral Traditions to Print', in Penny Griffith, Ross Harvey and Keith Maslen (eds), *Book and Print in New Zealand: A Guide to Print Culture in Aotearoa*, Victoria University Press, Wellington, 1997, pp. 17–43.

——, *Ngā Mōteatea: An Introduction. He Kupu Arataki*, Auckland University Press, Auckland, 2011.

Meads, Diana, Philip Rainer and Kay Sanderson, compilers, *Women's Words: A Guide to Manuscripts and Archives in the Alexander Turnbull Library Relating to Women in the Nineteenth Century*, National Library of New Zealand, Wellington, 1988.

Meredith, Paul and Alice Te Punga Somerville, '"Kia Rongo Mai Koutou Ki Taku Whakaaro": Māori Voices in the Alexander Turnbull Library', *Turnbull Library Record*, vol. 43, 2010/11, pp. 96–105.

Middleton, Angela, *Pēwhairangi: Bay of Islands Missions and Māori, 1814 to 1845*, Otago University Press, Dunedin, 2014.

——, 'Silent Voices, Hidden Lives: Archaeology, Class and Gender in the CMS Missions, Bay of Islands, New Zealand, 1814–1845', *International Journal of Historical Archaeology*, vol. 11, no. 1, 2007, pp. 1–31.

——, *Te Puna – a New Zealand Mission Station: Historical Archaeology in New Zealand*, Springer, New York and London, 2008.

Mikaere, Annie, 'Maori Women: Caught in the Contradictions of a Colonised Reality', *Waikato Law Review*, vol. 2, 1994, www.waikato.ac.nz/law/research/waikato_law_review/pubs/volume_2_1994/7 (accessed 11 January 2017).

Mikaere, Buddy, 'Musket Wars, Migrations, New Tribal Alignments', in Danny Keenan (ed.), *Huia Histories of Māori: Ngā Tāhuhu Kōrero*, Huia, Wellington, 2012, pp. 109–30.

Monture, Rick, *We Share Our Matters: Two Centuries of Writing and Resistance at Six Nations of the Grand River*, University of Manitoba Press, Winnipeg, 2015.

Moon, Paul, *Ka Ngaro Te Reo: Māori Language Under Seige in the Nineteenth Century*, University of Otago Press, Dunedin, 2016.

Moore, D., B. Rigby and M. Russell, *Rangahaua Whanui National Theme A: Old Land Claims*, Waitangi Tribunal, Wellington, 1997.

Morris, Ewan, 'Māori Monument or Pākehā Propaganda? The Memorial to Keepa Te Rangihiwinui, Whanganui', in Annabel Cooper, Lachy Paterson and Angela Wanhalla (eds), *The Lives of Colonial Objects*, University of Otago, Dunedin, 2015, pp. 231–35.

Munro, Jessie, *Letters on the Go: The Correspondence of Suzanne Aubert*, Bridget Williams Books, Wellington, 2009.

——, *The Story of Suzanne Aubert*, Second Ed., Bridget Williams Books, Wellington, 2009.

Nelson, Elizabeth, Sandra Smith and Patricia Grimshaw (eds), *Letters from Aboriginal Women of Victoria, 1867–1926*, History Department, University of Melbourne, Melbourne, 2002.

Ngata, A. T. and Pei Te Hurinui Jones, *Ngā Mōteatea: The Songs*, Part III, Auckland University Press, Auckland, 2006.

Nicholas, J. K., *Narrative of a Voyage to New Zealand*, vol. 2, Black and Son, London, 1817.

Nikora, Shelley, 'Riperata Kahutia: A Woman of Mana', MA thesis, Waikato University, 2009.

O'Brien, Karen, 'Boots, Blankets, and Bomb Tests: First Australian Petitioning and Resistance to Colonisation', *Griffith Journal of Law and Human Dignity*, vol. 2, no. 2, 2014, pp. 357–76.

Oliver, Steven, 'Tautari, Hemi and Tautari, Mary', from the Dictionary of New Zealand Biography. *Te Ara – the Encyclopedia of New Zealand*, www.TeAra.govt.nz/en/biographies/2t12/tautari-hemi (accessed 11 January 2017).

——, 'Te Kiri Karamu, Heni', from the Dictionary of New Zealand Biography. *Te Ara – the Encyclopedia of New Zealand*, www.TeAra.govt.nz/en/biographies/1t43/te-kiri-karamu-heni (accessed 11 January 2017).

——, 'Wyllie, Kate', from the Dictionary of New Zealand Biography. *Te Ara – the Encyclopedia of New Zealand*, www.TeAra.govt.nz/en/biographies/2w36/wyllie-kate (accessed 11 January 2017)

O'Malley, Vincent, *Agents of Autonomy: Maori Committees in the Nineteenth Century*, Huia, Wellington, 1998.

——, 'Reinventing Tribal Mechanisms of Governance: The Emergence of Maori Runanga and Komiti in New Zealand before 1900', *Ethnohistory*, vol. 56, no. 1, 2009, pp. 69–89.

——, *The Great War for New Zealand: Waikato 1800–2000*, Bridget Williams Books, Wellington, 2016.

O'Malley, Vincent and David Armstrong, *The Beating Heart: A Political and Socio-Economic History of Te Arawa*, Huia, Wellington, 2008.

Orange, Claudia, 'The Māori and the Crown', in Keth Sinclair (ed.), *The Oxford Illustrated History of New Zealand*, Oxford University Press, Auckland, 1993, pp. 21–48.

Orbell, Margaret, 'Maori Women's Writing: An Introductory Survey', *World Literature Written in English*, vol. 17, no. 1, 1978, pp. 252–56.

——, 'Tikawe's Last Song', *New Zealand Studies*, vol. 8, no. 2, 1998, pp. 22–24.

——, *Waiata: Maori Songs in History*, Second Ed., Penguin, Auckland, 2007.

O'Regan, Hana, 'The Fate of Customary Language: Te Reo Māori 1900 to the Present', in Danny Keenan (ed.), *Huia Histories of Māori: Ngā Tāhuhu Kōrero*, Huia, Wellington, 2012, pp. 297–324.

Owens, J. M. R., 'Christianity and the Maoris to 1840', *New Zealand Journal of History*, vol. 2, no. 1, 1968, pp. 18–40.
——, 'New Zealand Before Annexation', in Geoffrey W. Rice (ed.), *The Oxford History of New Zealand*, Second Ed., Oxford University Press, Auckland, 1997, pp. 28–56.
Parham, W. T., 'Fulloon, James Francis', from the Dictionary of New Zealand Biography. *Te Ara – the Encyclopedia of New Zealand*, www.TeAra.govt.nz/en/biographies/1f18/fulloon-james-francis (accessed 11 January 2017).
Parkinson, Phil G. and Penelope Griffith, *Books in Māori, 1815–1900: Ngā Tānga Reo Māori*, Auckland University Press, Auckland, 2004.
Parr, C. J., 'Maori Literacy, 1843–1867', *Journal of the Polynesian Society*, vol. 72, 1963, pp. 211–34.
Parsonson, Ann, 'Stories for Land: Oral Narratives in the Maori Land Court', in Bain Attwood and Fiona Magowan (eds), *Telling Stories: Indigenous History and Memory in Australia and New Zealand*, Bridget Williams Books/Allen & Unwin, Wellington, 2001, pp. 21–40.
Paterson, Lachy, '"A Sparrow Alone Upon the House Top": The *Te Pihoihoi* Press', in Annabel Cooper, Lachy Paterson and Angela Wanhalla (eds), *The Lives of Colonial Objects*, University of Otago Press, Dunedin, 2016, pp. 117–21.
——, *Colonial Discourses: Niupepa Māori, 1855–1863*, Otago University Press, Dunedin, 2006.
——, 'Kiri Mā, Kiri Mangu: The Terminology of Race and Civilisation in the Mid-Nineteenth-Century Māori-Language Newspapers', in Jenifer Curnow, Ngapare Hopa and Jane McRae (eds), *Rere Atu, Taku Manu! Discovering History, Language and Politics in the Maori-language Newspapers*, Auckland University Press, Auckland, 2002, pp. 78–97.
——, 'The *Te Waka Maori* Libel Case: A Discussion', *law&history*, vol. 4, no. 1, 2017, pp. 88–112.
Peart, Nicola, 'Where There is a Will, There is a Way – A New Will Act for New Zealand', *Waikato Law Review*, vol. 15, 2007, pp. 26–47.
Pedersen, Susan, 'Samoa on the World Stage: Petitions and Peoples Before the Mandates Commission of the League of Nations', *Journal of Imperial and Commonwealth History*, vol. 40, no. 2, 2012, pp. 231–61.
Pere, Joseph Anaru Te Kani, *Wiremu Pere: The Life and Times of a Maori Leader, 1937–1915*, Libro International, Auckland, 2010.
Perry, Adele, *Colonial Relations: The Douglas-Connolly Family and the Nineteenth-Century Imperial World*, Cambridge University Press, Cambridge, 2015.
Pierson, Ruth Roach, Nupur Chaudhuri and Beth McAuley (eds), *Nation, Empire, Colony: Historicizing Gender and Race*, Indiana University Press, Bloomington, 1998.
Pilditch, Jan (ed.), *The Letters and Journals of Reverend John Morgan*, vol. 1 & vol. 2, Grimsay Press, Glasgow, 2010.
Pomare, Maui, *Legends of the Maori*, vol. 2, James Cowan (ed.), Southern Reprints, Papakura, 1987 (first published 1934).
Porter, Francis (ed.), *The Turanga Journals 1840–1850: Letters and Journals of William and Jane Williams Missionaries to Poverty Bay*, Victoria University Press, Wellington, 1974.
Porter, Frances and Charlotte Macdonald (eds), *My Hand Will Write What My Heart Dictates: The Unsettled Lives of Women in Nineteenth-Century New Zealand as Revealed to Sisters, Family and Friends*, Auckland University Press/Bridget Williams Books, Auckland, 1996.
Purchas, H. T., *A History of the English Church in New Zealand*, Lyttleton Times, Christchurch, 1907.
Ramos, Gabriela and Yanna Yannakakis (eds), *Indigenous Intellectuals: Knowledge, Power, and Colonial Culture in Mexico and the Andes*, Duke University Press, Durham, 2014.
Rei, Tania, *Māori Women and the Vote*, Huia, Wellington, 1993.
Reid, Kirsty and Fiona Paisley (eds), *Critical Perspectives on Colonialism: Writing Empire from Below*, Routledge, New York, 2014.
Riddell, Kate, '"Improving" the Maori: Counting the Ideology of Intermarriage', *New Zealand Journal of History*, vol. 34, no. 1, 2000, pp. 80–97.
Rodman, Margaret Critchlow, 'The Heart in the Archives: Colonial Contestation of Desire and Fear in the New Hebrides, 1933', *Journal of Pacific History*, vol. 38, no. 2, 2003, pp. 291–312.
Rountree, Kathryn, 'Re-Making the Maori Female Body: Marianne Williams's Mission in the Bay of Islands', *Journal of Pacific History*, vol. 35, no. 1, 2000, pp. 49–66.
Salesa, Damon I., *Racial Crossings: Race, Intermarriage, and the Victorian British Empire*, Oxford University Press, Oxford, 2011.

Bibliography

Sampeck, Kathryn, 'Introduction: Colonial Mesoamerican Literacy', *Ethnohistory*, vol. 62, no. 3, 2015, pp. 409–20.

Scholefield, Guy H. (ed.), *The Richmond-Atkinson Papers*, vol. 1, Government Printer, Wellington, 1960.

Scott, Gary, 'Te Awa-i-taia, Wiremu Nera', from the Dictionary of New Zealand Biography. *Te Ara – the Encyclopedia of New Zealand*, www.TeAra.govt.nz/en/biographies/1t26/te-awa-i-taia-wiremu-nera (accessed 11 January 2017)

Shep, Sydney J. 'The Paper Record: Phormium Tenax and New Zealand Papermaking', *BSANZ Bulletin*, vol. 21, no. 3, 1997, pp. 135–64.

Shortland, Edward, *Traditions and Superstitions of the New Zealanders*, Longman, Brown, Green and Longmans, London, 1854.

Silva, Noenoe K., *Aloha Betrayed: Native Hawaiian Resistance to American Colonialism*, Duke University Press, Durham, 2004.

——, 'Nā Hulu Kupana: To Honor Our Intellectual Ancestors', *Biography*, vol. 32, no. 1, 2009, pp. 43–53.

Simmonds, Naomi, 'Mana Wahine: Decolonising Politics', *Women's Studies Journal*, vol. 25, no. 2, 2011, pp. 11–25.

Simon, Judith and Linda Tuhiwai Smith, *A Civilising Mission?: Perceptions and Representations of the New Zealand Native School System*, Auckland University Press, Auckland, 2001.

Simpson, Elspeth M., 'Halbert, Thomas', from the Dictionary of New Zealand Biography. *Te Ara – the Encyclopedia of New Zealand*, www.TeAra.govt.nz/en/biographies/1h4/halbert-thomas (accessed 11 January 2017)

Simpson, Miria, *Ngā Taumata: A Portrait of Ngāti Kahungunu: He Whakaahua o Ngāti Kahungunu, 1870–1996*, Huia, Wellington, 2003.

Simpson, Robert L., 'The Church in New Zealand', in Daniel H. Ludlow (ed.), *The Encyclopedia of Mormonism*, vol. 3, Macmillan, New York, 1992, pp. 1014–16.

Sinclair, Niigaanwewidam James and Warren Cariou (eds), *Manitowapow: Aboriginal Writings from the Land of Water*, Highwater Press, Winnipeg, 2011.

Sole, Tony, *Ngāti Ruanui: A History*, Huia, Wellington, 2005.

Sorrenson, M. P. K., 'Māori and Pākehā', in Geoffrey W. Rice (ed.), *The Oxford History of New Zealand*, Second Ed., Oxford University Press, Auckland, 1992, pp. 141–66.

Spiller, Peter, Jeremy Finn and Richard Boast, *A New Zealand Legal History*, Brookers, Wellington, 2001.

Stephens, Māmari, 'A House With Many Rooms: Rediscovering Māori as a Civic Language in the Wake of the Māori Language Act (1987)', in Rawinia Higgins, Poia Rewi and Vincent Olseen-Reeder (eds), *The Value of the Māori Language: Te Hua o te Reo* Māori, vol. 2, Huia, Wellington, 2014, pp. 53–84.

Stevens, Michael, 'Kāi Tahu Writing and Cross-cultural Communication', *Journal of New Zealand Literature*, vol. 28, no. 2, 2010, pp. 130–57.

Stokes, Evelyn, 'Mokau: Maori Cultural and Historical Perspectives', Report commissioned by the Ministry of Energy, Wellington, 1988.

Stoler, Ann Laura, *Along the Archival Grain: Epistemic Anxieties and Colonial Common Sense*, Princeton University Press, Princeton, 2009.

Sutherland, Yvonne, 'Nineteenth-century Māori Letters of Emotion: Orality, Literacy and Context', PhD, University of Auckland, 2007.

Tau, Te Maire and Atholl Anderson (eds), *Ngāi Tahu: A Migration History. The Carrington Text*, Bridget Williams Books, Wellington, 2008.

Te Awekotuku, Ngahuia, *Mana Wahine Maori: Selected Writings on Maori Women's Art, Culture and Politics*, New Women's Press, Auckland, 1991.

Te Rangi Hīroa, *The Coming of the Maori*, Maori Purposes Fund Board, Wellington, 1952.

Travers, W. T. L., *The Stirring Times of Te Rauparaha*, Whitcombe and Tombs, Christchurch, 1906.

van Toorn, Penny, 'Indigenous Life Writing: Tactics and Transformations', in Bain Attwood and Fiona Magowan (eds), *Telling Stories: Indigenous History and Memory in Australia and New Zealand*, Bridget Williams Books/Allen & Unwin, Wellington, 2001, pp. 1–20.

——, *Writing Never Arrives Naked: Early Aboriginal Cultures of Writing in Australia*, Aboriginal Studies Press, Canberra, 2006.

Bibliography

Venuti, Lawrence, 'Introduction', in Lawrence Venuti (ed.), *Rethinking Translation: Discourse, Subjectivity, Ideology*, Routledge, London, 1992, pp. 1–17.

Wade, William Richard, *A Journey in the Northern Island of New Zealand*, George Rolwegan, Hobart-town, 1842.

Waitangi Tribunal, *The Taranaki Report – Kaupapa Tuatahi* (Wai 143), Waitangi Tribunal, Wellington, 1996.

——, *Turanga Tangata Turanga Whenua: The Report on the Turanganui a Kiwa Claims*, vol. 1, Legislation Direct, Wellington, 2004.

Walker, Ranginui, *Ka Whawhai Tonu Matou. Struggle Without End*, Penguin, Auckland, 1990.

——, *Liberating Maori from Educational Subjection*, Monograph no. 16, Research Unit for Maori Education, University of Auckland, Auckland, 1991.

Wanhalla, Angela, 'Interracial Sexual Violence in 1860s New Zealand', *New Zealand Journal of History*, vol. 45, no. 1, 2011, pp. 71–84.

——, *In/visible Sight: The Mixed Descent Families of Southern New Zealand*, Bridget Williams Books, Wellington, 2009.

——, *Matters of the Heart: A History of Interracial Marriage in New Zealand*, Auckland University Press, Auckland, 2013.

——, 'The Politics of "Periodical Counting": Race, Place and Identity in Southern New Zealand', in Penelope Edmonds and Tracey Banivanua Mar (eds), *Making Space: Settler-colonial Perspectives on Land, Place and Identity*, Palgrave Macmillan, London, 2010, pp. 198–217.

——, 'William Speer's Album: A Scrapbook of Colonial Travel', in Annabel Cooper, Lachy Paterson and Angela Wanhalla (eds), *The Lives of Colonial Objects*, Otago University Press, Dunedin, 2015, pp. 104–9.

Warbrick, Paerau, 'Minute Books: An Integral Part of the Māori Land Court', in Annabel Cooper, Lachy Paterson and Angela Wanhalla (eds), *The Lives of Colonial Objects*, Otago University Press, Dunedin, 2015, pp. 129–33.

Ward, Alan, *A Show of Justice: Racial 'Amalgamation' in Nineteenth-Century New Zealand*, Auckland University Press/Oxford University Press, Auckland, 1995 (first published 1973).

——, 'Davis, Charles Oliver Bond', from the Dictionary of New Zealand Biography. *Te Ara – the Encyclopedia of New Zealand*, www.TeAra.govt.nz/en/biographies/1d3/davis-charles-oliver-bond (accessed 11 January 2017).

——, 'Pere, Wiremu', from the Dictionary of New Zealand Biography. *Te Ara – the Encyclopedia of New Zealand*, www.TeAra.govt.nz/en/biographies/2p11/pere-wiremu (accessed 11 January 2017).

Ward, Damen, 'Imperial Policy, Colonial Government and Indigenous Testimony in South Australia and New Zealand in the 1840s', in Shaunnagh Dorsett and Ian Hunter (eds), *Law and Politics in British Colonial Thought: Transpositions of Empire*, Palgrave, New York, 2010, pp. 229–47.

Warrior, Robert, *The People and the Word: Reading Native Non-Fiction*, University of Minnesota Press, Minneapolis, 2005.

Waru, Ray, *Secrets and Treasures: Our Stories Told through the Objects at Archives New Zealand*, Random House, Auckland, 2012.

Waymouth, Lyn, 'Parliamentary Representation for Maori: Debate and Ideology in *Te Wananga* and *Te Waka Maori o Niu Tireni*, 1874–8', in Jenifer Curnow, Ngapare Hopa and Jane McRae (eds), *Rere Atu Taku Manu! Discovering History, Language and Politics in the Maori-language Newspapers*, Auckland University Press, Auckland, 2002, pp. 153–73.

White, John, *Ancient History of the Maori: His Mythology and Traditions*, Government Printer, Wellington, 1887.

Williams, H. W., *Dictionary of the Maori Language*, Seventh Ed., Legislation Direct, Wellington, 2006.

Worden, Nigel, 'Cape Slaves in the Paper Empire of the VOC', *Kronos*, no. 40, 2014, pp. 23–44.

Wordsworth, Jane, *Women of the North*, Collins, Auckland, 1981.

Wyss, Hilary E., 'Native Women Writing: Reading Between the Lines', *Tulsa Studies in Women's Literature*, vol. 26, no. 1, 2007, pp. 119–25.

Yate, William, *An Account of New Zealand, and of the Formation and Progress of the Church Missionary Sociey's Mission in the Northern Island*, Seeley and Burnside, London, 1835.

INDEX

adultery. *See* pūremu
advertising, 21, 320
Ahimanawa, 86, 87–88
Ahu, Tai, 263
Ahuriri, 239, 242
alcohol, 62, 157, 246, 248, 249, 251, 303, 304
    use during land purchasing, 57–60
    fines, 181–82
    sexual violence, 233, 234, 235
amalgamation policy, 80, 231, 236, 263, 310
Amohanga, Te Wamo, 147
Amuamu, Rēnata, 108–9
Amuri Bluff, 77
Anata, Meri, 175, 177, 178, 180
Angus, George French, 23
Aperahama, Hera, 159
Aperaniko, 90, 99
Araheke, 36
Aramoho, 139
archives and sources, 1–25 *passim*
    Alexander Turnbull Library, 5, 6, 270, 296, 300
    Appendices to the Journal of the House of Representatives, 195
    Archives New Zealand, 6, 38, 195, 290
    Auckland War Memorial Museum, 5, 6
    colonial collection, 24
    digitisation, 6, 229
    He Pātaka Kupu Ture/The Legal Māori Archive, 229
    Hocken Collections, 6
    Huntington Library, 279
    legal archives, 230
    Lost Cases Project Database, 229
    National Library of New Zealand, 229
    Native Land Court minute books, 38, 41, 42, 118, 132
    Niupepa Māori, 6
    Papers of Sir Donald McLean, 1820–1877, 6
    Papers Past, 6, 229
Aroaro, 88
Aropaoa, 33
Ashley River, 77
Astle, William, 147
Atkinson, Arthur S., 297
Atkinson, Harry, 251
Aubert, Suzanne (Sister Mary Joseph), 176, 277, 279
Auckland, 30, 116, 117, 129, 145, 147, 153, 154, 280, 302, 305
    Catholic cathedral, 276

Australia, 27, 193, 278, 319
    Aborigines, 193
autonomy. *See* rangatiratanga
Awanui School, 300
Awatea, Mere, 139–40
Awitu, 146
Awitu, Mere, 145

Baker, Ebenezer, 262
Baker, James, 133
Ballance, John, 197, 199
Ballantyne, Tony, 8
Ballara, Angela, 150, 172
Balneavis, Henry, 303, 304
Banks Peninsula, 203
bankruptcy, 306
Barnard, 49–50
Barnicoat, John, 297
Barritt, Major, 284
Bathgate, J. W., 40
Bay of Islands, 218, 265, 295
Bay of Plenty, 113, 129, 130, 213, 223, 274
    prisoners of war, 21
    war, 72, 73
Bayly, Christopher, 263
Beckham, Thomas, 120, 144, 147, 148
Belich, James, 85, 96, 107, 114
Bell, Francis Dillon, 28–29, 119
Bezer, E., 96, 98
Biggs, Reginald, 106
Binney, Judith, 3, 104, 107, 108, 115, 132, 266
Bishop, Catherine, 314
Blake, Richard, 163, 164, 168, 170
Blake, Edward T., 170, 171
Bluff, 100
Boardman, A., 146
Boast, Richard, 25, 123, 144
Booth, James, 139–40
Borlase, Charles, 235
Bowen, George Ferguson, 158, 159, 277, 278
Bowen, Lady, 277, 278
Boyes, Annie C., 300
Brabant, H. W., 137, 138
Bradwell, Cyril, 282
Bricker, Victoria R., 260
Brind, D., 295
Brissenden, 170
British Army, 72, 89, 103, 115
    Waikato campaign, 85–86, 116, 143
    Taranaki, 160
British Empire, 193

Index

Brookfield, Frederic, 119
Brookes, Barbara, 150
Brooks, Lisa, 197, 298
Brown, Charles, 169
Brown, Elizabeth. *See* Tāhere, Pēti Parāone
Brown, George, 214
Browne, Thomas Gore, 72, 147
Bryce, John, 135, 136, 171, 198
Buck, George, 232, 232
Buller, Walter, 314
    the *Waka Maori* libel case, 251, 252, 253, 255
Burns, Patricia, 76
Butler (interpreter), 58, 59

Cadman, Alfred, 204, 207, 208, 216, 218
Caffrey, Michael, 231, 234
Cambridge University, 18
Cameron, Duncan, 85
Campbell, Hannah, 259, 260
Canada
    Coast Salish, 193
cannibalism, 41, 77, 78
Canterbury, 205, 207
Canvastown, 207, 208
Cape Colony, 299
Caplan, Jane, 198
Caselberg, John, 5
Chapman, Thomas, 274, 275
Chapman, Mrs, 274
Chatham Islands. *See* Rēkohu
Christianity, 1, 20, 230, 256–89 *passim*
    Christian marriage, 120, 294, 295
Church Missionary Society, 18, 256, 256, 295
Chute, Trevor, 89
Clarke, George, 269
Clarke, Henry T., 22, 196, 210, 211
Clarke, Martha, 24
Clark-Walker, G., 23
Cochrane's Land Mart, 116
Colenso, Eliza, 301
Colenso, William, 17
commissions, 2, 4, 203, 212, 258, 318
    Confiscated Lands, 169
    Hawkes Bay Native Lands Alienation, 237, 238
    Native Land Laws, 40, 61
    Mōkau, 57–60
    Old Land Claims, 28–29
    Pōkaikai, 89–99
    West Coast, 140, 142, 181, 222–24, 299
    Worgan, George B., 138
committees, Māori. *See* Rūnanga
Compensation Court, 11–12, 16, 46, 71, 89, 116, 209, 223, 258
    Bay of Plenty, 128–34, 212, 213, 214, 216
    'European Compensation Court', 144–48

Royal Commission, 169, 171
    Taranaki, 138–43, 160–61, 171
    Waikato, 118–27, 134–38
    War losses, 144–48, 303–4
Coney, Sandra, 150
confiscation, 116, 118, 223–24
    Bay of Plenty, 212–16 *passim*
    Taranaki, 219, 220
        creeping confiscation, 160
Cook Strait, 72, 76, 82
Cooper, 32
Cooper, G. S., 56
Coopers Bay, 310
Cosgrove, Bryony, 319
Cowan, James, 114
Cowell, Keke (Martha), 223
Crane, Peti, 259
Crawford, James C., 119, 120, 261
Creagh, Oliver, 216, 217, 218

Dacker, Bill, 100
Dalton, J., 58
Dalton, Lucy. *See* Takiora
Dargaville, 48
Davis (interpreter), 253
Davis, Charles Oliver, 33, 276
de Costa, Ravi, 193
de Thierry, Inuwaiti, 224
debt, 261, 303, 304
    Native Land Court costs, 60, 61
    to Pākehā, 225, 237, 239, 242, 254
desertion, 260–61
Dickie, A. J., 43, 50, 51
Didsbury, George, 237, 251
dog taxes, 73, 181
Dorsett, Shaunnagh, 230
Douglas, Edward, 210, 211, 212
Douglas, Mrs. *See* Te Korowhiti Tuataka
Dufaur, Edward T., 22
Dunedin, 100, 168

East Coast (North Island), 73, 116, 118
education
    informal, 19–20
    Māori women teachers, 61, 219, 308, 309, 310
    missionary 18–19, 23–24, 263, 301
    Native Schools, 300–301, 309–10
Ellesmere, Lake. *See* Te Waihora
Elsmore, Bronwyn, 102
England, 166, 266
    delegations to, 174, 192
    donors to missions, 272
    literacy, 19
Enoka, Ani, 261
Enoka, Atarete, 261

Index

Epee, 73
Erena, Ema, 308, 309

Fenton, Francis Dart, 30
    Compensation Court, 123, 124
    Native Land Court, 11, 43, 44, 46–52 *passim*, 121, 210
fines, 179–80, 182
    muru, 182
Finny, Guy, 194, 203
Fisher, T. W., 218
flour mill, 62
Foley, Jane. *See* Te Kiri Karamu, Hēni
foreshore, 158–60, 189
Fox, William
    West Coast Commission, 140, 222, 223
Foxton, 53
Freemans Bay, 276
Fulloon, Elizabeth Koka, 132, 133, 212, 214, 215
Fulloon, James, 131, 132, 133, 154, 212–16 *passim*
Fulloon, John, 132

Galloway Redoubt, 88
Gannon, Michael Joseph, 256
gold mining, 156–58, 189
Gorst, John E., 85, 151–54 *passim*
Grace (interpreter), 59
Grace, Sarah, 22
Grace, Thomas S., 19, 21, 22
Graham, 49
Graham, George, 99
Greenwood, Alma, 279, 282
Grey, Alexander, 218
Grey, Eliza, 298
Grey, Sir George, 17
    colonial politics period, 22, 141
    first governorship, 10, 36, 120, 298–89
    second governorship, 72, 85, 152, 154, 156
        war and peace policies, 85, 153
Greytown, 39, 43
Griffith, Penelope, 5
Grimshaw, Pat, 3, 150
Grindell, James, 237, 251
Gudgeon, Thomas, 89, 98

Haami, Bradford, 9, 202, 263
Hadfield, Octavius, 17
Halbert, Thomas, 28
half-caste, 283
    counted as Pākehā, 189
    education, 301
    land rights, 219, 220, 221, 225, 260
    position in society, 132
Hall, John, 142
Halse, Henry, 54
Hamlin, Job, 86, 88

Hamlin, James, 86
Hamlin, Elizabeth, 268
Hapurona, 84
Harden, Matapere (Mrs C. J.), 76, 77
Harris, 29
Harris, Charles, 40
Harvey, Megan, 193
Haselden, C. J. A., 205, 206
Hauhau, 288
    Hauraki, 157
    Poverty Bay, 104, 112
    Waikato, 314
    Taranaki, 91, 92, 95, 162, 163, 165, 166, 167
    see also Pai Mārire
Hauiti, Rūihi, 175, 274
Hauraki, 145, 157, 158–60
Hautōtara, 40
Havelock, 262
Hawaiki, 247, 250
Hawaiki, Mere, 170
Hāwera, 91, 96, 162, 164
Hawke, Joseph, 291
Hawkes Bay, 30, 39, 72, 103, 116, 118, 174, 237, 279
Hawkes Bay Native Lands Alienation Commission. *See* commissions
Head, Lyndsay, 20
Heaphy, Charles, 124
Heke Pōkai, Hone, 16, 72
Hēmara, Miriama, 32–33
Hēmi, Merania, 177, 180
Heni, Arama, 86–87
Hēpara, Maraea, 48–50
Heretaunga, 33–34, 187, 240, 243, 253
Hihina, Rīpeka Tīria, 46
Hihina, Māta, 46
Hikairo, Hārete, 223
Hikairo, Wiremu M., 49, 50, 237
Hikawera, 40–41
Hikutaia, 157
Hikutere, 170
Hill, Harold, 282
Hinckley, Ira Noble, 279–82
Hinehoea, 58
Hinemoa, 291–92, 320
Hinewai, 125, 126
Hinurere, Ihapera, 43–44
Hiraka, 246, 249
Hiraka, Ārihi, 177, 180
Hobbs, Richard, 222
Hōhepa, Pat, 318
Hōhepa, Rīria, 318
Hokianga, 63, 73, 220
Hone, Hōriana, 224
Hongi Hika, 16, 18, 23
Horotiu River, 117
Horowhenua, 52–57

horse rustling, 166, 167
Huakirau, Pare, 58, 59
Huanga, Rihi, 308
Hughes, William, 234, 236
Huka, 77
Hukanui, 134, 135
Humanitarianism, 27, 193
Huntly, 183
Hurinui, 187
Huriwai, Miriama, 207
Hutt, 235
Hutt River, 234

India, 263
interpreters and interpretation, 11, 12, 16, 65, 66, 196, 214, 231–2, 253, 258, 262
    Māori women interpreters, 200, 201, 202, 310
Ipika, 204
Irai, Miriama, 47–48

Jenkins, Kuni, 298
Jesus Christ, 267–71 *passim*, 275, 285, 286, 287
Jillet, Etara, 260
Jillet, Robert, 260
Johnson, Justice, 231, 232
Johnson, Miranda, 150
Jones, Alison, 298
Jones, Pei Te Hurinui, 5
Jones, Joshua, 57–60
Joseph, Robert, 279
Justice Department, 205, 308

Kahe Te Rau-o-te-rangi, 299
Kahutia, Riperata, 41–42
Kahutia, Kataraina, 42
Kahuwahine, Kataraina, 37
Kaiapoi, 77, 78, 79, 190, 272–273
Kaihau, Aihepene, 123–24
Kaihau, Hēnare, 183
Kaikaramu, 196
Kaikōura, 76, 77, 79
Kaimare, Rīria, 105, 106, 107, 111, 113, 114
Kaingaiti, 88
Kaipara, 32, 49
Kaitāia School, 300
Kaitangata, 77
Kaitoritori, Irihāpeti, 177, 180
Kaiuri, Rēwiri, 83
Kapapango, Hēnare, 109
Kapiti, 74, 78, 82, 142, 152
Karaki, Arama, 88
Karamo Takirau, 293, 294
karanga, 5, 150
Karauria, 40
Karipa, 203, 294
Karira, 36

Kate (ship), 212–16 *passim*
Kati, Pāora, 106
Katikati, 80, 196, 200
Katipa, Ema, 108, 110, 111
Katipa, Himiona, 109, 113
Kau, 58–59
Kaupokonui (Kaupukunui), 163, 166, 169
Kawakawa, 61
Kāwana Hunia, 57
Kaweka, 142
Kawepō, Rēnata, 112
Kāwhia, 74, 260, 302, 303
Kawiti, Maihi Parāone, 62
Kelly, 40
Kēmara, Ataneta, 176, 177, 179, 180
Kemp, James (and family), 24, 267, 271
Kemp, Charlotte, 270, 271, 272
Kemp, Henry T., 37, 49, 203, 204, 205
Kemp's Purchase (Kemp's Deed), 190, 203
Kendall, Thomas, 18, 23, 265, 295
Kennedy, 23
Kepa, Wiremu, 145
Kerei, Wharekauri, 175, 176 178, 179
Kererengū, 76, 77
Kerikeri Mission House, 23
Ketemarae, 169
Keteonetea, 90, 91
Kihau, Ellen, 296, 297
Kihi, Amīria, 44–45
Kihikihi, 154
King, Hannah, 18
King, John, 18
Kīngi, Hōne, 146
Kīngi, Ruiha, 22–23
Kīngi, Ngāhuia, 22
Kīngitanga, 38, 57, 151–56, 174, 189
    war, 72, 84, 85–86, 88, 116, 119, 146, 147, 160
King Country, 104, 107, 114, 121, 156, 157, 160
Kirikiri, 119
Kohanga Kārearea, 104
Koheroa, 85, 155
Kohimārama Conference, 151
Koka, Wī, 88
Kōkiri, Mere Paea, 297–98
Konehu, Miriama, 159
Kōrako, Mātene, 259, 260
Kōrako, Mere Hinehou, 260
Koroneho, Wiremu, 145
Kororāreka, 276
Kōruarua, Pīpī, 203–9
Kotahitanga Movement, 68, 171, 175, 182, 183, 184, 189, 194
    covenant, 177, 180
    levy, 177, 178, 180
    Māori Parliament, 172, 173, 174, 183, 320
    'Māori Women's Parliament', 174

Kōtiro Hinerangi, 218
Kui, Mere, 259, 260
Kuia, 86–87
Kuiatu, Maata, 261
Kūkūtai, Hōri, 121
Kūkūtai, Nini, 47, 154
Kūkūtai, Noa, 121
Kūkūtai, Waata, 148
Kurakitoro, Ākanihi, 143, 224, 300
Kuru, Mere, 157, 158, 189
Kyster, David, 235

land
    as marriage gift, 29
    Commissioner of Crown Lands, 206
    compulsory acquisition, 183
    Crown grant, 29, 46, 50, 51, 123, 124, 172, 173, 193, 199, 226
    customary title, 27, 38, 138, 149, 173
    deeds, 83, 85
    Horowhenua dispute, 52–57
    intimidation, 42
    leasing, 56, 176, 179, 240, 244, 246, 248, 254
    post-Treaty sales, 30–37
    preemption, 30
    pre-Treaty sales, 27–29
    restrictions, 224–27
    sales to missionaries and traders, 28
    scrip, 122, 123
    settler attitudes, 27
    subdivision, 63–64, 66–68, 196
    take raupatu, 53
    ten-owner rule, 39
    tuku whenua, 28
land blocks
    Akire, 220
    Heretaunga, 237, 240, 243
    Heretoa, 220
    Howata, 220
    Kaitawa, 220
    Ketemaraea, 220
    Mokau-Mohakatino No.1, 58
    Ngātirahira, 225, 226
    Ngā-waka-a-Kupe, 39–41
    Onewhero, 11–12
    Ōnaero, 142
    Ōpūora, 220
    Pakake-a-whiri Koka, 256
    Patumāhoe, 120–21, 123
    Porokaiaia, 53
    Pouparae, 28
    Pukekura, 247, 250
    Rākūkū, 220
    Rohitu, 246, 248
    Tātaraimaka, 153
    Te Aoroa, 220
    Te Aratira, 220
    Te Matapū, 220
    Te Ngāere, 22o
    Te Pōnui-a-Rina, 220
    Titirangi, 44–45
    Tūākau, 120
    Tūrangatapuwai, 220
    Tuimata, 120, 121
    Waihī, 227
    Waikareao, 254
    Waipā, 220
    Waipapa (No.1) Ngātirahiri, 44–45
    Wairoa, 121
    Whakapoungākau Pukepoto, 195, 196
landlessness, 208, 209, 224
Lee, Christopher, 9
Lee, George, 236
Lee, Samuel, 18
legislation
    Appropriation Act 1873, 16
    Electoral Reform Act 1893, 228
    Land Board Bill 1899, 187
    Land Claims Settlement Act 1856, 28
    Married Women's Property Act 1884, 261
    Mokau-Mohakatino Act, 1888, 60
    Native Land Court Amendment Act 1889, 201, 259
    Native Lands Act 1862, 38
    Native Lands Act 1865, 38–39
    Native Lands Act 1867, 16, 39, 3001
    Native Lands Act 1869, 259
    Native Lands Act 1873, 39
    Native Lands Settlement and Administration Bill 1898, 64, 68, 70
    Native Schools Act 1867, 19, 277
    Native Succession Act 1881, 259, 260
    New Zealand Settlements Act 1863, 116
    Pensions Bill 1899, 187
    Unsworn Testimony Ordinance 1844, 230
    Wills Act 1837, 259
Levin, 53
Lewis, T. W., 198
libel, 21
literacy
    acquisition, 18–24
    agency, 4–5, 6–7, 11–16 *passim*, 319
    forms, 13–15, 320
    illiteracy, 21
    practices, 21–24
    religious texts, 265
    scribes, 21–22, 202, 299, 302
    writing, 4–5, 9–10, 12–16, 25, 294, 296–302 *passim*
        declarations, 257–63
        diaries, 9
        journals, 9

letters, 9, 19, 21–25 *passim*, 31, 213, 317, 320
   as petitions, 202–9
      flax letters, 23
      hongi, 298
      love letters, 296
   telegrams, 168, 217
   whakapapa books, 9
   wills, 258–63, 318
  signing and signatures, 12, 13, 20, 21, 83–85, 122, 130, 170, 199, 229, 254, 262–63
Locke, Samuel, 241, 244, 254
Lord, Lucy. *See* Takiora
Luna (ship), 214
Lyons, Martyn, 202

Mabey, Charles, 234, 235
Macdonald, Charlotte, 5, 150, 320
Macdonald, J. E., 45–46
Mackay, Alexander, 40, 64, 122, 124, 204, 205
Mahora, 257–58
Mahuika, Api, 150
Mahupuku, Hāmuera, 40, 59, 186
Mahurangi, 33
Mahuta, King, 183–86 *passim*
Mair, William Gilbert, 199, 211
Mākāretu, 112
Makarini, Neri, 19
Makauri, 42
Makawhiu, 34
Maketū (Bay of Plenty), 80, 135, 136, 137, 274
Maketū (South Auckland), 125, 126
Maki, Hawira, 126
Makura, 77, 78, 79
mana
   chiefly mana, 53, 55, 72, 74, 150, 154, 185
   government mana, 201
   mana kīngi, 153
   mana motuhake, 182
   mana wahine, 5, 7, 41, 152, 158, 190, 217, 318
   mana whenua, 7, 27, 38, 53, 55, 142, 202
   whakapapa, 150
Manaia, 281
Manawapou, 91, 92, 95, 96
Mangahuia, 40–41
Mangakāhia, Mere, 172, 173, 186, 189
Mangarei, 146, 147
Mangatara, 49–50
Mangatāwhiri Stream, 85, 155, 156
Māngere, 145, 146
Mangōrei, 36
Maning, Frederick, 303, 305
Maning, Hauraki, 305–7
Maning, Maria, 305–7
Mantell, Walter, 203–4 *passim*
Manukau, 146
Manukau Harbour, 145, 315, 316

Manuwhiri. *See* Ngāpora, Tamati
Māori Affairs, Department of, 10
Māori King Movement. *See* Kīngitanga
Māori language. *See* Reo Māori
Maramarua, 145, 155
March, J. E., 207
marriage, 294–95
   certificates, 291, 294, 295, 296
   Christian, 120, 294, 295
   rights, 249, 259
   mixed race, 28–29, 132, 296
Marsden, Samuel, 16, 18, 295
Marshall, William, 148
Marston (barrister), 131
Mata, Peti (Betsy Moss), 296, 297
Mataatua (waka), 11
Matangarara, 92
Matara, Metiria, 36–37
Matarikoriko Reserve, 226
Matawhero, 107–8, 109, 114, 115
Mātenga, Ani, 31–31
Mathews, Joseph, 300
Mātire Piripi, 43
Mātao, Hetariki, 54, 55
Matau, Mereana, 90, 95, 96–98
Matimati, Meri, 310–11
Matua, Hēnare, 238, 247, 250
Mauaranui, Rīria, 28–29
Maungakirikiri, 163, 165
Maungarake, 32
Maunu, Tamati, 54
Mautaranui, Emeri Maraea (Emily Buckworth), 132, 212–18
McDonald, 42
McDonald, Hector, 53, 55–56
McDonnell, Capt., 94, 95, 96, 99
McDonnell, Thomas, 89–99 *passim*
McHardy, John, 235
McKay, Marian, 147, 148, 258
McKenzie, D. F., 20
McLean, Sir Donald, 227
   government agent, 103, 104
   land purchasing, 31–37 *passim*
   Native Secretary, 85, 152, 162–69 *passim*
   Native Minister, 17, 55, 100, 101, 134, 218, 219, 251
McLean, Douglas, 309
McRae, Jane, 21
Melbourne, 299, 200
Mercer, 311
Mercury Bay, 211
Meredith, Paul, 7
Meremere, 85, 86
Messenger, William, 59
Mete, Taare, 187
Meurant, Kenehuru (Eliza), 193

Index

Mihipō Pātene, Ani, 122–23
Mikaere, Buddy, 20
Miropiko, 134, 135
missionaries, 18, 22, 27, 150, 169, 265–82 *passim*,
    294, 295, 296
    education, 18–19, 23–24, 263, 301
        Institute of Nazareth, 276–79
    pre-Treaty land sales, 28
    Mormon, 279–82
missions
    Catholic, 265
        Holy Congregation
        Sisters of Mercy, 279
    CMS Northland, 266, 295
    Methodist, 288
    Presbyterian, 288
    Salvation Army, 283, 285
    Wesleyan, 272
Moerewarewa, Māta, 90, 91, 92–96, 97
Mohakatino River, 57
Moheko, Ria, 262
Moiki, 43
Mōkau, 57–60
Mōkau River, 57
Mokina, 146
Mokopuna, Raina, 175, 178
Monk, Richard, 68
Moncur, James, 301
Monro, H. A. H., 11
Moorhouse, William S., 48
Moreti, Maraea (Maria Morris)
    war experiences, 102–3, 108–13 *passim*
    Salvation Army, 283–85, 288–9
Morris, Ewan, 315
Morgan, John, 301
Morgan, Matire (Matilda Moncur), 301–4, 310
Morgan, Samuel, 301–4
Mormons, 279–82
Morpeth, W. J., 138, 202
Morris, George B., 210
Morris, Maria. *See* Moreti, Maraea
mortgage, 226, 227, 246, 249
Munro, Jessie, 277

Nahunia, Turuhia, 146
Naihi, Āporo, 275
Nairn, Frank, 234
Napier, 39, 239–51 *passim*, 284
Native Affairs, Department of, 16
Native Affairs Committee, 8, 64, 136, 192–95,
    203, 205, 209, 212, 218, 226, 228
Native Affairs Select Committee, 20
native assessors, 50, 59, 62, 66, 119, 232
Native Committees, 65–66, 69–70
Native Department/Native Office, 33, 124, 132,
    154, 198, 202, 204, 218, 238, 264, 305, 311

Native Hostelry, 119
Native Land Commissioner, 23
Native Land Court, 4, 10, 37–52, 108, 116, 132,
    183, 202, 209, 211, 229, 256, 264, 318
    forms, 13–15, 129
    interpreters, 16
    Māori opinion on court and land sales,
        60–70, 175, 178, 179
    Official Notice, 43
    operation 37–39, 237
    petitions concerning, 194, 224–26
    succession, 258–69
Native Land Purchase Department, 169
Neinukua, Miriama, 34–35
Nepo, Hana, 84
Nesbitt, Dr, 42
New Plymouth. *See* Ngāmotu
New Zealand Company, 28
Newland, William, 94, 95, 96, 98
Newman, John L., 84
Ngaauta, 220
Ngāene, 163, 165
Ngāere Swamp, 170
Ngāhauporoaki, 224
Ngāheko, Hāriata, 224
Ngāhina Nātanahira, 89–93 *passim*, 99
Ngakangioue, Ōhaka, 256
Ngaki, 80
Ngāmotu (New Plymouth), 73, 82, 96, 143, 162,
    171, 225
Ngāpahi, 161
Ngāpora, Tamati, 146, 155, 158
Ngārori, Piriira, 178, 181
Ngāroto, 122, 123
Ngāruawāhia, 116, 117, 122, 151–56 *passim*, 304
Ngata, Sir Āpirana, 5
Ngātapa, 114–14
Ngāwhakaheke, 59
Ngohi, 163, 165
Niania, Hōri, 239, 242–43
Nicholson, Albert H., 53, 56, 57
Nicol, Jock, 299
Nichol, Mākere, 299
Nīkora, Shelley, 41
Niniwa-i-te-rangi, 6, 319
    Land Court, 41, 60–61, 64–70, 71
    Kīngitanga, 183–86
    Māori-language newspapers, 186–89
Noake, Maillard, 168
North America, 193
Northland, 61, 72, 161, 279

Ōākura, 123
Ōamaru, 79
oaths, 262. *See also* ōhākī
    allegiance, 86, 119, 127

Index

court, 94, 139, 230
Ōeo, 163, 165, 166
ōhākī, 257, 270, 272, 273
Ōhauiti, 210, 211
Ōhinemuru, 156–58
Ōhui, 130
Ōkuratope pā, 16
O'Malley, Vincent, 171
Ōmihi, 76, 77, 79
    battle of, 76–80
Ōmuturangi, 163, 165, 166
Ōnaero, 141, 142
Onetū, 220
Ōpōtiki, 14–15, 48, 116, 118, 128, 129, 130, 131, 214
Ōpunake, 163, 165, 223
Ōpureora, 45–46
Ōrākau, 116
orality, 4, 5, 10, 25, 197, 252, 259, 288, 298,
    302, 317, 320
    land sales, 30
    ohāki, 259, 270, 272, 273
    whaikōrero, 150, 184
Ōrangikaupapa, 262
Orbell, Margaret, 292
Ōtaki, 20, 53, 260, 285, 297
Ōtākou (Otago Heads), 101, 262
Otago, 100, 101, 262
Ōtāwhao, 301
Ōtotoika, 257
Ouenuku, Rene, 51, 52
Ōweta, 112
Ōwhata pā, 103

Pāhuia, 267
Paihia, 43, 44
Pai Mārire, 29, 72, 73, 105, 288
    Bay of Plenty, 128, 131, 132
    East Coast, 41–42
    niu pole, 102–3
    Taranaki, 89, 90, 91, 95, 160
Paisley, Fiona, 227
Pākaitore (Moutua Gardens), 315
Pakipaki, 181, 238–50 passim
Pākirikiri, 174
Pāmaramara, 10
Pānapa, Arapera, 176, 179
Panepane, Pirihira, 272–273
Panga, Hāriata, 33–34
Papakura, 73, 86, 86, 87
    Pakakura Ambush, 85–89
Pāparatū, 107
Pāpāwai, 172, 183, 312
Paraea, Mereana, 202, 222
Parahaki, Mount, 80, 81
Parāone, Hiraina, 274–76
Parāone, Māta, 159

Parāone Hūkiki, Hōhepa, 274, 275, 276
Parata, Ani, 261, 262
Parata, Wī, 20, 194
Parawai
    Holy Trinity Church, 199
pardons, 86, 88–89, 114
Parehuiroro, 158
Paremataiti, Hera, 159
Parihaka, 73, 142, 161, 162, 164, 166, 169, 171, 223
Parikino, 176, 179
Parirua, Eruea, 193
Parkinson, Phil, 5
Parliament, New Zealand, 17, 27, 60, 116, 151, 160,
    186, 188, 243, 251
    House of Representatives, 100, 194, 212, 215
    Legislative Council, 185, 205, 237
Parnell, 287, 288
Parore, 48–49
Parororangi, 40
Parramatta, 18
Parris, Robert, 83, 84, 89, 93, 161–68 passim
Parsonson, Ann, 38
Pātaka, Hēmi Watikini, 83
Pātangata, 31
Pātara Te Tuhi, 154
Pātea, 89, 99, 164, 166, 168
Pātea River, 139
Pātuki, John Tōpi, 203, 262, 296
Patumāhoe, 123, 125
Patutahi, 107, 110
Pawa, Mere, 261
Peata, Sister, 276–79 passim
Pēkamu, Maraea, 143
pensions, 132, 187, 214, 216, 311, 312, 313
Pere, Wī (Wiremu), 28–29, 109, 112, 113, 187, 188
    land schemes, 255, 256
periodicals
    Auckland Star, 136
    Colonist, 84
    Daily Southern Cross, 86, 145, 148, 153, 156, 160
    Evening Post, 255
    Huia Tangata Kotahi, 60, 175, 186
    Journal of the Polynesian Society, 10, 76
    Māori-language newspapers, 24, 153,
        186–89, 197, 291, 320
    Missionary Register, 270
    New Zealand Herald, 11, 147, 148, 157
    Poverty Bay Herald, 255
    Press, 273
    Star, 171
    Taranaki Herald, 99
    Te Ao Hou, 10
    Te Karere Maori, 315
    Te Korimako, 274, 276
    Te Pihoihoi Mokemoke
    Te Puke ki Hikurangi, 64, 186

Te Tiupiri, 183, 186
    'Ladies Column', 186
Te Waka Maori o Niu Tireni, 12, 21, 237–55
Te Waka o te Iwi, 32
Te Wananga, 238, 245–51 *passim*
Wellington Independent, 42, 99
Wanganui Herald, 99, 182
War Cry, 283, 285, 286, 287
Perry, Adele, 2
Petere, Mere (Mary Petley), 13–15, 128–29
petitions, 1, 24, 134, 136, 142, 143, 183, 192–228, 320
    delegation to London, 174, 192
    letters as petitions, 202–9
    Public Petitions Committee, 193
    structure and conventions, 195–96, 197, 199
    women's suffrage petitions, 192, 228
Petley, John, 13, 128
Phillips, Jane Maria, 1, 202, 218–22
Phillips, John G., 221, 222
photography, 314
Pī, Arama Karaka, 16
Piako River, 20
Pīhama, Hone, 163, 165
Pihia, Īnia, 142
Pipitea pā, 262
Piripi, Hare, 58
Piripi, Matire, 262
Pirongia, 122, 301, 302, 304
Poharama, 120, 121
Pōhio, Horomona, 203
Pohiwa, 81, 82
Poho, Ema, 109
Poka, Mere, 84
Pōkaikai, 89–99
Pōkeno, 85, 125
police, policing, 80, 235, 304, 304
Pōmare II, 54
Pōmare, Māui, 10
Pōmare, Mere Naera, 141–43
Pōmare, Wiremu, 53, 54, 55, 57
Pompallier, Jean Baptiste, 120, 276–77
Pōnui, 219
population decline, 187–88, 188–89
Porirua, 50, 51
Poroumati, Emare, 285–88
Port Underwood, 143
Port Waikato, 11, 147
Porter, Frances, 5
portrait painting, 314, 315
Pōrutu, Rūhia, 261
Pōtae, Maangi, 312–13
Pōtangaroa, Te Wiremu, 32
Pōtatau Te Wherowhero, 38, 146, 151, 316
Potote, Paratene, 103
Pounara, Hera, 144–45
poverty, 208, 209, 224, 249, 290, 299, 301–13

Poverty Bay, 102, 103, 104, 112, 113, 115, 255, 256, 284
prisoners of war, 21, 77, 80–82
    Chatham Islands, 104–6
    of Te Kooti, 109–14 *passim*
    Pōkaikai massacre, 92, 93–95, 97
Privy Council (London), 262
prostitution, 105, 270
Provincial Councils
    Auckland, 118, 157
    Canterbury, 205
    Hawkes Bay, 118, 237
    Taranaki, 100, 225
Pūaha, Raiha, 50–52
Puakitehau, 121
Pūhara, Heke, 175–80 *passim*
publications
    Account of New Zealand (1835), 13, 266, 270
    Bible, 267, 283, 284
    Book of New Zealand Women (1991), 150, 319
    Books in Māori, 1815–1900 (2004), 5
    Book of Common Prayer, 295
    Dictionary of New Zealand Biography, 150, 319
    Legends of the Maori (1934), 10
    Letters on the Go (2009), 277
    Maori is My Name (1975), 5
    My Hand Will Write What My Heart Dictates, 5–6
    New Testament, 105
    Ngā Mahi a ngā Tupuna (1855), 10
    Ngā Mōteatea (1959–1970), 5
    Pūtea Whakairo (2004), 9
    Rangitāne: A Tribal History (1986), 10
    The Maori King (1864), 152
    Traditions and Superstitions of the New Zealanders (1854), 80
    Women's Words (1988), 5–6
    Womanscripts (1995), 5–6
Puckey, 146
Puhata, Ema, 11
Pūiti, Petera, 247, 250
Pukearuhe, 57
Pukehinahina (Gate Pā), 103
Pukekohe, 119
Pukepoto, 22, 210, 211
Pukepuke, 110
Puketapu, 35
Puketapu pā, 107
Puketea Pupurutu, 58
pūremu (sexual misconduct), 292–94
Pūrewa, Maraea, 159
Puri, Maraea, 175, 178
Pūriri, Hana, 176, 177, 179, 180
Pūtiki, 183, 314
Pūtutu, Ani, 121

Raglan, 155
Rakahuri, 77
Ramarihi, 22
rangatiratanga, 5, 38, 66, 172, 174, 182, 183, 187
Rangiamohia, 89–92, 93, 95
Rangiohia, 293
Rangihaeata, 82
Rangihatau, Huingapaura, 227
Rangiheihei, 125, 126
Rangihoua, 18
Rangingangana, 54
Rangiriri, 46, 47, 146, 147
Rangitāne, 41, 53
Rangitīkei, 74
Rangituma, Māora, 145
Rangiwakaoma (Castlepoint), 32
Rāpata, 15
rape. *See* sexual violence
Raru, 267–68
Raru, Tamati, 83
Raumoa, Raiha, 44
Raupongo, Rāwiri, 83
Raurongo, Eruera, 83
Rāwhitiroa, 86, 87, 88
Rees, William, 61, 64, 255, 256
Rei, Tania, 150, 172, 194
Reid, Kirsty, 227
Reihana, 154
Rēkohu (Chatham Islands), 94, 104–5, 111, 114
religion, 256–89
    baptism, 267, 271
    Baptists, 276
    Christian names, 6, 109, 268
    conversion narratives, 266–69, 283–386
    deathbed spirituality, 269–76
    Mormons, 279–82
Rennell (official), 220
reo Māori
    civic language, 25, 263
    dialects, 24
    orthography, 18, 26
    use by officials, 17, 24–25
Repudiation Movement, 238, 245, 255
Rerewaka, 76, 77
Rewa, 276
Rewa Te Rārangi Pouaka, 301
Rewe, Miriama, 48
Rewi Maniapoto, 47, 152, 154, 156, 304
Rhodes, Mary Ann, 262
Richmond, C. W., 53, 54, 55, 237
Rifleman (ship), 105, 106
rights
    women's economic, 10, 246, 249, 260–61
Ringa, Maria, 23, 265, 295
Rīpene, Here, 176–80 *passim*
Rīria, 119–20

roads, roadbuilding, 166, 167, 181, 224, 304
Robinson, George, 207
Rogan, John, 11, 49, 50, 121, 142
Rolfe, Emma, 224–27
Rolfe, Frederick W., 98, 225–27
Rolleston, William, 198
Rongo, Hariata, 15, 23–24
Rongopāmamao, 257–58
Rōpata, Metapere, 194
Ropia, Hōne, 121
Ropiha, Wiremu, 44
Ropitoi, Maraea, 176, 177, 179, 180
Rotorua, 80, 196, 201
    Rotorua Lakes, 221
Ruakituri River, 107
Ruapuke, 262, 296
Ruatāhuna, 112
Rūātoki, 216, 218
rūnanga and komiti (councils), 64–65, 69, 151, 160, 171, 231
    alternative to Native Land Court, 42
    Komiti nui a Hēnare Matua, 247, 250
    Heretaunga women's committee, 181–82
    Komiti Wahine o Rotorua, 181
    Komiti Wahine o Hinehauone, 182
    Ngāti Maru women's rūnanga, 158–60
    women's committees, 151, 158–60, 171–82
    Whanganui Native Women's Committee, 182
Rūrū, Atereta, 255–56
Russell, Andrew Hamilton, 138
Russell, Emily, 299
Russell, George F., 299
Russell, Henry, 12, 237–55 *passim*
Russell, Purvis, 237, 240, 241, 243, 244

Sainsbury, George, 251
Salvation Army, 104, 108, 282–88, 289
Seddon, Richard, 185, 218, 221
self reliant policy, 72–73
Selwyn, George Augustus, 120
Seth-Smith, H. G., 202
sexual misconduct. *See* pūremu
sexual violence, 110, 231–37, 263
    customary law, 231
    sexual morality, 231, 234, 235–36
Sharpe, Mrs, 306, 307
Sheehan, John, 22, 170, 197, 198, 238, 255
Shera, Jemima, 304–5
Shera, John, 304
Shortland, Edward, 80, 82
Silva, Noenoe K., 8
Simeon, Agnes. *See* Kurakitoro, Ākanihi
slavery, 74, 82, 237
Smith (missionary family), 274
Smith, Thomas H., 132
Somerville, Alice Te Punga, 7

Index

song. *See* waiata
South Island, 30, 74, 143, 202, 203, 208, 259
Spanish colonies, 193
Speedy, Major, 124
Speer, William, 296–97
Spencer, Grey, 98, 99
Stephens, Māmari, 263
Stevens, John, 64, 65
Stewart, Marian. *See* McKay, Marian
Stewart, R. O., 147, 148
Stockman, E. W., 84
Strang, 40
suicide, 10, 290, 291–92, 320
    whakamomori, 292
Supreme Court, 22, 183, 229, 231, 247, 250
    Dunedin, 100
    Wellington, 108, 231, 251
surveyors and surveying, 124, 168
    Commission of Enquiry, G. B. Worgan, 138
    opposition, 48–52, 54–56, 57, 73, 169, 170, 176, 179, 216–18, 304
Suther, Dr, 96
Swainson, George F., 54, 55
Sydney, 18, 27, 266, 298

Tāhere, Pēti Parāone, 129–30
Tahuroa te Hauokoeko, 41
Taiaroa, Hone Wīwī, 262
Taiaroa, Hōri Kerei, 100, 101, 203, 204, 206
Taiawhio, Sophia, 218, 221
Taihuka, Pera, 103, 104, 109
Taihuka, Pehimana, 109
Taingākawa. *See* Te Waharoa, Tupu Atanatiu Taingākawa
Taiporohēnui, 91, 97
Taipua, 132
Taita, 232, 232
Taka, Hōri, 86, 87, 89
Takaanini Te Tihi, Īhaka, 190, 120, 125, 126, 155
Takahaka, 79
Takamoana, Karaitiana, 238
Takapuahia, 35
Taki, Mere, 261
Takiora (Lucy Dalton, Lucy Lord), 218–22 *passim*, 319
    Government informant, 160–71
Tākitimu (waka), 185
Tamaihenga, Hōhepa, 318
Tamakeke, 204
Tamaterā, Miriama, 46–47
Tamihana, Harete, 45–46
tāmoko, 20–21
Tangiteruru, 81
Tanner, Thomas, 241, 244
Tapatu Ruta, 32
Tapsell, Philip [Jr], 134, 138

Tapsell, Philip [Sr], 265, 295
tapu, 150, 270
Tarakawa, Takaanui, 10–11
Taranaki, 86, 225
    confiscation and compensation, 116, 123, 141–43, 219
    Tītokowaru, 107, 160–71
    Waitara dispute, 82–84
    war (1863), 153
Taranaki Volunteer Rifles, 100
Taranaki wars. *See* wars
Tarapīpipi, Wiremu Tamihana, 152
Tarawera eruption, 196
Taro, Ākinihi, 145–46
tattooing. *See* tāmoko
Tauhinukorokio, 79
Taumārere, 62, 309
Taumo, 81, 82
Taumutu, 203, 204, 205
Taunakiwehe, Maraea, 195, 196, 199–202
Taupiri, 147, 298, 315, 316
Taupō, 156
Tauranga, 22, 45, 46, 86, 151, 197, 198, 211
    confiscation and compensation, 116, 118, 128, 144
Taurangaika Pā, 100
Taureka, 102
Tauroa, Hōri, 11–12
Tauroa, Rehara, 11–12, 16
Taurua, Ngāwaka, 100, 167, 168
Tautari, Mary, 61–64, 66, 71
Tautawe, Wikitōria, 223
Tauteka, 53–57
Tāwhā, Rōra, 204–9
Tāwhai, Graham, 63
Tāwhai, Hōne Mohi, 313
Tāwhai, Mākere, 313
Tāwhiao, King, 107, 151–56 *passim*, 162, 164, 304
Tāwhiti Stream, 92
Taylor, Richard, 19
Te Aho, Atareta, 39–41
Te Ahu, Ihaia, 22
Te Aohuna, 41
Te Aohuruhuru, 10
Te Aokauai, Meri, 32
Te Apatū, Āreta, 256
Te Ape, 295
Te Arama, 175, 178
Te Arora, Kūini, 177, 180
Te Ātahīkoia, Mohi, 187
Te Aute, 34–35, 239, 242
Te Awaitaia, Wiremu Nēra, 153, 154, 155, 156, 272
Te Awamutu, 152, 153
Te Hapimana, 119
Te Hāpuku, 32, 238
Te Hāpuku, Nēpia, 12, 241, 245, 252

Index

Te Hauke, 32, 174
Te Hēmara Tauhia, 32
Te Heuheu, 187
Te Hikawera, 204
Te Hira Wharewhenua, 157, 158
Te Hoko, Ēpiha, 83
Te Houanga, 48, 49, 50
Te Ia, 153, 154
Te Iringa, 41
Te Iwi, Ana Pāora, 123–27
Te Iwi, Pāora, 120
Te Kaewa, Hana, 262
Te Kaiuku, 81
Te Kani, Hirini, 102
Te Kapene, 146
Te Karai, 210
Te Kawau, 36, 76
Te Keene, 119
Te Keepa Te Rangihiwinui (Major Kemp), 57, 139, 314–15
Te Kihi, Rēneti, 44
Te Kiri Karamu, Hēni (Jane Foley), 103, 199–202 *passim*, 258
Te Koka, 298
Te Kōkako, Hōri, 83
Te Kōneke, 107
Te Kooti Arikirangi, 29, 73, 104–15 *passim*, 161, 283, 284, 288
    Ringatū religion, 104, 111
Te Korowhiti Tuataka (Mrs Douglas), 210–12, 222
Te Kura, Māta, 159
Te Mahuki, 161
Te Manuahura, Ruta, 134–38
Te Matai, 121
Te Mautaranui, 212–16 *passim*
Te Mautaranui, Koka, 132, 133
Te Mohi, 257, 258
Te Motu, Makareta, 84
temperance, 171
    Women's Christian Temperance Union, 194
Te Nahu, Ārihi, 12–13, 21, 237–55 *passim*, 319
Te Nahu, Hāpuku, 12, 241, 245, 252
Te Ngākau o te Otea, 45, 46
Te Ngū, Mohi, 119, 120, 125, 126, 155
Te Ngutu-o-te-manu, 161, 163, 165, 166
Te Oka, Wiremu, 86
Te Orama, 176, 179
Te Oro, 58
Te Orora, Kuīni, 175, 178
Te Ōwai, Māta, 106, 111
Te Paea, Nerehana, 54
Te Paea Tiaho, 151–6, 158, 189, 315–16, 319
Te Pakihi, 51, 52
Te Pātui, 86
Te Pātūtū, Hākopa, 273
Te Pātūtū, Rāhira, 273–74

Te Pehi, 78
Te Pewa, Erueti, 139, 140
Te Puke, 137, 138
Te Puru, 45, 46
Te Rangi, Hōri, 88
Te Rangiahuta, 35
Te Rangiātaahua, Ēpiha Pūtini, 151, 315–16
Te Rangiātaahua, Piripi, 293
Te Rangihīroa (Sir Peter Buck), 150
Te Rangitāke, Wiremu Kīngi, 83, 84
Te Rangiwawata, 128, 129
Te Raro, 40–41
Te Rata, Arapata, 90, 92
Te Rātōia, 92
Te Rau, Kereopa, 42, 102
Te Rau-o-te-Hua, 135, 136
Te Rau-o-te-Rangi, 141, 142
Te Rauparaha, 74, 82, 120
    South Island raids, 76–79 *passim*
Te Rauparaha, Ruta, 298, 299
Te Rāwhiti, Reihana, 47
Te Rerenga, Wētere, 57–58
Te Riki, Pāora, 262
Te Ringa, Rākira, 84
Te Rohu, Hepine, 175, 177, 178, 180
Te Ropia, 121
Te Roto, Wilson, 148
Te Teira Manuka, 82–83
Te Tīpene, 120, 121
Te Ua Haumene, 72, 93
Te Ua, Wikitōria, 176, 177, 179, 180
Te Unuhi, Hana, 35
Te Urukahika, 50–51
Te Uruorangi, Pane, 175–80 *passim*
Te Waharoa, Tupu Atanatiu Taingākawa, 185
Te Waiheke, Meri, 293–94
Te Waihora (Lake Ellesmere), 203, 204, 205
Te Wairama, 109
Te Waiukoukou, 41
Te Wārihi, 106
Te Whāiti, 112
Te Whakamanu, 41
Te Wharerata, 220, 221, 222
Te Whatanui, 52–54, 56
Te Whatanui, Rīria, 55–57
Te Whatanui, Tūtaki, 54
Te Wheoro, Rongonui, 177, 180
Te Wheoro, Wiremu, 158, 304
Te Whiroa, 41
Te Whiti-o-Rongomai, 142, 161, 162, 162, 164, 166, 171
Te Whiwhi, Jane, 298, 299
Te Whiwhi, Mātene, 53, 54, 56
Te Whiwhi, Pīpī, 298, 299
Te Wiiti, 54
Tekenui, 220

Teira, Ruiha (L. M. Plumbridge), 202, 223–24
testimonies
    courtroom, 73, 229–31
Thames (district). *See* Hauraki
Three Kings Wesleyan Mission, 103
Tiakitai, Ema, 176, 177, 179, 180
Tiakitai, Hōriana, 175–80 *passim*
Tieri, Hēra, 296, 297
Tikorangi, 224, 225
Timata Tītoko, 117, 147
Timu, Maremare, 176, 179
Tīpene, 12
Tipuna, Raina, 177, 180
Tiritiri, 134
Tito Hanataua, 90, 93, 96, 162, 163, 164, 165
Tītoki, 143
Tītokowaru, Riwha, 73, 100, 107, 161–71
    passim
Tīwai, Pīhama, 48
Tiwaia, Rāhera, 223
Toenga, 23
Toha, Mātire, 146–47
Tohi Te Ururangi, 80
Tohu Kākahi, 142, 161, 171
tohunga-ism, 288
Toke, Hōne, 109
Tokiriri, Heta, 59
Tokoahu, Enoka, 45, 46
Tomoana, Ākenehi, 172, 173, 174, 176–80
    passim, 189
Tomoana, Hēnare, 112, 238
Tongi, Koka, 176, 179
Tōnore, Airini, 262
Topa, Wikitōria, 105, 106, 107, 112
Topeora, 6, 74–76, 152, 189
Toro, Mere, 262
transportation (exile), 104, 116, 168, 171
translation, 16–17, 26, 68, 197–98, 208
travers, W. T. L., 76
Treaty of Waitangi, 5, 18, 20–21, 63, 80, 117, 172, 189, 203
    preemption, 30
trials
    civil, 230
    criminal, 86–88, 108, 128, 230
    sexual morality, 231, 234
tribal groups
    Kānihi, 169
    Kohereki, 88
    Kurukau-puke-puke, 77
    Māungaunga, 316
    Muaūpoko, 52–57
    Ngāi Tahu, 190, 207, 208, 262, 273, 296
        kerēme (claim), 202–3
        Ngāti Toa raids, 76–80
        Pakakohi prisoners, 100, 101, 102

Ngāi Tara, 10
Ngāi Te Rangi, 80, 128, 151, 212
Ngāi Tūhoe, 73, 112, 132, 217, 218
Ngāpuhi, 16, 18, 53, 54, 72, 161, 199, 298
Ngāti Apa, 53, 56, 57
Ngāti Awa, 132, 212–16 *passim*
Ngāti Hikairo, 301
Ngāti Hikawera, 39, 183
Ngāti Hinga, 83
Ngāti Hinewhanga, 42
Ngāti Ira, 77
Ngāti Kahu, 11–12
Ngāti Kahungunu, 12, 31, 41, 59, 112, 150, 151, 238, 279, 319
    delegation to Kīngitanga, 183–85
    effect of land sales, 39
    Heretaunga Block, 237
Ngāti Mahanga, 272
Ngāti Maniapoto, 84, 152, 154, 156
Ngāti Maru, 23, 41–42, 158, 159, 171, 189
Ngāti Mutunga, 143
Ngāti Pare, 119, 120
Ngāti Pareraukawa, 56
Ngāti Porou, 113, 150
Ngāti Pou, 74, 75, 76
Ngāti Pūkeko, 148
Ngāti Rango, 33
Ngāti Raukawa, 52–57, 74, 298
Ngāti Rua, 131
Ngāti Ruanui, 89, 90, 92, 96, 107, 162, 164, 218, 219, 221, 319
    Deed of Settlement, 99
Ngāti Tahinga, 311, 312
Ngāti Tama, 58
Ngāti Tamaoho, 120, 151, 316
Ngāti Tamaterā, 157
Ngāti Tamehariua, 45, 46
Ngāti Te-Karo, 241, 244
Ngāti Te-whare-kākahu, 241, 244
Ngāti Tīpā, 121, 316
Ngāti Toa, 52–53, 120, 152
    South Island raids, 74, 76, 77, 78
Ngāti Tūaho, 83
Ngāti Tūwharetoa, 272
Ngāti Whakaue, 80
Ngāti Whātua, 32–33
Pakakohi, 99–102, 168
Patutokotoko, 90
Rongowhakaata, 28, 112, 255
Tangahoe, 89, 92, 96, 99
Tainui, 74, 151, 316, 319
    government apology 1995, 149
Te Aitanga-a-Māhaki, 28–29, 41, 102, 255
Te Ākitai, 119, 120
Te Arawa, 134, 135, 136, 151, 199

Index

Te Āti Awa, 74, 100, 273
    Waitara dispute and war, 13, 38, 53, 72, 82–85, 153
    Tītokowaru, 162, 164
Te Uri-o-Hau, 33
Te Whānau-a-Tauwhao, 80
Tūhourangi, 293
Umutai, 219, 221
Wanganui, 90
Tū, Hamiora, 211
Tuahūriri, 273
Tuainuku, 55
Tucker, 42
Tuhua (Mayor Island), 80, 81, 82
Tūkino, 90, 91, 92, 95
Tukuiho, Maraea, 144
Tullock, Robert, 40
Tully, 40
Tukupane, 204
Tūmua, Wikitōria, 183
Tūnui, Tamihana, 148
Tūpaea, Hamiora, 247, 250
Tūpoki, Hita
Tūponga, 41
Tūranganui (Tūranga, Gisborne), 28, 42, 73, 102, 106, 107, 109, 111, 176, 179, 283
Tūrangatatu, 41
Turikatuku, 16, 23
Turipona, Rīpeka, 197–99, 209
Turipona, Wiremu, 199
Tūrori, Rōra, 272
Turumeke, Ema, 76–80
Tutariaria, 35
Tūteahuka, 273
Tūtere Konohi, 108
Tutereiao, Ria, 261, 262
Tūwehiwehi, Wiremu, 87

Uhuuhu, Māngai, 237, 245, 251, 254
United States, 193, 280
Urenui, 141, 142, 143
Urewera, 112, 212–17 *passim*
Uru, Katarina, 190–91
urupā (burial ground), 123–24, 171
Urupeni Pūhara, 245–50 *passim*
Utah, 282
utu, 74–76, 77, 115, 294

De Vattel, Emer, 27
Victoria, Queen, 83, 117, 119, 127, 151, 152, 160, 162, 164, 173, 182, 188, 189, 192, 278
Volkner, Carl, 128
Von Tempsky, Gustavus, 161
voting, 171–72, 174, 189, 190
    Māori male suffrage, 151, 160
    women's suffrage petitions, 192, 228

Waahi Marae, 183
Waerenga-a-Hika, 102, 103–4
Waha-Aruhe, 79
Wāhanga, 267
Wāhi River, 27
Waiapu, Ani, 270–72
Waiapu, James, 270, 271
waiata, 21–22, 73, 80, 290, 320
    kaioraora, 74–76
    mōteatea, 5, 315
    waiata aroha, 292
    waiata tangi, 74, 80–82, 291, 315
Waiau-uwha River, 79
Waiharakeke, 77
Waihī (near Hāwera), 163, 165, 166, 168, 169, 220
Waikākahi Pā, 204, 205, 206
Waikanae, 194, 314
Waikaremoana, Lake, 107
Waikato (chief), 18
Waikato, 82, 85, 86, 116, 118, 129, 130, 236, 304
Waikato River, 75, 76, 116, 153
Waimā, 63, 313
Waimata, 79
Waimate Plains, 169, 219, 220
Waingana, 35
Waioeka, 13–14, 128
Waipā, 121, 122, 123, 153, 154
Waipā River, 117
Waipahihi, 134, 135
Waipaoa River, 28
Waipatu, 176, 179
Wairaka, 11
Wairākau, Atareta, 176, 179
Wairarapa, 10, 30, 39, 43, 72, 172, 250
Wairau (man), 162, 163, 165
Wairau (family), 220, 221
Wairewa, 205
Wairoa (Clevedon), 86, 87
Wairoa, 193, 284
Waitangi, 68, 179
Waitangi Tribunal, 29
    Taranaki Report, 99
Waitara, 38, 44, 45, 163, 165, 167, 225
Waitara River, 82
Waitaria, 108
Waitetuna, 154
Waitōtara, 46, 223
Waiuku, 11–12, 146
Waiwhakawera, Ani, 311–12
Walker, Dr., 98
Wallis, James, 272
Wanganui. *See* Whanganui
Wano, Turi, 187
war, 72–115
    kūpapa, 73, 89, 90, 91, 94, 103, 112–14, 115, 134, 160, 168

musket wars, 72, 76–80, 82, 151, 161
    Ōmihi, battle of, 76–80
wars (1840s), 72
    Kororāreka, sack of, 276
self reliant policy, 72–73
Pai Mārire wars, 73
    Poverty Bay, 102–4
Taranaki war (Waitara), 13, 38, 72, 152, 153, 160, 273, 297
    Waitara dispute, 82–84, 153
Taranaki war (Pai Mārire), 72, 160, 161
    Pōkaikai Commission of Enquiry, 89–99
Taranaki war (Tītokowaru), 73, 99–100, 161, 168
    Pakakohi tribe, 99–102, 168
Te Kooti campaign, 73, 106–15
Waikato war, 72, 128, 145, 146, 160
    Koheroa, 85
    Meremere, 85, 86
    Papakura ambush, 85–89
    proclamation 1863, 119, 146
    Pukehinahina (Gate Pā), 103, 212
Waraurangi, 23
Ward, Damen, 231
Warrior, Robert, 8
Watkins Waru, Sarah, 268–69
Watt, Isaac Newton, 100, 101, 261
Watt, Rai, 100, 261
Weld, Frederick, 123
Wellington, 30, 142, 188, 195, 209, 232, 243, 253, 305
West Coast Commission, 140, 142, 222, 223
Wete, Here (Henry West), 296
Wetere, 155
Weterere, 83
whaikōrero, 150, 184
Whāingaroa, 272
whakamā, 290
Whakamairu, Hōriana, 279–82
Whakamairu, Īhaia, 279
whakapapa, 9, 38, 41, 83, 150, 279
Whakatāne, 11, 116, 128, 131, 132, 133, 148, 213–16 passim
Whakatāne Heads, 213, 215
Whakahua, Miriama, 108
Whanako, Hemaima, 21, 254
Whānau-a-Kai, 29
Whangamarino River, 155
Whanganui, 30, 138, 162, 163, 165, 314
Whanganui River, 285
Whangārei, 22, 43, 44
Whangaruru, 43, 44
wharenui, 20
Whareongaonga, 106
Whatu, More, 83

Whāwhā, Kararaina, 53–57
Whenuakura River, 139
White, Bennett, 131
White, Meriama (Mereana), 131–32
White, John, 240, 243
Whiteley, John, 57
Whitelock (militiaman), 98
Whitingara, Marara, 177, 180
Wilkinson, George T., 257, 258, 308, 309, 311
Williams, David V., 318
Williams, Henry, 18, 269, 294
William, King, 192
Williams, Jane, 18
Williams, Marianne, 18–19
Williams, William, 28–29, 102, 103
Williamson, John, 157
Wilson, J. A., 130, 131, 202, 225, 226
Wilson, J. N., 238, 240, 241, 243, 244, 251
Wilson, Capt., 170
Wirihana, 139, 140
Wirihana, Capt., 96
Wohlers, Johannes, 297
Women's Christian Temperance Union, 194
women's history, 3
Worgan, George B., 138, 140
Wyllie, William, 108, 109
Wyss, Hilary E., 263
Yate, William, 13, 266–72 passim, 288
    sexual scandal, 266